Felix Mendelssohn has long been viewed as one of the most historically minded composers in Western music. This book explores the
conceptions of time, memory and history found in his instrumental
compositions, presenting an intriguing new perspective on his ever-
popular music. Focusing on Mendelssohn's innovative development
of cyclic form, Taylor investigates how the composer was influenced by
the aesthetic and philosophical movements of the period. This is of key
importance not only for reconsideration of Mendelssohn's work and
its position in nineteenth-century culture, but also more generally concerning the relationship between music, time and subjectivity. One of
very few detailed accounts of Mendelssohn's music, the study presents
a new and provocative reading of the meaning of the composer's work
by connecting it to wider cultural and philosophical ideas.

BENEDICT TAYLOR is a Mellon Postdoctoral Research Fellow at the
University of Oxford. His research focuses on musical temporality
and subjectivity in the nineteenth and twentieth centuries, theory and
analysis, and aesthetics.

Frontispiece Felix Mendelssohn, portrait by Wilhelm Hensel from 1829.

Mendelssohn, Time and Memory

The Romantic Conception of Cyclic Form

BENEDICT TAYLOR

CAMBRIDGE
UNIVERSITY PRESS

CAMBRIDGE
UNIVERSITY PRESS

University Printing House, Cambridge CB2 8BS, United Kingdom

One Liberty Plaza, 20th Floor, New York, NY 10006, USA

477 Williamstown Road, Port Melbourne, VIC 3207, Australia

314-321, 3rd Floor, Plot 3, Splendor Forum, Jasola District Centre, New Delhi - 110025, India

79 Anson Road, #06-04/06, Singapore 079906

Cambridge University Press is part of the University of Cambridge.

It furthers the University's mission by disseminating knowledge in the pursuit of
education, learning and research at the highest international levels of excellence.

www.cambridge.org
Information on this title: www.cambridge.org/9781108970532

© Benedict Taylor 2011

First published 2011
First paperback edition 2021

A catalogue record for this publication is available from the British Library

Library of Congress Cataloging in Publication data
Taylor, Benedict, 1981–
Mendelssohn, time and memory : the romantic conception of cyclic form / Benedict Taylor.
    p.   cm.
Includes bibliographical references and index.
ISBN 978-1-107-00578-5
1. Mendelssohn-Bartholdy, Felix, 1809–1847 – Criticism and interpretation.   2. Cyclic form
(Music)   3. Instrumental music – 19th century – History and criticism.   I. Title.
ML410.M5T39   2011
780.92 – dc23   2011027654

ISBN 978-1-107-00578-5 Hardback
ISBN 978-1-108-97053-2 Paperback

Contents

Illustrations

Frontispiece: Felix Mendelssohn, portrait by Wilhelm Hensel from 1829 (original destroyed, photograph courtesy of Staatsbibliothek zu Berlin–Preussischer Kulturbesitz, Musikabteilung mit Mendelssohn-Archiv, MA BA 368).

Acknowledgements

My thanks must go to the numerous colleagues and friends who have figured in the writing of this book. Those who have helped with earlier stages and generously commented on drafts of this study's original incarnation as a PhD thesis include Nicholas Marston, Dean Sutcliffe, Daniel Chua, Roger Parker, Michael Quinn, Thomas Schmidt-Beste, Peter Ward Jones, Douglass Seaton and Michael Fend. John Deathridge, R. Larry Todd, Christopher Wintle and Rohan Stewart-MacDonald all provided advice and stimulating conversation, while later in my post-doctoral years Scott Burnham and my colleagues from the music department in Princeton revived my interest in pursuing this subject further.

My gratitude also goes to St Catharine's College, Cambridge and the Ruprecht-Karls-Universität Heidelberg where the original thesis was written; to Princeton University and the Humboldt-Universität Berlin for subsequent research stays; and to the Alexander von Humboldt Stiftung for allowing me the opportunity to take up this project again.

The use of material from the Bodleian Library, Oxford, the Staatsbibliothek zu Berlin, the Alte Nationalgalerie Berlin and the Walker Art Gallery, Liverpool, is gratefully acknowledged, as is the kind assistance of Alison Garnham with the Keller archive in Cambridge. Material from chapters 2 and 4 previously appeared as 'Musical History and Self-Consciousness in Mendelssohn's Octet, Op. 20', *19th-Century Music*, 32 (2008), 131–59, published by the University of California Press (© 2008 the Regents of the University of California), and 'Cyclic Form, Time and Memory in Mendelssohn's A-minor Quartet, Op. 13', *The Musical Quarterly*, 93 (2010), 45–89, published by Oxford University Press. The brief account of Mendelssohn's 'Reformation' Symphony in Chapter 6 is reused as part of a larger article on that work published in *Ad Parnassum*, 5/12 (October 2009), 115–27, and a highly condensed form of Chapter 5, originally presented at the conference 'Mendelssohn in the Long Nineteenth Century', held at Trinity College Dublin in July 2005, is forthcoming in Nicole Grimes and Angela Mace (eds.), *Mendelssohn Perspectives* (Aldershot: Ashgate, 2011).

Berlin, April 2011

Introduction

The early instrumental works of Felix Mendelssohn are quite extraordinary for their pioneering use of cyclic form. This series of pieces, dating from the latter half of the 1820s, takes up the idea of thematic recall and ongoing development across the separate movements of an instrumental work to a degree unprecedented in previous music and one unsurpassed until the late works of Franck some sixty years later. At a time when Beethoven was still alive, and predating virtually all other attempts in the medium, the young composer was developing a formal principle that would have a decisive impact on the idea of instrumental form for the next century and a half. In works such as the Piano Sextet (1824), the B minor Piano Quartet, Op. 3 (1824–5), the Octet (1825), Piano Sonatas in E and B♭ major (1826 and 1827) and the A minor and E♭ Quartets, Opp. 13 and 12 (1827 and 1829), the principles of thematic recollection and metamorphosis are fused into a new paradigm of musical form and unity. Even more intriguingly, after the age of twenty, with this succession of cyclic masterpieces behind him, Mendelssohn seemed to turn his back on this principle that he had so brilliantly espoused in these youthful works. His instrumental music would continue to grow in range and depth, but the radical formal designs and cyclic recall of these earlier pieces would be modified into the more subtle structures of his mature music and a more restrained process of cyclical thematic growth and transformation.

This book investigates this remarkable use of cyclic form in Mendelssohn's music, both in his works of the 1820s and throughout the subsequent development of this principle in his later music of the 1830/40s. This topic is set against the wider backdrop of the problem of instrumental form in the Romantic era; as the first composer in the generation following Beethoven who engaged convincingly with the compositional issue of musical form and large-scale coherence in instrumental music, Mendelssohn assumes considerable importance here, and these cyclic pieces form a significant part of his achievement. A further subtext of this investigation is a desire to contribute towards understanding cyclic form and its development across the nineteenth century more generally, a subject which has received remarkably little attention. Mendelssohn is without doubt the most pivotal figure here in its early development before Franck and the French school of the late nineteenth century.

This conception of cyclic form is one which has notable implications for other aspects of musical experience and perception, most specifically here the phenomenology of form and conceptions of musical time. A remarkable characteristic of Mendelssohn's music is the linking of formal sophistication and impressive musical logic with a distinctly poetic, quasi-narrative quality. This mixture of formal strength and poetic content provides particularly fruitful ground for hermeneutic reflection. Nowhere is such reconciliation between form and expressive content more apparent than in these cyclic works, where the often radical formal designs are intimately – indeed intrinsically – related to the expressive realisation of the music. Especially in this regard, the structure of cyclic works play with listeners' perceptions of form and time, which can have a major impact on our conceptions of music's expressive narrative.

The cyclic procedures found in Mendelssohn's music introduce, it will be argued, new and fascinating conceptions of temporal experience and aesthetic journey. Notions of musical memory and multiple time arise from such structural implications, which require new approaches in order to understand their full potential. To this end, I will be drawing on philosophical and literary views of time, subjectivity and memory ranging from Plato to Bergson in order to interpret Mendelssohn's procedures in these pieces. This study is therefore not just an explication of form, but a consideration of how Mendelssohn's cyclic procedures relate to our perception of form and, through a combination of analysis and interpretation, the particular expressive course of his music. Form merges with content, technique with expression, and analysis with hermeneutics.

Perhaps surprisingly, given the significance of this music and current interest in the concepts of musical memory, subjectivity and history, this topic has hardly been explored in any detail at all. Indeed, there has been little detailed analytical study of Mendelssohn's music in general, so a major study here has considerable significance not just in the realm of Mendelssohn studies but also in the wider context of the position and understanding of this composer within his time and the music of his century.[1]

---

[1] The one major work in this area is Friedhelm Krummacher's landmark study of the chamber
    music for strings, which originated as his doctorial thesis and was published in 1978 as
    Mendelssohn – Der Komponist: Studien zur Kammermusik für Streicher (Munich: Wilhelm Fink).
    While Krummacher's study is without doubt the most important analytical account of

It is a fact not gone unobserved by Mendelssohn scholars that it might seem rather ironic to write about the music of a composer famous for his own reservation about the capacity of words confronted with music. But though Mendelssohn's protestation that words are unclear and unwieldy in dealing with the aesthetic experience of music rings true to many music lovers, our understanding of music is nevertheless importantly shaped by the verbal commentary surrounding and often inextricably intermingled with it. One could reasonably argue that Mendelssohn's relative lack of prominence within scholarship (strikingly disproportionate given his music's importance and unceasing popularity) has been partly a consequence of this reticence to explain and justify his music in verbal terms, with the resultant lack of ready verbal handholds or engaging contexts from which it could be interpreted leaving a vacuum that was easily occupied by the malicious extramusical discourse promulgated later by rivals and critics. Thus my intention here in analysing and interpreting Mendelssohn's music is to provide a richer cultural, historical and philosophical context for understanding and appreciating these works, to transform and deepen our aesthetic receptivity to this music.

Though my discussion grows from a historical and biographical background closely connected with the composer and questions of authorial intent make their appearance in several places, no attempt is made to limit the wider discussion to ideas that Mendelssohn may have or could have known. If the primary reason why we are still interested in this music now is because it speaks to us of something that is felt to be meaningful and important, trying to overcome our own historical situatedness through the chimera of an abstract antiquarianism is not only impossible but of questionable value for its own sake. The aim of this study is to widen our appreciation of this music's aesthetic significance for us, a hermeneutic endeavour that is richer when taking into account the historical context and beliefs of Mendelssohn and his time, but also in considering how we as historically situated perceivers may view it.[2]

Mendelssohn's music, his focus on formal and thematic construction within movements unavoidably leaves a good deal of the cyclic aspects of these pieces unexplored. Also significant, though markedly personal in judgement, is Greg Vitercik's *The Early Works of Felix Mendelssohn: A Study in the Romantic Sonata Style* (Philadelphia, PA: Gordon and Breach, 1992), which contains valuable studies of Mendelssohn's Octet and Quintet, Op. 18.

[2] Without belabouring this methodological point, it will be apparent that these views have a substantial intellectual background in the German nineteenth- and twentieth-century hermeneutic tradition. To rehistoricise the terms of the debate, Mendelssohn himself had personal and intellectual contact with Friedrich Schleiermacher in 1820s Berlin, and his own views and activities (discussed in Chapter 2) support this critical reading of history.

In the chapters that follow, I will be taking up a broadly chronological account of Mendelssohn's cyclic works. The idea of cyclic form is one which might well be expected in the early nineteenth century, as I argue in Chapter 1. This outlines the notion of cyclic form, trying to elucidate a definition of this problematic term and exploring it from both theoretical and historical perspectives, before tracing the development of this idea in the music of composers preceding Mendelssohn and across Mendelssohn's early works prior to 1825. There follow accounts of four of the composer's most significant cyclic works from the subsequent years – the Octet Op. 20, Piano Sonata Op. 6 and the Quartets Opp. 13 and 12 – which take up the central four chapters of the book and form the heart of my study.

The past played perhaps a more important role in Mendelssohn's music than in that of any other composer. Chapter 2 approaches his first major cyclic work, the Octet, from the perspective of the composer's strong historical sense, taking up ideas of musical memory and history as found embodied within the cyclic structure of this piece. The Octet enacts a coming to self-consciousness of its own musical history, which closely parallels near-contemporary views in early nineteenth-century Germany. This chapter sets up a historically based theory from the biographical and cultural context of these works, exploring in particular the composer's extraordinary personal connections with Goethe and Hegel. This will lead to the development of theories in later chapters that are more wide-ranging, moving from Neoplatonism to Bergson, Proust and Freud, in order to investigate the implications for memory and musical time that Mendelssohn's work may suggest.

The following two chapters take up the themes of time and memory, in relation to two of the composer's subsequent cyclic works, the E major Piano Sonata Op. 6 and A minor Quartet Op. 13. These works enact a circular journey, a mytho-poetic homecoming to an idyllic state left at their opening, an idea found in Western culture since antiquity and seen particularly emphatically in German society in the early nineteenth century. Mendelssohn's music from these years, I will be arguing here, participates in these universal myths of the return to a lost golden age, the search for a vanished past and the regaining of time. Though starting out from the cultural context of early nineteenth-century Germany (above all the work of Schiller and Novalis), these chapters makes use of broader ideas of time, memory and history to illuminate Mendelssohn's music, specifically the theories of Bergson and Proust.

In Chapter 5, this musical capacity for memory is seen now in an altered light, taking on a darker, more troubled aspect. Ostensibly, Mendelssohn's

E♭ Quartet is one of his most relaxed and seemingly trouble-free works, though a closer inspection of the cyclic processes at work underneath this beguiling surface reveals a visage anything but so easy-going. Instead, the unexpected and unsettling recall of past experiences within this work is seen in a light analogous to the psychoanalytical notion of trauma, this part of the study approaching Mendelssohn's quartet from the theoretical standpoint of Sigmund Freud's later codification of this idea.

Historical and more specifically biographical aspects return in the final chapter, which explores the various reasons why the composer felt the need to move away from the particular cyclic designs adopted in his works from the later 1820s, and the consequences this has for the cyclic elements manifested in his subsequent music from the later 1830s onwards. Instead of the open recollection and reminiscence of his teenage years, the cyclic recall of his earlier music would be replaced by a more subtle process of thematic growth and metamorphosis and an even firmer command of musical form, which contrasts with the more overtly radical and immediately impressive designs of his youth.

The centrepiece of Mendelssohn's mature cyclic style is the Symphony No. 3 in A minor, a work started in 1829 but only completed twelve years later in 1842. The musical progression of the symphony mirrors the more general movement in Mendelssohn's music from the past-haunted landscape and ruins of the opening movement to the ultimately affirmative peroration of the close of the work; from the inescapable recall of the symphony's introduction at the close of the first movement to its final transformation in the fourth-movement coda, crystallising in a nutshell the development of Mendelssohn's cyclic technique across these years. But this cyclic progression is fused with broader aspects of the musical construction which cannot easily be examined out of context. My account of the symphony, then, stands not only for Mendelssohn's mature cyclic technique, but inevitably also as a paradigm and exploration of his mature music in general.

1 | The idea of cyclic form

The very term 'cyclic form' is confusing. Hans Keller was exaggerating only a little when he described it as 'one of the most senseless technical terms in the rich history of musicological nonsense'.[1] In fact, it is almost obligatory for commentators to offer some brief apology for their continued use of the term. Charles Rosen, for instance, states that '"cyclical form" is an ambiguous as well as a vague term', whilst James Webster, in his influential study of Haydn's 'Farewell' Symphony, prefaces his text with a disclaimer on the unsuitability of the terms 'cyclic' and 'through-composed', before going on to use them nevertheless.[2]

The term 'cyclic', as applied to music since c. 1750, can be used to describe:

1) a work where part of one movement is recalled in another (examples include Haydn's Symphony No. 46, Beethoven's Fifth and Ninth Symphonies, Mendelssohn's Octet, Schubert's E♭ Trio, Schumann's Piano Quintet, and later pieces by Franck, Brahms, Dvořák, Elgar and Mahler);
2) a work where separate movements are based on similar thematic material, often accompanied by the merging of individual movements (examples include Schubert's 'Wanderer' Fantasy, Mendelssohn's Third and Schumann's Fourth Symphonies, Liszt's B minor Sonata, and numerous works of Franck);
3) a collection of miniatures, which make full sense only when considered as a whole (archetypically the Romantic song-cycle, but also including piano collections such as Schumann's *Carnaval* or *Davidsbündlertänze*).

Of the three types of musical cyclicism given above, the last is least related to the other two, and it is confusing that a common terminology may be given to both a collection of miniatures and to an integrated multi-movement form involving recall or transformation of material across movements. The idea of a set of small-scale movements or fragments that

---

[1] Hans Keller, 'The Classical Romantics: Schumann and Mendelssohn', in H.H. Schönzeler (ed.), *Of German Music: A Symposium* (London: Oswald Wolff, 1976), p. 185.
[2] Charles Rosen, *The Romantic Generation* (London: Harper Collins, 1996), p. 88; James Webster, *Haydn's 'Farewell' Symphony and the Idea of Classical Style: Through-Composition and Cyclic Integration in his Instrumental Music* (Cambridge University Press, 1991), pp. 7–8.

form a cycle or chain does have, in common with the other two definitions, the notion of a collective bond whereby the individual part is dependent on the whole for its ultimate meaning and coherence, but it is confusing to conflate this with the idea of musical recurrence in (usually more substantial) instrumental forms or genres.

Here it is useful to distinguish between what can be termed a musical 'cycle' and what, conversely, may be taken to constitute 'cyclic form'.[3] A cycle, in its most general sense, refers to a succession of individual movements that go to make up a work, such as the mass, suite, sonata, symphony or song-cycle. It can be taken to refer to music from almost any period and is correspondingly wide in its definition. In practice, however, when referring to the music of the later eighteenth century onwards, the term cycle is usually reserved for a collection of miniatures (such as the song or piano cycle), as distinct from the conventional three- or four-movement sonata cycle. Cyclic form, on the other hand, is a more specific term used to describe a large-scale instrumental work, normally from the nineteenth or early twentieth century, in which the same or very similar thematic material is used in at least two different movements. It is thus a more specific term in definition and historical usage.

A work in cyclic form, then, is a particular type of cycle in which the connections between the individual parts are intensified and made explicit. As a consequence, the divisions between the two types are not necessarily clear-cut: a work can be a cycle and in cyclic form, though normally in practice the two are distinct. As a rule, for instance, most instrumental pieces in cyclic form consist of three or four large-scale movements with thematic connections or recall between them. But a work such as Beethoven's C♯ minor Quartet, frequently cited as an early example of cyclic form, has more similarity with a cycle of seven interdependent movements than a conventional four-movement quartet. Likewise, the song cycle or collection of piano miniatures can also involve cyclic recall, as is found in Beethoven's *An die ferne Geliebte* or Schumann's *Davidsbündlertänze*, *Dichterliebe* and *Frauenliebe und -leben*, though these would not usually be described as being in cyclic form.[4] A cycle can thus exhibit characteristics of cyclic form,

---

[3] This distinction is found, for instance, in *The New Harvard* and *The Oxford Dictionary of Music*.
[4] A further possibility for fusing these two types of cyclicism is given in the nineteenth century by collections of pieces that feature thematic cyclic recall within a multi-movement (sometimes multi-opus) cycle for often quasi-programmatic reasons, such as Grieg's 'Scenes from Folklife' Op. 19 (1871), Smetana's *Má vlast* (1874–9), and Dvořák's 'Nature, Life and Love' trilogy of overtures, Opp. 91–3 (1892). Grieg's ten books of *Lyric Pieces* provide an even more notable cyclical conception with the sixty-sixth and final piece, 'Remembrances' (Op. 71 No. 7, 1901), returning to the music of the first, 'Arietta' (Op. 12 No. 1, 1867), now transformed into a slow waltz.

and all cyclic forms are by definition a type of cycle, in its broadest sense, but the two concepts are not in essence the same thing. Their most general common characteristic, the idea of relationship of parts to whole, is too vague an attribute to support a common definition. The cyclic form of Mendelssohn's Op. 13 Quartet (1827) has nothing in common with the contemporaneous cycle that is Schubert's *Winterreise*. We have to recognise that we are dealing with two different, though not incompatible, concepts.

Hence cyclic instrumental works – those in cyclic form – are usually distinct from those musical cycles embodied in the song cycle or set of piano miniatures, and consequently the substantial literature on the song cycle or the notion of the cycle in the nineteenth century is of limited use in considering such instrumental pieces.[5] Indeed, it is difficult to establish when and where (let alone why) this terminology originated. One looks in vain for any description of a thematically unified multi-movement instrumental work as cyclic in the first half of the nineteenth century. References to the cycle or cyclic works, the *Zyklus* or *Kreis* in German, abound, but these refer to the collection of miniatures and not to what we have termed cyclic form above.[6] The term seems not to have been mentioned, for instance, by either Mendelssohn or Schumann to describe this formal principle, both of whom speak of the relationship of whole to parts and of intimate thematic connections within multi-movement works without using any term corresponding to cyclic. It seems that this terminology was codified well after the

---

[5] For an overview of the genesis, meaning and development of the concept of the cycle in relation to the genre of the Romantic song cycle, see Ruth Bingham, 'The Song Cycle in German-Speaking Countries, 1790–1840: Approaches to a Changing Genre', unpublished PhD thesis, Cornell University (1993); David Ferris, *Schumann's 'Eichendorff Liederkreis' and the Genre of the Romantic Cycle* (Oxford University Press, 2001), chapters 1 and 3; and Barbara Turchin, 'Robert Schumann's Song-Cycles in the Context of the Early Nineteenth-Century *Liederkreis*', unpublished PhD thesis, Columbia University (1981). In all three authors the notion of the cycle is taken to refer to a collection of miniatures and not in the sense I am using it here. The extensive literature relating the cycle-collection to the Romantic fragment is also less relevant applied to instrumental cyclic form, where individual movements are typically more autonomous and internally coherent and the cyclical recall helps integrate the larger work in a manner usually absent in the more 'incomplete' cycle collection. (See Richard Kramer, *Distant Cycles: Schubert and the Conceiving of Song* (University of Chicago Press, 1994), esp. pp. 8–9, or Ferris, *Schumann's 'Eichendorff Liederkreis'*, for a mildly revisionist deconstruction of the trope of unity in the fragment-inspired song-cycle.)

[6] For instance, Beethoven describes his Bagatelles Op. 126 as a 'Ciclus von Kleinigkeiten' in his sketches. Schumann, referring to his Op. 24 Heine *Liederkreis*, speaks of a 'Cyklus (zusammenhängend)' (letter to Clara Wieck, 24 February 1840, in Berthold Litzmann, *Clara Schumann, Ein Künstlerleben: Nach Tagebüchern und Briefen*, 2 vols. (Leipzig: Breitkopf & Härtel, 1902), vol. I, p. 407), but this, along with the Eichendorff set Op. 39, is one of his cycles that does not feature any thematic recall between songs. The sets which do – *Dichterliebe* and *Frauenliebe* – are conversely not designated as *Kreise*.

principle which it describes had become common practice. The first use of the term in musical aesthetics appears to be in 1857, in Vischer's *Ästhetik oder Wissenschaft des Schönen*, to denote a work exhibiting a spiritual unity across several movements, and 'cyclic form' was afforded its first individual entry in a music dictionary by Arrey von Dommer in 1865.[7] Its primary dissemination, however, seems to have arisen through César Franck and his pupils. While Franck himself was fairly reticent about the cyclic qualities of his compositions, Vincent d'Indy in particular was a keen activist for the Franck school and the 'principle of cyclic composition' which it espoused.[8]

The terminology 'cyclic form' is thus not the most happy of inspirations, since it is easily confused with the contemporary notion of the cycle and hence ambiguous in its definition. Furthermore, it is misnamed. Indeed, it could be argued that it is, by some definitions, often neither cyclic nor a form. The word cyclic derives from the Greek κυκλικός, circular, which in turn comes from the word for circle, κύκλος. The concept of cyclicism abstracted from the immediate discussion of common musical usage thus implies some sense of circular motion, an overall trajectory which returns to its starting point. A design which might merit the term cyclic is hence one where the end is near-identical to the beginning, thus creating a frame to the piece (a specific subsection of the literally recalling type of cyclicism, definition 1 above), or, potentially, a work in which the end can be thought of in some way as connecting up to the start, suggesting that the piece can start again or go round continuously in cycles. In both these designs the form created is circular, hence cyclic in this particular sense.

Properly, then, a work which ends with the music of the beginning is cyclic in the most literal sense. I will designate this specific type of musical cyclicism as being *circular*. However, a cycle can also mean more loosely the general idea of recall, the principle of return and repetition. A musical work need not only be one large cycle, but may consist of several returns or cycles. Hence any work in which music from a previous movement is recalled and reused in a later one can be termed cyclic. Thus, in itself, thematic affinity

---

[7] Friedrich Theodor Vischer, *Ästhetik oder Wissenschaft des Schönen: Zum Gebrauche für Vorlesungen von Dr. Friedrich Theodor Vischer*, 3 vols. (Reutlingen, Leipzig and Stuttgart: Carl Mäcken, 1846–57), vol. III (Stuttgart, 1857), § 786, pp. 950–2: 'Cyclische Compositionsform'; Arrey von Dommer, 'Cyclische Formen', in *Musikalisches Lexikon: auf Grundlage des Lexicon's von H. Ch. Koch* (Heidelberg: J.C.B. Mohr, 1865), pp. 225–7 (though this entry actually refers to the more general sense of a multi-movement symphony or sonata cycle). See further Ludwig Finscher, 'Zyklus', in Ludwig Finscher (ed.), *Die Musik in Geschichte und Gegenwart*, 20 vols. (Kassel and Stuttgart: Bärenreiter and Metzler, 1998), vol. IX, cols. 2528–37.
[8] See Vincent d'Indy, *Cours de Composition*, ed. Auguste Sérieyx, 3 vols. in 4 books (Paris: A. Durand, 1903–50), especially the chapter 'La sonate cyclique' (vol. II.i (1909), pp. 375–433).

between movements of a work – even possibly an ongoing development and resolution – should strictly speaking not really warrant the epithet cyclic. (Beethoven's Op. 131 Quartet or Schubert's 'Wanderer' Fantasy, two works that are often cited as being cyclic, are therefore slightly uncertain inclusions in the canon of cyclic works.) This term implies, rather, the idea of recurrence, which, however, must be distinguished from recapitulation determined by the demands of normative designs such as sonata form. Cyclic form, therefore, involves musical recall above the level of the individual movement.[9] In practice, however, a work with extremely close thematic links between movements – even if these do not constitute literal recall of previously heard material – is usually designated as cyclic.

A further conception of the cycle, at its broadest and most vague, relates to the idea of separate parts forming links on a chain. This notion is in many ways misnamed, as the resulting structure is not necessarily circular and hence has no apparent relation to the etymological meaning of the word, but is commonly accepted as a definition. This is 'cyclic' in the same sense as all multi-movement works are cyclic, insofar as they are parts of a whole. A work which features an ongoing development or continuity across its movements without recall or close transformation might be more aptly termed 'through-composed'.

Since a work in cyclic form is one in which material is reused in separate movements, its designation as a form is furthermore also partly misleading, if by form we mean a distinct architectonic design capable of being repeated and which can therefore serve as a generic archetype. The term cyclic does not define the structure of an individual movement or determine the shape of the overall work, but only more generally describes the relationship between its movements. Thus at the level of the individual movement, the cyclic principle is typically in dialogue with an underlying generic form such as the sonata. In this sense, cyclicism is more akin to a structural principle or even a deforming process which works above or against traditional form. Cyclic form is thus the name given to a range of structures which result from what we could call a cyclic principle. As a consequence there is no single structural design common to all works in cyclic form but only a range of

---

[9] An exception to this rule could be made for a single-movement structure whose coda corresponds to the introduction, since the resulting form is circular and exists outside the bounds of sonata-space. Examples include the first movements of Mozart's Quintet K. 593, Haydn's Symphony No. 103, Schubert's Ninth and Mendelssohn's Third Symphonies, and the overtures to Mendelssohn's *Die Heimkehr aus der Fremde* and *St Paul*, and that to Wagner's *Tannhäuser*. There seems, however, little point in designating such works as cyclic; at best, one can speak of a cyclic frame.

possibilities resulting from the multiple ways in which the cyclic recall or transformation of themes can be realised. Hence I will speak of cyclic forms, in the plural.

'Cyclic form', then, is a vague and ambiguous term which incorporates many differing definitions. Nevertheless, in this study I will be assuming that cyclicism, with regard to musical form, entails at the very least close thematic affinity between movements or, more properly, explicit recall of music from one in another. These two types can be designated *transformative* and *recalling* cyclicism. To insist on a division between these two would be problematic, since the boundaries can be blurred between what constitutes close allusion and literal reprise. Moreover, many works which recall past movements tend to feature such thematic interconnections; cyclicism should be seen as a continuum of possibilities between these two types.[10]

It may be useful here to clarify the above discussion by giving a schematic overview of some of the most common cyclic formal types that can be found in the nineteenth and early twentieth centuries, along with examples of works that fall under these classes. The following list is not exhaustive and neither are the given categories mutually exclusive: many cyclic works exhibit attributes of more than one type (pieces have been categorised below under what seems to constitute their most significant cyclic properties) and others may be difficult to place. The latter is particularly the case with works that feature the ongoing transformation of material across movements when this is not accompanied by any notable deformation of form, while what constitutes 'end-orientation' (especially when the entire work is pervaded by cyclic material) and the distinction between integration, reminiscence and disruption may be also open to debate.

1. End-orientated (circular) cyclic forms

i) *Multi-movement introduction–coda frame.* The most perfectly circular design, introduced by Mendelssohn in his A minor Quartet Op. 13 (1827). Later examples include Liszt's B minor Sonata (1853), Dvořák's Quartet No. 1 in A Op. 2 (1861), Grieg's Quartet in G minor Op. 27 (1878), Rheinberger's Organ Sonatas Nos. 8, 12 and 15 (1882–91),

[10] The notion of 'thematic' here should also be understood quite broadly, as incorporating the melodic, harmonic, textural or timbral qualities of themes – generally any salient aspect of the music that can be understood to recur in a more-or-less perceptible manner in a later movement.

Chausson's Piano Trio Op. 3 (1883) and Symphony in B♭ (1890), Rimsky Korsakov's *Scheherazade* (1888), Rachmaninov's Piano Trio No. 2 Op. 9 (1893) and Symphony No. 1 (1895), d'Indy's *Jour d'été à la montagne* (1905), Elgar's Symphony No. 1 (1908), Vaughan Williams' 'London' Symphony (1913/18) and Strauss' *Eine Alpensinfonie* (1915). In such pieces the course of the internal work may be heard as a response to the question of the framing music or a return to a different level of reality.

ii) *Coda recall.* Here the return to an earlier theme (often from the first movement, especially its closing section) forms the end to the whole work, this recall often being heard as the culmination of the process of the finale. This differs from 1.iii below by its typically more nostalgic or tranquil tone and more frequent use in a chamber-music context. Again the model for this design was set by Mendelssohn in his E major Piano Sonata Op. 6 (1826) and E♭ Quartet Op. 12 (1829). Brahms in particular was fond of this design, using it in his String Quartet Op. 67 (1875), Third Symphony (1883) and Clarinet Quintet Op. 115 (1891); other instances include Dvořák's and Elgar's *Serenade for Strings* (1875 and 1892) and Tchaikovsky's Piano Trio Op. 50 (1882, a negative version). Franck's String Quartet (1889) presents a particularly complex example where the boundary between the recall of past material and the present is blurred. Later usage includes Reger's Clarinet Sonata No. 3 (1909), Magnard's Fourth Symphony (1913), and d'Indy's Quartet No. 3 (1929).

iii) *Coda apotheosis.* Predominantly used in symphonic music, especially from the later nineteenth century on. Here the last part of the finale forms a distinct independent section featuring the recall or transformation of earlier themes. (In a weaker sense, the final bars may feature a brief reference back to a prominent earlier motive, often the beginning of the work, such as is found in Haydn's 'Hornsignal' Symphony (1765) and Mendelssohn's Piano Quartet Op. 3 (1825).) Growing possibly from the tendency in Beethoven's codas to form a substantial culminatory section in their own right, the first important model is provided by Mendelssohn's Octet (1825) and Symphony No. 3 (1842). From here it was taken up by Franck (Piano Trio in F♯ minor Op. 1 No. 1, 1840), Schumann (Piano Quintet, 1842, Symphonies Nos. 2 and 3, 1846 and 1850), Raff (Symphonies Nos. 3, 6, 7 and 11, 1869–76), Bruckner (Symphonies Nos. 3, 4 (the 1878 'Volksfest' finale being especially clear), 5, 6, 7 and 8, 1873–90), in Rimsky Korsakov's Third Symphony (1873), Dvořák's Symphony No. 5 (1875), Rheinberger's Organ Sonatas Nos. 4, 6, 13, 16–18 and 20 (1876–1901), Tchaikovsky's Fifth

(1888, a transformed variant of I.i), Stanford's Fifth and Sixth (1894 and 1905), d'Indy's Quartet No. 2 (1897), Symphony No. 2 (1903) and Piano Sonata in E (1907), Dukas' Piano Sonata (1901), Mahler's Seventh (1905) and Eighth (1906) and Nielsen's Fourth Symphony (the 'Inextinguishable', 1916).

2. Non-end-orientated cyclic forms

i) *Synthetic or integrative.* Probably the most common cyclic type, and correspondingly broad in the range of possible designs included. Here parts of earlier movements are heard returning (normally in the finale, frequently as the music nears its conclusion), either literally or in further transformation, as if binding up the course of the work and connecting the separate movements. In such designs the finale may run parallel to the first movement, mirroring the former course of events or offering a reworking of it (possibly suggesting that the earlier movement has been ongoing behind the later music, implying a separate aesthetic or temporal level); another common technique is to recall an earlier theme (often thematically related) within the coda before briefly reverting back to the finale's material to close the work. More loosely, such pieces may feature some type of motto theme that reappears across movements (similar works using an *idée fixe* appear under 2.iii). A precedent for this type might be seen in Haydn's Symphony No. 46 (1772) or Dittersdorf's Symphony in A, K. 119 (1788). The first really influential example is again Mendelssohn's Octet, being subsequently taken up in his B♭ Piano Sonata (1827) and A minor Quartet, Gade's Piano Sonata (1840), Symphony No. 1 (1842) and Violin Sonata No. 2 (1849), Schumann's Symphony No. 4 (1841) and Piano Quintet (1842), Franck's F♯ minor Piano Trio, Piano Quintet (1879), Violin Sonata (1886), Symphony in D minor (1888) and String Quartet, Fanny Hensel's Piano Trio in D minor Op. 11 (1847), Liszt's B minor Piano Sonata, Dvořák's String Quartet No. 4 in E minor (1870) and Symphony No. 9 (1893), Tchaikovsky's Serenade for Strings (1880), Parry's Symphony No. 2 (1883), Saint-Saëns' Violin Sonata No. 1 (1885) and Third Symphony (1886), Glazunov's Symphonies Nos. 2, 4 and 7 (1886, 1893 and 1902), d'Indy's *Symphonie sur un chant montagnard français* (1886), String Quartet No. 1 (1891) and Violin Sonata (1904), Mahler's Fifth Symphony (1902), Magnard's Symphonies Nos. 1 and 3 (1890 and 1896), Debussy's String Quartet (1893), Kalinnikov's Symphonies Nos. 1 and 2 (1895 and 1897),

Sibelius' First Symphony (1899), Ravel's String Quartet (1903), Rachmaninov's Symphony No. 2 (1907), Balakirev's Symphony No. 2 (1908), Enescu's Symphony No. 2 (1914), Fauré's Violin Sonata No. 2 (1917) and Elgar's Violin Sonata (1918).

ii) *Reminiscence.* In these works part of a past movement – often a lyrical second subject or slow-movement theme which had seemed to offer some temporary respite or a vision of potential happiness – is recalled as a passing reminiscence within the piece's finale, often as a nostalgic interlude before the final section. This technique is seen in Beethoven's Sonata Op. 27 No. 1 (1801), Schumann's Cello Concerto (1850), Raff's Quartet No. 2 (1857) and Symphony No. 4 (1871), Bruckner's Symphony No. 2 (1872), Smetana's Quartet No. 1 (1876), Tchaikovsky's Quartet No. 3 (1876), Brahms' Violin Sonata No. 1 (1879), Fibich's Symphony No. 1 (1883), Mahler's First Symphony (1888), Stanford's A minor Quartet Op. 45 (1891), Dvořák's Quartet No. 13 in G, Op. 106 (1895) and Cello Concerto (1895), Saint-Saëns' Quartet No. 1 (1899), Elgar's Second Symphony (1911), Violin and Cello Concertos (1910 and 1919) and Piano Quintet (1919).

A related though less integrated version is seen in several of Beethoven's cyclic works (the Cello Sonata Op. 102 No. 1 (1815), Piano Sonata Op. 101 (1816) and Symphony No. 9 (1824)), where the cyclic recall of themes occurs before or at the very start of the final movement, recalling and summing up the journey thus far before the finale proper can start. This Beethovenian model was later reused by Mendelssohn in his Violin Concerto (1844) and Schumann in his Piano Concerto (1845), in Bruckner's Fifth (1878) and Stanford's Second (1879) Symphonies, Franck's Quartet, and d'Indy's Quartets Nos. 1 and 2, Symphony No. 2 and Piano Sonata. Dvořák's Quartet No. 9 in D minor Op. 34 (1877) presents a variant of this procedure, where the recall comes at the very end of the Adagio third movement.

iii) *Disruptive or non-integrative.* A specific subset of cyclical formal types may be seen as belonging to a small group of non-integrative cyclic works. Typically in these pieces a part of a previous movement which is not 'wanted' – normally a passage with dark or painful connotations – is recalled in a subsequent one and can sometimes upset the balance of this later movement in which it recurs. Often this can take the form of a passage of minor-key music returning in a major-key final movement, which had seemed ostensibly to have dispelled the previous shadows of the work, a fateful breakdown of the traditional darkness-to-light archetype. Such disruptive cyclical procedures are found in

Beethoven's Fifth Symphony (1808) and Piano Sonata Op. 110 (1822), Mendelssohn's Piano Sextet Op. 110 (1824) and Quartet Op. 12, Schubert's Piano Trio No. 2 in E♭ (1827), Tchaikovsky's Fourth Symphony (1878), and Mahler's Second, Third and Tenth Symphonies (1894, 1896 and 1910). (Some circular, end-orientated designs may also fit this expressive type, such as the trios of Tchaikovsky, Rachmaninov and Chausson noted above. Additionally, many cyclic pieces classed above as integrative may at first suggest some sense of disruption but later subsume the cyclic interruption into the course of the music.)

The formal designs of programme symphonies after Berlioz normally also relate to this general formal category – the intrusion of the protagonist's *idée fixe* upon extraneous music – though in some examples the transformation or recall may be viewed as synthetic (2.i). Examples include Berlioz's *Symphonie fantastique* Op. 14 (1830) and *Harold en Italie* Op. 16 (1834), and those by Liszt (*Eine Faust-Sinfonie*, 1857), Rimsky Korsakov (*Antar*, 1868; *Scheherazade*), Raff (No. 5 'Lenore', 1872) and Tchaikovsky (*Manfred*, 1885). The effect of cyclic recall in Dvořák's Ninth Symphony may also be read in this light, while the (very different) reuse of material in Mahler's Fourth (1900) and Sixth (1904) Symphonies also straddles the line between integration and disruption.

3. Combined- or single-movement cyclic forms

i) *Linking of movements of multi-movement cycle.* Here the separate movements that constitute the composition are joined to each other, sometimes combined with thematic recall before the last movement (the Beethovenian model in 2.ii above). (This technique in itself does not necessarily constitute cyclicism, but in practice is normally associated with works using ongoing thematic transformation across their movements.) Examples include Beethoven's Sonata Op. 27 No. 1, Mendelssohn's Sonata Op. 6 and Symphony No. 3, Schumann's Symphony No. 4, Berwald's *Sinfonie sérieuse* (1842), *Sinfonie singulière* (1845) and Quartet in A minor (1849), Raff's Fantasy-Sonata (1871), and Parry's Fifth and Stanford's Seventh Symphonies (1912). Many nineteenth-century concertos follow this principle, often accompanied by the truncation of individual movements (tending towards 3.ii below), such as J.B. Cramer's Piano Concerto No. 8 in D minor (*c.* 1819), Mendelssohn's Piano Concerto No. 1 (1831), Alkan's *Concerto da Camera* No. 1 (1832), Moscheles'

Concerto No. 6 (1833), Clara Wieck's Concerto in A minor (1833–5) and those of Schumann (1845), Rubinstein (No. 3 in G, 1854), Liszt (1856 and 1861) and Saint-Saëns (Nos. 3 and 4, 1869 and 1875). An interesting further concept is provided by Schumann in his First Symphony (1841), where the end of one movement prefigures the opening theme of the next, an idea taken up in the Fourth Symphonies of Brahms (1885), Mahler and Sibelius (1911).

ii) *Multi-functional four-in-one designs (or similar).* A more specific variant of 3.i, the separate movements of the sonata/symphony cycle being heard as simultaneously forming parts of a single-movement (typically sonata) form, with the 'finale' section featuring the recapitulation of opening 'exposition' material. Schubert's *Wanderer* Fantasy (1822) forms a notable example; later uses include Alkan's *Concerto da Camera* No. 2 (1833), Berwald's Quartet in Eb (1849), Liszt's B minor Sonata, the Cello Concertos of Sullivan (1866) and Saint-Saëns (No. 1, 1872), Strauss' *Ein Heldenleben* (1898), *Sinfonia Domestica* (1903) and *Eine Alpensinfonie*, Enescu's Octet (1900), Schoenberg's *Pelleas und Melisande* (1903), Quartet in D minor Op. 7 (1905) and First Chamber Symphony Op. 9 (1906), Zemlinsky's String Quartet No. 2 (1914), and Sibelius' Symphony No. 7 (1924).

Historical context and development

The tendency for the separate movements of a musical composition to demonstrate such thematic connections actually dates back almost as long as Western art music. The cyclic and parody masses of the fifteenth and sixteenth centuries, for instance, often featured the reuse of a single *cantus firmus* or pre-existent melodic source throughout, in some cases opening each movement with the same plainchant intonation as a kind of unifying motto, while instrumental forms of the late sixteenth and seventeenth centuries, such as the canzone, suite or sonata, similarly can exhibit thematic relationships or recurrences of material between their movements. (Another notable example of a cyclic design, though not one normally defined as a multi-movement work, is the variation set which returns to its theme at the end, as exemplified in Bach's 'Goldberg' Variations.)

The specifically thematic cyclic formal construction under discussion here, though, is a feature largely of the nineteenth and early twentieth centuries. Such thematic connections are indeed rather less notable between movements in the eighteenth century, a fact which is perhaps surprising given the widespread appeal to the Baroque aesthetic of 'unity of affect' in music theory of the time. Thematic recall can occasionally be found in composers such as C.P.E. Bach or Boccherini, and in 'non-classical' forms and genres such as the instrumental fantasia (several of the most prominent early cyclic works stem from this tradition), but significantly the Viennese 'classical style' (at least when taken in reference to the music of Haydn and Mozart) is distinguished by the rarity of such thematic recurrences between movements.[11] Apart from one example in Haydn, his Symphony No. 46, in which the recall of the minuet in the finale is problematised by being treated rather as a joke, there seem to be no obvious examples of what one could call proto-Romantic cyclical practice in this tradition before Beethoven. Certainly, the separate movements of a classical sonata or symphony commonly demonstrate affinities in material, particularly between the outer movements, as Rudolf Réti has shown with Mozart's Symphony No. 40, or James Webster in relation to Haydn's Symphony No. 45.[12] But this is not the same thing as the literal (or near-literal) recall of past music, or the undisguised use of themes or motives from earlier movements, as is found so noticeably in music a few decades later.

The idea of cyclic form is hence essentially a Romantic one, which separates the procedures of Haydn, Mozart and even, to an extent Beethoven, from the next generation, that of Mendelssohn. The reasons for the relative lack of cyclic connections in the eighteenth century and the corresponding increase in the nineteenth are not easy to determine, though it is conceivable that the unifying potential of thematic recall was in part taken in the eighteenth century by the role of tonality, tying in with the traditional (and possibly simplistic) view of the sonata as evolving from a harmonic to a thematic basis across this period.[13] More broadly, a case can also be made for

---

[11] It should be noted, however, that several other Viennese composers of the age (such as Karl Ordonez, Dittersdorf and Vanhal) do experiment to a greater extent with thematic connections between movements. The question of possible *harmonic* connections or allusions between the movements of a classical-period work is another matter and has received more attention of late; see for instance Webster, *Haydn's 'Farewell' Symphony*, pp. 204–24; Ethan Haimo, 'Remote Keys and Multi-Movement Unity: Haydn in the 1790s', *The Musical Quarterly*, 74 (1990), 242–68, and *Haydn's Symphonic Forms: Essays in Compositional Logic* (Oxford: Clarendon Press, 1995), esp. pp. 64–9, 202, 231–2, 274–6; and Rohan H. Stewart-MacDonald, 'Elements of "Through-Composition" in the Violin Concertos Nos. 23 and 27 by Giovanni Battiata Viotti', *Ad Parnassum*, 3 (2005), 99–131.

[12] Rudolf Réti, *The Thematic Process in Music* (New York: Macmillan, 1951), pp. 114–37; Webster, *Haydn's 'Farewell' Symphony*, pp. 13–119.

[13] For a more detailed consideration of this issue viewed in relation to the music theory of the time see Mark Evan Bonds, *Wordless Rhetoric: Musical Form and the Metaphor of the Oration* (Cambridge, MA: Harvard University Press, 1991). Wilhelm Seidel also argues that even well

a change in several historical assumptions and epistemological structures which underlie the thought and belief systems of the time. These provide a useful cultural context for understanding and interpreting the growth of cyclicism in early nineteenth-century Germany, particularly as relating to Mendelssohn's music, and are therefore worth closer consideration here. Most notable are a group of related ideas: the revival of conceptions of time and history as circular, the growth of historicism and the historical self-consciousness of the age, the development of a modern condition of subjectivity, and the burgeoning theory of organicism.

The shape of history and historical self-consciousness

The view of history and historical progress as to some extent circular, and the propensity for cyclic systems of thought, is remarkably prominent among many leading intellectuals and artists of the early nineteenth century, above all in Germany. 'The True . . . is the circle that presupposes its end as its goal' Hegel famously declared in the Preface to the *Phenomenology of Spirit*.[14] For Johann Gottlieb Fichte, 'the collective journey, which mankind pursues, is no other than a way back to that point upon which it stood at the very beginning, and has no other goal but to return to its origin',[15] while for Goethe, similarly, 'the entire creation is and was nothing but a falling from and returning to the original source'.[16] Likewise, in the works of Schiller, Schelling, Hölderlin, Novalis, the Schlegel brothers, Kleist and Eichendorff; in England Wordsworth, Coleridge, Blake and Shelley; and,

into the nineteenth century coherence across a multi-movement work was understood to be realised through the generic succession of movements of defined tempo and tonality and a perceived aesthetic inner unity of psychological or expressive states rather than through the unity of material ('Schnell–Langsam–Schnell: Zur "klassischen" Theorie des instrumentalen Zyklus', *Musiktheorie*, 1 (1986), 214). It is also possible that the notion of musical unity was simply less important – or problematised – for composers and theorists in the late eighteenth century (see on this point Neil Zaslaw, *Mozart's Symphonies: Context, Performance Practice, Reception* (Oxford University Press, 1989), p. 416).

[14] Georg Wilhelm Friedrich Hegel, *Phenomenology of Spirit*, trans. A.V. Miller (Oxford University Press, 1979), p. 10, German original in Hegel, *Werke*, 20 vols. (Frankfurt am Main: Suhrkamp, 1979), vol. III, p. 23. Also see the 'Smaller' *Logic*: 'Philosophy exhibits the appearance of a circle which closes with itself' (*The Logic of Hegel*, trans. William Wallace (Oxford University Press, 1892), p. 25 / *Werke*, vol. VIII, p. 60), repeated in the conclusion to the 'Greater' *Logic* (*Science of Logic*, trans. A.V. Miller (London: Allen & Unwin, 1969), p. 842 / *Werke*, vol. VI, p. 571).

[15] Johann Gottlieb Fichte, *Die Grundzüge des gegenwärtigen Zeitalters*, Lecture 1, in *Johann Gottlieb Fichtes sämmtliche Werke*, 8 vols. (Berlin: Veit, 1845–6), vol. VII, p. 12, cited originally by M.H. Abrams in *Natural Supernaturalism: Tradition and Revolution in Romantic Literature* (New York: Norton, 1971), p. 218.

[16] Goethe, *Aus meinem Leben: Dichtung und Wahrheit*, part II, book 8, in *Poetische Werke: Vollständige Ausgabe*, 10 vols. (Essen: Phaidon Verlag, 1999), vol. VIII, p. 228. Unless otherwise stated, all translations are my own.

later, Carlyle and Marx – in all can be found the notion of a circular or progressive spiral journey which passes through discord and strife and back into unity. This tendency to view history and human progress in circular or spiral terms, as M.H. Abrams has shown, can be profitably viewed as a result of a Neoplatonist revival in contemporary philosophy and culture; in the words of Abrams, 'the basic categories of post-Kantian philosophy and many philosophical-minded poets can be viewed as highly elaborated and sophisticated variations upon the Neoplatonic paradigm of a primal unity and goodness, an emanation into multiplicity which is ipso facto a lapse into evil and suffering, and a return to unity and goodness'.[17]

This idea of history as cyclic is in fact an ancient and widespread one. Anthropological and ethnological researches support the validity, even historical primacy, of the conception of a cyclical, reversible time that can be found in many non-Western cultures and religions, and which stretches back in the Western tradition to Anaximander and Pythagoras.[18] In much ancient thought time is circular, consisting of the eternal recurrence of events throughout perpetual cycles of history.[19] At the time of the birth of natural science and philosophy in the work of the Pre-Socratics, the movement of the celestial bodies and the natural cycles of the day and seasons offered a strong justification for viewing the world in such light. This notion of time and the cosmos as cyclical can be found in Plato's Orphic flights of fancy and even in the more sober reasoning of Aristotle.[20] In the fifth century AD Proclus introduced the idea of the Great Circle to the Neoplatonist thought

[17] Abrams, *Natural Supernaturalism*, p. 159. Abrams provides an excellent survey of this tendency of post-Revolutionary thought to return to Neoplatonist conceptions and the cyclic view of history, to which I am greatly indebted here. More limited in scope but nevertheless useful is Marshall Brown's *The Shape of German Romanticism* (Ithaca, NY: Cornell University Press, 1979), relating specifically to the idea of the circle or spiral in German Romantic thought.

[18] See G.J. Whitrow, *Time in History: Views of Time from Prehistory to the Present Day* (Oxford University Press, 1988), pp. 19–96, and Mircea Eliade, *The Myth of the Eternal Return* (New York: Pantheon Books, 1954). Important anthropological accounts of time-conceptions in non-Western societies include Evans-Pritchard's *The Nuer* (1940) and Lévi-Strauss' *Structural Anthropology* (1958) and *The Savage Mind* (1962); see Nancy D. Munn, 'The Cultural Anthropology of Time: A Critical Essay', *Annual Review of Anthropology*, 21 (1992), 93–123, and Alfred Gell, *The Anthropology of Time: Cultural Constructions of Temporal Maps and Images* (Oxford: Berg, 1992) for critical assessments of this topic.

[19] Abrams, *Natural Supernaturalism*, pp. 34–7, also B.J. Bury, *The Idea of Progress: An Inquiry into its Origins and Growth* (London: Macmillan, 1920), pp. 7–13. The extent to which ancient thought still incorporated notions of progressive development is disputed; for a concise account see Whitrow, *Time in History*, pp. 37–51.

[20] Notable examples can be found in the myths related in Plato's *Republic, Phaedo, Phaedrus, Timaeus, Critias* and *Statesman*. Aristotle appears to support the uniqueness of the individual life (*On Generation and Corruption*, II.11), yet also the cyclical recurrence of human beliefs and institutions (*Metaphysics*, XI.8, *Meteorology*, I.3, *Politics*, IV.10) and time itself as something intrinsically cyclical (*Physics*, IV.13–14, a slightly obscure passage).

of Plotinus. All history and the events of the cosmos are part of a constant movement to and from the primal unity, the Neoplatonic One, identical with the Good, the True and the Beautiful, between which run innumerable smaller epicycles.[21]

The notion of indefinite cyclical recurrence was, however, inimical to Christianity, which introduced from Jewish millennialism the important idea of a single, linear progression to a finite end, the divine *eschaton*. The subsequent Hellenising of Christianity in the following centuries combined this circular progression of the Neoplatonists with the single historical trajectory of Christianity to result in the characteristic shape of the spiral. The end of time – the *telos* towards which the course of history is driving – will be the same as what was in the beginning, but yet greater. After the fall of man from the prelapsarian world of unity and his consequent division and alienation from the Good, the reformation of the world at the end of time will reunite all creation into the One, but now as part of a greater unity which consists of this multiplicity.[22] Such a notion was able to fit conveniently with several pre-existent aspects of Christian doctrine; 'I am the Alpha and the Omega, the beginning and the end', declares the Lord to St John.[23] Yet within this single progressive historical cycle, time, for the largely agrarian-based population of Europe, would still appear to follow a recursive cyclical course corresponding to the changing of the seasons and natural cycles of human life – 'a uniform and static experience' before the predicted second coming of Christ. To this extent, it had changed little since prehistory.[24] For the medieval world, the natural cycles of the seasons and the cosmic orbits of the planets thus reflected the divine order of creation, an order which was literally underpinned by the music of the spheres.[25]

The circular symmetries and unity in multiplicity characteristic of religious music before the age of scientific rationalism and secular humanism

---

[21] Proclus, *Elements of Theology*, trans. E.R. Dodds (Oxford: Clarendon Press, 1933), Prop. 25–39.

[22] Augustine's *City of God*, set against a Neoplatonist background, is undoubtedly the most important formulation of this Christian universal history; see particularly X.14 (on the progressive education of mankind), XII.13 (the rejection of earlier perpetual cyclic views of history), XXII.1 (the regaining of good from evil as being better than never having originally left this state) and XXII.30 (the final participation of the blessed in God, now with greater knowledge from this journey).

[23] *Revelation* I.8.

[24] Reinhart Koselleck, *Futures Past: On the Semantics of Historical Time*, trans. Keith Tribe (Cambridge, MA: MIT Press, 1985), p. 230.

[25] The mathematical ratios of the natural harmonic series occurring in music, which provided the basis for the idea of the harmonic underpinning of the entire cosmos, as found in the Pythagoreans and Plato and preserved by Boethius in his *De institutione musica*.

can be seen as a manifestation of this Neoplatonic order.[26] A fascination with abstract, often rather cerebral structures – complex contrapuntal forms and symmetries, crab canons and the like – is a characteristic trait of much fourteenth- and fifteenth-century Flemish polyphony. In the fourteenth century Machaut prefixed a retrograde canon with the legend 'Ma fin est mon commencement, et mon commencement ma fin', whose words form the solution to the canon.[27] The cyclic mass settings of the fifteenth and sixteenth centuries interlard common material throughout the separate movements of the mass, the pre-existent plainchant – the music of God, dictated to Gregory – functioning as a unifying spirit informing the separate parts of the whole. Scholars have likewise pointed to the static temporal quality of Renaissance modality and relative indifference of much baroque music to linear temporal order, in distinction to the emphatically progressive, dynamic temporality of tonal music after around 1750.[28]

The point at which this essentially cyclic model of time became replaced in Western Europe by a linear conception is subject to debate, but it is generally agreed that since the Renaissance, and above all during the Enlightenment, the notion of time as irreversible and progressive and the resulting temporalisation of experience increasingly took hold.[29] In many respects this can be viewed as a corollary to the rise of grand narratives of history resulting from the growth of modernism, bourgeois capitalism and secular humanism, alongside technological developments such as the capacity for ever-more accurate time-keeping. The 'long eighteenth century' is quintessentially the

---

[26] Good general overviews of the relationship of the art of the middle ages to Neoplatonist aesthetics can be found in Edgar de Bruyne, *The Esthetics of the Middle Ages*, trans. Eileen B. Hennesey (New York: Frederick Ungar, 1969), and Umberto Eco, *Art and Beauty in the Middle Ages*, trans. Hugh Bredin (New Haven, CT: Yale University Press, 1988).

[27] Illustrated in Nigel Wilkins, 'Rondeau (i)', in Stanley Sadie (ed.), *The New Grove Dictionary of Music and Musicians*, 29 vols. (London: Macmillan, 2001), vol. XXI, p. 646. Also illustrated is another canon actually written in the shape of a circle by Baude Cordier.

[28] See Walter Wiora, 'Musik als Zeitkunst', *Die Musikforschung*, 10 (1957), 27; David B. Greene, *Temporal Processes in Beethoven's Music* (New York: Gordon and Breach, 1982), pp. 7–27; Helga de la Motte-Haber, 'Historische Wandlungen musikalischer Zeitvorstellungen', in Diether de la Motte (ed.), *Neue Musik: Quo vadis? 17 Perspektiven* (Mainz: Schott, 1988), pp. 53–66; and generally on the change in temporal conception around 1750, Karol Berger, *Bach's Cycle, Mozart's Arrow: An Essay on the Origins of Musical Modernity* (Berkeley, CA and Los Angeles, CA: University of California Press, 2007).

[29] See Whitrow, *Time in History*, pp. 177–86; classic accounts of this development include Bury, *The Idea of Progress*, and Georges Poulet, *Studies in Human Time*, trans. Elliott Coleman (Baltimore, MD: Johns Hopkins Press, 1956). R.J. Quinones, in *The Renaissance Discovery of Time* (Cambridge, MA: Harvard University Press, 1972), dates this change to the Renaissance in northern Italy, France, England and Germany, while, conversely, Reinhart Koselleck sees this processes of temporalisation very much as a product of the eighteenth century.

century of the Enlightenment. From the revolutions in human thought of the preceding century – the decentring of the cosmos by Copernicus and Galileo, the development of the modern Dutch economy with its preoccupation with the individual in both mercantile and artistic forms and the rise of the middle class, the mechanistic physical universe of Newton's *Principia* and Locke's empiricist epistemology in the 1660s – the idea arose that humanity was in a state of development and progress, that mankind could control its own destiny. In a world where ancient belief in God and the established order of mankind was destabilised and subjected to the scrutinising eye of human reason, man was once again 'the measure of all things'. To quote the words of Alexander Pope's paean to humankind: 'Know then thyself, presume not God to scan; / The proper study of Mankind is Man. . . . / Sole judge of Truth, in endless Error hurl'd: / The glory, jest, and riddle of the world!'[30]

The eighteenth century is henceforth (perhaps rather simplistically) understood as the era of secular human progress, scientific, mechanistic and rationalistic. If the quintessential shape of history for the early nineteenth century is the circle or spiral, that of the eighteenth is, so to speak, the straight line, the path of history linear and unidirectional, moving imperturbably on to the forthcoming Utopia. As Turgot in 1751 defined the view of his age, 'the total mass of the human race, by alternating stages of calm and agitation, of good and evil, always marches towards greater and greater perfection'.[31] 'Without doubt this progress may be more or less rapid', agreed his follower Condorcet, 'but its course will never be retrograde.'[32] Hence it is hardly surprising that the music of the period strides confidently forward, seemingly unperturbed by the past. Humanity, it seems, will be able to find perfection and completion within time, to achieve closure through its own means.

Much of the Romantic movement in Western Europe can be read as a reaction against this insatiable linearity, a disillusioned realisation that this former dream of human progress was possibly too naïve.[33] What this

[30] Alexander Pope, *An Essay on Man*, Epistle II, lines 1–2 and 17–18, in Pope, *Poetical Works*, ed. Herbert Davis (Oxford University Press, 1966), pp. 250–1.

[31] Anne-Robert-Jacques Turgot, 'Plan de deux Discours sur l'Histoire Universelle', in *Oeuvres de Turgot et documents le concernant*, ed. Gustave Schelle, 5 vols. (Paris: Alcan, 1913–23), vol. I, p. 285.

[32] Nicolas de Condorcet, *Esquisse d'un tableau historique des progrès de l'esprit humain* (Paris: Agasse, 1795), p. 4.

[33] See Rudolf Wendorff, *Zeit und Kultur: Geschichte des Zeitbewusstseins in Europa* (Opladen: Westdeutscher Verlag, 1983), pp. 357–76. This is not to claim that the idea of progress stopped after 1800 – indeed it intensified in the nineteenth century – but for many intellectuals and thinkers this notion had become problematised and was forced to incorporate non-linear or cyclic elements (Hegel's spiral is a good example).

century of unstoppable progress had resulted in was the failure of the French Revolution, which after the euphoria of its beginnings disintegrated into the Terror and a series of wars that were to ravish Europe for the next two decades. The Romantics were hence the generation who grew up in the wake of the failure of humanity to reach its own secular Utopia. For this generation the linear teleology of the Enlightenment seemed simplistic. In the 'Prologue in Heaven' from Goethe's *Faust*, written in 1797 as the poet was resuming work on his masterpiece, the errant linear strivings of life on earth described by the archangel Michael are transcended by Raphael's account of the celestial harmony of the spheres, which move in circles.[34] For some – the paintings of David, the 'heroic' music of Beethoven's middle-period – the revolutionary hope is perpetuated through the Napoleonic years, but by the restoration of absolute monarchies at the Congress of Vienna, this final glimmer is extinguished.

The governing paradigm of history now had to be reformulated. After Wordsworth's glad confident morning turned to a bloody carnage, a secular theodicy is created to explain the failure of the revolution. Time and again this takes the form of a return to Neoplatonist conceptions of history as cyclic – a notion antithetical to linear progress – or fused with the idea of a (possibly indefinitely postponed) teleology, resulting in the shape of the spiral. Such views, as outlined at the start of this section, are the mark of so many artists and intellectuals of the generation that reached maturity in the aftermath of the French revolution.

In this febrile context, the pervasiveness of cyclical formal structures in nineteenth-century literature and music can be seen as a profound reflection of the cultural concerns of the time. The concept of returning to the past in some sense in order to progress into the future was a fundamental trope of early Romantic thought; variants of the idea can be found in Schiller, Friedrich Schlegel and in the historical dialectic of Hegel.[35] In part this

---

[34] Goethe, *Faust: Eine Tragödie*, 'Prolog im Himmel', lines 243–70, in *Poetische Werke*, vol. V, p. 124. See Jane K. Brown, *Goethe's Faust: The German Tragedy* (Ithaca, NY: Cornell University Press, 1986), pp. 42–59, which provides a useful account of Goethe's drama, its relation to Neoplatonism and contemporary thought.

[35] See Schiller's *Über die ästhetische Erziehung des Menschen* and *Über naive und sentimentalische Dichtung*, in *Sämtliche Werke*, 5 vols. (Munich: Carl Hanser, 1962), vol. V, pp. 570–669, 694–780. Constantin Behler comments that 'Schiller's aesthetics can be said to represent the purest, most precise, and most influential version of what can be called the classical German theory of modernity, in which typically an idealised image of ancient Greece anchors a critique of an alienated present that is dialectically to be overcome in a utopian third stage of history' (*Nostalgic Teleology: Friedrich Schiller and the Schemata of Aesthetic Humanism* (Berne: Peter Lang, 1995), p. 3). Likewise, see Friedrich Schlegel's *Philosophie der Geschichte*, 2 vols. (Vienna: Klang, 1829), Lecture 18, where the future is to be formed from a regeneration of the past. Hegel's entire philosophy, it has been claimed, was spurred on by the failure of radical

tendency was created by the need for German artists and intellectuals to build a specifically German artistic and literary tradition, as is seen notably in the work of Goethe. The desire to find a suitable starting point or model for such a tradition reflected acutely the birth-pangs of German national identity, in the face of centuries of cultural and artistic dominance from its European neighbours and the recent Napoleonic occupations. Commonly this is seen in Romantic thought as a spiritual return to the glories of ancient Greece, as articulated originally by J.J. Winckelmann and later taken up by Goethe, Schiller and Hölderlin,[36] or the longing for the supposed lost unity of the Christian middle ages when the Germanic lands had been united under the Holy Roman Empire (whose thousand-year reign had finally crumbled under Napoleon in 1805).[37]

The defining characteristic of cyclic works is this same idea of recurrence, the return to the past. Whether this is as the telos of a work or as part of the journey to an eventual new state, such a structure is antithetical to the straightforward linearity of the eighteenth century or indeed the archetypal heroic paradigm of middle-period Beethoven. In this context it is indeed notable that several of Beethoven's compositions most significant for their use of cyclicism belong to a brief period around 1815–16. The coincidence with the date of the Congress of Vienna and the ensuing period of restoration is surely not entirely by chance. The extent to which the return to the past and the sense of history becomes more prominent in Beethoven's music increases dramatically in the period which saw the restoration of pre-1789 political systems across Europe and the ultimate dissolution of the Enlightenment dream of progress, the same point that saw the return to non-linear interpretations of history in the intellectual thought of the time.[38]

modernism as seen in the French Revolution and the consequent need for continuity with the past. Both Schlegel and Hegel were closely connected with Mendelssohn, the former being his uncle by marriage, the latter a frequent guest of the Mendelssohn household in the 1820s and his philosophy lecturer at university.

[36] Representative examples include Winckelmann's *Gedanken über die Nachahmung der griechischen Werke in der Malerei und Bildhauerkunst* (1755), Goethe's theoretical works (such as 'Antik und modern') and his literary emulation of classical models (*Iphigenie, Römische Elegien*), Schiller's *Ästhetische Erziehung* and *Über naive und sentimentalische Dichtung*, and Hölderlin's novel *Hyperion*.

[37] This idea informs the thought particularly of the Romantics, such as the Schlegels, Wackenroder, Tieck and Novalis, whose *Die Christenheit oder Europa* (1799) is probably the most prominent illustration of this tendency.

[38] A useful consideration of Beethoven's later music and its relationship to the political events of the time is provided by Stephen Rumph, *Beethoven After Napoleon: Political Romanticism in the Late Works* (Berkeley, CA and Los Angeles, CA: University of California Press, 2004). Rumph touches on several aspects of the cyclical procedures of this music in relation to the national ideology of the time and the Hegelian view of history (pp. 18–25 and 112–20).

The sense of the past articulated in cyclic music from the early nineteenth century can furthermore be seen to reflect the heightened sense of historical self-consciousness present to the generations living after 1800. The idea of history and time played a more prominent part in the nineteenth century than it possibly ever had before.[39] This was the age of heightened historical self-consciousness and the birth of historicism. Intellectuals like Wilhelm von Humboldt saw in such historical consciousness a key to modern self-identity and cultural nationhood; 'one cannot understand the present without knowing the past, and the relationship between the two', as Goethe was to claim.[40] From the establishment of museums and national galleries, the preservation of early artefacts and paintings, unprecedented philological concern with ancient sources, the Gothic revival and neo-classical trends in architecture and visual arts, the early nineteenth century witnessed an unparalleled interest in and awareness of the works of the past.[41] In music, the decades after 1820 saw the Bach revival and the invention of the modern musical canon, in both of which Mendelssohn played a pivotal role.[42] The idea of 'inventing' traditions became further a key part in the creation of national identity in the rising tide of nationalism that spread across Europe.[43] Such views are particularly marked in the Restoration period, that era between the Congress of Vienna in 1815 and the failed

[39] For overviews of the importance of time to German intellectuals of the era see Wendorff, *Zeit und Kultur*, esp. pp. 339–400, and Koselleck, *Futures Past*. It is arguable that this sense of historicity first grew in the eighteenth century as the reverse face (and determiner) of the notion of progress; the importance of history to such figures as Turgot and Condorcet is clearly evident in their works cited above.

[40] Goethe, *Italienische Reise*, bk. I, 25 January 1787, in *Poetische Werke*, vol. IX, p. 211.

[41] Other examples of this historical tendency include the Palestrina revival in music and the Nazarene movement in art (one of whose most important figures, Philipp Veit, was Mendelssohn's cousin). Relevant scholarship in this field includes Walter Wiora, *Die Ausbreitung des Historismus über die Musik: Aufsätze und Diskussionen* (Regensburg: Bosse, 1969), James Garratt, *Palestrina and the German Romantic Imagination: Interpreting Historicism in Nineteenth-Century Music* (Cambridge University Press, 2002), and more generally, Stephen Bann, *Romanticism and the Rise of History* (New York: Twayne, 1995), Susan Crane, *Collecting and Historical Consciousness in Early Nineteenth-Century Germany* (Ithaca, NY: Cornell University Press, 2000) and John Edward Toews, *Becoming Historical: Cultural Reformation and Public Memory in Early Nineteenth-Century Berlin* (Cambridge University Press, 2004).

[42] The most comprehensive account of Mendelssohn's activities on behalf of historical music is provided by Susanna Großmann-Vendrey in *Felix Mendelssohn Bartholdy und die Musik der Vergangenheit* (Regensburg: Bosse, 1969).

[43] Eric Hobsbawm and Terence Ranger (eds.), *The Invention of Tradition* (Cambridge University Press, 1992). The success of James Macpherson's Ossianic works in the later eighteenth century, for instance, reflected this urge to find an origin for a specifically northern European artistic and cultural tradition. The *Nibelungen* craze in Germany from the 1820s onwards was similarly an attempt to validate a specifically Germanic artistic heritage.

revolutionary uprisings across Europe of 1848 which was later given the unflattering sobriquet of *Biedermeier*, to which most of the examples of early Romantic cyclicism belong.

In a review of 1835, Robert Schumann even speaks of the cyclic tendency in music as explicitly forming a type of historical consciousness: a composer 'no longer persisted in developing an idea only within one movement, one hid this idea in other shapes and modifications in following movements. In short, one wanted to integrate *historical interest*... and as the entire age became more poetic, dramatic interest as well.'[44] Such cyclic works intrinsically demonstrate the presence of the past within the present; one's own time and the present cannot be understood in isolation, but must be viewed in light of what led up to it, the journey which explains the arrival. Indeed, as in Montaigne's adage, often the journey is more important than the arrival: for the early Romantics, the hope of the final Utopia – the very idea of a triumphant goal to human striving – was becoming increasingly suspect, and was often postponed indefinitely or made synonymous with a circular return to the past.

Subjectivity

This idea of historical self-consciousness closely relates to a further distinction between the cyclical music of the nineteenth century and the circular or cyclic designs manifested in earlier music: the idea of subjectivity.[45] By subjectivity, in this context, I mean the notion of music as somehow embodying an autonomous aesthetic persona, broadly congruent but not identical to the biographical creator – what Carl Dahlhaus has defined as the 'aesthetic' as opposed to the 'biographical' subject of a work.[46] This aesthetic subject

---

[44] Robert Schumann, 'Sonaten für Pianoforte' (*Neue Zeitschrift für Musik* (*NZfM*), 2 (1835)), in *Gesammelte Schriften über Musik und Musiker*, ed. Martin Kreisig, 2 vols. (Leipzig: Breitkopf & Härtel, 1949), vol. I, p. 59, emphasis mine.

[45] The brief description here is obviously a drastic oversimplification of the issue. The idea of musical subjectivity relates closely to a range of interrelated notions arising at that time which cannot be covered here. These include the rise of the autonomy of instrumental music and the work concept; the emancipation of art from religious function and growth of the aesthetic idea of originality; and the change in aesthetic views of artistic creativity from (neo-)classical *mimesis* to the self-expression of 'Sensibility' and Romanticism. It is also possible to argue for the earlier appearance of certain aspects of this musical subjectivity with the aesthetics of *Empfindsamkeit*; see especially Laurenz Lütteken, *Das Monologische als Denkform in der Musik zwischen 1760 und 1785* (Tübingen: Niemeyer, 1998).

[46] Carl Dahlhaus, *Ludwig van Beethoven: Approaches to his Music*, trans. Mary Whittall (Oxford University Press, 1991), p. 31. The concept of a musical persona takes up an idea suggested by Edward T. Cone, *The Composer's Voice* (Berkeley, CA: University of California Press, 1974),

is allocated the qualities of human consciousness with a temporal sense and the capacity to think and develop in relation to its surroundings. In a useful formulation, Michael Steinberg has described this sense of subjectivity as denoted by what he calls two 'fictions of modern music': music 'can and does speak in the first person', and 'has the capacity of memory, a sense of past, present and future, and a means for their articulation'.[47]

This conception of music as forming some type of aesthetic presence, a subjective persona that seems intrinsically related to the movement of our conscious states and experience of time, is a commonplace of our listening habits and understanding of Romantic music. The belief that music may be closely connected to the nature of human consciousness is again an idea with a long provenance, but it is particularly pronounced in the early nineteenth century, where it relates to the wider importance attached to the notion of subjectivity during this period. (To this extent, I am less concerned here with precisely *how* music may model a sense of subjective presence – an extremely tricky undertaking, in part because it is not just music that seems to resist full conceptual formulation but time, the self and consciousness too – than with the historical fact that this supposed connection between music and subjectivity was recognised and perceived as significant at this time.[48])

As Steinberg argues, since the Enlightenment music has been heard as articulating the relationship of the individual to society, self to other, that is such a feature of the modern human condition. Rather than the individual being literally the 'subject' of a feudalist despot, the history of modernism – defined in broadly Marxist terms as the age of the rise of the secular bourgeois individual in Western Europe – is characterised by the capacity for the individual to negotiate his or her relationship between self and external society. It is this capacity for social interaction that Steinberg terms subjectivity.

This change in societal structure is replicated by a significant shift in philosophical systems underpinning the beliefs of the time. For the pre-moderns, the presence of God as a metaphysical given assures a meaningful

---

later developed by Carolyn Abbate in *Unsung Voices: Opera and Musical Narrative in the Nineteenth Century* (Princeton University Press, 1991). See further Raymond Monelle, *The Sense of Music: Semiotic Essays* (Princeton University Press, 2000), chapter 6, 'Text and Subjectivity', pp. 147–69.

[47] The definition is taken from Michael P. Steinberg, *Listening to Reason: Culture, Subjectivity, and Nineteenth-Century Music* (Princeton University Press, 2004), p. 9.

[48] Cf. Richard Klein, 'Thesen zum Verhältnis von Musik und Zeit', in Richard Klein, Eckehard Kiem and Wolfram Ette (eds.), *Musik in der Zeit: Zeit in der Musik* (Göttingen: Velbrück Wissenschaft, 2000), p. 62.

order to the world and man's place within nature. With the existence of a transcendent God now in question, the inheritance of the Enlightenment demand for reason, the post-1790 generation had to generate the totality of the cosmos from only the basic epistemological grounds of the Cartesian *cogito*, without allowing God into the equation. Epistemology attempts to construct a metaphysics; God and the Absolute are marginalised or even discarded.[49] This is why the philosophical systems of the post-Kantian philosophers are primarily epistemological. The philosophical idealism of Fichte, Schelling and Hegel attempts to reconstruct the universe from the basic opposition of subject and object, self and other. The subjectivity so commonly attributed to the Romantics finds its philosophical justification in the subject-generated world of Fichte's *Science of Knowledge* and Schelling's *System of Transcendental Idealism*. The progression of history becomes in their work the process of the mind understanding its own past, as epitomised in that seminal *Bildungsreise* of the spirit's movement to self-consciousness, Hegel's *Phenomenology of Spirit*. In such a system, the transcendent eschatology of Christian thought is replaced by an immanent one, where the telos is the return back into the self, hence describing a circular journey.[50]

The importance of the rise in subjectivity in philosophy at this time does not just present an inert background to what I am describing as musical subjectivity, since art, and above all music, was seen as providing a vital role in articulating this notion of subjective identity.[51] For Steinberg, this 'modern articulation of subjectivity relied importantly on music'.[52] Music is a language of subjectivity, a mode of cultural experience and understanding privileged by early German Romantic thinkers. Hegel had claimed that 'music takes as its subject-matter the subjective inner life itself',[53] while Schleiermacher held that music conveys the 'movements of self-consciousness', not

[49] See Charles Taylor, *Sources of the Self: The Making of Modern Identity* (Cambridge, MA: Harvard University Press, 1989), esp. pp. 127–98.
[50] Again, for an elegant account of this philosophical development see Abrams, *Natural Supernaturalism*, pp. 65ff. Robert C. Solomon also provides an accessible historical critique of this conception of the all-encompassing self – what he terms the 'transcendental pretence' – in *Continental Philosophy since 1750: The Rise and Fall of the Self* (Oxford University Press, 1988).
[51] For a good account of the development of subjectivity in German philosophical thought of the time and its relation to aesthetics, above all music, see Andrew Bowie, *Aesthetics and Subjectivity: From Kant to Nietzsche* (Manchester University Press, 2003) and *Music, Philosophy, and Modernity* (Cambridge University Press, 2007).
[52] Steinberg, *Listening to Reason*, p. 9.
[53] Georg Wilhelm Friedrich Hegel, *Aesthetics: Lectures on Fine Art*, trans. T.M. Knox, 2 vols. (Oxford: Clarendon Press, 1975), vol. II, p. 909 / *Werke*, vol. XV, pp. 158–9.

conceptual ideas 'but true states of life'.[54] Music also famously occupies the highest position among the arts in the metaphysical system of Arthur Schopenhauer, where its pattern of tension and release across time functions as an idealised mirror of the Will, analogous to the movement of human consciousness.[55] For the Romantic mind, time *is* indeed human conscious-ness. The external mechanism of Newton's seventeenth-century clockwork universe is replaced by Kant's subject-generated contingency of human time. For Schelling, time is 'not something which runs independently of the self, but rather, time is the *self itself*'.[56] Since music 'has time in itself', it correspondingly exhibits a close relationship to self-consciousness.[57]

Music was heard to enact the journey of the aesthetic subject spoken of by Dahlhaus in an artistic *Bildungsreise* comparable to that crystallised in the novel of the period – the *Bildungsroman* epitomised in Goethe's *Wilhelm Meisters Lehrjahre*.[58] As Scott Burnham has influentially formulated it, the middle-period works of Beethoven were heard as the discourse of an aesthetic self across time – a 'telling presence' that both enacts and nar-rates a heroic mytho-poetic journey that remains a powerful trope to this day.[59] Musical works were commonly seen as a succession of different psy-chological 'soul-states', a progression described by E.T.A. Hoffmann in his famous review of Beethoven's Fifth Symphony and found in the writings of A.B. Marx and future critics like Robert Schumann.[60] This feature is made explicit in Berlioz's programmatic support for his *Symphonie fantastique*,

---

[54] Friedrich Schleiermacher, *Ästhetik*, ed. Rudolf Odebrecht (Berlin: de Gruyter, 1931), p. 394, quoted by Bowie, *Aesthetics and Subjectivity*, p. 232.

[55] Arthur Schopenhauer, *Die Welt als Wille und Vorstellung*, vol. II, chapter 39, in *Werke* (*Zürcher Ausgabe*), 10 vols. (Zurich: Diogenes Verlag, 1977), vol. IV, pp. 535–8.

[56] Friedrich Wilhelm Joseph Schelling, *System des transzendenten Idealismus*, in *Sämtliche Werke*, ed. K.F.A. Schelling, 14 vols. (Stuttgart: Cotta, 1856–61), vol. III, p. 466. Emphasis in the original.

[57] Schelling, *Philosophie der Kunst*, in *Sämtliche Werke*, vol. V, pp. 493 and 491.

[58] Friedrich Schlegel was pointing to this enhanced sense of subjectivity when he famously declared the French Revolution, the philosophy of Fichte, and Goethe's *Wilhelm Meister* as the defining characteristics of his age (*Athenäums-Fragment* No. 216). See on this point Isaiah Berlin's discussion in *The Roots of Romanticism*, ed. Henry Hardy (London: Chatto & Windus, 1999), pp. 93–9.

[59] Scott Burnham, *Beethoven Hero* (Princeton University Press, 1995). Burnham argues that 'Beethoven's music successfully models human self-consciousness' (p. 142); in Beethoven the human is the subject for the first time in Western music.

[60] For instance, A.B. Marx claims that Beethoven, in the 'Eroica', elevated music from undifferentiated feeling to 'the sphere of the clearest and most definite consciousness' (A. B. Marx, *Ludwig van Beethoven: Leben und Schaffen*, 2 vols. (Berlin: Janke, 1828), vol. I, p. 265). On the notion of music for Schumann forming some type of psychological progression, see Anthony Newcomb, 'Once More "Between Absolute and Programme Music": Schumann's Second Symphony', *19th-Century Music*, 7 (1984), 233–50.

where the cyclic thematic techniques (the successive thematic transforma-tions the work's *idée fixe* undergoes) enact the journey of a subjective persona (here the symphony's protagonist) across the work. (As this example shows, the idea of the narrative or spiritual development of a musical 'persona' within a piece of music is often intrinsically bound up with the thematic development or transformation of a musical subject.[61])

In cyclic pieces, the recurrence of music from past movements adds a further, deeply significant, aspect to this concept of musical persona: the idea of memory. The recall of the past within the present consciousness of the music opens up an entirely new dimension to the discourse, the consciousness of separate levels of time. Cyclic music *has a history*. The progression of the musical work across time becomes transparent to itself. Previously latent relationships between the music of separate movements become explicit, establishing a form of musical self-consciousness. Through its capacity for memory, the identity of the work as a unified whole becomes clear to itself, taking up the idea of the construction of self-identity through memory that is such a feature of the modern age.[62]

Indeed, it could be argued that this sense of subjectivity may be bet-ter expressed through music than through philosophical concepts. This is certainly how many nineteenth-century thinkers, philosophers as well as musicians and artists, viewed it, who looked to music to illuminate notions of time, self-consciousness and subjective identity for which full conceptual formulation appeared problematic, if not impossible.[63] In the cyclic music

---

[61] Scott Burnham has again described this idea aptly as 'the almost universal critical concept of the anthropomorphic subject, the musical theme that acts as a dramatic protagonist whose tribulations and triumphs comprise for the listener a deeply engaging psychological process' (Review-Article 'E.T.A. Hoffmann's Musical Writings', *19th-Century Music*, 14 (1991), 295).

[62] This idea was given its classic formulation by John Locke (*An Essay Concerning Human Understanding*, II.27, 'Of Identity and Diversity'), and remained, problematically, part of our modern understanding of self-identity. On this link between music and self-consciousness, see further Bowie, *Music, Philosophy, and Modernity*, pp. 138–65, and, on self-consciousness and Romantic art more generally, James H. Donelan, *Poetry and the Romantic Aesthetic* (Cambridge University Press, 2008).

[63] See Bowie, *Aesthetics and Subjectivity*, p. 34: 'Although music is manifested in sensuous material, it does not necessarily represent anything and may in consequence be understood metaphorically as articulating or evoking what cannot be represented in the subject, namely the supersensuous basis of subjectivity which concepts cannot describe.' As Manfred Frank and Andrew Bowie have both argued, this point also undercuts the arguments advanced by some critics attacking the supposed notion of the unified self and subjective identity in modernity, since the resistance of the self and self-consciousness to adequate philosophical formulation was already recognised by numerous contemporary thinkers, while art (and music in particular), as a conveyer of meaning itself irreducible to verbal determination, avoids the pitfalls inherent in the critique of language.

of Mendelssohn and Schumann, as with that of Franck, Elgar and Mahler after them, the complex textures and shifting play of temporal states create a multilayered conception of time and a richness and complexity to the musical journey unequalled in other music. Music, the most fundamentally temporal art, is heard to encapsulate the entire range and subtlety of modern subjectivity within its own structure.

Organicism

This idea of the art-work as embodying a type of consciousness, a living, evolving organism, connects to a further important contemporaneous idea, the concept of organicism. Across the eighteenth century the reigning neo-classical aesthetic of *mimesis* gradually gave way to this new conception of a work of art as an organic, self-sufficient entity. This was supported by the shift in models of creativity from the empiricist-based epistemological system of Locke – the mind as a *tabula rasa*, reflecting what it sees – to the Romantic idea of the creative overflow of genius; from art as imitation of nature to art as manifestation of the spirit of its creator.[64] The organicist theory emphasises both the natural, living quality of the art-work and its inner unity and connectedness of parts, even when the latter may be difficult to perceive. Indeed, the two aspects are interconnected; because the work is thought of as having grown naturally and 'spontaneously from the vital root of genius', its unity is ensured, as every part connects to and is dependent on each other.[65]

Organicism thus emphasises qualities such as life, change and growth, yet also unity and the idea of natural cycles. Such aspects can be seen as congruent with many features of the Neoplatonist thought of an earlier age, effectively updating this concern with the unity of the whole by replacing God in the centre by the individual artist-genius. This interest in the unifying of separate parts is one of the underlying motivations for the cyclical thematic techniques, the recall or metamorphosis of material across the separate movements of an instrumental piece. This spreading out of connections across the inter-movement span of a work runs alongside the consequent subordination of the autonomy of the individual movement in favour of the logic of the overall design. In the classical formulation, the

---

[64] A classic overview of organicist theories of the time and their philosophical roots is provided by M.H. Abrams, *The Mirror and the Lamp: Romantic Theory and the Critical Tradition* (Oxford University Press, 1953), pp. 156–225.

[65] Edward Young, *Conjectures on Original Composition* (1759; repr. Leeds: Scolar Press, 1966), p. 12.

parts are only fully explainable through the whole, and the whole through the parts.

This cultural backdrop is hardly insignificant, since the use of cyclical form arose in music at around the same time as the notion of organicism in Britain and Germany, and the notion of the cycle – natural recurring patterns such as the life-cycle or seasons – is deeply bound up with the idea of organicism. Starting in Britain with figures like Young and Gerard, and spreading to Germany with Herder, Goethe and Kant, the concept of an organic living spirit informing the work of man and nature and the essential coherence and unity of the whole became a dominant paradigm whose influence still remains to this day. The idea informs much of Goethe's thought, most famously theorised in *Die Metamorphose der Pflanzen* (1790), and was taken up by the younger generation of Romantics both in Germany and in England.

In music theory of the time, organicism became the predominant model of musical composition, replacing eighteenth-century rhetorical, physio-logical and mechanistic theories. Deriving from the nature philosophy of the German Romantics and idealist philosophers, the concept was taken up by several of the leading musical critics and theorists.[66] In his famous 1810 review of the Fifth Symphony, E.T.A. Hoffmann explicitly describes Beethoven's music in organicist, natural terms ('the beautiful tree, leaves, blossom and fruit, springing from one seed'), commenting on the hidden deeper unity of the parts and calling attention to the thematic metamor-phoses of the opening motive across the work.[67] (The criterion of unity, as used perhaps uncritically in the twentieth century as a normative demand for a work of art, is hence justified in this particular context as a valid historical premise governing the music of the time.)

This move to an organicist model is coupled with an increasing empha-sis on the thematic aspect of music by contemporary theorists. For figures

---

[66] See Lotte Thaler, *Organische Form in der Musiktheorie des 19. und beginnenden 20. Jahrhunderts* (Munich: Emil Katzbichler, 1984); a good summary of this relationship between organicism and musical theory in the early nineteenth century is also given by Ian Bent in *Music Analysis in the Nineteenth Century*, 2 vols. (Cambridge University Press, 1994), vol. I, pp. 7–17. Other useful considerations of this topic include Ruth Solie, 'The Living Work: Organicism and Musical Analysis', *19th-Century Music*, 4 (1980), 147–56; David L. Montgomery, 'The Myth of Organicism: From Bad Science to Great Art', *The Musical Quarterly*, 76 (1992), 17–66; and Severine Neff, 'Schoenberg and Goethe: Organicism and Analysis', in Christopher Hatch and David Bernstein (eds.), *Music Theory and the Exploration of the Past* (University of Chicago Press, 1993), pp. 409–33.

[67] E.T.A. Hoffmann, 'Beethovens Instrumental-Musik', from *Kreisleriana*, in *Poetische Werke*, 6 vols. (Berlin: Aufbau Verlag, 1963), vol. I, p. 102.

like Reicha, Marx and Lobe, the construction and development of thematic material was the primary aspect of musical composition. In Marx's
words, 'each musical creation evolves, just as do organisms in nature, from
a germ . . . called a "motive"'. 'The motive is the primary configuration of
everything musical, just as the germinal vesicle . . . is the primal configuration of everything organic – the true primal plant or animal.'[68] All three theorists were connected in the capacity of teacher, confidant or friend with the
most significant cyclic composers of the younger generation, Mendelssohn,
Berlioz, Schumann, Franck and Liszt.

It is also clear that this type of organic interconnectedness (at both a
technical and a spiritual level) was not only known by the composers in
question but was also perceived as a significant aspect of their cyclic works.
Speaking of Beethoven's C♯ minor Quartet in a letter of 1828, Mendelssohn
enthuses

That is one of my principles! – the relationship of all 4 or 3 or 2 or 1 movements of
a sonata to each other and to their respective parts, so that one already knows, from
the simple beginning throughout the entire existence of such a piece, the secret that
is in the music.[69]

Referring to Mendelssohn's A minor Quartet two years later, the critic
Ludwig Rellstab likewise describes the lied 'Frage' that serves as a motto
for the quartet as 'a song whose poetic content and musical expression
weaves a secret thread, establishing a spiritual bond between the individual
movements'.[70] Robert Schumann's account of Mendelssohn's own Third
Symphony leaves further unmistakable evidence of the importance of this
organic process to composers at this time. In this important review of 1842,
Schumann imputes two types of organicism to this highly cyclic work. First,
the extreme level of thematic interconnection between movements and the
corresponding unity of the whole is noted ('the symphony is distinguished
by the intimate relation of all four movements to one another. . . . More
than any other symphony, it constitutes a tightly woven, complete whole')

---

[68] Cited in Bent, *Music Analysis in the Nineteenth Century*, vol. I, p. 14; Adolph Bernhard Marx,
'Form in Music', in *Musical Form in the Age of Beethoven: Selected Writings on Theory and
Method*, ed. and trans. Scott Burnham (Cambridge University Press, 1997), p. 66.

[69] Mendelssohn, letter of 22 April 1828 to Adolf Lindblad, in Lotte Dahlgren (ed.), *Bref till Adolf
Fredrik Lindblad från Mendelssohn, Dohrn, Almqvist, Atterbom, Geijer, Fredrika Bremer,
C.W. Böttiger och andra* (Stockholm: Albert Bonnier, 1913), p. 20.

[70] Ludwig Rellstab, review of first edition of Mendelssohn's Quartet Op. 13, in *Iris im Gebiet der
Tonkunst*, I:51 (24 December 1830), n.p., cited by Thomas Grey, '. . . *wie ein rother Faden*: on
the origins of "leitmotif" as critical construct and musical practice', in Ian Bent (ed.), *Music
Theory in the Age of Romanticism* (Cambridge University Press, 1996), p. 199.

and, second, the cyclic relationship of the finale's coda to the opening of the first movement is described in terms of the natural cycle of day. 'Many will expect the symphony to conclude in the character of the last movement, while instead, rounding out the whole in cyclic fashion, it recalls the opening introduction of the first movement. We find this conclusion poetic; it is like an evening mood corresponding to a beautiful morning.'[71]

The difference between the few examples of thematic recall in classical-period works and those found later in Romantic music is often related to this ideal of organicism. The return of music from a past movement in the former is normally heard as an intrusion, something external which disrupts the fabric of normative form – a quotation from outside. In Romantic cyclicism, the recall usually becomes part of the fabric of the work, pointing to a higher unity, a feature which has important implications for the perception of time and musical narrative.[72] In such cyclicism, even when the recall does not arise logically it is usually integrated into the subsequent course of the music, a feature which may be seen as a variant of the 'breakthrough' (*Durchbruch*) principle, where an event occurring outside the immanent flow of the music – imposed through transcendent means, a *deus ex machina* – is stabilised by its following retrospective integration into the immanent fabric of the musical discourse.[73] The difference between the reprise of the third movements in the finales of Beethoven's Fifth Symphony and Mendelssohn's Octet is that the return in the latter is integrated into the course of the finale, arising seamlessly out of its own thematic material, which is therefore retrospectively seen as related. This softens the distinctions between movements; it is not just heard as a quotation of something past, but subsumes both scherzo and finale, past and present, into a more complex conception of time.

The quotation of the minuet in the finale of Haydn's Symphony No. 46 can similarly be seen as an ironic, self-conscious comment on the work, rather than an instance of later Romantic cyclicism. The quotation is not integrated at all into the movement but proceeds from a fermata at a slower tempo, distinctly separate from the rest of the finale. This obvious reminiscence

---

[71] Robert Schumann, 'Sinfonien für Orchester', *Gesammelte Schriften*, vol. II, p. 133.

[72] Though, as noted above, a small number of nineteenth-century cyclic works belong to a specific subset of non-integrative cyclic formal types that relate to the idea of disruptive cyclicism.

[73] The idea of 'breakthrough' arose from the writings of Paul Bekker on Mahler (see *Gustav Mahlers Sinfonien* (Berlin: Schuster, 1921), pp. 44ff.) and was subsequently taken up by Adorno in his monograph on the composer. For a discussion of this concept see James Buhler, 'Breakthrough as a Critique of Form: The Finale of Mahler's First Symphony', *19th-Century Music*, 20 (1996), 125–43.

of a prior movement breaks down the autonomy of the finale in the same way as Haydn's 'knowing' manipulations of generic expectations in sonata movements (for instance, the false recapitulation) have been analogised with the broadly contemporaneous irony of Laurence Sterne and the early German Romantics.[74] The thematic similarity between the material of the two movements is exposed by their juxtaposition, but there is no attempt at making this an organic synthesis. (If this is integrative, it can be so only through a Romantic awareness of the gap between the disunified quality of the music and the totality to which it points, something which has to be posited ironically by the listener rather than forming an inherent quality of the music.[75] This is notably different from the later nineteenth-century practice, where cyclic recall is normally strongly integrative and synthetic. To invert categories, in Friedrich Schlegel's definition, Haydn's would be 'Romantic' art, Mendelssohn, Schumann, Franck and the rest 'classical'.[76]) Charles Rosen's view of cyclic recall as relating to the fragment is applicable here, but not, I would argue, for most of the later Romantic examples.[77] This is the only time in 106 symphonies that Haydn recalls part of an earlier movement in a later one, which suggests that this one instance should be seen more as a pun on musical form and the idea of the autonomy of individual movements than as a generic structural principle.

Origins and precursors of nineteenth-century cyclicism

The development of cyclic form is gradual and multifaceted, and it is impossible to give clear cut-off dates for what constitutes 'proto-cyclicism' and what alternatively is 'true' Romantic cyclicism. The origins of nineteenth-century cyclical practice are hence not straightforward. Two broad lines

[74] Rey M. Longyear, 'Beethoven and Romantic Irony', *The Musical Quarterly*, 56 (1970), 647–64; Mark Evan Bonds, 'Haydn, Laurence Sterne, and the Origins of Musical Irony', *Journal of the American Musicological Society*, 44 (1991), 57–91.

[75] See Daniel K.L. Chua, 'Haydn as Romantic: A Chemical Experiment with Instrumental Music', in W. Dean Sutcliffe (ed.), *Haydn Studies* (Cambridge University Press, 1998), pp. 120–51.

[76] See Friedrich Schlegel, *Über das Studium der griechischen Poesie* (1795), or the *Athenäums-Fragment* No. 116, which set out the incompleteness requisite of Romantic art. In David Ferris' reading, the distinction can be read as one between dynamic organicism (the 'Romantic', incomplete and infinitely striving) and formal organicism (the 'classical'; complete, perfect and unified), which highlights a 'basic contradiction in the doctrine of organicism' (*Schumann's 'Eichendorff Liederkreis'*, pp. 62–3).

[77] Rosen, *The Romantic Generation*, pp. 88–92. Rosen himself applies this theory only to Mendelssohn's Octet, in the context of Romantic cyclical practice.

of development may be traced.[78] The first grows out of the performative tradition of the improvised keyboard fantasy, as exemplified in the works of C.P.E. Bach, where a freer approach to form may be integrated by the reuse of common thematic material across its parts, sometimes accompanied by the running together of sections.[79] Merged with the classical sonata this resulted in the mixed genre of the *sonata quasi fantasia*. Cyclic works which arise out of this tradition include Beethoven's Piano Sonata Op. 27 No. 1 (1801), Hummel's Fantasy in E♭, Op. 18 (1805), E.T.A. Hoffmann's Piano Sonata in F (1807), Dussek's Fantasy in F, Op. 76 (1811), Schubert's 'Wanderer' Fantasy (1822) and the Fantasy for Violin D. 934 (1827).[80]

The second category consists of works from the classical symphonic and instrumental genres, such as Haydn's Symphony No. 31, the 'Hornsignal' (1765), where a cyclic design is suggested by the brief allusion to the horncall of the opening movement in the last bars of the finale, and the Symphony No. 46 (1772) discussed above, Ordonez's String Quartets Op. 1 (*c.* 1760s), Vanhal's Symphony in A major A9 (*c.* 1775–8), which returns to the music of the opening at the close of the finale, and Dittersdorf's Symphony in A major K. 119 (1788), whose finale, entitled *Recapitulante*, recalls themes from earlier movements within its rondo structure. The music of composers working outside Vienna if anything features such thematic recall more frequently. Examples include C.P.E. Bach's Sonata H. 151 (Wq. 51/2, 1760) and Keyboard Concertos H. 473 and 475 (Wq. 43/3 and 43/5, 1772); Boccherini's Quintets in A major and C major Op. 25 Nos. 3 and 4 (G. 297–8, 1778)

[78] The role opera played in popularising the idea of recurring themes may also be significant, especially given the rise of reminiscence themes in French *opéra comique* of the late eighteenth century (of which Grétry's *Richard Coeur-de-Lion* (1784) is normally cited as the first example). This technique's influence on the *idée fixe* of Berlioz and the programmatic cyclic tradition that followed him is clear.

[79] Examples include the *Fantasies* H. 227 and 289 (Wq. 122/5 and 61/3). See further, David Schulenberg, *The Instrumental Music of Carl Philipp Emanuel Bach* (Ann Arbor, MI: UMI Research Press, 1984), pp. 138–45, and, more generally, Peter Schleuning, *Die freie Fantasie: Ein Beitrag zur Erforschung der klassischen Klaviermusik* (Göppingen: Kümmerle, 1973).

[80] The original version of Schumann's *Fantasie* Op. 17 also recalled the end of the first movement at the close of the work. The use of the designation 'fantasia' to connote an instrumental work with greater formal freedom (and in this context cyclic connections or through-composed links between movements) is echoed in later symphonic works such as Schumann's Fourth Symphony and Sibelius' Seventh. Similar fantasia-like structural experiments (such as the running on of movements, conflation of sections into a single movement or the cyclical recall of material) also mark the instrumental concerto after 1820, to a degree greater than in other instrumental genres. Spohr's Violin Concerto No. 8 in A minor, 'In modo di scena cantante' (1816), J.B. Cramer's Concerto No. 8 in D minor (*c.* 1819) and Weber's *Konzertstück* Op. 79 (1821) are three of the earliest models; later concertos by Mendelssohn, Moscheles, Alkan, Clara Wieck, Herz, Schumann, Rubinstein and Liszt participate in this tradition.

and Symphonies in D minor Op. 12 (G. 506, 1771) and C minor Op. 41 (G. 519, 1788); Viotti's Violin Concerto No. 21 (*c.* 1792–7); Anton Reicha's Symphonies Opp. 41 and 42 (1799/1800) and String Quartet Op. 52 (1805); Clementi's Piano Sonatas in G major Op. 40 No. 1 (1802) and G minor Op. 50 No. 3 ('Didone abbandonata', 1821); Dussek's Piano Sonata in A♭, Op. 64 (1807); and Méhul's Symphony No. 4 (1810). Most significant in this early development is perhaps the Piano Sonata in C minor (*Figurata*) Op. 18 (1802, pub. 1820), by Ludwig Berger, later to become Mendelssohn's piano teacher. The *Figurata* of the sonata's title refers to the six-note germinal motive stated at the start, which is explicitly used to generate the material of all three movements. Berger's work originated as a bet to see whether the composer could write an entire sonata based on a single motive.[81] If the accolade of 'first cyclic work' had to be awarded to a piece, Berger's Sonata would be one of the strongest candidates for that title.

Beethoven and Romantic cyclicism

Most famous of the pre-Romantic cyclic composers is undoubtedly Beethoven, despite the fact that cyclical procedures, in the fully fledged forms later encountered in nineteenth-century music, are far less prevalent or significant in Beethoven's music than common opinion might suggest. It would nevertheless be misleading to suggest that Beethoven's role and status for the Romantics was not of singular importance here. Beethoven was central to all subsequent composers who tackled the problem of large-scale instrumental form, many of whom wished to be seen, or were claimed by supporters, as heirs to his musical and spiritual legacy, and the cyclic elements of several of his works would serve both as inspiration and as legitimation for many later musicians.[82] Within only a few years, the cyclic tendencies of Beethoven's later music would be taken up and developed further by the first generation of Romantic composers. Subsequent figures would continue to draw on Beethoven for inspiration, though this was

---

[81] A good account of Berger's sonata and its relation to the idea of organic growth is given by Montgomery, 'The Myth of Organicism', 27–30.

[82] Vincent d'Indy, for instance, was often at pains to stress his teacher Franck's position as direct descendant of Beethoven, as part of the nationalist ideology of his time. While Beethoven was undoubtedly an influence on Franck, Mendelssohn's early works and the thematic technique of Berlioz – with the possible addition of Schubert's 'Wanderer' Fantasy and the example of Franck's teacher Anton Reicha – are actually far more developed and realistic models for Franck's early efforts in the style.

nearly always mediated through the achievement of the first generation of
composers after him.

Cyclical procedures, in the sense later understood by the term, are definitely emergent in several of Beethoven's works, chief amongst these being
the Piano Sonatas Op. 27 No. 1 and Op. 101, the Cello Sonata Op. 102
No. 1, the Symphonies Nos. 5 and 9, and *An die ferne Geliebte* Op. 98.
Both the Sonata Op. 27 No. 1 and the Fifth Symphony are, by their structural incorporation of parts of earlier movements in their finales, cyclic in
the strict sense above. Other works famous for cyclic recurrence such as
the Ninth Symphony, the Piano Sonata Op. 101 and Cello Sonata Op. 102
No. 1 are not structurally cyclic but use thematic recall as a rhetorical gesture, ultimately external to the unfolding of events even if calling attention
to them. Here music from previous movements is recalled as if constituting
a memory, summing up the journey so far, before the music can continue
into the finale. The intention here is similar to later Romantic cyclical usage,
even if the structural implications of such recall are slight. By binding up
the movements and increasing the sense of continuity across the inter-
movement span of the work, Beethoven contributes to a stronger and more
potent sense of aesthetic journey across the music. Other works such as the
sonatas Opp. 106 and 110 similarly blur the demarcation of movements'
thematic individuality.

Of the handful of earlier works in cyclic form, the Op. 27 Sonata is
designated *Sonata quasi una fantasia*, which allies it with the performative
tradition of the improvised fantasy (the later sonatas, Op. 101 and Op. 102
No. 1, can similarly be seen to draw upon this tradition). The Fifth Symphony, meanwhile, is a fascinating work on the cusp of two eras, encoding
this fissure within its very structure. Ostensibly, this is the epitome of the
progressive, heroic work, more so, in a way, than the 'Eroica', since this teleological journey is acted out unflinchingly across the course of the entire
symphony. The Fifth Symphony is the apogee of the eighteenth-century
confidence in progress, but simultaneously embodies the nagging fear that
the conquered past may come back to haunt the present – the cold horror
of the return to the scherzo in the middle of the finale – that such triumph
of the human spirit, even the possibility of such a triumph, is not final
but only a chimera. The moment of doubt that disturbs even this most
celebrated of heroic works points to the reality of the future, the collapse
of the revolutionary daydream by 1815, within which the obsessive hammering of the C major tonic for twenty-nine bars at the symphony's close
seems merely feverish. As Hoffmann understood, the struggle of the symphony is still heard resonating even in the silence following the conclusion,

personifying the 'infinite yearning which is the essence of romanticism'.[83] While the symphony is not as fully developed a cyclic work as those of the Romantic era which followed it, it foretells in this one gesture the future of Romantic cyclicism.

The extent to which Beethoven's late works are cyclic is rather questionable, in contrast to popular supposition. Opus 131 may possibly feature an allusion to its opening fugal subject in the second subject of the finale, but this example is hardly as distinct or thorough-going as later cyclical use. The conjectured thematic links between several of the late quartets – the idea of a common four-note motivic cell which interpenetrates all five, as Deryck Cooke has theorised – do suggest something nearing cyclic procedure, though the arcane way in which Beethoven often handles this suggests a creator more wishing to hide or subvert the unity to which such connections point.[84] The works of 1815–16 – the Op. 101 Sonata, the C major Cello Sonata, and *An die ferne Geliebte* – all suggest an organic unity and coherence that the later works question as much as they confirm. It would be wrong to suggest that none of these pieces relate to cyclicism or the later works of the Romantics, since for Mendelssohn, at least, they provided the starting point for his more extensive structures and were seen as such (see the letter of 1828, quoted on page 33). But, as so often with these works, their qualities seem even more enigmatic and inscrutable the more they are examined.

An die ferne Geliebte is the work of Beethoven that most closely approximates later Romantic cyclicism, and the strongest example before Mendelssohn.[85] Here, an early prototype of Mendelssohn's more complex design in his Opp. 6 and 13, the implicit affinity between the last and first songs is realised when the music of the opening is recalled near the end of the song-cycle. The effect is not just of passive memory but of a linking of past and present; the memory of the past grows out of the present and indeed becomes part of the present, the two converging into a new variant

---

[83] E.T.A. Hoffmann, 'Beethovens Instrumental-Musik', *Poetische Werke*, vol. I, p. 101.

[84] See Deryck Cooke, 'The Unity of Beethoven's Late Quartets', *The Music Review*, 24 (1963), 30–49.

[85] *An die ferne Geliebte* is in fact in many ways closer to the instrumental cyclic forms than to the Romantic song cycle in structure. As David Ferris argues, 'What *An die ferne Geliebte* has, which is lacking in virtually every other Romantic cycle, is a clear sense of unity and coherence ... For this reason, [it] is much closer to the continuous instrumental forms that provide us with familiar exemplars of organic unity' (*Schumann's 'Eichendorff Liederkreis'*, pp. 10–11). Likewise, for Richard Kramer, '*An die ferne Geliebte*, the work commonly taken to define the [song-cycle] in its pure, most elemental state, stands ironically at the periphery of it' (*Distant Cycles*, p. 9). The best account of the cyclic qualities of this work has been given by Christopher Reynolds, 'The Representational Impulse in Late Beethoven, I: *An die ferne Geliebte*', *Acta Musicologia*, 60 (1988), 43–61.

which combines memory and actuality into one.[86] A fundamental point of the Romantic conception of cyclicism is that a return to something past may be yet part of an onward, teleological trajectory, a circular journey which is still progressive. As such, it introduces a new conception of time and narrative process.

A further important figure of the 1820s is Franz Schubert, who deserves to be mentioned in this context even though overt thematic cyclicism does not play a prominent part in his instrumental music. Beyond the 'Wanderer' Fantasy (his most celebrated cyclic work and highly influential later for composers such as Schumann and Liszt) and the C major Violin Fantasy, the only other clear example of cyclicism in Schubert's output is the Piano Trio No. 2 in E♭, Op. 100 (1827). The recall of the andante second movement in the finale of this work should be seen as representative of an essentially Romantic conception of cyclicism, albeit differing from Mendelssohn in its replacement of a dynamic, progressive conception of time with a more static circularity.[87] More common in Schubert's music is the recurrence of small harmonic/motivic gestures or distinctive sonorities between movements, which, while less openly cyclic in a formal sense, nevertheless undoubtedly contribute to a sense of aesthetic journey. Such features are present in the last two symphonies and the late piano sonatas and chamber music (the String Quartet in G, D. 887, is a good example).[88] This aspect of Schubert's music is one of the reasons why it has frequently been assigned the quality of memory and reminiscence, a feature which is traditionally opposed to the teleological dynamism of Beethoven's heroic works and allies it more with the disillusioned spirit of Restoration Vienna.[89] The composition of

[86] See Rosen, *The Romantic Generation*, pp. 166–74, and interpretations by Joseph Kerman, 'An die ferne Geliebte', in Alan Tyson (ed.), *Beethoven Studies 1* (New York: Norton, 1973), pp. 123–57, and Nicholas Marston, 'Voicing Beethoven's Distant Beloved', in Scott Burnham and Michael Steinberg (eds.), *Beethoven and his World* (Princeton University Press, 2000), pp. 124–47.

[87] The notion of a fatalistic circularity or indefinite wandering to Schubert's works from *c.* 1822, taking *Winterreise* as its hermeneutical support, is a feature of much discussion of the composer; a good example is Scott Burnham, 'Landscape as Music, Landscape as Truth: Schubert and the Burden of Repetition', *19th-Century Music*, 29 (2005), 31–41.

[88] See Charles Fisk, *Returning Cycles: Contexts for the Interpretation of Schubert's Impromptus and Last Sonatas* (Berkeley, CA and Los Angeles, CA: University of California Press, 2001). Claims for the cyclic properties of some of Schubert's other works have also been made by Martin Chusid in 'Schubert's Cyclic Compositions of 1824', *Acta Musicologica*, 36 (1964), 37–45.

[89] See Carl Dahlhaus, 'Sonata Form in Schubert', in Walter Frisch (ed.), *Schubert: Critical and Analytical Studies* (Lincoln, NE: University of Nebraska Press, 1986), p. 8: 'In Schubert, unlike in Beethoven, the most lasting impression is made by remembrance, which turns from later events back to earlier ones, and not by goal-consciousness, which presses on from earlier to later.' Also see the issue of *The Musical Quarterly* dedicated to the matter of Schubert and memory (*The Musical Quarterly*, 84 (2000), 581–663).

Schubert's works at much the same time as Mendelssohn was exploring similar notions of memory in music suggests a fascinating common concern.

Cyclic form in Mendelssohn's early works

Mendelssohn's early works experiment with ideas of cyclicism to a degree unmatched in the music of his contemporaries. In Mendelssohn's music, the principle of cyclic thematic recall becomes fused for the first time with the process of onward thematic development and the organic interconnection of material between separate movements, the formal principle which became a quintessential property of most future cyclic works. Such thematic recall is moved from its position as an extraneous rhetorical gesture, as in Beethoven's music, and integrated into the movement as a fundamental part of its structure. Mendelssohn's earliest examples commonly demonstrate thematic affinities between movements, while his subsequent works increasingly bring these relationships to the surface and, by the Piano Sextet of 1824, feature the literal recall of music from earlier movements. The remainder of this chapter will explore the development of this cyclic tendency in Mendelssohn's early works up to 1825 and his first full essays in the form.

Both Mendelssohn's earliest published compositions, the Piano Quartets Opp. 1 and 2 (completed in October 1822 and May 1823 respectively) demonstrate definite yet unostentatious similarities in material between individual movements typical of much classical-period music. The former is clearly indebted to Mozart, while the latter is one of the earliest illustrations of Mendelssohn's creative encounter with the music of Beethoven. The C minor Quartet Op. 1, written when the composer was just thirteen, proceeds from an antecedent phrase built out of a complex of three motives (i, ii, and iii) which are taken up and modified in the remaining three movements (see Ex. 1.1). The first movement's second subject, taken from the preceding bridge-passage figuration and marked by the characteristic grace-note of motive iii, is similarly echoed in the second movement (second theme, b. 27), in aspects of the scherzo (see particularly the section following the double bar, b. 37), and in the finale's second theme (b. 20), which likewise relate to motive iii.

Meanwhile, the F minor Piano Quartet concerns itself with an interrelationship of material that goes beyond the affinities between movements seen in Op. 1 and manifests itself in a predilection for a design approaching the monothematic construction of the four-movement cycle. Thus the first movement's second subject clearly grows from the three-note descent of the first bar, via a transitional passage in the piano which sequences out

Ex. 1.1   Piano Quartet in C minor Op. 1 (1822): motivic connections.

this motive into a descent of over an octave (bb. 29–36, see Ex. 1.2). The adagio second movement is built on both this descending third and the characteristic contour of the first movement's first subject (the rising sixth $\hat{5}$–$\hat{3}$–$\hat{1}$[–$\hat{7}$]), which in turn is taken up in the second theme (b. 25). In this movement's recapitulation, the reprise of the second subject is substituted for by the barely distinguishable first theme, now transformed into the texture of this second theme.[90] Both the third movement intermezzo and finale take up this sixth-motive, the melodic sequence from F minor to the Neapolitan G♭ in the latter ([c]–c♭–b♭) being prepared by the descending chromatic c–b♯–b♭ in the second bar of the intermezzo (x, Ex. 1.2). The finale of this quartet, like that of its predecessor, is a genuine monothematic

---

[90] On this point, see the good account given by Greg Vitercik, 'Mendelssohn as Progressive', in Peter Mercer-Taylor (ed.), *The Cambridge Companion to Mendelssohn* (Cambridge University Press, 2004), pp. 72–5.

Ex. 1.2 Piano Quartet in F minor Op. 2 (1823): thematic connections.

movement, thus completing the tight interrelationship of parts evidenced in the work. The concern in this work with the logical development of fundamentally lyrical material points its way to the sophisticated procedures of Mendelssohn's later music from the 1830s.

A further composition from this period, the String Quartet in E♭ (March–April 1823), was not published by Mendelssohn and had to wait until 1879 before seeing the light of day. The quartet continues the practice observed in Op. 1, where relatively understated relationships between the four movements are suggested by affinities in thematic construction and contour between several of their themes. Again, this is partly achieved through surface similarities in melodic decoration (the grace-notes of the first movement's second subject, second movement's first subject, and the minuet and trio) and a common underlying construction of themes (the rising triadic contour seen particularly between the trio and opening fugue

Ex. 1.3 Violin Sonata in F minor Op. 4 (1823): opening themes of first two movements.

Ex. 1.4 Clarinet Sonata (1824): thematic transformation of outer movements.

subject of the finale). None of the techniques displayed in these early pieces go much beyond the achievement of the Viennese classics, but nonetheless they clearly demonstrate Mendelssohn's ready assimilation and mastering of this tradition.

In the years 1823–4 Mendelssohn wrote three instrumental sonatas for solo instrument and piano, of which the only one to be published in his lifetime was the F minor Violin Sonata Op. 4 (May–June 1823). While there is no direct quotation of earlier movements in this work, the intrusion of a cadenza in the finale's coda, returning to the recitative-like gestures of the previously anomalous, unaccompanied opening of the first movement, imparts a strong sense of cyclic reprise and rounding-off. Relationships between the thematic material of the separate movements are relatively inconspicuous, though the opening of the Poco adagio picks up the descending c–ab anacrusis of the first movement, reinterpreted now as $\hat{3}$–$\hat{1}$ in Ab major, before touching on F minor in its opening bars, highlighting if only momentarily the connection between the two movements (Ex. 1.3).

Both the other two instrumental sonatas feature far more overt connections between musical themes. The finale of the Clarinet Sonata in Eb (completed in April 1824) takes up the scalic descent of the first movement's main theme, in what must be the clearest example of thematic transformation found so far in Mendelssohn's music (Ex. 1.4).

Ex. 1.5 Viola Sonata (1823–4): thematic connection between last two movements.

The implications of this relationship appear to be more an attempt to unify the sonata through the close matching of its outer movements – an affinity which is strengthened by the parallels between the structures of these two movements and by the related textures of their respective second subjects – than an expressive device, as it would later become in Mendelssohn's music. Nevertheless, this sonata marks an important change from the relatively understated relationships of the previous instrumental works, and points its way to the future use of cyclic form.

The Viola Sonata in C minor, written between November 1823 and February 1824, similarly demonstrates close relationships between its movements. The substantial set of variations that functions as the work's finale takes up a close transformation of the material of the preceding Menuetto second movement for its theme (Ex. 1.5). Further relationships are established, moreover, by the affinity between the continuation of this second movement and the first theme of the opening movement. It is unclear why Mendelssohn did not publish this composition, given its impressive musical quality. Possibly the later reuse of the main theme of its minuet in modified form as the third movement of his First Symphony necessitated the discarding of one of these two works.[91]

This latter work – the Symphony No. 1 in C minor (March 1824) – is one of the most impressive of Mendelssohn's early compositions, and, along with the Op. 3 Quartet and D major Piano Sextet, a piece which suggests an attainment of compositional maturity well over a year before the more celebrated Octet. The formative musical idea of this work is a concise $\hat{5}$–$\flat\hat{6}$–$\hat{5}$) neighbour-note motive, sometimes continued down in scalic

---

[91] Mendelssohn seems to have been uncertain about the inclusion of the minuet in the symphony in any case, since he later replaced this movement with an orchestration of the scherzo from the Octet in performances of the symphony in London in 1829, before eventually deciding on the original movement upon publication in 1834. It is also possible that there was simply not a sufficient market for the solo viola to justify having such a work engraved.

Ex. 1.6 Symphony in C minor Op. 11 (1824): thematic working.

descent or repeated in sequence at degree 8̂. Nearly all of the symphony's themes incorporate this figure, normally as their head-motive (Ex. 1.6); elsewhere, the motive can often be found permeating the musical texture (for instance, in the first movement, bb. 53–4 and 65–6; third movement, b. 114; finale, second theme, bb. 52–5).

For the first movement's E♭ major second subject, the motive is retained at its opening pitches g–a♭–g, thus being reinterpreted as 3̂–4̂–3̂) in the major. This second subject is later recapitulated in the submediant, so it is only in the C major coda of the finale that this major-mode version on 3̂ is finally heard in the tonic major (b. 274). In addition, this motive's emphasis on ♭6̂ is further gives rise to a preponderance of ♭VI harmonies across the work. The recapitulation of the second theme in the first movement

Ex. 1.7a Piano Quartet in B minor Op. 3 (1824–5): motives x and y.

is shifted unexpectedly to A♭ major (thus sounding its opening motive at the pitches c–d♭–c heard earlier in the first theme's sequence at bb. 4–5), and the second-movement Andante is marked by the deft employment of ♭VI for the successive appearances of its transitional theme (C♭ (b. 17); F♯ (b. 59, enharmonic ♭VI of the secondary tonal area of B♭); and C♭'s enharmonic equivalent B (b. 63)).[92] The use of a similar chromatic motive as the basis of an instrumental work would be demonstrated a few months later in the Op. 3 Piano Quartet; meanwhile, in the later 'Italian' Symphony (1833/4), this same $\hat{5}$–♭$\hat{6}$–$\hat{5}$ neighbour figure would become a unifying thread across the last three movements.[93]

The successor to the two youthful piano quartets, the B minor Quartet Op. 3 (written between November 1824 and January 1825 and dedicated, with permission, to Goethe) shows far closer thematic links between movements, an increasing concern with motivic saturation and economy, and a growth and development of material which fully warrants the much-abused term organic. The quartet is pervaded by a chromatic gesture deriving from the chromatic turn figure of the opening bars (motive *x*), which itself soon gives rise to a related chromatic ascent deriving from this opening (*y*, Ex. 1.7a).

These two primary ideas run throughout the work, infusing themselves into much of its texture and being used as the basis for the principal themes of all four movements (Ex. 1.7b). These include the derivation of the scherzo from the opening Neapolitan-inflected turn (*x*) and the transformation of the second movement and scherzo's rising chromatic upper-voice into the finale's first theme (*y*). A subsidiary thematic idea, introduced as the first movement's second subject (b. 110, itself growing from b. 24), is taken up in a modified version as the second idea of the finale. The very last bars of

---

[92] The most detailed consideration of this piece is given by Wulf Konold in *Die Symphonien Felix Mendelssohn Bartholdys: Untersuchungen zu Werkgestalt und Formstruktur* (Laaber Verlag, 1992), pp. 39–85; also see Vitercik, *The Early Works of Felix Mendelssohn*, pp. 53–63.

[93] See John Michael Cooper, *Mendelssohn's Italian Symphony* (Oxford University Press, 2003). This motive is particularly prominent in the 1834 revision; Cooper surmises that Mendelssohn may have been dissatisfied with the symphony in its earlier manifestation due to its lack of cyclic unity, a deficit which the later concentration on this motive in the revisions to the last three movements was intended to rectify.

Ex. 1.7b Piano Quartet in B minor Op. 3: derivations of opening chromatic motive.

Ex. 1.7c Ludwig Berger: *Sonata Figurata* (1802): germinal motive.

the finale return to the original motive, recalling the work's opening in a highly effective closing gesture.

Such organic interconnections are indeed extremely appropriate given the work's dedication to Goethe. The germinal idea here is not dissimilar to that used by Berger in his *Sonata Figurata* (Ex. 1.7c),[94] though Mendelssohn's

---

[94] It is likely that Mendelssohn was aware of this piece, though this particular sonata was not one of the thirteen works by Berger found in Mendelssohn's library (Thomas Christian Schmidt, *Die ästhetischen Grundlagen der Instrumentalmusik Felix Mendelssohn Bartholdys* (Stuttgart: M & P, 1996), p. 33). The Mendelssohns' relationship with Berger is tricky to determine; the elder composer taught both Felix and his elder sister Fanny between 1819 and 1821 (thus at the time Berger's Sonata was published), though it appears that he was never fully accepted by the children's parents or attained the level of artistic influence and respect afforded to Carl Friedrich Zelter.

Ex. 1.7d Piano Quartet in B minor Op. 3: motivic–harmonic parallelism.

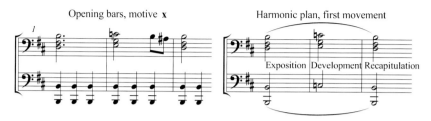

material proves far more susceptible to development and the fluid propagation of new variants across the course of the work, as is seen immediately by the growth of the initial figure into motive *y* in bar 9.

Indeed, the growth and metamorphosis of material in this work is not only thematic but harmonic, as the Neapolitan C♮ of the turn-motive in bar 2 is paralleled in a large-scale move to C major at the start of the first movement development section. In effect, the motivic model of the first three bars encapsulates in microcosm the structure of the movement, a notable example of organic growth from an initial seed or kernel which gives the appearance of containing the subsequent course of events within it (Ex. 1.7d).

This development section itself is a remarkably original conception, prescient of Mendelssohn's later structures: changing tempo up from *Allegro molto* (♩. = 72) to *Più allegro* (♩. = 112), it presents a further transformation of the chromatic ascent (*y*), preparing the melodic structure and texture of the scherzo,[95] and returns wholesale at the end of the recapitulation as a coda, mirroring the idiosyncratic parallel structure Mendelssohn was to use on several occasions later. The B minor Piano Quartet, taken as a whole, fully endorses Goethe's and Zelter's confidence in the composer, and represents as much as any work of Mendelssohn's his coming of age.[96]

It is the D major Piano Sextet of April–May 1824 (posthumously published as Op. 110), however, which constitutes Mendelssohn's first real essay in literal cyclic recall. Following the precedent set by Beethoven, its finale is interrupted by the recall of the grim minor-key 'minuet', echoing that in Beethoven's Fifth Symphony. Mendelssohn's arrangement differs substantially from Beethoven's, however, in that this cyclic recall occurs virtually at

---

[95] The Scherzo itself is slightly faster still, marked as *Allegro molto* (♩. = 126).

[96] An earlier piano quartet in D minor of Mendelssohn's had been responsible for the famous appraisal of the composer by Goethe, Zelter and Lobe as a musical genius whose precocity outmatched even that of Mozart's, whose prodigious abilities Goethe had experienced over a half-century before.

the end of the movement, being seen retrospectively as the goal of the music and thus determinedly altering the course of the work.

In this piece, the climactic reappearance of the D minor minuet in the Allegro vivace is as much the result of the work's harmonic argument as an outgrowth of its thematic process. Thematic and other more general musical relationships exist between the outer two movements, such as the parallel construction of their expositions and the loose affinity exhibited between the two second subjects (an affinity that is moreover echoed in the slow movement), which in themselves are not unusual for classical instrumental works. But in common with Beethoven's Fifth (if diverging from Mendelssohn's later example), the recalled material is not closely related thematically to the surrounding movement but is rather a shock disruption of the minor mode of the third movement.

The second movement's F♯ major represents an extreme sharpening of the major third of the tonic D major, a rarefied six-sharp Adagio directed to be played *con sordini* (possibly owing to the example of the Largo cantabile e mesto from Haydn's D major Quartet Op. 76 No. 5). This movement is counterbalanced by an immediate return to the tonic *minor* for the third movement scherzo and F major, its minor third degree, for its trio, setting up a harmonic dualism which will run throughout the finale and finally culminate in the return of the scherzo in the coda. The sharpward tendencies of the first two movements (circumscribing D major, its dominant A, F♯ major, and its dominant C♯) are thus contradicted by a turn flatwards to D minor in the third movement.

Throughout the course of the finale, an emphasis on the flattened sixth scale degree (b♭) becomes increasingly prominent, implying the tonic minor, D minor, at the expense of the ostensible D major tonality of the piece. Brief hints are given at b. 86 in the uneasy chromatic turn a–b♭–g♯–a that is familiar from the Op. 3 quartet and has appeared as a motive in several of the Sextet's themes. The development starts with a strange transition that leads to B♭, a brief tonicisation of this crucial ♭$\hat{6}$ scale degree, and in its second half sustains a dominant pedal on A that all the time threatens to slip up to B♭, strongly suggesting D minor. The bridge passage between first and second subjects is extended in the recapitulation, dwelling on the D minor hues suggested by the flattened-sixth b♭. The closing section, greatly expanded from that of the exposition, returns to the a–b♭–g♯–a turn, obsessively reiterating the b♭–a half-step, which comes to a shuddering halt on a dominant minor ninth ($V^{♭9}$, bb. 207–8), precipitating the return of the D minor third movement. This recalled minor-key agitato passage stretches for a full 37 bars, a dark twist to a movement that had initially seemed so carefree. The final Allegro con fuoco, based on the opening music of the finale, leads out of this third movement reprise, presenting a large i–I$^{\flat7}$–IV–iv–$\flat$II–[V]$^6_4$–V^7–i cadence which affirms D major only in the last three bars, retaining the D minor key signature to the end. Underneath the ostensible high spirits of the D major finale has been the shadow of this D minor minuet, whose tonality has gradually been encroaching on the movement and at its end finally breaks through.

The D major Piano Sextet is an attractive piece which points in more than one way to the composer's later works. One can only speculate as to why Mendelssohn chose to discard this piece; perhaps the unusual scoring (piano, violin, two violas, cello and bass) or the lack of thematic integration of this recalled material (anomalous within the rest of his oeuvre) may be cited as possible reasons. Besides the Sextet's important status as the first work of Mendelssohn's to feature the explicit cyclic recall of previous music in a later movement, the work exudes a Mozartian lyricism and melodic expansiveness that would be taken up again, if in a more sophisticated manner, in the A major Quintet Op. 18. The precarious balance in this work between major and minor modes of the tonic, the light and dark sides of the music's experience, is one that would become typical of Mendelssohn's music. Running throughout the Sextet is a darker undercurrent which threatens to upset the entire course of the work when it erupts in the finale, and is contained only with great difficulty. One is reminded in this context of the resigned statement that the composer penned to his father in 1830 on hearing of Goethe's critical illness, an expression that Eric Werner sees as 'entirely Goethean in spirit' as it is characteristic of Mendelssohn's Jewish heritage. 'In the midst of all merriment I never forget that the core and essence of all things is serious – yes, often tragic. And in serious moments I again think that true seriousness must be gay, and not dark and cold . . . I am convinced of this.'[97]

---

[97] Letter of Felix Mendelssohn to his father, 14 December 1830, quoted by Eric Werner, *Mendelssohn: A New Image of the Composer and his Age*, trans. Dika Newlin (London: Free Press of Glencoe, 1963), p. 171.

2 | Musical history and self-consciousness

The Octet Op. 20

Genieße mäßig Füll und Segen!
Vernunft sei überall zugegen,
Wo Leben sich des Lebens freut!
Dann ist Vergangenheit beständig,
Das Künftige voraus lebendig,
Der Augenblick ist Ewigkeit.

(Goethe, *Vermächtnis*[1])

Towards the end of the finale of Mendelssohn's Octet, the musical past becomes increasingly drawn into the present. Reminiscences of earlier movements are heard fleetingly amidst the seemingly irrepressible drive of the music to its final bars. In the central, developmental section of this movement's irregular structure, the theme of the quicksilver third-movement scherzo is caught three times, always in a new key, but is never securely held – and then 'all has vanished'.[2] The climactic coda – the apotheosis of the whole composition – unfurls in a series of three increasingly explicit references back to the music of the Octet's earlier movements. First comes a passage which sounds strangely familiar yet without being like anything previously heard in the finale, which manages to allude unmistakably to the Allegro moderato opening movement without ever quite quoting it. There follows a distant echo of the crisis that had befallen this movement's development section, whose darker hues had spilled out to form the slow movement – the insistent repeated minims and the revisiting of the C and F minor tonal areas of those two movements. Finally, the irrepressible sweep of this section is consummated by the explicit reappearance of the closing theme of the Allegro over the pulsating quavers of the finale's own closing theme. The finale and opening movement have closed and merged into one

---

[1] 'Enjoy in measure plenitude and blessing! / Let reason be present everywhere, / Where life delights in life! / Then the past is still abiding, / The future lives on before us, / The moment is eternity.'

[2] Goethe, *Faust I*, line 4398 (*Walpurgisnachtstraum*): 'und alles ist zerstoben' – literally, 'turned to dust' (*Poetische Werke*, vol. V, p. 230).

another, tying up the work with a return full-circle in an ecstatic meeting of parts to whole. The entire edifice has turned round on itself in one gigantic, interconnected organic system, which has grown away from and returned back into itself. Beginning and end, first and last, are one and the same.

It is the process of its own becoming, the circle that presupposes its end as its goal, having its end also as its beginning; and it is only by being worked out to its end, is it actual.[3]

If reception history is anything to go by (which admittedly in Mendelssohn's case is not always the best judge), the Octet in E♭ major for strings Op. 20, occupies a pivotal position within Mendelssohn's music. Robert Schumann, a colleague who deemed this work a composition of 'consummate perfection', recounts how the Octet remained Mendelssohn's favourite piece of his youth.[4] Judging by its subsequent reception, this work, alongside the Overture to *A Midsummer Night's Dream* that followed barely a year later, has become emblematic of a popular image of Mendelssohn that is as limited in scope as it is enduring. This youthful work is celebrated for being the miraculous product of teenage prodigy who at sixteen finds his mature voice, a legend which has sustained the myth of the young Mendelssohn emerging from nowhere like a musical Minerva, a fully formed genius at the age of sixteen. As John Horton expressed it, in a phrase that has been imitated and paraphrased countless times since, 'not even Mozart or Schubert accomplished at the age of 16 anything quite so accomplished as this major work of chamber music'.[5] Notwithstanding Spohr's series of 'double quartets', which the elder composer was quick to point out were anyway a different concept from Mendelssohn's work, as the first – and so far only really enduring – composition for eight strings, the Octet has effectively created a genre of which it is both the originator and sole surviving member. The third movement of this work has provided the embodiment of the 'Mendelssohnian scherzo' (particularly, one might add, to those whose knowledge of Mendelssohn's scherzos is rather limited) – a movement of mercurial deftness that has proved inimitable and defining to this day.

---

[3] Hegel, *Phenomenology of Spirit*, p. 10 / *Werke*, vol. III, p. 23.
[4] Robert Schumann, 'Erinnerungen an F[elix] Mendelssohn vom Jahre 1835 bis zu s[einem] Tode', in Heinz-Klaus Metzger and Rainer Riehn (eds.), *Felix Mendelssohn Bartholdy*, *Musik-Konzepte* 14/15 (Munich: Edition Text + Kritik, 1980), p. 107.
[5] John Horton, *The Chamber Music of Mendelssohn* (London: Geoffrey Cumberlege / Oxford University Press, 1946), p. 60. Horton's formulation itself perhaps owes something to Schumann's in his *Erinnerungen*: 'He wrote the Octet in his 15th [*sic*] year. No master of the past or present can boast such consummate perfection at such an early age' ('Erinnerungen an Mendelssohn', p. 107).

But, most importantly for the present study, this work is also one of the first and most significant compositions in cyclic form. The cyclic recall of parts of the work's earlier movements across the course of the finale is both a groundbreaking new formal paradigm and the climax of the work's expressive journey. The Octet provides an important new model for the form or paradigmatic 'plot' of an instrumental work, as would be used countless times following Mendelssohn. It displays the ceaseless onward drive of the archetypal Beethovenian 'Heroic' model, but simultaneously subsumes the past within its course. Indeed, the goal of the work seems to be the fusion of the two, the past and the present melding into one. This process can, I believe, usefully be viewed as a musical expression of views of time and history prominent around this age, most notably those by two of Mendelssohn's most important mentors or teachers, Goethe and Hegel.

This present chapter will be approaching the Octet from the standpoint of this cyclic formal design, offering readings of the work from the perspective of these two leading figures of German culture. This approach will lead to the creation of a new model for understanding cyclic form, relating to ideas of subjectivity, memory, time and history, which will be of major importance for consideration of much of the later cyclic music of the nineteenth century.

Musical memory and self-consciousness: 'the Circuitous Journey'

For on the circumference of a circle, beginning and end are the same (Heraclitus, Fragment B. 103)

It is the Octet's large-scale cyclic trajectory, in which its separate elements become fused into one, which constitutes the work's groundbreaking quality and creates a compelling formal paradigm that would become defining for so many later nineteenth-century pieces. Previous themes are heard returning in later stages of the work as if memories, arising from within the consciousness of the music, as is prefigured in several of Beethoven's cyclic designs such as the Ninth Symphony or the sonatas Opp. 101 and 102 No. 1.[6] What is new about Mendelssohn's process, however, is that the *telos* of the work is formed out of the realisation of these memories. Rather than in Beethoven's examples, where almost uniformly the recalled

---

[6] See Elaine Sisman, 'Memory and Invention at the Threshold of Beethoven's Late Style', in Scott Burnham and Michael Steinberg (eds.), *Beethoven and his World* (Princeton University Press, 2000), pp. 51–87.

past is an inessential rhetorical gesture that takes place before the real finale gets underway, in Mendelssohn's work the cyclic recall – the articulation of the music's self-consciousness – is the goal of the whole piece, to which the entire composition has been striving.[7] The telos is formed out of the synthesis of past and present.

This paradigm would become defining for later music: the cyclic model established by Mendelssohn in this work would become probably the most common type in the next century.[8] By recalling the past movements towards the end of the finale, binding the separate parts of the work up into one, Mendelssohn creates a design that would be taken up and imitated from Schumann and Franck to Bruckner, Tchaikovsky, Elgar and Mahler. To overstate the case mildly, it is hard to find a large-scale instrumental work from the end of the Romantic era that does not, in some way, incorporate a brief reminiscence of or passing allusion to one of its earlier movements as it nears its conclusion.

The prevalence of this design in later music is not just due to the influence of this one piece of Mendelssohn's, but points, I feel, to a deeper affinity of the times to this formal idea. This design is particularly fascinating for its resonances with a structure that became especially prevalent in literature and philosophy at the time, and remained a potent idea well into the twentieth century. This circular narrative design, which M.H. Abrams has entitled 'the Circuitous Journey', is found in so many of the writings of contemporary poets and philosophers, underlying much of their views on time and history. Indeed, Abrams outlines several of these characteristics of the philosophy and literature of the age, almost every one of which can be seen to be shared by Mendelssohn's work. These are:

 i) A self-moving and self-sustaining system
 ii) An immanent teleology
iii) Unity lost and unity regained

---

[7] The one work of Beethoven's that differs from this description in providing an example of *end*-orientated cyclic recall is, as noted, the song-cycle *An die ferne Geliebte*. Another work that stands behind the Octet is the Fifth Symphony, which in the recall of its third movement midway through the finale is often viewed as an immediate model for Mendelssohn's work. The crucial distinction between the two is that Beethoven's (like his Piano Sonata Op. 110 and Mendelssohn's own Piano Sextet of the preceding year) is an example of what I have termed 'disruptive' or 'non-integrative' cyclicism, differing in function and effect from the Octet's 'integrative' procedure. Haydn's Symphony No. 46 or Dittersdorf's Symphony in A, K. 119, are probably closer (if in all likelihood unknown) precedents for Mendelssohn.

[8] For Charles Rosen, for instance, this work of Mendelssohn's provided the 'supreme model' for most of the later experiments in cyclical form. 'Only rarely', however, 'was a similarly convincing simplicity achieved.' Rosen, *The Romantic Generation*, pp. 90–2.

iv) Progress by reversion – the Romantic spiral
 v) Redemption as progressive self-education
vi) The spiral journey back home.[9]

Famous examples of this circular journey can, according to Abrams, be found in Hegel's *Phenomenology of Spirit*, Hölderlin's *Hyperion*, Wordsworth's *Prelude*, and, later in the twentieth century, Proust's *A la recherche du temps perdu* and Eliot's *Four Quartets*. The beginning of the work is the end, but we only realise this at the end, which is reached through the coming to self-consciousness of the journey taken to get there. Indeed, the end can only be reached through this realisation of the journey it has taken, in summary.

Mendelssohn's Octet, then, may be seen as an innovatory musical expression of notions of time and historical consciousness that were extensively prevalent in early Romantic thought. This idea of a retrospective recapitulation of past history as a necessary step towards the attainment of the final goal – the notion of recapitulating the past in order to progress on to the future – is a recurring trope of the Romantic era. Such historical self-consciousness is one of the defining characteristics of Mendelssohn's age, and a fundamental category of what may be termed modernity. Mendelssohn, one can argue here, is the first fully to articulate this modern conception of subjectivity and historical self-consciousness in music, and this particular work, the Octet, is the first in which this is carried out.

Of all the examples cited above, perhaps the most promising parallel is that of Hegel. Mendelssohn, of course, knew the philosopher personally, and later attended Hegel's lectures on aesthetics as a student at the University of Berlin.[10] Even three years before studying under Hegel, it would hardly be surprising to find close affinities between Mendelssohn's work and the world and ethos of Hegel and Hegelianism. Mendelssohn was probably the most deeply cultured and widely read composer in history and certainly one of the most intelligent. The grandson of the 'Jewish Socrates' Moses Mendelssohn and 'the spiritual heir' of the humanist tradition of Goethe and classical Weimar, his grasp of philosophy and the classics was far beyond the level of

---

[9] Abrams, *Natural Supernaturalism*, pp. 172–95. The seventh and final category, 'Philosophical systems as a literary plot', obviously cannot apply directly to music (although one could note the prevalence in the nineteenth century of musical works with literary associations or allusions – a quality that is shared by the present piece).

[10] This was during the winter semester 1828–9; Mendelssohn's notes for these lectures still exist, though they are currently in private ownership and scholars have not yet been given the chance to study them in detail.

any comparable musician of the age.[11] (At the age of eleven Mendelssohn had taken to writing mock Homeric epics, and Goethe later commented with approval on the composer's translation of Latin authors. At the time of the Octet Mendelssohn was busy translating one of the seminal texts of classical aesthetics, Horace's *Ars Poetica*.) Growing up in the heady cultural milieu of 1820s Berlin, Mendelssohn could hardly fail to take on board aspects of Hegel's outlook, even if it is fair to assume that he would have been unlikely to have conceived a musical work as a musical embodiment of Hegel's philosophy. As Scott Burnham remarks, in 1820s Berlin, everybody was a Hegelian.[12]

The closest analogy for Mendelssohn's design is that found in Hegel's celebrated *Phänomenologie des Geistes*. I will contend that numerous features of the design and structure of Mendelssohn's Octet, and the approach to history and time evinced therein, form remarkable parallels with Hegel's famous work of 1807, and, more generally, with the ethos of Hegelianism and the Hegelian system. At the same time, Hegel is not the only personal acquaintance of Mendelssohn's with whose work the Octet forms notable correspondences. In true dialectical fashion, after much valuable insight, when taken to an extreme the connection between Mendelssohn and Hegel inevitably falters, which is when the figure of Goethe, waiting patiently in the wings, steps forward for the last part of the chapter. Thus the Octet affords us a chance to explore two of Mendelssohn's most extraordinary personal connections, those with Goethe and Hegel, and the importance such associations may have for the aesthetic conception of his music.

The Octet as a phenomenology of spirit

The basic premise of Hegel's *Phenomenology* and indeed his entire philosophy, to which the former was designed as a prolegomenon, is the notion of history as a necessary, self-sustaining organic process, tracing the coming to self-consciousness of an idea (namely spirit or *Geist*) over time. 'History is

---

[11] John E. Toews, 'Musical Historicism and the Transcendental Foundation of Community: Mendelssohn's *Lobgesang* and the "Christian German" Cultural Politics of Frederick William IV', in Michael S. Roth (ed.), *Rediscovering History: Culture, Politics and the Psyche* (Stanford University Press, 1994), p. 183.

[12] Scott Burnham, 'Criticism, Faith, and the *Idee*: A.B. Marx's Early Reception of Beethoven', *19th-Century Music*, 13 (1990), 187. A useful survey of early nineteenth-century musical culture in Berlin is provided in Carl Dahlhaus (ed.), *Studien zur Musikgeschichte Berlins im frühen 19. Jahrhundert* (Regensburg: Bosse, 1980).

nothing but the development of the idea of freedom', as he was to contend
later in the *Lectures on the Philosophy of History*. 'The history of the world
is this process of development and realisation of spirit.'[13] The structure
of Hegel's philosophy is a circle, or more precisely a spiral, moving out
dialectically from an initial unity through contradiction and back, returning to a recognition and awareness of the self: 'Only this *self-reinstating*
identity, or this reflection-into-self in other-being . . . is the true' (Preface to
the *Phenomenology of Spirit*).[14] Or, as formulated in the *Logic*:

> Progress is a *return* to the *ground*, to the *original* and *true* . . . The essential thing for
> science is not so much that something pure and unmediated is the beginning, but
> that in its totality it is a self-contained circle in which the first also becomes the last
> and the last the first . . . The line of scientific progress thus becomes *a circle*.[15]

Within this system, art, a manifestation of the highest mode of spirit,
Absolute Spirit, is a mode of consciousness, a form in which spirit reflects
on itself. It is a manifestation of the Idea in sensuous form, the category of
Beauty arising out of the convergence of the sensuous and the ideal ('the
pure appearance of the Idea to sense').[16] As Charles Taylor argues, the 'Idea'
here is to be understood in the Platonic sense, though Hegel imbues this
concept with a dynamic, generative quality not normally associated with the
earlier philosopher.[17] Following Kant's demand that the work of art, to be
considered as such, must be an end in itself, complete and self-contained –
to be 'purposive yet without purpose' – the art-work must, for Hegel,
furthermore embody the qualities of a self-sustaining inner teleology and
organic wholeness.[18]

This notion of a self-generating organic system, coming to self-knowledge
at its end through the recollection of its own history in an overall circular or spiral journey, is strongly reminiscent of the process seen in both
Mendelssohn's Octet and later in the Piano Sonata Op. 6 and Quartet Op. 13.
In fact, the Hegel scholar John Toews has characterised Mendelssohn's music
in decidedly Hegelian terms as the unfolding of an idea over time. Especially

---

[13] Georg Wilhelm Friedrich Hegel, *Lectures on the Philosophy of History*, trans. J. Sibree (New
York: Dover, 1956), pp. 456–7 / *Werke*, vol. XII, pp. 539–40, translation slightly altered; also
cf. p. 19 / 32.

[14] Hegel, *Phenomenology of Spirit*, p. 10 / *Werke*, vol. III, p. 23.

[15] Hegel, *Science of Logic*, p. 70 / *Werke*, vol. V, pp. 70–1, emphasis in original.

[16] Hegel, *Aesthetics*, vol. I, p. 111 / *Werke*, vol. XIII, p. 151.

[17] Charles Taylor, *Hegel* (Cambridge University Press, 1977), p. 328.

[18] Immanuel Kant, *Kritik der Urteilskraft*, §15 ['Eine formale objektive Zweckmäßigkeit aber
ohne Zweck'], in *Immanuel Kant: Werke*, 12 vols. (Frankfurt am Main: Suhrkamp, 1977),
vol. X, p. 144.

in Mendelssohn's early cyclic works, unity is provided 'by the recognisable continuity of a pre-given musical subject through a series of transformative variations or episodes', a process in which the musical theme or idea evolves towards 'full self-disclosure'.[19] The subject is initially given in 'undeveloped or not fully interpreted form', the process of the music being to reveal the subject 'as the hidden identity tying together its various movements'.[20] In Mendelssohn's work, one could say, spirit has found a way of reflecting on itself, enacting its own coming-to-self-consciousness within the work of art itself.[21]

As will be illustrated, the Octet operates as a giant interconnected organic system, embodying its own internal teleology and generative process. The large-scale recall of music from past movements in the course of the finale is only the clearest manifestation of the interconnection of all four movements achieved by Mendelssohn in this work, an ideal towards which he had been working in his compositions of the previous year, such as the B minor Piano Quartet. This relationship of 'all 4, 3, 2 or 1 movements to each other and their respective parts'[22] that Mendelssohn set as one of his compositional principles is manifested in a process of organic development and growth that occurs both internally to movements and further at a higher, 'meta-movement' level across the four-movement structure of the composition.

Without delving too deeply into the construction of the first three movements, some discussion of these earlier stages of the Octet is useful in establishing the nature of Mendelssohn's procedure, the entire organic system that he constructs, which will find its consummation in the cyclic recall of the finale. The following analytical section charts this organic growth of material across the Octet, initially seen within the first movement and then successively at higher levels, between first and second movement and then third and fourth, culminating in the wholesale reprise and transformation of the work's closing bars

---

[19] Toews, 'Musical Historicism and the Transcendental Foundation of Community', pp. 186–90.
[20] Toews, *Becoming Historical*, p. 230. Conversely, Andrew Bowie has interpreted Hegel's own *Logic* from an explicitly musical standpoint that reads like a summary of Mendelssohn's cyclic style: 'A theme emerges, disappears, reappears in changed form, and is finally made part of a wider movement, which ends such that the varying themes, which contrasted with and replaced each other, are seen as belonging together.' *Aesthetics and Subjectivity*, p. 156.
[21] On the role of the 'Idea' in the theory of A.B. Marx, and how this relates to Hegel and to Mendelssohn's music, see Arno Forchert, 'Adolf Bernhard Marx und seine "Berliner Allgemeine musikalische Zeitung"', in Carl Dahlhaus (ed.), *Studien zur Musikgeschichte Berlins im frühen 19. Jahrhundert* (Regensburg: Bosse, 1980), pp. 381–404.
[22] Mendelssohn, letter of 22 April 1828 to Adolf Lindblad, in Dahlgren, *Bref till Adolf Fredrik Lindblad från Mendelssohn*, p. 20.

1							2			C
1¹	1²	1¹ (→Tr)	1²	on V	2	2	(developed)			C
1^{1.1} 1^{1.2}		1^{1.1} 1^{1.2}			2.1 2.2 2.1 2.2	(1²)(1^{1.1})(2.1)				
E♭	V/f	E♭ V/f f	V/g	g V/B♭	B♭	V/g G	V/c V/A♭ g	V/B♭	B♭	
1 9	21	37	45	52	59	68	75 77	84 88	93	113 127

Fig. 2.1 Octet in E♭, Op. 20 (1825), first movement exposition: thematic and harmonic structure.

Cyclicism and the organic growth of material across the Octet

Organic growth: the first movement

For Friedhelm Krummacher, the thematic process of the first movement's exposition is the first time that Mendelssohn comes close to the ideal of organicism that is such a notable characteristic of his mature music.[23] Both thematically and harmonically, this opening movement reveals a continual process of growth out from its opening phrase that indeed justifies the analogy with the aesthetic ideal of organic growth and unity claimed by several commentators.

The exposition is built on a double-phrase construction of its two main subject groups, a design that contributes greatly to the unusually broad scale of the movement (Fig. 2.1). (Indeed, in its scope and breadth this movement immediately bids to be set beside another work in E♭, the first movement of Beethoven's Third Symphony, an analogy which, as we shall see, is not just incidental.[24]) The two main sentential-like phrases of the first subject group (bb. 1–20 and 21–37, themselves split into two unsymmetrical parts), are immediately repeated, bb. 37–59. This repetition, however, is far from being an exact replication of the proceeding music. The exposition is formed from an ever increasing series of harmonic waves expanding out by step from the tonic E♭. The supertonic, F minor, implied by the harmonic sequence of the

---

[23] Friedhelm Krummacher, *Mendelssohn – Der Komponist: Studien zur Kammermusik für Streicher*, p. 156.

[24] This gigantic movement was indeed longer still in the first version of 1825, more than double the apparent length at 731 bars to the present 318. Substantial cuts were introduced by Mendelssohn when revising the work in 1832, most significantly to the recapitulation of the first subject, and by renotating the original crotchet note values to quavers reducing two bars in the written score to one.

Ex. 2.1 Octet, first movement: harmonic reduction of exposition, bb. 1–68.

opening theme, bb. 1–4 to bb. 5–7, is more strongly suggested by the V/ii at b. 25, this subsidiary phrase bb. 21–37 forming a complement to the first. On the return to the first period (b. 37), the passing movement to ii is more strongly articulated, establishing V / F minor for the consequent four bars, 41–5. The second phrase of the first theme (b. 45) is now given in F minor. This new tonic in turn is used as the starting point for another expansion up a step to V / G minor for the reiteration of the second period (b. 52), which leads to a sustained dominant pedal of B♭ (bb. 59–67) in preparation for the second theme group.

This second-subject group shows a parallel construction to the first, offering an immediate repetition in G of its initial phrase (again split into two unequal components – the static legato theme of bb. 68–75 and the derived staccato figure of bb. 75–6), returning to the tonality of the preceding section (bb. 52–7) now transformed into the major (although the e♭ in b. 78 retains a hint of the previous minor mode). This G major then moves, via C minor, to a temporary A♭ (b. 86), which, however, proves unstable and leads eventually to the confirmation of V/V for the closing theme (b. 113). C minor, the relative minor comparatively absent from the exposition, will become in turn the focus of the first part of the development.

In short, we are presented with a series of overlapping harmonic expansions up a step of ever increasing scale, which become progressively more firmly established (Ex. 2.1). Greg Vitercik has likened this pattern – suggesting a process of growth and transformation – to 'the vision of organic growth Goethe had propounded in [his] *Metamorphose der Pflanzen*, in which the development of a plant is held to reveal the progressive transformation of a single, fundamental cell.' 'It is not … unreasonable', he continues, 'to find evidence of Goethe's influence in the structural organisation of the composer's first fully mature work.'[25]

Complementary to this harmonic and formal procedure is the dense process of thematic manipulation, juxtaposition and development present

---

[25] Vitercik, *The Early Works of Felix Mendelssohn*, p. 75.

Ex. 2.2   Octet, first movement: first and second thematic families, archetypal versions.

across the exposition. Thematically, most of the material of the movement relates back to just two main families of musical ideas, which can be
described in their ideal form as an ascending arpeggio figure, typified by
the opening theme, and a turning motive passing by conjunct step, found
in its reply (b. 12) and used as the movement's second subject (Ex. 2.2).
So basic are these two different motives that it is tempting to view them
much as a Goethean *idealer Pflanzentypus* – an abstract, ideal type that
is not physically present but lies behind all representations that are generated from it, much like a Platonic Idea or Schoenbergian *Grundgestalt*.
While the former idea is associated more with the first subject and its traditionally 'masculine' qualities and the latter with the more lyrical second
subject group, elements from both these families intercross within each
group, forming contrasts, juxtapositions and latent relationships between
the two. Krummacher has spoken rightly of the innumerable connections
Mendelssohn's method makes both backwards and forwards between the
hidden affinities established by the juxtaposition of seemingly unrelated
motives.[26]

The probable source for this formal conception is the first movement of
Beethoven's *Eroica* Symphony, from which Mendelssohn takes the idea of
setting up a quasi-dialectical generative process between two basic musical
ideas. The genius of this design is that, like the *Eroica*, by contrasting two distinct families of musical motives which are fairly open-ended and inclusive
in what they can be seen to incorporate, it can effectively make 'thematic'
many passages of music which would otherwise just be seen as anomalous. The simplicity of the juxtaposition of arpeggiated and scalic/conjunct
groups of motives means that almost anything introduced into the music
can be viewed as relating to one or other family; the thematic relationships

---

[26] Krummacher, *Mendelssohn – Der Komponist*, p. 302.

Ex. 2.3a Octet, first movement: derivation of second ('turn') family from opening theme.

established in such a design are partly due to the nature of the material of tonal music itself.[27]

In fact, both these two families derive from the same source – the very opening bars of the Octet. As R. Larry Todd has demonstrated, the arpeggiated opening theme, soaring up from the first violin's low g across over three octaves to a high ab³, conceals what is essentially a four-note turning figure, the underlying voice-leading being reducible to the neighbour-note prolongation of scale-degree $\hat{3}$, g–f–ab–g (Ex. 2.3a).[28] This same figure is indeed found explicitly in the upper voice of the theme's accompaniment in the second violin (the last note, g¹, b. 9, being taken over registrally by the third violin, Ex. 2.3b).

This 'subthematic' motive – a category Dahlhaus has reserved for the procedures found in the late works of Beethoven that so influenced the young Mendelssohn – can be seen to generate innumerable related figures across

[27] I am influenced here by David Epstein's detailed analysis of Beethoven's movement in *Beyond Orpheus: Studies in Musical Structure* (Cambridge, MA: MIT Press, 1979), pp. 111–38.

[28] R. Larry Todd, 'The Instrumental Music of Felix Mendelssohn Bartholdy: Selected Studies Based on Primary Sources', unpublished PhD thesis, Yale University (1979), pp. 291–2. This particular neighbour-note background figure can be related to an archetypal changing-note schema [$\hat{3}$–$\hat{2}$ ... $\hat{4}$–$\hat{3}$] identified by Leonard B. Meyer and treated at greater length by Robert O. Gjerdingen in *A Classic Turn of Phrase: Music and the Psychology of Convention* (Philadelphia, PA: University of Pennsylvania Press, 1988), pp. 55–9.

Ex. 2.3b Octet, first movement: turn figure in accompaniment, bb. 1–9.

Ex. 2.4 Octet, first movement: variants of second ('turn') family of motives.

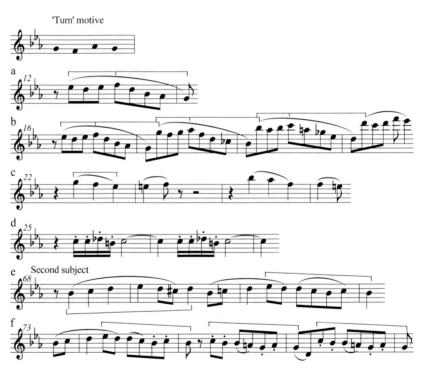

the course, not only of the exposition, but indeed of all four movements of the work. The winding motive of bb. 12–13 that follows on from the 'signal' answer to the first phrase clearly incorporates this neighbour-note turning figure into what is essentially a 1̂–2̂–3̂ ascent barely hidden by the octave displacement of the final g (Ex. 2.4a). In the consequent phrase, this figure is sequenced out across four bars into a linear progression moving

Ex. 2.5 Octet, first movement: reduction of exposition, opening group.

in tenths with the bass from e♭² up an octave to e♭³ (Ex. 2.4b). The legato phrase (bb. 22–3, Ex. 2.4c) that answers the transformation of the opening arpeggios into semiquavers in b. 21 is both the inversion of this previous 1̂–2̂–3̂ ascent and a further transformation of the neighbour-note turn of the subthematic motive. This is immediately followed by a closely derived figure in semiquavers (b. 25, Ex. 2.4d), which links up retrospectively the arpeggiated semiquaver pattern of b. 21 with the turn-family of motives.

At the cadence of this second period (b. 36) – a characteristic plagal IV turning to half-diminished ii$_{♭5}^7$ that grows out of the harmonies of the opening theme and will become so significant later in the work – this three-note ascent 1̂–2̂–3̂ is heard once again. Throughout the opening course of the Octet, clear cadential endings are continually undercut by the predilection for ending phrases on degree 3̂ in the upper voice. In Schenkerian terms, the middleground of the first-subject group can be read as prolonging this 3̂, starting from the first sonority of the piece – the throbbing measured tremolo with g¹ in violin II – and the first note of the melody line in the first violin (g), through the weak first perfect cadence of b. 9 (again with this g in both upper parts), the momentary cadence of b. 13, and the melodic close of b. 21 (violins I and II; Ex. 2.5).

The importance of this procedure lies in the life and sense of incompletion with which it endows the movement; while the formal-architectonic construction of phrases is kept by the composer, the articulation of musical paragraphs is undercut, as if the flow of the music continues unabated across the ends of musical phrases, ever pressing on. This open-ended quality is one of the most remarked-upon features of Beethoven's 'Heroic' style; here Mendelssohn imbues his work with this similar quality of forward striving that Scott Burnham has read as a mark of the *Goethezeit*.[29]

The second subject is nothing other than a further variant of this turning motive; a conjunct winding figure that unfurls out from its pedal b♭ and returns back to it again. This idea is successively developed into a pendant

---

[29] Burnham, *Beethoven Hero*, pp. 112–46.

Ex. 2.6 Octet, first movement: variants of first (arpeggiac) family of motives.

phrase (bb. 75–7) that is little more than a modification of the second theme's second half, which is at the same time equivalent to the inversion of this theme (Ex. 2.4e and f). Much of the seemingly 'a-thematic' material of the movement – most particularly, the extraordinary semiquaver scalic passage in all eight voices that forms the celebrated retransition back to the recapitulation, and numerous similar passages of apparent standard passagework – may be seen to relate to and grow from this group of motives.

Similarly, the first group of motives, the arpeggiated family that grows from the opening theme of the Octet, exhibits a comparable process of development and modification (Ex. 2.6). The first theme is continued in the bass of b. 9, in a new variant that emphasises degree $\hat{6}$, treated as an appoggiatura to $\hat{5}$, which will form an important feature later in the work (Ex. 2.6b). This figure will be inverted at the reiteration of these bars at b. 45 in F minor (Ex. 2.6c), and is later used in leading to the minor-key section of the development (b. 131). The new semiquaver figure of b. 21 is, as suggested, a further derivation of the opening motive, articulating an E♭ arpeggio that is now confined to a single octave (Ex. 2.6d). Most memorably, this opening theme provides the basis for the exposition's closing theme (bb. 113–27, Ex. 2.6e).

A striking feature of the thematic process in this exposition is the juxtaposition and drawing together of seemingly disparate motives from these two families of themes. Across the course of the movement the two families

Ex. 2.7 Octet, first movement: interspersion of second- and first-subject material, bb. 68–72.

Ex. 2.8 Octet, first movement: relationship between tail of second subject and first-subject theme, bb. 86–9.

commonly interfuse with one another. This is seen not just by the alternation of arpeggiac and conjunct motives within phrases (bb. 9–13; 21–5) but also with the second subject, whose fourth bar is filled in the first violin with an echo of the first theme's head motive (b. 71, Ex. 2.7); the rather static second theme is heard as a momentary interpolation within the more dynamic process of the movement as a whole, as is underscored by the sustained pedal point upon which it rests.

As Krummacher has indicated, though, the relationship between themes is not just one of static juxtaposition but involves the forming of new connections between themes that had at one stage seemed unrelated. The continuation of the second period of the second subject is a noteworthy example. The semiquaver figure of the first subject group's second phrase (b. 21) had seemed to be more closely related to the arpeggiac motive than to the turning figure. However, after the pendant to the second theme has continued at b. 84, the semiquaver motive enters in inversion, continuing the melodic sequence initiated by the preceding theme (b. 88, Ex. 2.8). The two figures – the first drawn openly from the second subject and conjunct in motion, the second deriving from the first theme and (save for one passing note) fundamentally arpeggiac – are revealed as being interchangeable, establishing a connection between the first subject and the arpeggiac family of motives and the second theme.

This growth of material across the exposition culminates in the closing theme, which forms a climactic metamorphosis of the opening theme, repeatedly emphasising the scale-degree $\hat{6}$ prominent in the later variant of b. 9. The theme presented here is in a sense the apotheosis of the opening subject, its ultimate goal across the course of the exposition, and it is this

Ex. 2.9 Octet, first movement recapitulation: new counterpoint to first-subject material, bb. 227–31.

version that will be recalled – if again in a further transformation – at the close of the work.

In the final published version of 1832 the recapitulation is drastically shortened by cutting almost the entire first-subject group after the opening phrase, which then leads straight to the second subject, presented without internal repetitions and given over a dominant pedal. This expedient was one which would be followed by Mendelssohn in many of his mature instrumental works, and indeed would become a quintessential trait of the composer's approach to form; by giving only the head of the first subject group Mendelssohn articulates the return to the tonic but saves giving a further rehearing of material already worked out and developed considerably within the exposition and development sections.[30] Notable within this brief first-subject passage is the introduction of a new cantabile line in the second violin as a countermelody to the winding figure of $1^{1.2}$ (b. 228, Ex. 2.9), which substitutes for the lyrical counterpoise to the missing 1^2 (b. 22, Ex. 2.4c). Effectively, Mendelssohn combines material from the first and second phrases in contrapuntal conjunction, synthesising the two passages into one at the recapitulation. The coda, which functions as the goal of the movement's process of transformation, presents new variants of both the conjunct 'winding' theme (bb. 294–7, 303–4) and of the closing theme (bb. 305–6).

In this imposing opening movement, Mendelssohn can clearly be seen to be emulating the achievement of Beethoven, above all the model of the 'Eroica', in the dynamic internal teleology and continual growth, contrast, opposition and subsequent revealing of latent relationships between two

---

[30] See Krummacher's summary of Mendelssohn's formal approach in 'Zur Kompositionsart Mendelssohn: Thesen am Beispiel der Streichquartette', in Carl Dahlhaus (ed.), *Das Problem Mendelssohn* (Regensburg: Bosse, 1974), pp. 169–84; trans. Douglass Seaton as 'On Mendelssohn's Compositional Style: Propositions Based on the Example of the String Quartets', in Douglass Seaton (ed.), *The Mendelssohn Companion* (Westport, CT and London: Greenwood Press, 2001), pp. 551–68.

basic subthematic concepts. (For many writers this feature of Beethoven's music has proved attractive as a musical presentation of a type of process that is often seen as 'Hegelian', although this view is admittedly not always without its problems.[31]) In this, Mendelssohn is taking up the teleological drive and organicist conception associated with Beethoven's 'Heroic' style. Where he will go beyond this model is in the subsequent extensive thematic connections he establishes between movements, which fuse this linear momentum with a broader circular movement resulting in a spiral trajectory that is quintessentially Hegelian or even Goethean.

This process of 'organic' unfolding and development of material, both thematic and harmonic, is followed in each of the following movements. Greg Vitercik has contributed one of his most impressive analyses to the process of the third-movement scherzo, whose second theme grows almost imperceptibly from a tiny detail of the first theme – the b♭ of b. 4. This note, which appears unobtrusively as a consonant skip from the preceding g, is gently emphasised in the counterstatement with an accent on the metrically weak fourth quaver beat, and filled in with a passing note (g–a–b♭, b. 12). This three-note ascent – the inversion of the melodic line at b. 4 – becomes steadily more significant in the ensuing bars, being metrically realigned at b. 16 and subsequently broken up across the eight-part texture in almost pointillistic imitation. The second theme is formed out of this texture, being nothing more than a succession of ascending thirds strung together (Ex. 2.10).

---

[31] Indeed, for one of the most celebrated proponents of this view, 'Beethoven's music *is* Hegelian philosophy' (Theodor W. Adorno, *Beethoven: The Philosophy of Music*, ed. Rolf Tiedermann, trans. E. Jephcott (Cambridge: Polity Press, 1998), p. 14, my emphasis). The literature on Beethoven and Hegel is prodigious: see, for instance, Christopher Ballantine, 'Beethoven, Hegel and Marx', *The Musical Review*, 33 (1972), 34–46; Janet Schmalfelt, 'Form as the Process of Becoming: The Beethoven-Hegelian Tradition and the "Tempest" Sonata', in Christopher Reynolds, Lewis Lockwood and James Webster (eds.), *Beethoven Forum 4* (Lincoln, NE: University of Nebraska Press, 1992), pp. 37–71; Reinhold Brinckmann, 'In the Time(s) of the "Eroica"', in Scott Burnham and Michael Steinberg (eds.), *Beethoven and his World* (Princeton University Press, 2000), pp. 1–26, and numerous writings of Carl Dahlhaus.

This view can be problematic: as Stephen Rumph has rightly argued, it is mistaken to connect the notion of an irresistible linear teleology to Hegelian views of history, while the notion of an evolving organic system is likewise hardly unique to Hegel (*Beethoven After Napoleon*, pp. 212–20). The idea of a continuous, unilinear teleological progression might adequately characterise eighteenth-century views of history and historical progress, but it is a poor match for the post-revolutionary theories of thinkers such as Hegel. In this sense, Beethoven's 'heroic' works could be thought of as perpetuating an outdated – indeed predominantly French – eighteenth-century ideal, vainly sustaining an already-doomed revolutionary hope throughout the Napoleonic era. A more nuanced reading of this music's Hegelian qualities is given by Burnham in *Beethoven Hero*, pp. 121–4.

Ex. 2.10 Octet, scherzo: motivic growth of second subject from first.

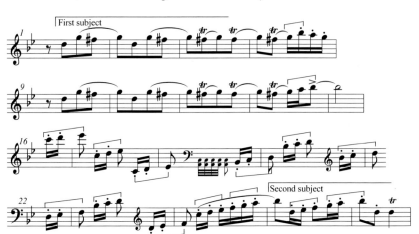

In Vitercik's words,

> The second theme . . . represents the end product of a motivic process that spans
> the first theme and transition, gradually transforming a fleeting melodic detail in
> the first theme into the generating motive of the second theme. Perhaps the most
> delightful, and typically Mendelssohnian, aspect of this process is that the themes
> bear absolutely no resemblance to one another; the logic of the thematic derivation
> is as absolute as it is evanescent.[32]

No less significant is the recapitulation, which manages to re-present the
material of the exposition without ever quite touching the ground. Vitercik
again has demonstrated the deftness with which Mendelssohn manipulates
latent aspects of the harmonic structure of the exposition while managing
to avoid any firm cadence in the tonic until three bars before the end: in
common with so many of his later sonata-form movements, the recapitulation is given over a dominant pedal, avoiding strong articulation of the
tonic (and therefore any sense of closure) until the very last bars of the
movement.[33]

The second movement Andante, meanwhile, is a remarkable example
of an organic conception of music. David Montgomery has described
this movement as an exceptional case of organicism, where the larger
form of the movement seems to be foreshadowed in a 'complex motivic

---

[32] Vitercik, *The Early Works of Felix Mendelssohn*, p. 105.

[33] *Ibid.*, pp. 104–20. One of the most notable features in the recapitulation is the process of
recontextualisation made to the D major episode from the exposition (bb. 31–6; 43ff.).

Ex. 2.11a Octet, first movement: climax of development section, bb. 137–43.

prototype . . . based upon an abstraction of Goethe's luxurious super-plant [the *Urpflanz*]' – the harmonic and motivic complex presented at the beginning.[34] More specifically, many details of this movement stem from the material of the first movement, in particular that of the development section, thus forming the first link in this work's nexus of cyclic inter-connections.

Thematic connections between movements: the Andante and first movement

The development section of the first movement represents a crisis-point within that movement. After the exposition's closing theme has continued across the double bar, a transition on $1^{1.2}$ (Ex. 2.6b), presented simultaneously in inversion (bb. 131–6), leads to a vehement statement of part of the first subject's second phrase, transformed into a new C minor context (b. 137). While the rushing semiquavers in the lower parts are recognisable, the double-dotted descending arpeggio in the treble and repeated crotchets seem less familiar. It is only when this two-bar unit is repeated at b. 139 that we realise that these three crotchets, heard off the beat and now outlining a descending third, are none other than a version of the lyrical reply to this semiquaver figure from b. 22 (compare Ex. 2.11a with Ex. 2.4c above). Moving from C minor via a diminished seventh implying V^7 of F minor, the passage ascends in a series of movements up a fourth to B♭, which soon collapses to a $^6_4$ of D♭ major. This key is only transitory, though, and returns through a German sixth back to C, which is heard now as V of the evident goal of F minor (b. 147). The crotchet figure is gradually liquidated; a forlorn hint of a new theme glides across in the first violin, before the music settles on to the tonic F minor for a statement of the second subject theme

---

[34] Montgomery, 'The Myth of Organicism', 26.

Ex. 2.11b Octet, slow movement, opening.

(b. 164). This climax unmistakably echoes that in the development section of Beethoven's 'Eroica' Symphony, the passage having reached a climactic impasse on a dissonant minor ninth and subsequently disintegrating in trudging crotchets. More importantly, however, it is the material from this aporia in the first movement that spills out to become the starting point of the slow movement.

Both aspects of the Andante's opening bars derive from the development section of the first movement (Ex. 2.11b). Starting from an empty fifth that reveals itself in the second bar to be C minor, the repeated quaver figure on the last three beats of the bar is merely a further metamorphosis of the hammering crotchets of the first movement's development, while the theme that enters in the second bar is made up of the same descending third that went with this rhythm.

In this manner, the development material has become separated into its constituent rhythmic and thematic elements. Furthermore, in harmonic layout, the opening section of the Andante follows that of the development remarkably closely. Following its initial presentation in b. 2 the *siciliano* theme is repeated immediately in sequence on the subdominant, F minor, but then, miraculously, its a♭ is taken up in b. 4 by the violins, entering for the first time, reinterpreted now as 5̂ of D♭ major. Within the space of its opening four bars the movement has passed from C minor, via F minor, to D♭ major, where it remains for the next twelve bars. The remarkable tonal latitude opened up by the slow movement – the progression from C minor, via an ascending fourth, to the Neapolitan D♭ – is almost exactly that traced in the preceding movement's development section, which has already served as the source of its thematic content.[35]

---

[35] The connection between the two movements was further clarified by Mendelssohn in his 1832 revision; in the original 1825 version the start of the first-movement development had returned to a statement of the first theme in the tonic, before moving to G minor for the equivalent of b. 137. By excising these bars Mendelssohn downplayed the more literal parallel between the

As Montgomery suggests, this opening thematic-complex works like a generating prototype for the rest of the movement. For instance, the transition theme, starting on E♭ minor (b. 29), is simply another metamorphosis of the opening third motive, whose rising harmonic sequence is continued in the following bars (bb. 33–5), now without the motivic connection in evidence but with a series of rising overlapping suspensions that prefigure the second theme. In turn, this passage is used as a harmonic template from which is formed the true second subject at b. 41.[36]

The tonal ambiguity initiated by the first four bars of the Andante is reflected further in a tonal precariousness that runs until the very last bars of the movement. The statement of the siciliano theme in D♭ is rounded out to an eight-bar antecedent phrase, closing on the dominant A♭ (bb. 4–11). Two ensuing bars of dominant prolongation lead to another two bars which seem to suggest the start of the expected consequent phrase, but the following bar immediately slips back to C minor, suggesting the entire passage has just been a lengthy interpolation of the Neapolitan ♭II degree within C minor. The next eleven bars attempt to restore the sense of C minor as the true tonic, though this is continually offset by repeated emphasis on the Neapolitan scale degree D♭. The close is equivocal: the tierce de Picardie and preceding D♭ in the melody line suggest V / F minor as much as C (b. 27).

The problem for establishing C minor as the tonic here is that the only real – if itself partial – statement of a theme has been given in the wrong key, D♭, and the prominent F minor in b. 3 and the ending on a D♭-inflected C♮ chord suggest that this tonality might be better viewed as V / F minor. (D♭ is, after all, mildly more relatable to an F minor context than C minor.) What also gives the theme at b. 4 the sense of being the genuine article is the way it enters seraphically in the four upper voices, the spatial separation from the preceding, and the manner in which it is rounded out to a proper 4+4 periodic phrase (the repetition at bb. 6–7 sounds unexpected, since we have already heard this one-bar motive four times in the movement). In short, the melody at b. 4 had sounded in immediate retrospect as if it had been

succession of events in the development and those in the exposition, but simultaneously saved unnecessary reduplication of the first theme and tautened the section's harmonic progression, making the relation of this passage to the slow movement even more apparent.

36   See Vitercik, *The Early Works of Felix Mendelssohn*, pp. 97–100: 'What is peculiar about the process … is the elusiveness with which it is realised. The individual steps of the transformation are clear enough, but as a result of the interpenetration of surface and middle-ground processes, no trace of clear relation between the opening theme and the E♭ major theme remains at the end of the process' (p. 98).

the actual start of the movement, though this impression is subsequently refuted when the music returns back to C minor at b. 16.

The first theme here is not recapitulated later in the work, the music leading straight from the developmental section of bb. 56–75 to a presentation of the second subject in C major, slipping to A♭.[37] The closing bars of the movement take up this equivocation between C and F minor from the close of the first subject, brief remnants of the first theme being all that is left of this material. The oscillations between C and F – and the tints of D♭ that function as an intermediary between the two – are more equivocal than ever. The final C♮ chord is unresolved; whatever the movement was expressing, it seems to have left something unsaid.

One almost expects the following movement to start in F minor, and so resolve the issue between C minor and V / F minor. Instead of which, the scherzo's half-lit G minor seems to form some kind of disjunction with what has preceded it. In terms of the Octet's narrative or its unfolding of musical plot there seems to be a qualitative leap up a step or dialectical loop from the unresolved interiority of the slow movement to the breezy, if slightly sinister outdoor skittishness of the scherzo. One is reminded of the connection the latter movement has with the *Walpurgisnacht* scene of Goethe's *Faust I*; if, as R. Larry Todd conjectures, one can read the Octet as some type of musical expression of Goethe's drama, then this contrast between the slow descent into suffering and insanity of Gretchen and the fantastical interlude provided by the *Walpurgisnaght's* dream episode seems a nigh-on perfect analogy for this musical disjunction.[38]

The progression of the work seen across its first three movements is hence somewhat akin to a dialectical process (or in Goethean terms, a process of *Polarität und Steigerung*), where the initial condition gives way to its contradiction. Thus the exposition gives rise to its Other, the C minor-dominated development section, which in turn is taken up at a larger level in the ensuing second movement. The subtle disjunction in the centre, between second movement and scherzo, forms a type of dialectical step up, while the scherzo and finale similarly exist in a complementary relation to each

---

[37] This excision of the first subject from the recapitulation (cut by the composer in 1832) seems to have contributed significantly to the sense of continued organic growth and evolution across the movement; see Krummacher, *Mendelssohn – Der Komponist*, p. 405; Vitercik, *The Early Works of Felix Mendelssohn*, pp. 101–3; Montgomery, 'The Myth of Organicism', 47.

[38] Fanny Mendelssohn relates that Felix was inspired by this scene of *Faust* when writing the Octet's scherzo, see Sebastian Hensel, *Die Familie Mendelssohn 1729–1847: Nach Briefen und Tagebüchern*, 3 vols. (Berlin: B. Behr, 1879), vol. I, p. 154. Todd has proposed a 'Faustian' reading of the entire Octet from this source (*Mendelssohn: A Life in Music* (New York: Oxford University Press, 2003), pp. 149–52), an idea that will be considered later in the chapter.

other, the former being subsumed into the latter across its course. Finally, the movement of the work will turn back into itself in the finale's coda, which brings back the music of the first and second movements, now at a higher level. In this movement the threads that have interlaced the entire work are recalled and bound up together in a synthesis of the preceding parts that looks beyond any prior model and is pre-emptive of virtually all future attempts at cyclicism.

Cyclic recall: the finale

The form of the finale is, as Krummacher has argued, the first irregular structure of Mendelssohn's oeuvre, being irreducible to any exact formal type though suggesting elements of several.[39] Most basically, the movement can be heard against a general tripartite sonata/sonata-rondo model, with structural divisions articulated by the return of the opening theme-complex in the tonic at b. 189 – corresponding to the start of a developmental section that proceeds from a sonata-rondo-like statement of the principal theme – and the build-up over a dominant pedal of bb. 327–55 heralding a telescoped recapitulation-coda. In common with several later examples of this type of sonata deformation, though, this last section is less a reprise of the exposition than an apotheosis of the piece, which presents substantially new (or, rather, old) material recalled from earlier movements.[40]

The irregular form of the movement is pre-empted in the nature of the material and the manner in which it is set out in the opening pages. Nearly all the material for the finale is given at the start in a thematic complex consisting of four main elements (*a*, *b*, *c* and *d*, Ex. 2.12). While each of the four ideas is clearly distinct, they nevertheless share common features: the rising fourth of *b* is taken from the immediately preceding answer of *a*, which is heard continuing underneath; the rhythm and phrase-structure of *c* are virtually identical to those of the statement of *b* that it completes; and *d* returns obviously to the quavers of *a*, outlining a new, cadential-sounding harmonic progression.

One of the most salient points about this thematic exposition is that it is so cursory; by the sixty-third bar (of a 439-bar Presto movement) all the main material for the movement has been heard. This brevity is

---

[39] Krummacher, *Mendelssohn – Der Komponist*, pp. 373–5. Krummacher also asserts, probably correctly, that this finale is in fact the most freely formed movement of any of Mendelssohn's (p. 185).

[40] See James Hepokoski, *Sibelius Symphony No. 5* (Cambridge University Press, 1993), p. 6. A later example of Mendelssohn's is the finale to the 1833 version of the 'Italian' Symphony.

Ex. 2.12 Octet, finale: opening thematic complex.

chiefly due to the nature of the themes used: the first is already given in
fugal presentation, leaving little potential for development; the second and
third, while open-ended, are likewise rather too forthright for any intricate
development; and the fourth sounds like an ending already, if a curiously
incomplete one, lacking any real melody. In short, it is not immediately
obvious that an extended finale structure can be created from just these
four distinctive motives. The following section (bb. 63–189) merely consists
of an expanded variation of the first, which now moves to the dominant.
From the perspective of a sonata-based design, this functions as the second
half of the exposition which establishes the secondary tonality, a format
used by Mendelssohn in another fugal-sonata hybrid, the scherzo of the
Op. 18 Quintet, and familiar from similar formal experiments such as the
finales of the 'Jupiter' Symphony and Beethoven's Op. 59 No. 3.

The opening material has already been presented and varied once by the
end of the exposition. What the movement really requires is the injection of
new material that will sustain it for longer than the 190-odd bars taken to
reach its secondary area. This want is initially satisfied by the introduction
of a new countertheme at b. 189. An extended transition in the first violin

Ex. 2.13 Octet, finale, countersubject (a^2).

leads back to a restatement of the opening theme in the tonic, in the manner of a sonata-rondo return. This reprise, however, is combined with a new fugal countersubject in long note-values (a^2), whose head-motive sounds like an inverted version of theme *b*. This second theme, when reached, then soon proves susceptible to the fugal treatment for which it had seemed predisposed (b. 213).[41] Primarily, however, this need will be fulfilled by the gradual reintroduction of elements from past movements. To put it simply, the cyclic recall in the finale of the Octet is motivated by the immanent demands of the movement, the return of past music completing the vacant potential of the finale's own thematic substance. The nature of the material presented in the opening thematic-complex is thus intrinsically related to the finale's form: the movement *demands* the introduction of further melodic material.[42]

In fact, the exposition had already hinted at this relationship to music previously heard, prefiguring the process of the coda which will be formed from the ever more unambiguous recall of these past ideas. Theme *a*, as Todd suggests, recalls the second subject of the first movement, and both this and theme *b* demonstrate affinities to the scherzo – the former to the scherzo's semiquaver accompanimental figure, the latter to the rising fourth head-motive of its main theme.[43] The twice-heard cadence to B♭ towards the end of the exposition outlines a plagal cadence familiar as a characteristic sonority from the first movement (I, bb. 34–7), being preceded by a winding chromatic line in crotchets that further recalls that movement's coda (bb. 137–45 and 149–65). Later in the development section, a *fortissimo* statement of the countersubject a^2 seems to offer a distant echo of the first movement development in its strident rhythm and descending arpeggiation (b. 243, Ex. 2.13).

---

[41] This theme, as numerous commentators have spotted, bears a striking resemblance to one from Handel's *Messiah*, 'and He shall reign forever', which is itself treated as a fugue.

[42] In this sense the analogy with the progression of Hegel's dialectic is quite justifiable; in Hegel's view the superseding of one element by another, its antithesis, is spurred on either by internal contradictions in the former or by an absence or need felt within it.

[43] Todd, 'The Instrumental Music of Felix Mendelssohn Bartholdy', p. 292.

The first explicit instance of cyclic recall is the appearance of the scherzo theme at b. 273. Though its material had been prepared by the rising fourth of theme *a* immediately preceding it and the accompanimental quavers of *b*,[44] this sudden flashback to the earlier movement, set off from its surroundings by the unexpected drop in dynamic to *pianissimo*, is nonetheless startling. It is both an organic outgrowth of the finale's material and yet an interruption. Charles Rosen has aptly described the qualitative difference between Mendelssohn's procedure here and earlier precedents for this cyclic recall – most famously Beethoven's in his Fifth Symphony. Rather than occurring after a fermata, bringing the movement to a momentary halt, the cyclical interruption is 'integrated seamlessly into the texture'. 'We find ourselves back in the scherzo almost without being able to put our finger on the exact point that it returns.'[45]

The scherzo is fleetingly heard twice, in F and E♭, interspersed with closely related material drawn from themes *a* and *b*. The spatial separation created here by the division of the eight instrumental voices into two quartets – one given the scherzo theme, still at its original *pianissimo*, the other those of the finale – almost suggests that the scherzo has been going on in the background throughout the music of the finale, having been continually present 'behind' the movement, at some different level. This passage culminates in a *fortissimo* statement of the scherzo theme in G minor, its original key, alongside the repeated minims of theme *c* with which it is contrapuntally counterpoised. After being sequenced from G up to E♭, the scherzo theme is heard in inversion in the bass against theme *c*. From this, a brief passage – inspired, no doubt, by the finale of Mozart's last symphony – combines five of the themes heard so far in a remarkable display of compositional ingenuity: the continuation of the scherzo's inversion is heard against *b*, entering in stretto (Vla II, b. 313; Vln IV, b. 314), the inversion of *c* (Vln II and III, Vla I, b. 313), *a²* (Vln I, b. 315), and *a*, which reappears at b. 317.

By pitting the two movements alongside each other, Mendelssohn may be envisaging an all-encompassing synthesis of finale and scherzo, akin to the contrapuntal display of Mozart's 'Jupiter' finale. This is certainly how Rosen reads the passage:

[44]   This connection between the two has been noted by several scholars. Indeed, Krummacher argues that the finale's opening material is inherently scherzo-like from the start, so that the lapse into the earlier movement, when it comes, is merely the logical outgrowth of its own latent characteristics (*Mendelssohn – Der Komponist*, p. 186).

[45]   Rosen, *The Romantic Generation*, pp. 89–90.

What is astonishing is the complete ease with which a synthesis [is] accomplished. The integration into the new movement is now total, although, at the same time, the earlier movement is still heard as a quotation.[46]

But, alternatively, the contrapuntal conjunction can be viewed not as an accommodation of the separate elements to each other but as a struggle between the two. This is suggested by Todd's view, interpreting the movement from the perspective of Goethe's *Faust* where the diabolical scherzo subject and resolute Handelian theme, characterising the forces of Evil and Good respectively, battle to gain supremacy of Gretchen's soul.[47]

The culmination of this process of cyclic recall occurs in the coda. This final section of the movement comprises a series of references, becoming ever clearer, to earlier parts of the Octet. At no stage is the allusion actually equivalent to a direct quotation; in a sense, the process of assimilation and synthesis of the two movements is one that is ever becoming – the two approaching each other asymptotically. However, the last reference is so close that it is hard not to see it as a fusion of the music of the finale and the opening movement, a union of the two which is simultaneously both but yet neither precisely.

This climactic amalgamation of scherzo and finale material leads on to this final section of the piece, preceded by a pedal-point of twenty-eight bars on the dominant. Leading out of the contrapuntal *tour de force* of the preceding bars, the music recapitulates the second and third themes of the opening thematic exposition over a sustained dominant pedal, continuously building up tension which is finally released as the dominant resolves down to a tonic $^6_3$. The new passage heard now, the first of the coda's three allusions, seems unmistakably to conjure up the first movement without in fact being a direct citation (b. 355, Ex. 2.14).

The first two phrases return to the arpeggiac construction of the first movement's main theme, specifically the passage of bb. 32–6, highlighted the second time around by the prefatory crotchet linear ascent (bb. 371–3)

---

[46] *Ibid.*, p. 92.

[47] Todd, *Mendelssohn: A Life in Music*, p. 152. That Mendelssohn was well aware of this diabolical nature is suggested by a letter of his from Paris in which he expresses astonishment at the incongruity of the decision to play the scherzo in church during a mass: 'finally, on Monday – laugh, if you wish! – my Octet will be played in a church for the Beethoven commemoration; this is the most ludicrous thing the world has ever seen, but it was impossible to dissuade them, and I must say I am looking forward to experiencing a solemn mass alongside the scherzo.' Letter 15/17 March 1832 to his mother, in Felix Mendelssohn Bartholdy, *Reisebriefe von Felix Mendelssohn Bartholdy aus den Jahren 1830 bis 1832* [*Briefe* vol. I], ed. Paul Mendelssohn Bartholdy (Leipzig: Hermann Mendelssohn, 1861), pp. 326–7.

Ex. 2.14 Octet, finale, coda, first part: allusions to first movement, bb. 355–71.

which matches the quavers of I: 32–3.[48] Particularly characteristic are the
Db and Cb trills and the associated I^7 and iv harmonies of bb. 357 and 361,
which recall innumerable instances of these – or closely related – sonorities
in the first movement.[49] The soaring line of b. 363 that answers this passage
likewise seems to hark back to the closing theme of the first-movement
exposition, particularly in the 4̂–3̂ and 6̂–5̂ appoggiaturas.

Yet elements of this section can also be seen to be prefigured in the
finale's own exposition. The phrase starting at b. 355 does stem from the
first movement, but it is also a metamorphosis of the finale's own cadential
passage from towards the end of the exposition (bb. 137–45 and 149–65),
which had seemed even then to allude to the earlier movement. In addition,
the quavers of theme *a* clearly continue in the inner parts throughout
the section, as they will until the very end of the work. In its thematic
construction the coda is thus as close to being part of the first movement
as it is a development of the material of the finale. This might account for
one of the extraordinary attributes of this coda – the fact that it manages
to sound familiar without having been previously heard. The remarkable
thing about this section is the sense in which it simultaneously sounds like
a return to the world of the first movement while still forming a logical

---

[48] The first movement, it will be recalled, was originally written in double-note values, so the
notated correspondence was initially exact.

[49] Specifically the first theme and the near-identical half-diminished ii^7 at b. 7, and the cadential
passage bb. 34–6 already cited.

Ex. 2.15 Octet, finale, coda, second part: recall of rhythm and harmonic progression of first-movement development and second movement, bb. 387–95.

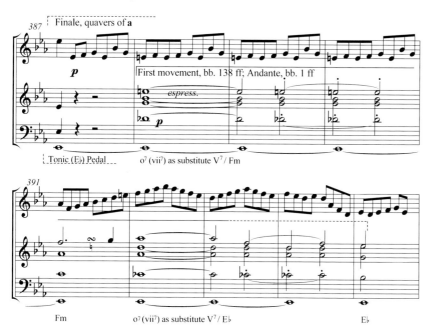

continuation of the finale. The coda of Mendelssohn's Octet belongs to both finale and first movement, without being either exactly.

The second part of the coda returns to the world left behind in the slow movement. Under the quavers of *a*, the lower voices reiterate the same progression from the first movement's development that had spilled out to form the Andante (Ex. 2.15). The rhythm is the same – the three repeated minims (again, corresponding in note values exactly to Mendelssohn's 1825 notation) heard both at I: 138 and II: 1 – and the harmonic progression – a diminished seventh, functioning as C^7, moving to F minor – almost identical. Again, this passage is not altogether unfamiliar from the finale, since its gestures had seemed echoed in the A major section of the development (bb. 243ff.). Here, however, as Vitercik has shown, the progression that has been a recurring agent in so many of the Octet's themes is anchored down to a E♭ context, the e♮ leading to ii in the violin neutralised by the tonic pedal in the bass and the harmonies returning back to E♭ via a diminished ii^7 at b. 392.[50]

[50] Vitercik, *The Early Works of Felix Mendelssohn*, pp. 133–6.

Ex. 2.16 Octet, finale, coda, final transformation: return of first-movement theme alongside finale's material, bb. 403–11.

Finally, Mendelssohn gives us the most explicit recall of the section – the return of the exposition's closing theme, in rhythmic transformation, now combined with the quavers of *d* (b. 403, Ex. 2.16). The fleeting glimpses of past themes have become clearer and clearer, culminating in this transparent reference to the first movement in the very last bars.

This latter figure (*d*) had all along seemed to be curiously missing something; a closing section but without an actual theme. The union of the first-movement theme with this passage from the finale's opening complex finally reveals how this passage has all along been the accompaniment to the earlier theme, adumbrating a harmonic progression that has been familiar from the very first bars of the composition.[51] The finale's closing theme finds its completion in the fusion with the first-movement theme, its latent potential now realised as it ties the two movements up. And this earlier theme finds its final metamorphosis in union with the finale's theme (Ex. 2.17). The transformed return of the theme that was the goal of the first movement's exposition alongside the finale's closing theme is the completion of

---

[51] *Ibid.*, p. 136: 'What had seemed to be a carefully controlled drive towards closure within the confines of the finale is revealed – in a thrilling instant – to be the beginning of a gigantic cadential gesture that encompasses the whole of an unusually expansive four-movement work.'

Ex. 2.17 Octet: transformation of first-movement closing theme into finale's coda theme.

what was latent but incomplete. By merging finale and first movement the work has found a telos which is the fusion of the two.

In this sense, I feel, one can genuinely speak of a synthesis. Unlike a simple combination of themes, both parts are here fused and transformed into something new. The closing section contains both the first movement and finale together, yet is neither exactly, the synthesis merging both parts, simultaneously dissolving their individual identities and hence transcending them. The two, in other words, are *aufgehoben*, in Hegel's celebrated use of the term. The goal of the entire work is this all-encompassing synthesis of the separate parts of the Octet into one, where beginning and end are one.

The path of the Octet, then, true to Hegel's system, has followed one gigantic organic process, whose initially linear course has wrapped around on itself and returned to its beginning. The goal of this process, the return back into itself, has been realised through the coming to self-consciousness of its own history. This is attained through a process of recollection, where previous themes return within the finale as if memories of the music's journey. First the scherzo theme returns at the central point of the finale, initially as if in conflict, but subsequently being subsumed into the movement through the intensive contrapuntal working-out of the following passage. Then an increasing tide of recollections sweep in, all the while growing in explicitness: the first movement's exposition, then its development and the slow movement, its dialectical other, and finally returning full-circle into the first movement's closing theme which is at last synthesised with the finale as the telos of the work.[52]

---

[52] As Toews describes it, 'this theme becomes the unifying "hidden" core of the ensuing musical moments (that operate more like historical episodes or scenes than structural oppositions), and goes through a process leading to a "return" in which the various moments are "remembered" as elements of the same subject' (*Becoming Historical*, p. 230). Toews is referring specifically to the 'Reformation' and 'Italian' Symphonies, taken by the author as paradigms of Mendelssohn's early cyclic style.

The coda to Mendelssohn's Octet thus presents a recollection and summary of the journey of the piece, an explicit realisation of the music's own history, whose goal is none other this same self-consciousness. As Hegel was to write, in the penultimate sentence of his famous work,

The *goal*, Absolute Knowing, or Spirit that knows itself as Spirit, has for its path the recollection of the Spirits as they are in themselves and as they accomplish the organisation of their realm.[53]

And this coming to self-consciousness brings the movement of the whole structure round back into itself in one giant circle. Again,

It is only as this process of reflecting itself into itself that it is in itself truly *Spirit*.... The movement is the circle that returns into itself, the circle that presupposes its beginning and reaches it only at the end.[54]

The moment in which this self-knowledge is attained, where the underlying idea that has lain behind all the different surface manifestations is recognised, is the supreme synthesis. The linear has become verticalised, the ('spatial') temporal progression fused into an instant.

[As to] the moments of which the reconciliation of Spirit with its own consciousness proper is composed; by themselves they are single and separate, and it is solely their spiritual unity that constitutes the power of this reconciliation. The last of these moments is, however, necessarily this unity itself and, as is evident, it binds them all into itself.[55]

Indeed, in this epiphanic moment, when everything comes together into a unity and this unity is recognised by the music, the journey of the spirit through time is completed and history, in some form, is at an end.

In the Notion that knows itself as Notion, the *moments* thus appear earlier than the fulfilled whole whose coming-to-be is the movement of those moments. In *consciousness*, on the other hand, the whole, though uncomprehended, is prior to the moments. Time is the notion itself that *is there* and which presents itself to consciousness as empty intuition; for this reason, Spirit necessarily appears in Time just so long as it has not *grasped* its pure Notion, i.e., has not annulled Time.[56]

---

[53] Hegel, *Phenomenology of Spirit*, p. 493 (*Werke*, vol. III, p. 591). See further p. 492 (pp. 590–1):
'As its fulfilment consists in perfectly *knowing* what *it is*, in knowing its substance, this knowing is its *withdrawal into itself* in which it abandons its outer existence and gives its existential shape over to recollection.... But recollection, the inwardising of that experience, has preserved it and is the inner being, and in fact the higher form of this substance. So although this Spirit starts afresh ... it is none the less on a higher level than it starts.'
[54] *Ibid.*, pp. 487–8 (p. 585).   [55] *Ibid.*, p. 482 (p. 578).   [56] *Ibid.*, p. 487 (p. 584).

ning now.

The meaning of this passage is disputed – whether Hegel is seriously suggesting that time and history is completed when *Geist* comes to full self-knowledge – that is, with his own philosophy. But it does seem to suggest that time, in some sense, is qualitatively changed, whether suspended or effectively ceases, when this self-knowledge is reached.

When, one might ask, does the moment occur in which this unity is realised, in which the movement binds up all its parts to each other? What happens if time does cease? The Octet, notably, is continually pressing onwards, 'zieht uns hinan',[57] to this final synthesis. Perhaps this point is never reached – like many of the Romantics of the day, the supreme reconciliation and integration of every individual into the whole is always imminent but never arrives – the two approaching each other asymptotically, 'bad infinity', as Hegel would call it. Or, more likely, given Mendelssohn's classical leanings – the desire to reconcile and harmonise, the elective affinity to the aesthetic maxims of his friend Goethe and teacher Hegel – the final realisation of this process is reached in the very last passage that synthesises first movement and finale into one. This realisation achieved, the piece ends; time ceases. The 'frame' at either side of the music is the annulment of time; the silence at the end of the work is the sound of eternity.

The Octet and musical history

The process enacted in the Octet of bringing back and synthesising the music's own internal history is fascinating given Mendelssohn's highly developed historical consciousness and knowledge of the musical past. Indeed, one might wonder if this analogy can be taken further: might Mendelssohn's work actually outline a comparable process within the context of musical history taken in a wider sense? Might not the 'historical interest' within such cyclic works themselves parallel a broader attitude towards music history and the musical past as a whole? After all, to take the analogy with Hegel further ('seriously', as Hegel would have it), if the Octet were *fully* comparable to the *Phenomenology of Spirit*, Mendelssohn's work would have to recapitulate and synthesise the entire previous course of music within itself, forming a summation and apogee of history.[58] As Hegel would demand

---

[57] 'Draws us onward' – the final line of *Faust II*.
[58] The finale of Beethoven's Ninth has been read in not dissimilar fashion by Lawrence Kramer as a possible enactment of a Hegelian progression of history from east to west, from ancient Greece, via the Christendom of the German middle ages to the present day ('The Harem Threshold: Turkish Music and Greek Love in Beethoven's "Ode to Joy"', *19th-Century Music*, 22 (1998), 78–90).

of modern philosophy, 'everything that at first appears as something past and gone must be preserved and contained; it must itself be a mirror of the whole history'.[59]

Such an idea might indeed seem rather attractive on a number of counts. The Octet is habitually read as the culmination of Mendelssohn's musical 'apprenticeship', the first emergence of his mature voice in what is, like Hegel's *Phenomenology*, his first major work. The offspring of the series of string symphonies and chamber music written between the ages of eleven and fifteen that move stylistically from Handel and C.P.E. Bach to Haydn and Mozart, the Octet is usually viewed as growing out of these past influences and synthesising them into something unique and individual. This formation seems borne out by Zelter's famous declaration the previous year, 'from today on you are a boy no longer; I proclaim you a journeyman in the name of Mozart, in the name of Haydn, and in the name of the elder Bach'.[60]

The references and allusions to past historical styles that some commentators see embodied in the music of the Octet – the *siciliano* topic of the Andante's opening and *stile antico* suspensions of its second subject, the Handelian fugue of the finale and the Beethovenian ambition of the first movement, the thoroughly modern (and entirely Mendelssohnian) scherzo – only seem to encourage such a view.[61] Like Hegel's work, it presents 'a gallery of past images, a moving pageant of historical scenes', which are drawn together at the end into a higher synthesis.[62] This finale – like that of Mozart's 'Jupiter' Symphony, which served as a model for Mendelssohn's work[63] – seems to sum up and crown this glorious history, a trope which was indeed particularly prevalent at the time. As the French critic Saint-Foix wrote apropos Mozart's final symphony,

[59] Georg Wilhelm Friedrich Hegel, *Lectures on the History of Philosophy*, trans. E.S. Haldane and F.H. Simson, 3 vols. (London: Kegan Paul, 1896), vol. I, p. 41 (*Werke*, vol. XVIII, p. 61). See further the close of the lectures, vol. III, pp. 552–3 (*Werke*, vol. XX, p. 461): 'The latest philosophy contains therefore those which went before; it embraces in itself all the different stages thereof; it is the product and result of those that preceded it.'

[60] Hensel, *Die Familie Mendelssohn*, vol. I, p. 140. This was on the occasion of Mendelssohn's fifteenth birthday, 3 February 1824. The language used by Zelter (*Gesell*) explicitly refers to the tradition of an apprentice, having served his time and learned his craft, being promoted to the status of an independent 'Journeyman'.

[61] See Todd, *Mendelssohn: A Life in Music*, pp. 151–2.

[62] Hegel, *Phenomenology of Spirit*, p. 492 / *Werke*, vol. III, p. 590.

[63] Mendelssohn knew Mozart's work well, having first heard it in 1821 at a performance in Leipzig *en route* to his first visit to Goethe in Weimar. The finale to Mozart's symphony is already the model for the String Symphony No. 8 in C major (1822).

With a sovereign grace, eloquence, and force, the master in his thirty-second [*sic*] year gathers up all the elements his most glorious predecessors have used and reveals to us all that music has achieved up to his time, and what it will do nearly a hundred years later.[64]

In fact, the idea of embodying the progress of music history within the structure of an individual piece is even found in the music of one of Mendelssohn's leading contemporaries, Louis Spohr's Symphony No. 6 in G major ('Historische Symphonie') Op. 116, whose four movements are meant to depict the progression of music from Bach and Handel (1720) to Haydn and Mozart (1780), Beethoven (1810), and finally (1840) the present day.[65]

The analogy is deceptive, though. For it is only with great difficulty that one attempts to trace any historical development of styles across Mendelssohn's work. We start out with a soaring Beethovenian movement, move back to the eighteenth century with the second-movement *siciliano*, and continue regressing to a polyphonic church-style. To outline the matter with drastic simplicity, Beethoven leads to Mozart, to Palestrina, via Mendelssohn, to Handel, and back again to Mendelssohn. The musical order of styles simply does not match the historical chronology suggested: the musical progression is non-chronological. Whatever the Octet might be thought of as depicting, it is certainly not the progression of music history to *c.* 1825.

On deeper reflection, this is not really that surprising. Mendelssohn, for all his highly developed historical sense and the personal and cultural connections with Hegel, was neither a believer in musical or artistic progress, nor, really, a Hegelian, in the strong sense. Within the terms of the Octet's own history, the recurrence and synthesis of the past into the music's telos does indeed follow remarkably closely a Hegelian process, but to go further and make the inference that the internal process of Mendelssohn's

---

[64] Saint-Foix, quoted by Elaine Sisman, *Mozart: The 'Jupiter' Symphony* (Cambridge University Press, 1993), p. 34. The idea of music history having reached a zenith (or perhaps as having already passed its high-noon) is echoed in much criticism and journalistic writing of the time. One of the standard contemporary guides to music history, Raphael Georg Kiesewetter's *Geschichte der europäisch-abendländischen oder unsrer heutigen Musik* (Leipzig: Breitkopf & Härtel, 1834), voiced such sentiments, while A.B. Marx, who at this stage was at the start of his close musical friendship with Mendelssohn, contended later that this peak had already been reached: with Beethoven, musical art had 'come of age' (Marx, *Musical Form in the Age of Beethoven*, pp. 174–5).

[65] Mendelssohn in fact admired Spohr's Symphony following its appearance in 1839, though he voiced disapproval of the composer's tongue-in-cheek portrayal of the modern age as trivial and superficial, denoted by Spohr through parodying the operatic style of Auber.

work somehow encapsulates Hegel's view of history in the broader sense is doomed to failure. This point is where the analogy between Mendelssohn and Hegel becomes strained, and points to fundamental differences between the two figures and their attitudes to history. The two may have a great deal in common, but when taken too far the congruence between their views ultimately breaks down.

Whether or not Hegel actually believed in the idea of unremitting progress so often attributed to him – in a sense, whether he himself was quite as 'Hegelian' as some of his subsequent followers were – is a moot point. Certainly, while the movement of the spirit through world history was hoped to be a progressive journey, moving incrementally to greater knowledge, Hegel's views on art and this rather whimsical modern notion of an artistic form of progress are far less straightforward. His love for the Greeks, in common with many German intellectuals after Winckelmann, knew almost no bounds, and indeed he famously declared in the *Aesthetics*: 'Of all the masterpieces of the classical and modern world – and I know nearly all of them, as one should and can – the *Antigone* of Sophocles seems to me to be the most magnificent and satisfying work of art of this kind.'[66] (Indeed, Mendelssohn himself was known on occasion to comment sardonically at the fulsome love for the German Christian medieval past shared by followers of Hegel.[67]) But since art is one particular manifestation of *Geist*, and the journey of this spirit through history is understood to be a process of gradual improvement and nearing to perfection, one can infer from his system that art has a teleological demand. (Whether or not Hegel was artistically sensitive enough actually to believe this is beside the point.)

How important the influence of Hegel was for Mendelssohn is unclear. Mendelssohn's relationship with Hegel was certainly not as close as that with figures such as Goethe or Zelter, or the family circle in which he grew up. Thomas Schmidt states quite categorically that 'Mendelssohn was not a "Hegelian"'. Schmidt is right not to exaggerate the relationship between the two, though his discussion of Hegel's potential influence on the formation of Mendelssohn's aesthetic views seems to understate the similarities there are.[68] Julius Schubring relates that Hegel's visits to the

[66] Hegel, *Aesthetics*, vol. II, p. 1218 (*Werke*, vol. XV, p. 550); one of many references to this work in Hegel's writings. Mendelssohn was later to write incidental music to Sophocles' tragedy.
[67] 'One thanks God that these highly prized middle ages are over never to return. Don't say this to any Hegelian, but it is true, and the more I read and think on the subject, the more clearly I feel this.' Letter to his sisters, Naples, 28 May 1831, *Briefe*, vol. I, p. 154.
[68] Schmidt, *Die ästhetischen Grundlagen der Instrumentalmusik Felix Mendelssohn Bartholdys*, p. 59.

Mendelssohn house in the 1820s, as the teenage composer was growing up, were motivated more by the philosopher's love of whist than that of wisdom.[69] Zelter reports in a letter to Goethe that Mendelssohn would mimic Hegel's manner of delivering his lectures very well, though again quite what this proves is unclear.[70] Eric Werner has gone rather further, though, suggesting that Mendelssohn was indebted in more serious ways to Hegel's views. Listing the affinities in their aesthetic outlook, Werner even cites a letter purportedly written from Hegel to Mendelssohn in 1829, in which the philosopher responds to questions the composer had put to him concerning the aesthetics of music and in particular the relationship between music and words. The former discussion is not especially convincing, however, being composed of general points that might be shared by anyone from the time, and the original source for the letter – unspecified by Werner – has never been found.[71] Others, like Susanna Großmann-Vendrey, quite sensibly treat Hegel as one of several formative figures whose viewpoints, while not necessarily matching precisely, are broadly congruous with Mendelssohn's.[72]

Certainly, Mendelssohn was not an unreserved admirer of Hegel. Part of this may be due to the understandable antagonism Hegel's pronouncement on the death of art and the indeterminacy of instrumental music would have produced in any promising young composer. ('It is unbelievable,' he later protested after Hegel's lectures, 'Goethe and Thorwaldsen are still living, and Beethoven died only a few years ago, and yet Hegel proclaims that German art is as dead as a rat. *Quod non!* If he really feels thus, so much the worse for him, but when I reflect for a while on his conclusions

---

[69] Julius Schubring, 'Erinnerungen an Felix Mendelssohn Bartholdy', *Daheim*, 2 (1866), 373ff., trans. (anon.) in *Musical World*, 31 (12 and 19 May 1866) and repr. in R. Larry Todd (ed.), *Mendelssohn and his World* (Princeton University Press, 1991), p. 222.

[70] Letter, Zelter to Goethe, 22 March 1829, *Briefwechsel zwischen Goethe und Zelter*, ed. Max Hecker, 3 vols. (Frankfurt: Insel Verlag, 1987), vol. III: 1828–32, p. 153.

[71] Werner, *Mendelssohn: A New Image*, p. 80, given as an 'unpublished letter, 30 June 1829' (a date when Mendelssohn would have been in England). Werner has become mildly notorious for the unreliability of his scholarship. A debate conducted across several issues of *The Musical Quarterly* brought the matter to wider attention in the late 1990s (see the original article by Jeffrey S. Sposato, 'Creative Writing: The [Self-] Identification of Mendelssohn as Jew', *The Musical Quarterly*, 82 (1998), 190–209, and the responses this prompted). Despite claims to the contrary, though, it has never been conclusively proved that Werner ever deliberately falsified evidence as his sternest critics accuse him of doing, despite his numerous inaccuracies and conflations when transcribing source material.

[72] Susanna Großmann-Vendrey, 'Mendelssohn und die Vergangenheit', in Walter Wiora (ed.), *Die Ausbreitung des Historismus über die Musik: Aufsätze und Diskussionen* (Regensburg: Bosse, 1969), pp. 73–82.

they appear to me very shallow.'[73]) Much of Mendelssohn's later progress would stem ultimately from his desire to take up these challenges. (Indeed, in both these senses – concerning his historical self-consciousness and the question of the comprehensibility of instrumental music – Mendelssohn can be said to be one of the first, if not the first, musical 'modern'.) As with Goethe, artistic creation, not dry, obtuse theorising, was the critical consideration for Mendelssohn, an attitude which would contribute ultimately to the breakdown of his friendship with a theorist of similar predisposition, A.B. Marx.

In terms of documentary evidence, the case is inconclusive. Mendelssohn obviously had personal contact with Hegel, undoubtedly knew something of his philosophy and later studied under him, though quite how far one can go in relating their aesthetic and philosophical viewpoints remains a matter of personal discretion. I have suggested here that the two do have a great deal in common, though this is likely to be as much through common affinities in outlook and mutual interests as from any direct influence of Hegel on the younger composer. Pushed too far, though, the relationship becomes strained. The parallels between the two – Hegel's philosophy and Mendelssohn's music – can be taken far, but at this last 'historical' stage the two finally must diverge. In place, a new model must be formed that satisfies the conditions more closely.

The figure to whom Mendelssohn's aesthetic viewpoint corresponds the most closely in this matter is undoubtedly that other great figure of German culture and Mendelssohn's most important spiritual mentor, Goethe. Goethe's and Hegel's viewpoints were not entirely incongruent, but yet the two differed in several significant ways. Both Goethe and Hegel, not dissimilarly to Mendelssohn a generation later, constitute the 'Klassiker', not 'Romantiker', in German culture – classical, rational, marked by a distrust of what they saw as the spiritual and emotional immaturity of Romanticism. In Goethe's famous phrase, 'Classicism is health, Romanticism sickness'.[74]

---

[73] Letter to his sisters, Naples, 28 May 1831, *Briefe*, vol. I, p. 155. For Hegel, art, religion, philosophy, history, and even political institutions and laws are all manifestations of *Geist*. However, as seen by the supposed decline of Greek art with the rise of philosophy (a theme later rehearsed by Nietzsche), philosophical formulation and self-consciousness necessarily follow after art has peaked – in Hegel's famous image, 'The owl of Minerva spreads her wings only at the falling of the dusk' (*Philosophy of Right*, Preface; *Werke*, vol. VII, p. 28). Since the history of *Geist* has been philosophically formulated for the moment by none other than Hegel, art is presumably necessarily in a period of decline. This was hardly going to be music to Mendelssohn's ears.

[74] Goethe, *Maximen und Reflexionen*, No. 1031: 'Klassisch ist das Gesund, romantisch das Kranke' (*Poetische Werke*, vol. II, p. 588). Also see the conversation reported by Eckermann,

(Mendelssohn, similarly, living in a generation apparently marked by the prizing of adolescent emotions and the quest for novelty often at the expense of lucidity, harmonious balance and artistic maturity, was wont to complain at times of the Parisian neuroticism and mawkishness (*Pariser Verzweiflungssucht und Leidenschaftssucherei*) of his contemporaries.[75]) The bond between Goethe and Hegel was respectful yet guarded. Hegel, later in life, would write to Goethe in a spirit of intellectual kinship, expressing his profound debt to Goethe's example:

When I survey the course of my spiritual development, I see you everywhere woven into it and would like to call myself one of your sons; my inward nature received from you nourishment and strength to resist abstraction and set its course by your images as by signal fires.[76]

Goethe's relationship to Hegel was more wary: whilst he was broadly in accord with Hegel's 'classical' leanings, the love for the antique past and the distrust of the youthful Romantic movement, Hegel's abstraction and proverbial philosophical obscurity were less affectionately taken.

Nature does nothing in vain . . . Her workings are ever alive, superfluous, and squandering in order that the infinite may continually be present because nothing can abide. With this I even believe I come close to Hegel's philosophy which, incidentally, attracts and repels me; may the genius be gracious unto all of us![77]

Throughout his life, indeed, Goethe remained rather eclectic in what he favoured from philosophers, taking from them primarily only those aspects of their thought that accorded with what were already his own views. Yet Goethe seemed to have sensed that both he and Hegel were after similar concerns, albeit from opposing angles, and was eager to hear about

---

2 April 1829, in Johann Peter Eckermann, *Gespräche mit Goethe in den letzten Jahren seines Lebens*, ed. Otto Schönberger (Stuttgart: Reclam, 1998), p. 343. Mendelssohn similarly relates a conversation with Goethe where the poet 'complained about the universal tendency of the young people of the day to be so languishing and melancholic' (Letter, Weimar, 24 May 1830, *Briefe*, vol. I, p. 4).

[75] Letter to his mother, 23 May 1834, *Briefe aus den Jahren 1833 bis 1847 von Felix Mendelssohn Bartholdy* [*Briefe*, vol. II], ed. Paul and Karl Mendelssohn Bartholdy (Leipzig: Hermann Mendelssohn, 1863), p. 41. On this occasion Frédéric Chopin and Ferdinand Hiller had played to Mendelssohn on a visit to Düsseldorf.

[76] Hegel to Goethe, Berlin, 24 April 1825, cited by Walter Kaufmann, *Hegel: A Reinterpretation* (New York: Doubleday, 1966), p. 351.

[77] Goethe to Zelter, Weimar, 13 August 1831, *Briefwechsel zwischen Goethe und Zelter*, vol. III, p. 515, this translation taken from Kaufmann, *Hegel*, p. 353. It is not clear quite how much of Hegel's writings Goethe actually knew in detail; in fact, Goethe's statement is virtually a direct paraphrase, not of Hegel, but of Aristotle (see *On the Soul*, 434a30–1; 415b3–7; 415a30).

Hegel's *Aesthetics* from Mendelssohn on the occasion of his young protégé's last visit to Weimar in 1830. ('Yesterday I had to tell him about Scotland, Hengstenberg, Spontini, and Hegel's *Aesthetics*.'[78]) For both Goethe and Hegel, the problem of man's relationship with time, the intersection of the temporal and the eternal, the contingent and the absolute, was one of the central questions they faced.

Mendelssohn and Goethe

'Mein Felix fährt fort und ist fleißig. Er hat soeben wieder ein Oktett für acht obligate Instrumente vollendet, das Hand und Fuß hat.' (Letter, Zelter to Goethe, 6 November 1825[79])

Johann Wolfgang von Goethe was probably the greatest cultural figure in early nineteenth-century Germany and certainly one of the most significant influences on Mendelssohn, and his aesthetic and philosophical views.[80] As the composer wrote in 1830, following his last meeting with the elderly poet, 'when he is gone, Germany will take on a different form for artists. I have never thought of Germany without feeling heartfelt joy and pride that Goethe lived there; and the rising generation appears on the whole so weak and sickly that my heart sinks. He is the last, and a happy, prosperous period for us closes!'[81] Schumann explicitly described Goethe as Mendelssohn's role-model, and later in life, in his Leipzig apartment, Mendelssohn would keep a bust of Goethe in his composing study.[82]

    The artistic relationship between the two figures and the similarities and common outlook demonstrated in their work has been the focus of an increasing number of studies.[83] But I would like to look at one topic in

---

[78] Letter from Mendelssohn to his family, Weimar, 24 May 1830, *Briefe*, vol. I, p. 5.

[79] 'My Felix improves and is hard-working. He has just again finished an Octet for eight obligato instruments, which is well done.' *Briefwechsel zwischen Goethe und Zelter*, vol. II: 1819–27, p. 414.

[80] For detailed accounts of the influence of Goethe on Mendelssohn here see particularly Großmann-Vendrey, 'Mendelssohn und die Vergangenheit', pp. 77–82, and Thomas Schmidt, *Die ästhetischen Grundlagen der Instrumentalmusik Felix Mendelssohn Bartholdys*, pp. 46–52.

[81] Letter to his father, Rome, 10 December 1830, *Briefe*, vol. I, p. 83.

[82] Schumann, 'Erinnerungen an Mendelssohn', p. 103.

[83] For instance Reinhard Szeskus, '*Die erste Walpurgisnacht*, Op. 60, von Felix Mendelssohn Bartholdy', *Beiträge zur Musikwissenschaft*, 17 (1975), 171–80; Wulf Konold, 'Mendelssohn und Goethe', in *Felix Mendelssohn Bartholdy und seine Zeit* (Laaber Verlag, 1984), pp. 93–110; Lawrence Kramer, '*Felix culpa*: Goethe and the Image of Mendelssohn', in R. Larry Todd (ed.), *Mendelssohn Studies* (Cambridge University Press, 1992), pp. 64–79, and 'The Lied as Cultural Practice: Tutelage, Gender, and Desire in Mendelssohn's Goethe Songs', in *Classical Music and*

particular: Goethe's views on time and history, and their resonances with Mendelssohn's aesthetic conception as exemplified in the Octet.

One of the major themes of Goethe's work throughout his life is the question of man's relationship with time, the opposition between the eternal and the temporal, and the relationship of our present time with the achievements of the past. 'My field', the poet once wrote, 'is time'.[84] In brief, this revolved around the problem of man's ephemerality and the search for the eternal within the transient confines of human life, in a world where religious certitude was becoming increasingly questioned. As many authors have noted, this was a typical concern of the age, but Goethe's struggle with this issue was particularly notable.[85] Especially given the infancy of Germany's entry onto the stage of European culture and the dawning historical self-consciousness of the age, a pressing concern for the young author in the 1770s and '80s was the relationship of the new literary tradition he hoped to build with the glories of the vanished classical past. The famous journey to Italy in 1786–8 at last seemed to provide him with an answer. For Goethe, this was a question of situating the past within a living tradition. Unlike the efforts of the youthful *Sturm und Drang* movement, of which he had been the leading literary embodiment, the poet now at last began to realise the full importance of an artistic tradition.[86] Hence, partly, the reason for the classicising strain in Goethe's work from the late 1780s onwards, the movement away from the adolescent rebellion and Promethean striving of *Götz von Berlichingen, Die Leiden des jungen Werthers* and the *Urfaust* to a more mature, harmonious, consciously 'classical' art, which is not afraid to allude to and grow from its illustrious predecessors (a progression that is likewise mirrored in Mendelssohn's own creative

Postmodern Knowledge (Berkeley, CA and Los Angeles, CA: University of California Press, 1995), pp. 143–73; Leon Botstein, 'Neoclassicism, Romanticism, and Emancipation: The Origins of Felix Mendelssohn's Aesthetic Outlook', in Douglass Seaton (ed.), *The Mendelssohn Companion* (Westport, CT and London: Greenwood Press, 2001), pp. 1–23; Julie D. Prandi, 'Kindred Spirits: Mendelssohn and Goethe, *Die erste Walpurgisnacht*', in John Michael Cooper and Julie D. Prandi (eds.), *The Mendelssohns: Their Music in History* (Oxford University Press, 2002), pp. 135–46; and John Michael Cooper, *Mendelssohn, Goethe, and the Walpurgis Night: The Heathen Muse in European Culture, 1700–1850* (University of Rochester Press, 2007).

[84] Literally, 'Ich hatte Zeit, mich zu fassen', a celebrated line written by Goethe's character Wilhelm Meister to his wife Natalie (*Wilhelm Meisters Wanderjahre*, bk I, ch. i, in *Poetische Werke*, vol. VII, p. 391).

[85] For a general introduction to Goethe's thought here in relation to that of his contemporaries, see Deirdre Vincent, *The Eternity of Being: On the Experience of Time in Goethe's* Faust (Bonn: Bouvier Verlag Herbert Grundmann, 1987), pp. 159–74.

[86] See Michael Beddow, 'Goethe on Genius', in Penelope Murray (ed.), *Genius: The History of an Idea* (Oxford: Blackwell, 1989), pp. 98–112.

development).[87] History and artistic tradition are conceived as a dynamic process, imbued both with continuity and an ongoing organic growth and development from what has preceded it, rather akin to the historical vision of Hegel. On the other hand, in contradistinction to Hegel, for Goethe the past is never and can never be superseded. In this, Goethe is not too distant from what Hegel's actual opinions appear to be, though this is not entirely supported by his system.

Goethe's outlook here, as Susanna Großmann-Vendrey has shown, is remarkably similar to Mendelssohn's own views on the subject.[88] Großmann-Vendrey has called attention to a letter the composer wrote from Italy articulating his views on the relationship of his music to the past, which the composer insists can never be repeated but can only be continued, through an inner spiritual necessity; any similarity between his own music and that of his great predecessors results not from 'dry, sterile imitation' but from a spiritual penetration into the essence of the past and a shared empathy with the eternal truth within it which gives rise to this correspondence.[89] The paradox here, as James Garratt points out, is that, in defending himself against the charge of imitation, Mendelssohn is himself almost directly paraphrasing one of Goethe's own letters from Italy.[90] Likewise, the existence of an artistic tradition and his own position as a continuation and outgrowth from this heritage is a notion that assumed great importance for Mendelssohn. In the conversations reported by Lobe, the composer insists that there are no completely new paths in music – just a 'continuation slightly farther' down the one and true path.[91] The series of

---

[87] For instance, E.M. Wilkinson has suggested that Goethe's *Faust* is the first great modern work that tries to keep the European tradition alive by constantly alluding to and recalling it ('Goethe's *Faust*: Tragedy in the Diachronic Mode', *Publications of the English Goethe Society*, 42 (1971–2), 116–74).

[88] Susanna Großmann-Vendrey, 'Mendelssohn und die Vergangenheit', pp. 77–82: 'Goethe und das geschichtliche Verständnis Mendelssohns'.

[89] Letter to Zelter, Rome, 18 December 1830, *Briefe* [5th ed., 1863], vol. I, p. 97; also see the composer's letter of 13 July 1831 to Eduard Devrient (Eduard Devrient, *Meine Erinnerungen an Felix Mendelssohn-Bartholdy und seine Briefe an mich* (Leipzig: J.J. Weber, 1869), p. 115).

[90] James Garratt, 'Mendelssohn and the Rise of Musical Historicism', in Peter Mercer-Taylor (ed.), *The Cambridge Companion to Mendelssohn* (Cambridge University Press, 2004), pp. 66–7. Garratt has further suggested how 'Hegelian' Mendelssohn's argument concerning this point seems to be ('Mendelssohn's Babel: Romanticism and the Poetics of Translation', *Music & Letters*, 80 (1999), 29–31). The two passages in question were originally discussed by Susanna Großmann-Vendrey in 'Mendelssohn und die Vergangenheit', p. 80.

[91] See Johann Christian Lobe, 'Conversations with Felix Mendelssohn', trans. Susan Gillespie, in R. Larry Todd (ed.), *Mendelssohn and his World* (Princeton University Press, 1991), pp. 193–4. Similarly, Mendelssohn's political and artistic views were strongly characterised by the idea of liberal reform, as opposed to revolution (see the composer's letter to his sister Rebecca, Düsseldorf, 23 December 1837, *Briefe*, vol. II, p. 72; also cf. pp. 38–47).

historical concerts he organised in Leipzig, where the music of the past was played in order up to the present day, played an important role in deepening the public's awareness of their cultural past as well as in the formation of the Austro-German symphonic canon.[92] Most significant here were his encounters with Goethe himself, where, as Mendelssohn relates, he played the music of the various great composers to the elderly poet on the piano 'in chronological order', so that he could understand the development of music.[93]

This deeply respectful attitude to the great achievements of the past is characteristic of the composer's aesthetic outlook throughout his entire life. Mendelssohn's principles on this matter and their relation to the aesthetic idea of the 'classical' have been subject to much inquiry, especially in German scholarship. Carl Dahlhaus has conjectured that for Mendelssohn certain models of composition stood out as models or ideal paradigms of their kind, the *classici auctores* Bach and Handel for the liturgical passion and oratorio, Gluck and Mozart for the *opera seria* and *buffa*, Haydn and Beethoven for the string quartet and symphony, an idea further taken up by Wulf Konold.[94] Garratt has gone on to analogise this historical tendency in Mendelssohn's music with the idea of 'translation' between the past and present – the idea of the partial appropriation of a historical style, in dialogue with the composer's own contemporary idiom – to explain some of this composer's more 'historicist' works.[95] In a similar vein, Michael Steinberg has argued

[92] On this point and Mendelssohn's historical activities in general as a performing musician, see Großmann-Vendrey's larger study, *Felix Mendelssohn Bartholdy und die Musik der Vergangenheit.*

[93] Letter, Mendelssohn to his family, Weimar, 25 May 1830, *Briefe*, vol. I, p. 8: 'Vormittags muss ich ihm ein Stündchen Clavier vorspielen, von allen verschiedenen großen Componisten, nach der Zeitfolge, und muss ihm erzählen, wie sie die Sache weiter gebracht hätten; und dazu sitzt er in einer dunklen Ecke, wie ein Jupiter tonans, und blitzt mit den alten Augen'. Goethe later related the incident to Zelter: 'wer versteht irgendeine Erscheinung, wenn er sich von dem Gang des Herankommens [nicht] penetriert? Dazu war denn die Hauptsache, dass Felix auch diesen Stufengang recht löblich einsieht und glücklicherweise sein gutes Gedächtnis ihm Musterstücke aller Art nach Belieben vorführt. Von der Bachischen Epoche heran hat er mir wieder Haydn, Mozart und Gluck zum Leben gebracht, von den großen neuern Technikern hinreichende Begriffe gegeben und endlich mich seine eigenen Produktionen fühlen und über sie nachdenken machen' (letter, Goethe to Zelter, Weimar, 3 June 1830, *Briefwechsel zwischen Goethe und Zelter*, vol. III, p. 338). Also cf. Karl Mendelssohn-Bartholdy, *Goethe und Felix Mendelssohn Bartholdy* (Leipzig: Hirtel, 1871), p. 41.

[94] Carl Dahlhaus, 'Mendelssohn und die musikalische Gattungstradition', in Dahlhaus (ed.), *Das Problem Mendelssohn* (Regensburg: Bosse, 1974), pp. 56–60; Wulf Konold, 'Funktion der Stilisierung: Vorläufige Bemerkungen zum Stilbegriff bei Mendelssohn', in Heinz-Klaus Metzger and Rainer Riehn (eds.), *Felix Mendelssohn Bartholdy, Musik-Konzepte* 14/15 (Munich: Edition Text+Kritik, 1980), pp. 4–5.

[95] Garratt, 'Mendelssohn's Babel', 34–46. The importance in connection with this matter of Mendelssohn's own published literary translation of Terence's *Andria*, completed in 1825 and

that Mendelssohn's conception of the classical was the antithesis of the historicising strain of thought that arose in the nineteenth century and found a culmination in the historical performance movement, the wish to situate each document from the past within its historical context, thus turning history into a desiccated archive of marmoreal relics from the past.[96] For Mendelssohn, rather, the great works of the past were constantly alive, reinventing themselves anew. There is no antithesis between the classical and the modern; the truly classical is the eternally modern (the traditional *stile antico e moderno*), as summed up in Mendelssohn's words 'dass alles Alte Gute neu bleibt'.[97] This attitude is demonstrated perfectly in the music Mendelssohn wrote for the revivals of Sophoclean tragedy, the settings of *Antigone* and *Oedipus Coloneus*.

Goethe's views on time and history are seen throughout much of his work, but are perhaps crystallised most profoundly in *Faust*, his life's work, begun in the early 1770s and completed only the year before the poet's death in 1832. As one Goethe scholar has stated, 'Faust's understanding of and relation to time is at the heart of Goethe's drama', in fact 'the central theme of the play'.[98] After all, Faust's wager – the entire linchpin of the story – is concerned with the joys of the fleeting moment and the desire to clasp hold of this, an entirely original addition of Goethe's to the original sixteenth-century morality tale:

Werd' ich zum Augenblicke sagen:	Were I to say to the fleeting moment:
Verweile doch! du bist so schön!	Yet tarry a while! You are so fair![99]

commented upon with approval by Goethe, has been well made by Leon Botstein in 'Neoclassicism, Romanticism, and Emancipation', pp. 6–8.

[96] Michael P. Steinberg, 'Schumann's Homelessness', in R. Larry Todd (ed.), *Schumann and his World* (Princeton University Press, 1994), pp. 57–65, condensed in *Listening to Reason*, pp. 100–22.

[97] Mendelssohn, letter to his sister Rebecca, 23 December 1834, *Briefe*, vol. II, p. 73. See Großmann-Vendrey, 'Mendelssohn und die Vergangenheit', p. 81.

[98] Ilse Graham, 'The Grateful Moment: The Element of Time in *Faust*', in *Goethe: Portrait of the Artist* (Berlin: de Gruyter, 1977), p. 315.

[99] Goethe, *Faust I*, lines 1699–700. This idea of the transient 'beautiful moment', it will be recalled, is alluded to by Nietzsche to characterise both Mendelssohn and Goethe, whose work, too good for the diseased, *décadent* Romanticism of the later nineteenth century, was in both cases effectively ignored. Mendelssohn, 'that halcyon master', was the 'beautiful incident [*schöne Zwischenfall*] of German music', characterised here in virtually identical terms as Goethe in *Twilight of the Idols* ('So dass Goethe . . . bloss ein Zwischenfall, ein schönes Umsonst gewesen wäre'). Friedrich Nietzsche, *Jenseits von Gut und Böse*, § 245; *Götzen-Dämmerung*, 'Streifzüge eines Unzeitgemässen' § 50 (*Sämtliche Werke (Kritische Studienausgabe)*, ed. Giorgio Colli and Mazzino Montinari, 15 vols. (Berlin and New York/Munich: de Gruyter/Deutscher Taschenbuch Verlag, 1980), vol. V, p. 188; vol. VI, p. 152).

Now this is especially interesting since, as we know, there is a direct Faustian connection between Goethe's drama and Mendelssohn's Octet. The scherzo of Mendelssohn's work, on his sister's authority, was inspired by the Walpurgisnight's Dream episode of Part I of *Faust*:

Wolkenzug und Nebelflor	The train of clouds and veil of mist
Erhellen sich von oben.	Lighten from above,
Luft im Laub und Wind im Rohr –	Air in leaves and wind in reeds –
Und alles ist zerstoben.	And everything has vanished.[100]

'To me alone he told his secret', claimed Fanny:

The whole piece is to be played staccato and *pianissimo*, the individual tremolos coming in here and there, the trills passing away with the quickness of lightning; everything is new, strange, and yet so insinuating and pleasing. One feels so near the world of spirits, lightly carried up into the air; one would like to take up a broomstick and follow the aerial procession. At the end the first violin takes flight with feather-like lightness – and all has vanished.[101]

This piece of evidence has inspired R. Larry Todd to propose a Faustian reading of the Octet as a whole, based on the first part of Goethe's drama, which had been published as far back as 1808.[102] Such a theory, naturally, is intriguing. While there is no proof that anything more than the scherzo was connected with Goethe's play, one cannot rule out an association from this lack of evidence, especially given Mendelssohn's congenital reticence concerning disclosure of the extramusical content of his music. While on the face of it, it might seem a little far-fetched to hold that Mendelssohn's work was designed as an enactment of Goethe's narrative, one must concede that, at the time of the Octet, Mendelssohn was just beginning his brief though fruitful artistic friendship with A.B. Marx, an advocate of basing musical compositions on extramusical literary or historical ideas, and that numerous works from the following years would base themselves on literary texts – even two of Goethe's poems in *Meeresstille und glückliche Fahrt*. Perhaps the most celebrated work written under this aesthetic, the overture to Shakespeare's *A Midsummer Night's Dream*, was written less than a year after the Octet. This example itself is instructive, since, as is well known, Marx had instructed the initially enthusiastic composer entirely to redraft the exposition to his Shakespearean overture as he believed the original did

---

[100] Goethe, *Faust I*, lines 4395–8.
[101] Fanny Mendelssohn, cited in Hensel, *Die Familie Mendelssohn*, vol. I, p. 151.
[102] Todd, *Mendelssohn: A Life in Music*, pp. 149–52.

not characterise strongly enough the course of the action.[103] One could easily infer from this that a work written the year before this encounter with Marx – and moreover one with this known literary connection to at least one of its movements – could reasonably be expected to be more imprecise and general in any allusions made to its literary model.

The extent to which one wishes to take this Faustian analogy is obviously a matter of personal opinion, since it can never be proved, barring the discovery of a further document from the composer or sibling stating this. Either way, the intimate link between Mendelssohn's work and Goethe's – at least within one movement – and the two figures, their aesthetic outlook and close artistic and spiritual relationship, is undeniable. At any rate, the connection provides a nice 'hermeneutical window', in Kramer's phrase, on to the Octet.[104] In 1825, the year in which Mendelssohn composed his octet, Goethe had resumed work on the second part of his *magnum opus* which had been projected as early as 1796; the elderly poet even gave Mendelssohn an autograph copy of excepts from its first act in 1830 (Fig. 2.2).

It seems in this context therefore hardly surprising to discover that the views on time held by Goethe and articulated by him in *Faust* are echoed in the process of his protégé's Octet. The Octet, as demonstrated above, enacts an organic, evolving spiral process that is not only strongly 'Hegelian' but also comparable to that theorised by Goethe (and seen, arguably, in *Faust*).[105] But, more than this, the treatment of time and history found in Goethe's writings, and above all in *Faust*, is mirrored in the Octet.

The presence of aspects of the music of the past within Mendelssohn's work should be understood in relation to the allusive nature of Goethe's work.[106] This incorporation of earlier music in Mendelssohn's work, both in the Octet and in his music in general, reveals the eternal presence of the past in the present, the continued validity for the present of the great achievements of history. In the same sense that Mendelssohn's work, like Goethe's before him, participates in the great artistic tradition lying behind

---

[103] Adolph Bernhard Marx, *Erinnerungen aus meinem Leben*, 2 vols. (Berlin: Janke, 1865), vol. II, p. 232.

[104] Lawrence Kramer, *Music as Cultural Practice, 1800–1900* (Berkeley, CA and Los Angeles, CA: University of California Press, 1992), pp. 6–20. Leon Botstein has claimed in this context that we might profitably hear all of Mendelssohn's music as a 'parallel to the second part of Goethe's *Faust*' ('Neoclassicism, Romanticism, and Emancipation', p. 4).

[105] An example of this organic approach in relation to Goethe's play is Peter Salm's *The Poem as Plant: A Biological View of Goethe's Faust* (Cleveland, OH and London: Case Western Reserve University Press, 1971).

[106] Jane Brown has even suggested that 'allusiveness per se is the defining quality of art for Goethe'. *Faust: The German Tragedy*, p. 177.

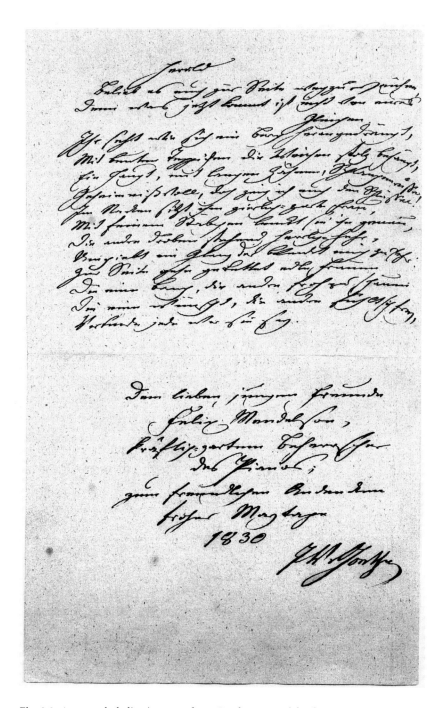

Fig. 2.2 Autograph dedication page from Goethe to Mendelssohn, containing excerpts from Part II of *Faust*.

it through its intertextual references back to that tradition, the present moment contains and to an extent validates all previous points by its growth from and participation within this historical continuum. Like the Helen episode of *Faust* (Part II, Acts 2 and 3), to be refound, in order to take up its new existence in the present, the past must first become fully aware of its own historical status.[107] This past is not presented as it actually existed historically, 'but as it existed – and could therefore continue to exist – in essence'.[108] It is a product of an unrepeatable moment in history yet contains the essence of that entire history within it, an idea that is infinitely repeatable. This recapturing of the past reveals the 'higher unity' of time that Goethe claimed to have found in Part II of *Faust* – the sense of the past and present as one.[109] However, on the other hand there is no sense in which this past is ever superseded: Mendelssohn's piece charts no historical progression, in terms of forming a culmination or improvement of what has preceded it, which is where Mendelssohn demonstrates his fidelity to Goethe's maxims and where he departs from Hegel, to whom in other respects he often comes quite close.

The very process of the Octet is that of a metamorphic spiral, which continually presses towards this transcendent moment – one which contains all that precedes it, an instant in which time past, present and future can be glimpsed as one, a moment *sub specie aeternitatis*. This moment of highest intensity is the *höchste Augenblick*, spoken of by Faust, in time but above it.[110] Hence the Octet's continual pressing onwards, constantly striving to

---

[107] This comparison between the historical attitude of Mendelssohn to music and that encapsulated in this act of Goethe's has been specifically cited by Walter Wiora in *Die Ausbreitung des Historismus über die Musik*, 'Diskussion', p. 84. The Helena scenes of Part II had not been finished by the time of the Octet, though Goethe had drafted some of them (for instance, the *Classical Walpurgisnacht*) as early as 1800.

[108] Vincent, *The Eternity of Being*, pp. 38–9. The idea of the incorruptibility of the essential truth of an art-work is articulated by Goethe frequently. A good example is found in *Wilhelm Meister*, where the organic, inner relationships that Wilhelm finds in *Hamlet* and which themselves are timelessly valid contrast with the 'accidental' historically specific external context which surrounds this essential core (*Wilhelm Meisters Lehrjahre*, bk V, ch. iv, in *Poetische Werke*, vol. VII, pp. 187–9).

[109] Note Goethe's famous account of his impressions on seeing Cologne Cathedral in *Dichtung und Wahrheit* III/14: 'One feeling that overwhelmed me and became inexpressibly fascinating was the sensation of past and present being one, a perception that introduced something spectral into the present.' *Poetische Werke*, vol. VIII, p. 401. See, likewise, Mendelssohn's response to the ruins of the Forum in Rome (letter, 8 November 1830, *Briefe*, vol. I, p. 51).

[110] Goethe, *Faust II*, line 11586. The idea of the epiphanic moment has a long history, and literature and philosophy in the nineteenth and twentieth centuries is particularly rich in examples, from Blake, Wordsworth, Shelley and Kierkegaard to Proust, Joyce, Woolf and Heidegger. The notion of the moment in specifically German music and its reception has been taken up by Berthold Hoeckner in *Programming the Absolute: Nineteenth-Century German Music and the Hermeneutics of the Moment* (Princeton University Press, 2002).

encapsulate linear time into one instant, the synthesis of previous moments into one. As in Goethe's *Faust*, this envisaged moment is the realisation of the participation of the individual/contingent with the whole, the capacity to envisage all life within a single moment, 'to adopt that perspective of eternity that Goethe regarded as the ultimate achievement of great art'.[111] This moment, found through time yet itself above time, contains within it the eternal. It is in itself a kind of eternity: the paradox of the timeless moment.

To persist with its literary counterpart, if viewing the Octet as a Faustian quest or narrative, we can take the analogy further, to the eventual Fifth Act of Part II and the death of Faust:

Zum Augenblicke dürft' ich sagen:	Then, to the moment, I could say:
Verweile doch, du bist so schön!	Yet tarry a while, you are so fair!
Es kann die Spur von meinen Erdetagen	The traces of my days on earth
Nicht in Äonen untergehn –	Cannot disappear from eternity –
Im Vorgefühl von solchem hohen Glück	In presentiment of such high fortune
Genieß' ich jetzt den höchsten Augenblick.	I now enjoy the highest moment.[112]

Upon reaching this highest moment, on realising the eternal participation of the contingent and transient within the whole, Faust dies. While (arguably) forfeiting his wager with Mephistopheles, he has nevertheless transcended its very terms and has hence overcome the finite limitations of human striving.[113] Likewise, on the realisation of this eternity, found within the instant, the music ceases. No more needs to be said; the rest is silence. In this manner, we can see the meeting and affinity of the ideas of Goethe and Hegel. This analogy with Goethe's *Faust* and the poet's views on time and history offers us an alternative – though not entirely incompatible – perspective from that of Hegelian synthesis and the path to self-consciousness, outlined above.[114]

Perhaps, one could suggest, the temporal nature of music, its ability to suggest the past and present, and prefigure the future, to combine a

---

[111] Vincent, *The Eternity of Being*, p. 38.

[112] Goethe, *Faust II*, lines 11581–6. This scene had again been drafted by Goethe earlier, around 1800.

[113] The same idea is theoretically formulated in Goethe's 'Studie nach Spinoza' (1784–5): 'ein eingeschränktes lebendiges Wesen teil an der Unendlichkeit oder vielmehr, es hat etwas Unendliches in sich' (Johann Wolfgang von Goethe, *Kunsttheoretische Schriften und Übersetzungen*, in *Berliner Ausgabe* (22 vols.), vols. XVII–XXII (Berlin: Aufbau Verlag, 1965–78), vol. XVIII, p. 141; cf. Spinoza, *Ethics*, V, Prop. 22–34; Leibniz, *Discourse on Metaphysics*, § 8–9).

[114] Walter Kaufmann has outlined several parallels to Goethe's *Faust* in Hegel's *Phenomenology* and the numerous debts which the philosopher acknowledged to his elder colleague (*Hegel*, pp. 116–19).

multitude of elements at any given time and to portray an immanent unity within a multiplicity of temporal events, is inherently assuming to encapsulate eternity in the moment. This aspect of music was noted by Goethe himself, in a letter written barely a week before his death to Mendelssohn's teacher, Zelter:

> Fortunately the character of your talent relies on tones, i.e., on the moment. Now, since a sequence of successive moments is always itself a kind of eternity, it was given to you to be ever constant in that which passes and thus to satisfy me as well as Hegel's spirit, insofar as I understand it, completely [by finding eternity in the moment].[115]

This abiding idea of Goethe's – 'permanence in transience' (*Dauer im Wechsel*)[116] – is perfectly crystallised in the process of Mendelssohn's piece. The eternal is represented in the finite, mediated through the finite world, through art. Music, by its temporal quality, its uniquely potent ability to enact the temporal states of human consciousness, can offer a glimpse of this eternal unity even through its transience – the revelation of the hidden unity and harmony of nature in which Goethe found the idea of the beautiful.[117]

The Octet is not just 'the first work of Mendelssohn's maturity', the composition in which the prodigiously talented composer seems to have found his own individual voice and musical direction, but is also the first work in which his historical attitude and views are encapsulated within his music's actual structure. The 'historical interest' within his music reveals the eternal verity of the past, within not just Mendelssohn's work, but the entire past tradition of music the composer inhabited so deeply. Through its cyclic structure, the Octet captures and renews its past, crystallising this quest into the course of its own history. This search for the transcendence of time – the finding of eternity in an instant, the *schöne Augenblick*, the eternal truth underlying the surface change and discontinuity – would be resumed in Mendelssohn's cyclic works from the following years, which would provide even more radical and remarkable examples of this quest.

---

[115] Goethe to Zelter, 11 March 1832; *Briefwechsel zwischen Goethe und Zelter*, vol. III, p. 639, translation taken from Kaufmann, *Hegel*, p. 357. This was in fact Goethe's last letter to Zelter, the poet dying eleven days later.

[116] Graham, *Goethe: Portrait of the Artist*, p. 2. Cf. Goethe's poem of the same name: 'Lass den Anfang mit dem Ende / Sich in *eins* zusammenziehn! / Schneller als die Gegenstände / Selber dich vorüberfliehn!' (*Poetische Werke*, vol. I, p. 69 / 440).

[117] 'Das Schöne ist eine Manifestation geheimer Naturgesetze, die ohne dessen Erscheinung ewig wären verborgen geblieben.' Goethe, *Maximen und Reflexionen*, No. 183, in *Poetische Werke*, vol. II, p. 502.

3 | Returning home

The E major Piano Sonata Op. 6

Ich lebe mein Leben in wachsenden Ringen,
die sich über die Dinge ziehn.
Ich werde den letzten vielleicht nicht vollbringen,
aber versuchen will ich ihn.

Ich kreise um Gott, um den uralten Turm,
und ich kreise jahrtausendelang;
und ich weiß noch nicht: bin ich ein Falke, ein Sturm
oder ein großer Gesang.

Rilke, *Das Stundenbuch*, 'Das Buch vom mönchischen Leben'[1]

In the years following the Octet, Mendelssohn repeatedly returned to the idea of cyclic form in his instrumental music. The Piano Sonatas in E, Op. 6 (1826), and B♭ (1827, Op. post. 106) were followed by the String Quartet in A minor Op. 13 (1827), and two years later by the E♭ Quartet Op. 12. This series of cyclic works is quite remarkable by any standard, and shows the composer exploring the formal and expressive implications of cyclic thematic recall and unification long before any other musician was seriously to take up this design.

The idea of the return to the past as forming the ultimate goal of a musical work is articulated for the first time in two of these works from the years 1826–7, the E major Piano Sonata Op. 6, and the Quartet in A minor Op. 13. In these two pieces, the end towards which the entire composition has been striving is found through the return to the very opening, which is achieved only in the last bars of the work. Unlike the process seen in the Octet from the preceding year, though, this goal is not formed so much by the transformation and synthesis of the past into the present, but through a circular journey back to a home left at the outset, the wistful refinding of a part of the past previously lost, a process that distils an unmistakable sense of recollection or nostalgia.

---

[1] 'I live my life in ever-growing circles, / that draw themselves over things. / I will, perhaps, not complete the last, / but I shall attempt it. / I circle around God, round the age-old tower, / and I circle thus for thousands of years; / and I know not yet: am I a falcon, a storm / or a great song.'

The following chapter focuses on the E major Piano Sonata Op. 6. This piece will be contextualised within a group of themes relevant to its interpretation – Neoplatonism, the return home, the myth of a lost golden age – that in turn provide a useful context to the discussion of the Op. 13 quartet in Chapter 4, which takes the ideas raised here further and views them in a wider historical context. Thus these two chapters may be seen as forming a pair, related through their common themes of musical memory, nostalgia, and the search for a timeless essence underlying the surface change.

The myth of the golden age

The idea of the return to the past, or to the past as recreated in memory, as the telos of a musical work again shares close parallels with an idea which is remarkably prevalent in literature and philosophy from the early nineteenth century, above all in Germany. The notion of a lost golden age, a vanished Arcadia or a primal Edenic state of innocence and harmony, figures prominently in the writings of German intellectuals and poets such as Winckelmann, Goethe, Schiller, Hölderlin, Fichte, Schelling, Hegel, Novalis, the Schlegels, Wilhelm von Humboldt and Eichendorff.[2] In the work of these figures, this lost paradise is sought either to be recaptured through a circular movement back to this initial state or to be regained at a higher level through a tripartite spiral journey (as we have seen with Hegel).[3] For Schelling, to take an example, 'The golden age . . . is to be sought not by an endless and restless progress and external activity, but rather by a return to that point from which each of us has set out – to the inner identity with the absolute'.[4] Likewise, in Heinrich von Kleist's essay *Über das Marionettentheater* of 1810, the history of man is formulated in allegorical terms as tracing a great circle, moving away from and back to an initial unity, while the idea of a lost golden age similarly 'runs like a unifying thread' through the work of Novalis.[5]

---

[2] The idea of a golden age stretches back to Hesiod and Ovid, but is a virtual obsession for German thinkers at this time. A comprehensive survey of this conception since antiquity and especially in early nineteenth-century Germany is provided by Hans Joachim Mähl in *Die Idee des goldenen Zeitalters im Werk des Novalis* (Heidelberg: Carl Winter, 1965).

[3] Constantin Behler labels this process 'nostalgic teleology', identifying it with a fundamental schema in the work of Schiller and his contemporaries which 'looks back to an earlier ideal "unity of human nature" and posits its recovery as the goal or telos of education, morality, and history' (*Nostalgic Teleology*, p. 3).

[4] Schelling, *System der gesammten Philosophie und der Naturphilosophie insbesondere*, in *Sämtliche Werke*, vol. VI, pp. 563–4, cited by Abrams, *Natural Supernaturalism*, p. 356.

[5] Peter Küpper, *Die Zeit als Erlebnis des Novalis* (Cologne: Böhlau, 1959), p. 130.

For some, this past is irretrievably lost, a regret expressed in Friedrich Schiller's poems 'Die Götter Griechenlands' and 'Resignation', and theoretically formulated in *Über naive und sentimentalische Dichtung*. 'All nations . . . have a paradise, a state of innocence, a golden age. Nay, more than this, every man has his paradise, his golden age.' For Schiller, though, one 'can no longer return to Arcadia'; mankind must instead be led on 'towards Elysium'.[6] For Kleist, famously, 'paradise is barred and the cherub behind us; we must make the journey round the world and see if it is perhaps open again somewhere on the other side'.[7] The journey of man is thus not so much a circle but rather an ellipse or eccentric path which leads asymptotically closer to the goal the further it moves away, without perhaps ever ultimately reaching it. Such is also the view of Friedrich Hölderlin in his novel *Hyperion* of 1797–9, for whom this goal is in a state of eternal becoming – the journey of life (and human history) an unceasing cyclical process of youthful aspiration, disillusion, and renewed endeavour.

For others, this redemptive end for human striving is still dreamt of as possible, and the final circular homecoming of the spirit can be prefigured through art. Novalis' three works *Die Lehrlinge zu Sais*, *Heinrich von Ofterdingen* and *Hymnen an die Nacht* all promise an ideal perfectibility, a quality denied only by the incompletion of the former two. Joseph von Eichendorff's *Ahnung und Gegenwart* (1812) revisits a similar theme, where the return of the protagonist to the place of the opening at the end of the novel, the completing of the circle, is accomplished through the action of religious grace.[8] Mendelssohn's works from these years, I suggest, can be aptly viewed as a musical parallel to such ideas of a circular homecoming and the regaining of Eden found so prominently in the literature of the early Romantics in Germany.

The Sonata in E major Op. 6

The E major Sonata is the first of Mendelssohn's works which alludes openly to Beethoven's late music – a group which includes the later Sonata in B♭,

---

[6] Friedrich Schiller, *Über naive und sentimentalische Dichtung*, in *Sämtliche Werke*, 5 vols. (Munich: Carl Hanser, 1962), vol. V, pp. 747 and 750.

[7] Heinrich von Kleist, *Über das Marionettentheater*, in *Werke und Briefe*, 4 vols. (Berlin and Weimar: Aufbau Verlag, 1978), vol. III, p. 476. For elucidation of this highly symbolic essay see Helmut Sembdner (ed.), *Kleists Aufsatz über das Marionettentheater: Studien und Interpretationen* (Berlin: Erich Schmidt, 1967).

[8] The hero, Friedrich, resolves to become a monk at the end of the story. See Marshall Brown, *The Shape of German Romanticism*, p. 149.

Fig. 3.1 Piano Sonata in E major Op. 6 (1826), autograph score, first page.

the A minor and E♭ Quartets. This connection between Mendelssohn's early works and Beethoven's late ones has often been mentioned, though rarely have such comments gone beyond noting apparent parallels in thematic construction, which often either serve tacitly to denigrate Mendelssohn's music for not being identical to Beethoven's work in all other aspects of its design or implicitly to legitimise it through such association. Most interesting from the present viewpoint is the correspondence between those pieces containing echoes of Beethoven's music and the cyclic designs pursued within them; while Beethoven's music is hardly as developed in this cyclic aspect as Mendelssohn's, it is nonetheless surely not without significance that Mendelssohn's most cyclic works are, almost without exception, those which allude so openly to Beethoven.[9] That Mendelssohn perceived a 'cyclic' tendency in Beethoven's late works is undeniable; his encounter with the latter's music here may be seen as one of the most artistically significant instances of creative 'misreading' in the nineteenth century.[10]

The opening of Mendelssohn's sonata, as has been often noted, recalls unmistakably that of Beethoven's A major Sonata Op. 101, one of the elder composer's works most prominent for its use of a proto cyclic design.[11] Contemporaries such as Schumann saw the similarities between the two as due to an 'inner spiritual affinity',[12] though for some more recent commentators the differences are viewed invariably to Beethoven's advantage, proving indicative for them of the divergence between Beethoven's and Mendelssohn's music. Charles Rosen, for example, has claimed that Mendelssohn here 'dispensed with the most original aspect of Beethoven's invention'. Beethoven's work 'begins not by establishing the key of A, but in the middle of the transitional modulation to the dominant. ... Under the modest lyric surface is a powerful dynamic process. Mendelssohn, however, starts by accepting the central key as E major, and this results in a more conventional and placid form.' This criticism does point to an important

---

[9] The Octet, despite the use of some of Beethoven's middle-period works as a point of departure, is perhaps exceptional here in that the allusions are never as overt as those in Opp. 6, 12, 13 or 106.

[10] The terminology is of course Harold Bloom's (*The Anxiety of Influence: A Theory of Poetry* (Oxford University Press, 1973)). A nuanced and perceptive application of Bloom's theories to Mendelssohn's (and other composers') creative encounters with Beethoven's music is given by Mark Evan Bonds in *After Beethoven: Imperatives of Originality in the Symphony* (Cambridge, MA: Harvard University Press, 1996).

[11] See, for instance, William S. Newman, *The Sonata since Beethoven* (Chapel Hill, NC: University of North Carolina Press, 1969), pp. 299–300, Joscelyn Godwin, 'Early Mendelssohn and late Beethoven', *Music & Letters*, 55 (1974), 272–7, Peter Schleuning, 'Felix Mendelssohn Bartholdys Klaviersonate E-Dur, op. 6', *Mendelssohn-Studien*, 16 (2009), 231–50.

[12] Schumann, 'Sonaten für Pianoforte' (*NZfM*, 3 (1835)), *Gesammelte Schriften*, vol. I, p. 124.

divergence between the two works, though the rather facile comparative evaluation Rosen makes between the two misses the fundamental point of Mendelssohn's sonata.[13]

As the third movement of the 'Italian' Symphony a few years later clearly demonstrates, Mendelssohn was perfectly capable, when he wished, of taking up the harmonic implications of such a design (which, as Jonathan Kramer has demonstrated, is in many ways a more remarkable piece than Beethoven's).[14] Mendelssohn's departure here must instead be understood as an intentional misreading of Op. 101 that deliberately attaches particular significance to this tonic start.

As anyone who has looked beyond the opening page of the sonata will realise, Mendelssohn's opening is in fact at the same time the end of his work; where Mendelssohn differs from Beethoven is that his sonata actually starts from its end.[15] In T.S. Eliot's famous lines, 'In my beginning is my end . . . . In my end is my beginning.' 'What we call the beginning is often the end / And to make an end is to make a beginning. / The end is where we start from.'[16] The work starts from 'home' and ends there, the entire course of the composition between these two outer points being designed as a circular return to this opening state. In this, Mendelssohn takes up the cyclic structure only hinted at in Beethoven's model, in its brief return to the opening theme in the transition preceding the finale, and develops it further into a design that spans the entire work. Mendelssohn's opening is in fact the start of a far more radical and unified design that completely transcends the (comparatively undeveloped) suggestion of Beethoven's model. The course of the first movement is the progressive movement away from the 'home' of the beginning, articulated in a highly organic process of thematic evolution across the exposition. What in Beethoven's work is a 'dynamic [harmonic] process' is transformed into a more subtle method of thematic growth and

---

[13] Rosen, *The Romantic Generation*, p. 571. In harmonic terms, the start of Beethoven's Op. 101 is undoubtedly more daring than Mendelssohn's sonata, but conversely the latter enacts a far more sophisticated process of thematic evolution across both its first movement and the work as a whole.

[14] As Kramer has shown, Mendelssohn's movement is a remarkable example of an end-weighted hypermetric accent (Jonathan Kramer, *The Time of Music: New Meanings, New Temporalities, New Listening Strategies* (New York: Schirmer, 1988), pp. 91–3; also see Konold, *Die Symphonien Felix Mendelssohn Bartholdys*, p. 292).

[15] This idea of musical temporality has been taken up by Jonathan Kramer in 'Multiple and Non-Linear Time in Beethoven's opus 135', *Perspectives on New Music*, 11 (1973), 122–45, being elaborated further in *The Time of Music*.

[16] T.S. Eliot, 'East Coker', I and V, and 'Little Gidding', V, from *Four Quartets* (*Collected Poems 1909–1962* (London: Faber, 1974), pp. 196, 204 and 221).

metamorphosis which goes beyond any previous model and is characteristic of what would become one of Mendelssohn's unique achievements.

The opening of Mendelssohn's sonata, as with Beethoven's, evokes immediately the topos of the Pastoral – the relaxed $^6_8$ time signature, the parallel tenths between the two outer voices and the sustained pedal tonic and dominant in the inner voice all pointing to this association.[17] The pastoral, of course, has notable connotations with the idea of Arcadia – as exemplified in the *Eclogues* of Virgil or the idealised seventeenth-century landscapes of Poussin and Claude. Its use here might recall for us Schiller's injunction for the modern 'sentimental' poet of setting himself 'the task of creating an Idyll', which will lead mankind onwards towards his Elysium.[18] While the melodic phrases of the opening theme give the appearance of artless simplicity in their appealing song-like lyricism, melodic interest is sustained across the entire opening paragraph through the evasion of melodic closure until the eighteenth bar, which sees the start of a new section, underpinned by a more unstable semiquaver figuration in the left hand, growing out of the material developed across the opening paragraph. The first cadence to the tonic at b. 4 is weakly articulated through the continuing dominant pedal in the tenor inner voice and the descent, which reaches only to degree $\hat{3}$, in the melody; the following four bars develop the characteristic opening neighbour-note motive, heard now in inversion, before elaborating the descent of bb. 2–3 ($\hat{8}$–$\hat{3}$) into a scalic descent from $\hat{3}$ to $\hat{7}$ an octave below (Ex. 3.1). The consequent phrase (bb. 8–17) retraces this opening with an increased thickening of texture, and a contrapuntal elaboration and extension of its second half that leads to the first full cadence at b. 18.

From here rhythmic and motivic activity is increased. A new theme, rising out from the depths of the rippling texture, takes up the descent from this upper g♯² to d♯ seen already in bb. 7–8 and modified at bb. 15–16 in the consequent (Ex. 3.1, second theme). In fact, its initial arpeggiation is merely a simplification of the opening thematic idea that, in conjunction with this subsequent scalic descent, has underlain all the melodic material so far in the movement (the arpeggiation $\hat{3}$–$\hat{5}$–$\hat{8}/\hat{3}$) followed by descent from this head-note). The following bars extend this new idea through their changing

---

[17] Robert S. Hatten provides an extensive list of pastoral tropes found in Beethoven's Op. 101 in *Musical Meaning in Beethoven: Markedness, Correlation, and Interpretation* (Bloomington, IN: Indiana University Press, 1994), pp. 97–9. The link Hatten makes between the pastoral and religious in Beethoven's work is particularly apt for consideration of Mendelssohn's sonata. See also Sisman, 'Memory and Invention at the Threshold of Beethoven's Late Style', for a further account of the pastoral topos and its significance in Beethoven's music of these years.

[18] Schiller, *Über naive und sentimentalische Dichtung*, *Sämtliche Werke*, vol. V, p. 750.

Ex. 3.1 Piano Sonata Op. 6, first movement, exposition: successive derivation of material from opening theme.

harmonic context until a new variant of this theme is heard in C♯ minor (b. 27), which prefigures directly the second subject (b. 40). This secondary theme will itself metamorphose into a closing variant (b. 56), which leads to the return of the opening theme heard now in the dominant, metrically realigned and in conjunction with the rippling semiquavers that have been present since the start of this onward development at b. 18. In this return to the opening subject, Mendelssohn not only demonstrates the underlying coherence of the exposition by returning to the underlying theme, but also turns the exposition into a miniature (if harmonically open) circle of its own. Since the development section itself is highly abridged and leads back to the restatement of the recapitulation – heard now over a dominant pedal and transformed through elision, metrical displacement and the widening of tessitura – the entire first movement can be seen as a series of increasing circles; the whole work is in fact a larger circle, formed out of these smaller epicycles – the 'circle of circles' (*Kreis von Kreisen*) as Hegel would formulate it.[19]

---

[19] Hegel, *The Logic of Hegel* [Shorter Logic], p. 24 / *Werke*, vol. VIII, p. 60. Also see the 'Longer' Logic (*Science of Logic*, p. 842 / *Werke*, vol. VI, p. 571). The quintessential Neoplatonic formulation of this idea is given by Proclus in the *Elements of Theology*, Prop. 33 (p. 37): 'All that proceeds from any principle and reverts upon it has a cyclic activity. For . . . it links its end to its beginning, and the movement is one and continuous, originating from the unmoved and to the unmoved again returning. Thus all things proceed in a circuit from their causes to their

Fig. 3.2 A contemporary depiction of Arcadia: Karl Friedrich Schinkel, *Griechische Ideallandschaft mit rastenden Hirten* (1823). Continuing in the pastoral tradition of Poussin, the artist has added his name and date to the bottom left of the sarcophagus, simultaneously asserting his authorship and creating a personal *momento mori.*

This process of continuous lyrical evolution of essentially song-like melodic material is quite remarkable in its sophistication and apparent ease at fusing seemingly antithetical categories of closed melodic formal syntax with a dynamic growth and development of thematic material. In a word, Mendelssohn solves at one stroke in this work the nineteenth-century problem of maintaining a logical evolving structure and thematic development within a Romantic sonata style in which the emphasis is placed on lyrical melody, an achievement that he was both the first and perhaps the only really successful figure to realise.[20] The Op. 6 sonata is probably the first of Mendelssohn's works where this characteristic trait is fully demonstrated.

causes again. There are greater circuits and lesser, in that some revert upon their immediate priors, others upon the superior causes, even to the beginning of all things. For out of the beginning all things are, and towards it all revert.'

[20] This capacity for organic development amidst lyrical song-like themes is one of Mendelssohn's most significant achievements and will be taken up again later in this study. See on this point Donald M. Mintz, 'The Sketches and Drafts for Three of Felix Mendelssohn's Major Works', unpublished PhD thesis, Cornell University (1960), pp. 132ff.

Ex. 3.2 Piano Sonata Op. 6, second movement: rhythmic interplay of $\frac{2}{4}$ and $\frac{3}{4}$.

This ongoing movement away from the home of the opening is continued in the two following movements.[21] The second movement already shows a progression away from the opening part of the sonata, an intermezzo-like minuet movement in the unexpected key of F♯ minor. Though this section is measured in triple time, the pairings of notes suggest rather a hemiolic $\frac{2}{4}$ with something of a march about it, a rhythmic play which persists throughout the first section (Ex. 3.2). The subtle metrical disjunction is exploited at the cadence preceding the double bar, where the measured downbeat C♯ minor goal (b. 8[1]) is heard to jut in a beat early, a surprise accentuation of the unaccented second beat of the two-note pairing. This play is continued over the double bar, the second bar of every two-bar group emphasising the notated triple metre at the expense of the duple expectation set up in the previous bars, alternating briefly with duple phrasing (bb. 14–15) before switching back to triple (bb. 16–17). This nine-bar template is then repeated

---

[21] The autograph manuscript of the sonata, now in the Bodleian Library, reveals that Mendelssohn was keen to emphasise the cyclic connection between the movements by adding, prior to publication, the present *attacca* designation between the first two movements and changing the key signature at the ends of both in preparation for the following movement, thus running the separate movements on to each other and creating a composite one-movement structure. See further R. Larry Todd, 'A Mendelssohn Miscellany', *Music & Letters*, 71 (1990), 62–3.

in condensed form in bb. 18–25, the metric play made now even more evident through the arpeggiated chords. In the reprise (b. 34) the opening phrase's pattern is again changed to reconfirm $\frac{3}{4}$, with a new walking figure in the bass formed from the inversion of the main theme.

In the persistent rhythmic play of the opening – this constantly reinterpreted ambiguity between $\frac{2}{4}$ and $\frac{3}{4}$, the march-like flavour – and the repeated pedals in inner voices, this movement suggests associations of outdoors and movement, possibly even a forest or woodland scene as Schumann would later paint – the distorted echoes of horncalls in the pedals sifting through the inner voices, the uncertain rhythmic play, where nothing is quite what it seems. 'How it surges and drives and gushes forth! Everything is as green and auroral as in a spring landscape', exclaimed Schumann.[22] This theme of solitary wandering through nature is a characteristic trope of much Romantic literature. In the famous *Märchen* of Hyazinth and Rosenblütchen from *Die Lehrlinge zu Sais*, Hyazinth, having left his Arcadian home of the opening, wanders 'through valleys and wildernesses, over mountains and streams', in search of the key to a mysterious yearning awakened in him by a travelling stranger who visited his contented parental home at the start of the story.[23] The theme of wandering through the forest likewise plays a significant role in Tieck's enigmatic tale *Der Runenberg*. This movement, through the connotations with the forest and the trope of journeying so beloved by the German Romantics, might form a comparable progression 'through strange lands', a journey away from the security of the E major home of the first movement, as found in the stories and novels of Novalis, Tieck and Eichendorff.

Throughout the sonata, the onward movement away from the idyllic Arcadian landscape of the opening movement is repeatedly offset by allusions back to (or distant intimations of) the opening theme of the work, which will return explicitly in the sonata's closing bars. The opening material of this second movement may be seen to bear a distant relationship to that of the first movement (the $\hat{3}$–$\hat{5}$–$\hat{8}$ arpeggiation at the middleground level, with movement around the upper-neighbour $\hat{5}$–$\hat{6}$–$\hat{5}$), which

---

[22] Schumann, 'Sonaten für Pianoforte', *Gesammelte Schriften*, vol. I, p. 124. Schumann's own F♯ minor Piano Sonata Op. 11 takes this movement of Mendelssohn's as a model for its own minuet. Opus 6 is also an influence behind Schumann's third movement, whose recitative gestures view Beethoven's late sonatas distinctly through the lens of Mendelssohn's reworking of them.

[23] Novalis, *Die Lehrlinge zu Sais*, in *Schriften. Die Werke Friedrich von Hardenbergs (Historische-kritische Ausgabe)*, ed. Paul Kluckhohn, Richard Samuel, Gerhard Schulz and Hans-Joachim Mähl, 6 vols. (Stuttgart: Kohlhammer, 1960–2006), vol. I, p. 94.

Ex. 3.3 Piano Sonata Op. 6, second movement, 'menuetto' and trio themes.

alongside the 'Tempo di Menuetto' marking, suggests some type of self-conscious allusion to the past (Ex. 3.3). Leading on without transition from this minuet is a trio in the submediant, D major. The music of this section is, now even more clearly than that of the minuet, related to the opening of the first movement: the syncopated dominant pedal in the bass (held over from the preceding minuet and forming a link between the two sections though the common note A), the relaxed melody moving by conjunct motion around $\hat{3}$ and its upper neighbour note, and the imitative contrapuntal elaboration of its second half following the double bar revealing the affinity between the two movements.

Midway through this section, the music appears to approach a stasis over diminished-seventh harmonies (Ex. 3.4c). The effect is of a momentary stilling of time, the music dwelling over these repeated, quasi-hypnotic sonorities. These diminished sevenths had first appeared in the opening movement, forming a 'strangely articulated cadence' which closed the exposition (Ex. 3.4a), and had reappeared as mysterious staccato octaves in the bass that seemed to cast a cloud over the course of the development section (Ex. 3.4b).[24] Interrupting the elaboration of the opening theme in G major, their octaves continue throughout the remainder of the section and persist into the recapitulation, which is destabilised over a dominant pedal. The resulting tension in the first movement between the music of the idyllic beginning and the growing infiltration of these sonorities suggests wonderfully the gradual introduction of discordant elements into

---

[24] Godwin, 'Early Mendelssohn and late Beethoven', p. 275.

Ex. 3.4a Piano Sonata Op. 6, first movement, close of exposition: stream of diminished sevenths (first explicit appearance).

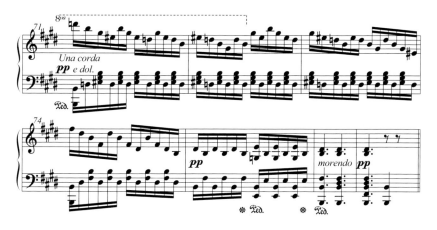

Ex. 3.4b Piano Sonata Op. 6, first movement, development: juxtaposition of main theme and diminished sevenths.

Ex. 3.4c Piano Sonata Op. 6, second movement, trio, central section: return of diminished sevenths.

the initially unspoilt Arcadian scene – the impetus for the outward movement away from this home, or even the dreamlike unreality of the entire setting.

In their later appearance in the trio these diminished sevenths form through their sensuous play of sonority a moment of pure stasis, a suspension of the onward progress of the music, suggesting, perhaps, an opening to memory. A similar passage from Mendelssohn's overture *The Hebrides* has been aptly described by R. Larry Todd as 'an intrusion of orchestral timbre', the 'shimmering prolongation of a diminished-seventh harmony' functioning 'as a special coloristic effect . . . which does not bear on the basic thematic material'.[25] The static intervallic equivalence of the constituent minor thirds, the blurring pedal effect and the marked *pianissimo, una corda* sonority,[26] result in a slowing of the musical passage through time, the remembered music issuing from afar, an effect of spatial or even temporal distance. In all later instances in the sonata, the allusion to the music of the opening is preceded by this same shimmering diminished-seventh sonority, a kind of enactment of memory or the movement to a different state of time. The contrast between movement and momentary stasis in Mendelssohn's sonata is in this respect not unlike that explored within the Romantic novel of the period – what Brown has spoken of as the 'freezing' of time, the opposition of impetuous movement (associated with the Gothic) with the static reflective time of the pastoral, the intersection of the eternal and temporal worlds.[27]

The heart of the composition is reached in the third movement, a blending of fugue and recitative that forms the expressive core of Mendelssohn's work. The opening A minor *Adagio e senza tempo*, marked 'Recitativo', owes clearly to the example of Beethoven's late sonatas, above all the third movement of the Sonata in A♭, Op. 110, though the conjunction with fugal writing is nowhere hinted at in Beethoven's work and is one of Mendelssohn's most extraordinarily original conceptions. This treatment of recitative as a fugue was to be taken up a year later by the composer in the A minor Quartet, one of numerous features that connect these two closely related works. Even more so, perhaps, than the *Arioso Dolente* from Op. 110, this mixture of

---

[25] R. Larry Todd, 'Mendelssohn's Ossianic Manner, with a New Source: *On Lena's Gloomy Heath*', in Jon Finson and R. Larry Todd (eds.), *Mendelssohn and Schumann* (Durham, NC: Duke University Press, 1984), p. 142. A similarly shimmering, suspended effect is achieved in the famous *Venetianisches Gondellied* Op. 19 No. 6, bb. 22–3.

[26] This same designation *pianissimo, una corda* is used in a slightly later piano work, the *Fantasia on 'The Last Rose of Summer'* Op. 15 (1827), to comparable effect for the recall of fragments of the opening melody throughout the darker, more impassioned (and somewhat enigmatic) central part of the work.

[27] Marshall Brown, *The Shape of German Romanticism*, pp. 210ff. This effect might be seen as equally applicable to the later A minor Quartet, where the 'static' memory is provided by a song of Mendelssohn's inserted into the 'prose' of the quartet. The very regularity or repetition of rhythm in a poem (or, by implication, a Lied), through its interpolation within a prose narrative, constitutes an interruption of the linear impetus of time; in Brown's words, 'as temporality without forward movement, rhythm and rhyme . . . constitute the ground or "tonic chord" of human time' (p. 212).

the archaic and the deeply expressive, almost operatic, forms the anguished centrepiece of the sonata.

Growing out of the four fugal entries on V of A minor and its dominant, the music moves initially through flatward regions, returning back through Am to Em, then, driven by an expressive rising chromatic bass line, further to Bm, F♯m and the dominant of F♯m – breaking off into a reiterative-like arpeggiation *senza tempo* on a Neapolitan sixth, followed by a diminished seventh serving as V/V in F♯. On its second appearance this section is more intense. Gone are the ordered subject–answer pairings of the first presentation: stretto entries on the dominant of E minor propel the music even more impassionedly to a climax on three successive diminished-seventh arpeggios that present the complete set of chromatic pitches.

From the analogy with the Romantic literary tales taken up earlier, it is hard not to interpret this passage as forming some sort of trial or ordeal within the musical journey, particularly some type of inner soul-searching. In *Die Lehrlinge zu Sais*, for instance, Hyazinth travels on his journey 'through a ragged, wild country; mist and scudding clouds enveloped his path . . . time became slower and an inner unrest lay upon him' – a journey that should be understood as much as inner and spiritual as outward and spatial.[28] This same sense of temporal lassitude can be encountered in Mendelssohn's largely unmeasured writing ('senza tempo'), free of temporal fixed points, and the succession of diminished sevenths that result in almost complete disorientation in terms of tonal space and as a consequence musical time.

In the midst of this impassioned movement there comes a visionary major-key episode, twice interrupting at the height of the preceding fugue, leading out of the diminished sevenths into which the climax had disintegrated.[29] Set off from the fugue each time through this haze of diminished sevenths, the effect is unmistakably one of movement to and from different aesthetic or temporal levels. Marked *pianissimo dolce, una corda*

---

[28] Novalis, *Die Lehrlinge zu Sais, Schriften*, vol. I, p. 94. See Gordon Birrell, *The Boundless Present: Space and Time in the Literary Fairy Tales of Novalis and Tieck* (Chapel Hill, NC: University of North Carolina Press, 1979), p. 18.

[29] This entire section owes something to the Andante of the 'Hammerklavier' sonata, seen, beyond the similarities in melodic construction of this major key episode, in the choice of keys preceding it (F♯ minor, followed by the Neapolitan G; see also Godwin, 'Early Mendelssohn and late Beethoven', p. 276). The importance of this sonata to Mendelssohn is demonstrated, not just in his own homage from the following year, the B♭ Sonata (even published posthumously as Op. 106), but in a mock letter he wrote, purportedly from 'Beethoven', to his sister Fanny, in which the composer mentions with characteristic understatement that he did not write this work 'out of thin air'. (Werner, *Mendelssohn: A New Image*, pp. 108–9.)

Ex. 3.5 Piano Sonata Op. 6, third movement, visionary episode in F♯ major.

again, this passage recalls more unmistakably than ever the opening of the sonata, heard now as if a distant vision (Ex. 3.5).

What causes this deep sense of distance, of memory or nostalgia, is not just the position of this andante passage as the calm pool in the midst of the minor-key adagio or the preparation through the familiar blur of diminished-seventh sonority, nor the *lontano* effect of the *pianissimo, una corda* marking, but also surely the tonal remoteness of this passage. While the first appearance, in F♯ major, is comprehensible as a major-key transfiguration of the F♯ minor second movement, this tonality itself, through its very unusualness, is surely not also without symbolic value. F♯ major is associated with connotations of distance and transcendence – the furthest point, after all, from a 'neutral' C major key signature.[30] What seems to confirm this impression is that on its second appearance the visionary passage returns now in B♭ major – the tritonal pole of the sonata's overall tonic of E major. It is this last appearance which will lead, via the familiar rippling diminished sevenths of the first movement, to the finale, the homecoming to E major, and with it eventually the cyclic return of the sonata's opening in the coda.

There is the sense here that at the furthest point of remove – the remotest stage of the journey, when one is farthest away and despairing over ever finding one's goal – we are in reality at our closest, that we are in possession of the truth sought for; the darkest hour precedes the dawn. The vision of the opening – shimmering distantly in the tritonal realm of B♭ major – is in fact the solution, the goal of the piece, which is only now realised, at the furthest point, and the darkest moment of the work. This quintessentially Neoplatonist notion – rather like the despairing of Odysseus when he is in fact already, without his knowing it, standing on the shore of Ithaca – is one

---

[30] On the symbolic properties of this key (and its enharmonic equivalent G♭) see Hugh Macdonald, '[G♭]', *19th-Century Music*, 11 (1988), 221–37.

much loved of the Romantics.[31] Schiller, in his poem 'Odysseus', expresses this theme succinctly:

Alle Gewässer durchkreuzt', die Heimat zu finden, Odysseus;
Durch der Scylla Gebell, durch der Charybde Gefahr,
Durch die Schrecken des feindlichen Meers, durch die Schrecken des Landes,
Selber in Aides' Reich führt ihn die irrende Fahrt.
Endlich trägt das Geschick ihn schlafend an Ithakas Küste,
Er erwacht und erkennt jammernd das Vaterland nicht.[32]

Odysseus, having crossed all waters to find his homeland;
Past the baying of Scylla, past the peril of Charybdis,
Through the terrors of the fiendish sea, through the horrors of land,
Led even within Hades' realm by his erring journey.
Finally destiny brought him, sleeping, to Ithaca's coast,
He awoke and, lamenting, did not recognise his fatherland.

This mythic circular journey is one of the most potent ideas in Western thought, a Neoplatonic streak found repeatedly in religious thought and Christian eschatology:

[A]t that very moment when you will realise with horror that, far from getting nearer to your goal, you are, in spite of all your efforts, actually further away from it than ever, I predict that at that very moment you will suddenly attain your goal and will behold clearly the miraculous power of the Lord who has all the time been loving and mysteriously guiding you.[33]

In Novalis, the quest the protagonist has set out for – be it the goddess of wisdom, an otherworldly vision of radiant female beauty or, that archetypal Romantic symbol, the blue flower – is revealed to be that which had been present all along, the home mistakenly discarded at the outset. In the *Märchen* of Hyazinth and Rosenblütchen, the idealistic youth Hyazinth leaves his childhood love and the contentment of his idyllic home in search of the mysterious goddess – the mother of all things – he learnt of through the travelling stranger. After many years of wandering through foreign lands

---

[31] *Odyssey*, bk. XIII. The image of Odysseus' wanderings and travails as part of his circular route back to the land of his ancestors is one particularly beloved of Plotinus (see *The Enneads*, I.6.8, V.9.1).

[32] Schiller, 'Odysseus', *Sämtliche Werke*, vol. I, p. 250.

[33] The quotation is taken from Fyodor Dostoyevsky's *The Brothers Karamazov*, trans. David Magarshack, 2 vols. (Harmondsworth: Penguin, 1958), vol. I, p. 64. Here, the Orthodox monk, the Elder Zossima, offers a peasant woman advice, in a strain typical of Neoplatonist-influenced Christianity.

Ex. 3.6 Piano Sonata Op. 6: comparison of finale bb. 5–6 with second movement bb. 14–15.

he at last comes to the dwelling place of Isis, where he dreams he lifts the veil of the divine woman – only to see his sweetheart Rosenblütchen, whom he had left behind long before. Fragments Novalis jotted down telling of the resolution of the main story of *Die Lehrlinge* similarly indicate that at the climax of the story, on lifting the veil of Isis, the hero sees '– wonder of wonders – himself', a circular, Neoplatonic reinterpretation of the well-known Delphic/Socratic axiom 'know thyself!' (γνῶθι σεαυτόν).[34] The professedly linear quest has turned circular, the goal of the story revealed to be the return to itself, to its beginning.

The emphatic E major of the finale forms a joyful confirmation of the homecoming, the return back to the tonality and ultimately the music of the opening left behind at the start of the work. 'Now the wayside became once again richer and more varied, the sky soft and blue, the path more even. Time passed ever more quickly, as he saw himself nearing his goal.'[35] Gestures throughout the course of its sonata-form structure suggest echoes of earlier stages on the way of the sonata – the sequence of rising thirds and falling fourths in the continuation of the opening reminiscent of the second movement (Ex. 3.6), the climactic disintegration of the development into diminished sevenths in imitative octaves between the two hands recalling the use of those harmonies in the comparable part of the first movement.

In the development Mendelssohn introduces an extended passage of imitative sequential writing based on the head-motive of the first theme, increasing the sense of movement and mounting excitement, a stretto effect that perfectly mirrors the quickening of time described by Novalis. Even the

[34] Novalis, Paralipomena to *Die Lehrlinge zu Sais*, *Schriften*, vol. I, p. 110. Cf. Plato [attrib.], *Alcibiades I*, 124b; *Phaedrus*, 230a; *Charmides*, 165a; *Philebus*, 48c–d; Plotinus, *The Enneads*, V.3; Proclus, *Elements of Theology*, Prop. 83. The entire story of Novalis' later (and similarly unfinished) novel *Heinrich von Ofterdingen* is likewise a complex elaboration upon this circular journey, in which the outward *Bildungsreise* of the first part ('The Expectation') was to be reflected in the more spiritual homeward journey of the second ('The Fulfilment'), culminating in self-knowledge, the overcoming of time and mortality and the regaining of the golden age.

[35] Novalis, *Die Lehrlinge zu Sais*, *Schriften*, vol. I, p. 94.

Ex. 3.7 Piano Sonata Op. 6, finale, coda: transition to cyclic return of sonata's opening theme.

two brief allusions to earlier movements correspond to the original order presented in reverse, a retrograde journey back to the opening that will at last culminate in the recovery of this lost golden age.[36]

Towards the end of this movement the music disintegrates into a stream of diminished-seventh harmonies over a dominant pedal, once again returning to the gesture that has run throughout the piece and the apparition of memory it prompts. Out of this dying fall, growing from a rising second, emerges finally the opening theme of the sonata (Ex. 3.7), joined in the third bar of the form presented in the recapitulation. The effect is of returning to the true theme which has all along lain behind the work. The piece has finally reached its home.

[36] Cf. Birrell, *The Boundless Present*, p. 67: 'From the point where the reversal occurs, [Hyazinth's] accelerating journey forward through time brings him backward through time to the point of departure . . . The process leading to the attainment of the second Golden Age leads simultaneously and symmetrically to the recovery of the first.'

In his depictions of this homecoming, Novalis repeatedly returns to this idea of a heard music. In the tale of Hyazinth and Rosenblütchen, on lifting the veil of the goddess, 'a distant music was heard', as Rosenblütchen sinks into Hyazinth's arms.[37] In the 'Arion' and 'Atlantis' tales from *Heinrich von Ofterdingen*, song forms the actual means for the reuniting of the past golden age with the present and mankind with nature, while in the novel's main story Heinrich associates the symbolic blue flower, his love for Mathilde and music together in a heady Platonic mixture: 'visible spirit of song', he exclaims, 'she will dissolve me into music!'[38] The third *Märchen* from *Heinrich von Ofterdingen* ('Fable and Eros') suggests even a cyclic quality to this otherworldly music – an underlying theme behind this enchanted stream of sounds which unifies the music to itself. Though 'the music changed ceaselessly . . . still it appeared that only *one* simple theme united the whole'[39] – a conception which seems a remarkable distillation of Mendelssohn's sonata.

Novalis' account of this distant ethereal music, both here and in *Die Lehrlinge zu Sais*, must surely be intended to allude to Plato's description of the music of the spheres, the union of masculine and feminine and resulting circular homecoming taking on allegorically a cosmic significance.[40] Music for Novalis is 'heavenly knowledge on earth' – an echo or recollection of the lost golden age of harmony when the heavens were united with mankind.[41] While philosophy 'is really homesickness', music, conversely, can enable the mind to be 'for short moments in its earthly home'.[42] Through its play of tones 'all love and goodness, future and past, animate themselves in the soul' – foreshadowing the fusion and overcoming of time set as the goal of earthly endeavours and envisaged at the close of *Heinrich von Ofterdingen*.[43]

This homecoming might suggest a physical return to the place of the opening, but the enactment through music also suggests the possibility of this return being temporal – a return to memory, a refinding of something

---

[37] Novalis, *Die Lehrlinge zu Sais, Schriften*, vol. I, p. 95.

[38] Novalis, *Heinrich von Ofterdingen, Schriften*, vol. I, p. 227.

[39] *Ibid.*, p. 293: 'Die Sterne schwangen sich, bald langsam bald schnell, in beständig veränderten Linien umher, und bildeten, nach dem Gange der Musik, die Figuren der Blätter auf das kunstreicheste nach. Die Musik wechselte . . . unaufhörlich, und so wunderlich und hart auch die Übergänge nicht selten waren, so schien doch nur *ein* einfaches Thema das Ganze zu verbinden.'

[40] See Plato, *The Republic*, 617b.   [41] Novalis, *Heinrich von Ofterdingen, Schriften*, vol. I, p. 209.

[42] Novalis, *Das Allgemeine Brouillon*, fragments 857 and 245, in *Schriften*, vol. III, pp. 434 and 283.

[43] *Ibid.*, p. 283. See the poem 'Die Vermählung der Jahrszeiten' ('The Marriage of the Seasons'), with which, according to Tieck, Novalis was to conclude his work: 'Wären die Zeiten nicht so ungesellig, verbände / Zukunft mit Gegenwart und mit Vergangenheit sich' (*Schriften*, vol. I, p. 355).

lost. The music, through the preceding diminished seventh complexes, can remember (or press towards remembering) the opening – its home – left behind. Hence the sonata joins the opening theme *in medias res*, through a blur, the vision gradually emerging from the preceding diminished sevenths, its insubstantiality emphasised by a return to the diminished-seventh cadential sonorities which finally lead the work to its conclusion.

Despite this sense of completion and perfection, perhaps this homecoming is itself somehow unreal. The sonata possesses a certain dreamlike, wistful quality, rather like those mythical, consciously allegorical fairy tales of Novalis, to which it corresponds in so many ways.[44] Schumann spoke of a 'reflective sadness' common to both Mendelssohn's work and Beethoven's Op. 101.[45] ('Et in Arcadia ego' reads the inscription on the tomb of an earlier fellow-traveller in many an Arcadian painting.[46]) As if bearing out this view, following every occasion that the piece circles back to the music of the opening or a close allusion of this – at the end of the exposition and first movement, the transition following the initial F♯ vision back to the recitative of the third movement and again in the transition to the finale, finally now at the very end – we hear the particular diminished-seventh figuration that first appeared closing the initial circle of the exposition (Ex. 3.4a), a dissolving of time and space, a blurring of world and dream.[47]

Or this return might alternatively be to a deeper spiritual or metaphysical 'home', the refinding of an ultimate reality ongoing behind the work at a different level of time – as Schlegel would believe, regaining the ideal realm, the true essence behind the phenomenal manifestations of this world.[48] The

[44] 'All *Märchen*', Novalis declared, 'are simply dreams of those homeland worlds that are everywhere and nowhere' ('Denkaufgabe' fragment 195, *Schriften*, vol. II, p. 564; see also in this context the *Allgemeine Brouillon* fragment 986, where Novalis claims a *Märchen* is like 'a musical fantasy' (*Schriften*, vol. III, p. 454)).

[45] Schumann, 'Sonaten für Pianoforte', *Gesammelte Schriften*, vol. I, p. 124.

[46] The classic example can be found in Poussin's *Les Bergers d'Arcadie* of 1638. See Erwin Panofsky's famous essay 'Et in Arcadia ego: Poussin and the Elegiac Tradition', in *Meaning in the Visual Arts* (New York: Doubleday, 1955), pp. 295–320.

[47] 'Die Welt wird Traum, der Traum wird Welt': Novalis, *Heinrich von Ofterdingen*, *Schriften*, vol. I, p. 319.

[48] In Friedrich Schlegel's highly Neoplatonic formulation, man lives in two worlds – the eternal and the temporal. While the former demands self-expression and consistency, the temporal seeks organic change and fulfilment. Since the ideal is seen as the source of the real world, this movement towards fulfilment is essentially negative, a return back to the source, the removal of imperfection. Self-consciousness is therefore essentially temporal consciousness, the awareness of the two worlds and their movement, through time, from the real to the ideal. This movement is in fact the definition of time itself, which (pre-empting Hegel by several years) cannot be consummated without abolishing time itself. Schlegel, *Jena Lectures* (1800–1), this summary taken from Marshall Brown, *The Shape of German Romanticism*, p. 177.

cyclic recall of this half-remembered dream in the sonata hence embodies an example of Platonic anamnesis, a return to something always 'known' but veiled in the shrouds of time.[49] One could in fact describe the process of Mendelssohn's sonata as the perfect musical equivalent of this Platonic (or Neoplatonic) world-view, in explicitly thematicising the search for an unchanging essence through the transient, temporal medium that is music, and suggesting its regaining in a return to the unity and wholeness of the opening material, heard consequently as an underlying and enduring deeper reality, the music's source and spiritual home.

By the same token, this aspect can be viewed from a more specifically religious perspective. The completing of the circle in Mendelssohn's work – like the intentions of Novalis and Eichendorff (and unlike the asymptotic, infinitely incomplete cyclicism of some of the other Romantics) – is achieved through the action of religious grace and perfectibility, expressing a Neoplatonic journey from unity and contentment, away through division, alienation and contradiction, back to the One.

One small detail of the music that might hold significance for such an interpretation is the difference between the end of the first movement and that of the fourth. At the close of the first, following the rippling diminished sevenths, a submediant chord undercuts the initial tonic close, extending the final cadence through another echo of the opening theme to a second set of tonic chords. The effect is beautiful and unmistakably nostalgic. At the end of the work this longing glance is missing; the music simply concludes without any wistful digression (Ex. 3.8). The homecoming is complete, perfect; nothing remains to be desired. In both movements, the preceding *una corda* pedal marking is removed for the very last tonic chords, played *pianissimo* but *tutte le corde* – an affirmation of the presence or reality of the home that has finally been reached.

'Let us flee then to the beloved fatherland': Plotinus, taking his guidance from the *Iliad*, saw this homecoming as the soundest counsel, a return to the Beautiful and Good.[50] The notion of home might well have been significant

---

[49] Cf. Plato, *Meno*, 81e; *Phaedo*, 73–5; *Phaedrus*, 274–5; *Philebus*, 34b. Novalis' writings are filled with examples of such Platonic recollection. *Heinrich von Ofterdingen* is particularly rich in examples, such as the discussion of dreams in the first chapter – 'echoes from a lost golden age of harmony' – the uncanny sense Heinrich has in Chapter 5 of having known the miner's song previously, and the retrospective recognition of Mathilde – whom Heinrich feels he has already known 'for an unthinkable time' – as the blue flower of his opening dream (Chapters 6 and 7). Again, such anamnesis is closely connected by Novalis with art, and especially music, as languages communicative of this divine wisdom.

[50] Plotinus, *The Enneads*, I.6.8, citing the *Iliad*, II.140 (trans. Stephen MacKenna (Harmondsworth: Penguin, 1991), p. 54).

Ex. 3.8a and b Piano Sonata Op. 6: comparison of endings of first movement and finale.

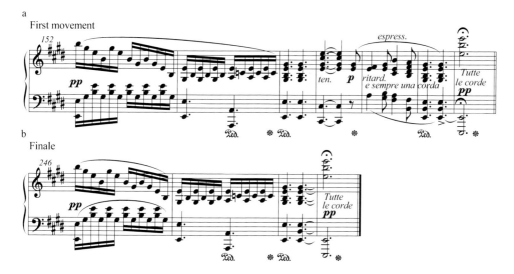

for Mendelssohn, even more so than for his contemporaries, given his family background and heritage.[51] The question of a 'Jewish' sensibility in the composer is of course highly fraught. All the same, there is unquestionably a nostalgic quality, a wistful backwards glance in these early cyclic pieces, which the composer would leave behind in his later music. 'What attracts and moves us here', wrote Schumann, 'is not the foreign and strange, not the new, but simply the dear, the familiar and homely.'[52] The sonata enacts an impossible return to the Rose-Garden – 'the passage which we did not take / Towards the door we never opened' – the unobtainable lost world of spiritual childhood and innocence before the fall.[53] For Mendelssohn, here, as for Eliot, 'the way forward is the way back'. 'Where are we travelling then?' asked Novalis. 'Always homewards.'[54]

---

[51] The notion of a Jewish exile and homelessness has been around since at least the sixth century BC, as enshrined in the book of Isaiah's account of the Israelites' exile to Babylon.

[52] Schumann, 'Sonaten für Pianoforte', *Gesammelte Schriften*, vol. I, p. 124. The original German is more succinct: 'Was uns hier berührt und anzieht ist nicht das Fremde, nicht das Neue, sondern eben das Liebe, Gewohnte.'

[53] Eliot, 'Burnt Norton', I, *Collected Poems*, p. 189. Gerald Abraham, in one of his more perceptive comments on the composer, spoke of the 'sweet, Virgilian purity' of Mendelssohn's music (*A Hundred Years of Music* (London: Duckworth, 1938), p. 61).

[54] Novalis, *Heinrich von Ofterdingen*, *Schriften*, vol. I, p. 325.

4 | In search of lost time

The A minor Quartet Op. 13

> I would enshrine the spirit of the past
> For future restoration.

Wordsworth, The Prelude (1805), XI

In the year following the E major Piano Sonata, Mendelssohn composed two further cyclic works, the String Quintet No. 1, Op. 18, and the Piano Sonata Op. 106, both of which were to be suppressed in some form by the composer. The A major Quintet, as known in its final, published version of 1832, is not obviously a cyclic work. The original 1826 version of the quintet, however, had a third-movement minuet and contrapuntal trio instead of the present andante second movement, which was written in 1832 following the death of Mendelssohn's friend and violin teacher Eduard Rietz (the dedicatee of the Octet). As Friedhelm Krummacher has shown, the finale of the quintet incorporates an allusion to the music of the discarded *Canone doppio* trio within its development section (the new fugal theme of b. 177, Ex. 4.1), the thematic resemblance strengthened by the similar rising accompanimental figure in the cello.[1]

By discarding this movement in 1832 Mendelssohn seems to have indicated that such cyclic connections were not of overriding importance for understanding the piece, or at least less important than the traditional four-movement structure now adopted (the quintet had originally lacked a true slow movement).

Meanwhile, the Sonata in Bb, dating from the spring of 1827, was held back by the composer and received publication only posthumously in 1868. The reasons for the composer's reticence over its publication appear to be relatively straightforward: as virtually every commentator has noticed, the parallels of the first movement and transition to the finale with Beethoven's 'Hammerklavier' Sonata in the same key, Op. 106, are immediately apparent, and moreover, unlike with Op. 101, not necessarily to Mendelssohn's

---

[1] Krummacher, *Mendelssohn – Der Komponist*, p. 108; also see pp. 238–9. The original minuet is reproduced on pp. 586–90.

Ex. 4.1 String Quintet in A major Op. 18 (1826): connection between trio theme of discarded 1826 minuet and finale's new development theme.

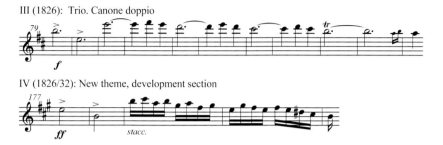

III (1826): Trio. Canone doppio

IV (1826/32): New theme, development section

advantage. This connection was only emphasised by Julius Rietz's posthumous assignment of the opus number 106 to the sonata, even if a more considered account of this piece might point as much to the influence of Weber (prominent especially in the finale). As a cyclic work it is less significant than the E major Sonata for this study, its cyclical nature established by the return of the B♭ minor scherzo in the finale as an episode within its development section, the recall being justified by the similarity between the descending arpeggiac figuration of the finale's main theme and that of the darker, quintessentially Mendelssohnian scherzo movement which returns (Ex. 4.2). The structure is to this extent, like the Op. 18 Quintet, comparable to that already seen in the Octet (if without the subsequent allusions of the latter's coda), or more generally in Haydn's Symphony No. 46 and Beethoven's Fifth. Beyond this, the thematic affinity between the primary themes of the first and third movements, both built from a rising-third motive, contribute to the close interrelationship of the sonata's movements.

More idiosyncratic is the unusual tonal layout of the four movements, the outer movements in B♭ major and second-movement scherzo in B♭ minor polarised with a slow movement in E major, recalling the tritonal harmonic argument seen in the E major Sonata. Since these two sonatas, Mendelssohn's sole mature contributions to the genre, were written within a year of each other and share each other's tritonal tonality within their course, it might be fascinating to speculate on whether the two formed a conscious pair, a 'multi-work' which was split when the composer decided only to publish the first. (The two cyclic string quartets from these years, Opp. 13 and 12, are similarly tritonally separated in A minor and E♭ major, the latter even referring to the former's tonality for a significant section in its

Ex. 4.2 Piano Sonata in B♭ major Op. [post.] 106 (1827): thematic connections.

opening movement and in thematic content forming a reworking of several of the earlier work's ideas.[2])

The masterpiece of these years, however, is the A minor Quartet, started in the summer of 1827 and completed that autumn. In this work, several of the ideas developed in the Octet and Op. 6 Sonata are taken up and developed to an unprecedented degree; this quartet would remain the most thorough-going and complex cyclic work for over half a century, until Franck's own quartet at the very least. The Op. 13 Quartet is fascinating for its use of a cyclical formal structure and the implications this has for our perceptions of musical time and memory. Indeed, such is the far-reaching nature of

---

[2] This connection is explored more fully in Chapter 5. The only other chamber works from this period, the Octet Op. 20 and Quintet Op. 18 (1825 and 1826), while differing in instrumental numbers, also share this unusual tonal feature (E♭ major / A major).

Mendelssohn's treatment of time in this quartet that one must look forward nearly a century for a comparable literary and theoretical formulation of this conception that does justice to the intricacy and sophistication of his music. While the historical theories drawn from Hegel, Goethe and the Romantic writers in Germany outlined earlier are still pertinent here, the exceptional treatment of form and time demonstrated in this work requires a wider theoretical underpinning, one which draws on ideas taken from the later theories of Bergson and Proust.

The A minor Quartet Op. 13

Several different strands of cyclicism interfuse in Op. 13. These are, namely, the cyclic frame provided by the recall of the quartet's introduction as the coda to the finale, the ongoing development and metamorphosis of material both within and across individual movements, and the literal (or near-literal) recall of music from earlier movements in the finale. As may be gathered from the above, the quartet's cyclical technique is formed primarily through its thematic processes, from which in turn unfolds the work's expressive and emotional journey. A detailed analysis of the formal and thematic techniques carried out across this quartet is therefore necessary prior to consideration of the wider questions of time, narrative and memory arising from their use.

Cyclic recurrence: the introduction–coda frame

The most evident and far-reaching manifestation of cyclicism in the A minor Quartet is the cyclic frame imparted by the recall of the opening motto-introduction to the first movement as the coda of the last, a procedure I shall term the meta-movement introduction–coda frame. The basic, underlying plot of the work can be seen as the process by which the A major introduction-motto, initially outside the emotional and spiritual world of the following A minor first movement, gets drawn into the course of the music and is finally regained in the work's coda. Here, in the coda, the music leads on into a quotation from an earlier song, 'Frage' Op. 9 No. 1, which is hence heard as the goal of the entire work. After a half cadence in b. 13, the introduction had repeated a questioning three-note figure associated with the words 'Ist es wahr?' ('Is it true?') in the song. This is all that was

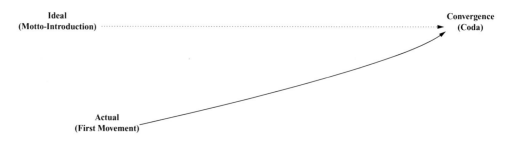

Fig. 4.1 Quartet in A minor Op. 13 (1827): paradigmatic formal trajectory.

directly heard of this music, the introduction immediately subsiding onto the dominant and an anxious e–f oscillation in the viola part accelerating the music into the A minor first movement. We are expected to hear the entire work encased within the introduction–coda frame as some response to this question posed, since at its recall in the coda the question is now answered by the subsequent continuation of this music from the song, picked up at the reprise of this figure in b. 13, with minor modification.

This strategy gives rise to what I shall call a two-level aesthetic presence: something initially outside is gradually incorporated into the music and finally attained as the work's culmination, a narrative which can be interpreted in terms of a quest for a non-present ideal vision which is finally reached through the terms of the real present and correspondingly actualised (Fig. 4.1).[3]

Such a structure can be seen as a form of the concept of breakthrough, discussed earlier in relation to cyclicism. Here, the transcendent ideal is glimpsed at the outset, but this fugitive vision is lost, and must be regained through the immanent process of the music; the breakthrough, as it were, is the initial event which must be actualised subsequently. This quest can be interpreted in a number of ways – a mythical fall from grace, followed by a long, agonising process of redemption leading to final reconciliation

---

[3] This can be viewed against the backdrop of contemporary Romantic conceptions of the real and ideal and their eventual synthesis, a theme which runs throughout much late eighteenth- and early nineteenth-century thought, from Schiller through Schlegel, Novalis and Schelling, and ultimately to Hegel. See, for instance, Schiller's *Aesthetic Education of Man*, where the fusion of the real and ideal – the 'form' and 'sense' drives – is to be achieved through art and the corresponding 'play' drive; Friedrich Schlegel's early essay 'Über die Grenzen des Schönen' (1794), which likewise considers the potential union between nature/reality and art/the ideal; or Schelling's *System of Transcendental Idealism*, whose philosophical system is designed as a progressive fusion of the real and ideal, an objective in which art holds a privileged status.

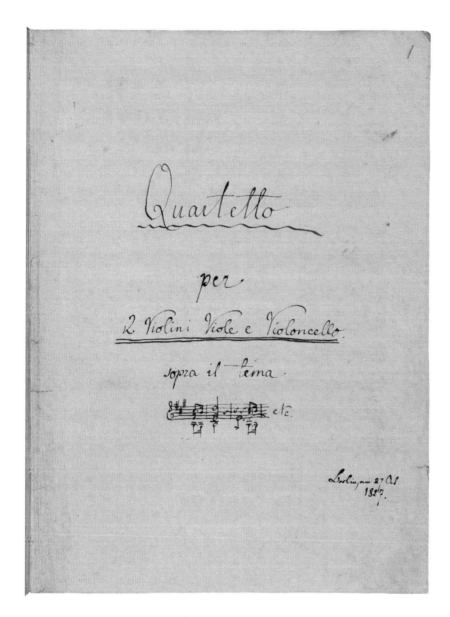

Fig. 4.2 Quartet Op. 13, autograph score, title page.

and parousia, or as part of a flashback narrative, the internal events being recounted as the past.[4]

---

[4] See, for example, Hans Kohlhase, 'Brahms und Mendelssohn: Strukturelle Parallelen in der Kammermusik für Streicher', in Constantin Floros, Hans Joachim Marx and Peter Petersen (eds.), *Brahms und seine Zeit: Symposion Hamburg 1983* [*Hamburger Jahrbuch für*

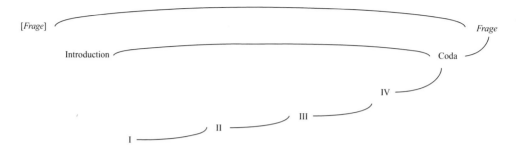

Fig. 4.3 Quartet Op. 13: outline of multilevel cyclic structure.

This formal procedure, by linking beginning and end, creating a long-range teleology across the entire work, an initial problem or question which is only solved and explained retrospectively at the end, closely relates to the emotional journey and expressive world of the piece. Form and expression are intrinsically bound up. This design was to prove highly influential in subsequent music. In their different ways, cyclically framed works such as Dvořák's A major Quartet Op. 2, Brahms' Third, Chausson's Bb minor and Vaughan Williams' 'London' Symphonies, and, most clearly of all, Elgar's First Symphony, derive from this source.

With Mendelssohn's work, an extra layer of cyclicism is added by the incorporation of the quotation from 'Frage'. Mendelssohn took the novel step of publishing the quartet with the song, entitled 'Thema', facing the first page, as a kind of hermeneutic clue to the work, along the lines of Beethoven's *schwer gefasste Entschluss* in Op. 135. 'You will hear its notes resound in the first and last movements, and sense its feeling in all four', wrote Mendelssohn to his friend Adolf Lindblad. 'I think I express the song well, and it sounds to me like music.'[5] Thus we are presented with two levels of 'otherness' in a work with three aesthetic layers: enclosing the interlying four-movement course of the quartet is the introduction–coda frame, and, likewise, outside this is the presence of this musical *objet recherché*, at first not even heard (save for the 'Frage' motive) but enigmatically present on the printed page like a Schumannesque sphinx, similarly outside the work but subsequently incorporated (Fig. 4.3).

Musikwissenschaft, 7] (Laaber Verlag, 1984), p. 63: '[The introduction–coda frame] establishes the relation to the programmatic model and corresponds to the "once upon a time" of the story or the framed narration of the novella, so beloved in the nineteenth century. It appears as if Mendelssohn wanted to compose out different time dimensions through the contrast in mode, tempo and expressive quality with the following Allegro section.'
5 Dahlgren, *Bref till Adolf Fredrik Lindblad från Mendelssohn*, p. 20.

Ex. 4.3 Quartet Op. 13, first movement: *a* and *b* themes.

The full poetic and expressive implications of this feature must be left until later; in the broad context of the quartet's formal aspects it signifies the full resolution and telos of the entire work, in an aesthetic layer at one further remove.

Internal thematic working and recall

Beyond this recall of the external motto-frame, there is a literal recall of themes from the first two movements and the introduction to the finale in the finale, and an ongoing development of common thematic ideas throughout and across the four-movement span. The three cyclic characteristics above are indeed intrinsically related; it is the common underlying thematic affinities of the material throughout this work that enable the literal recall to occur organically within the immanent conditions of the musical process, and the two of these in conjunction which can lead to the final goal of the coda, the recollection of the opening and the resolution of the work. Consequently, an understanding of the internal thematic working is necessary for full comprehension of the overall form.

Two main strands of thematic ideas run through the work, one (*a*), associated with the opening, almost hymn-like tranquillity of the major-key introduction and relating in mood and emotional orbit to the underlying thread of 'Frage', and the other (*b*) a descending minor scale from degree $\hat{5}$ to $\hat{1}$, commonly with a characteristic dotted anacrusis, an abstract shape which lies behind most of the four internal movements' material (Ex. 4.3).

Internal non-recurring variants

All the material for the work is derived from these two families of ideas.[6] The internal relationship of thematic variants to movements is a type of

---

[6] The thematic connections between the material of the quartet's movements have been little scrutinised – rather surprisingly, given the clear cyclic links stemming from the recall of material in this work. The best account is given by Hans Kohlhase in 'Studien zur Form in den Streichquartetten von Felix Mendelssohn Bartholdy', in Constantin Floros, Hans Joachim Marx and Peter Petersen (eds.), *Zur Musikgeschichte des 19. Jahrhunderts* [*Hamburger Jahrbuch für Musikwissenschaft*, 2] (Hamburg: Karl Dieter Wagner: 1977), pp. 77–80, some of this material being subsequently reused in 'Brahms und Mendelssohn', pp. 62–4.

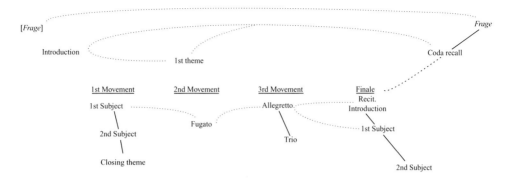

Fig. 4.4 Quartet Op. 13: detailed outline of multilevel cyclic structure showing internal links within movements.

Ex. 4.4 Quartet Op. 13, third movement, intermezzo and trio themes.

branching, such that the second subject of the finale may not be immediately recognisable as relating to the first of the third movement, or that to the closing idea of the first, yet they are nevertheless related through a preceding variant in each movement (Fig. 4.4). In other words, simplifying slightly, each movement is monothematic and in addition relates to the others, though the variants derived over the internal course of each movement do not always obviously manifest affinities to other variants in different movements.

For instance, the *Allegro di molto* trio of the third movement, probably the section least obviously relating in thematic substance to the rest of the work, is nevertheless connected by being a transformation of the *Allegretto con moto* intermezzo material, which itself is clearly drawn from an ongoing transformation of the principal *b* shape. This procedure is matched in the scherzo of the E♭ Quartet: the trio is loosely related thematically (in Op. 13 the common descending triads $\hat{5}$–$\hat{1}$, $\hat{2}$–$\hat{5}$, in itself unremarkable in the context of tonal music, Ex. 4.4), but linked as compellingly by the differences between the sections – in both quartets a light, wistful, minor-key allegretto contrasted with a faster, airy tonic-major trio; a contrasting yet complementary parallel to the scherzo.

Ex. 4.5 Quartet Op. 13, finale: derivation of second subject from first.

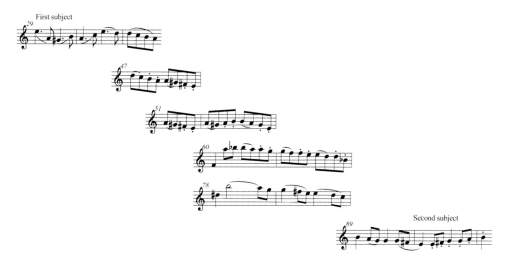

   The finale's second subject likewise, in its determinedly ascending trajectory, seems in its immediate context unrelated to the descending figure *b*.
Here, one has to follow an organic process of transformation across the preceding part of the exposition, this material itself relating back to numerous
thematic strands of past movements, to trace its derivation (Ex. 4.5).
   A process of successive melodic diminution to the tail of the finale's first
subject grows into a reprise of the quaver figuration forming the complement to the recitative sections at the introduction to the movement (this
material in turn being derived from the corresponding diminutions at the
tail of the first movement's first subject). The lapse back into this introductory recitative material is manifest explicitly at b. 60; from b. 78 a new variant
of this appears, marked now by the shift from even quavers to a dactylic
crotchet–two-quavers rhythm, but outlining the same melodic diminution
of a descending scale (which here even more clearly points up the relationship, implicit throughout the whole work, between this quaver tail-piece
and the principal *b* shape which precedes it). This leads directly into the
second subject, b. 90, formed of the same dactylic scalic-figure, but which
now turns on itself and climbs upwards. The connection between this theme
and the basic material of this work is hence composed out across the fabric
of the movement.
   While these variants in the two movements just described may not be
used to produce further derivations over the course of the work, they can
be interpreted in the light of stages on the musical journey. The quartet's
narrative is not narrowly linear, in the sense of a leads to b, to c, to d,

Ex. 4.6 Quartet Op. 13, first movement: derivation of themes in exposition.

and so on, but is a more complex process, with an overall linear trajectory but with numerous 'dead-ends' or interrelating, chiastic strands. The
trio provides a vital input of energy, the archaising D minor fugato of the
second movement giving way to the life-impulse of its own fugal writing
and the first sight of the final A major of the work's resolution, glimpsed at
the outset but only now realised. Likewise, the purposeful defiance of the
finale's second subject's upward trajectory contrasts with the surrounding
material, again providing grit to the ensuing musical and emotional struggle
of the final stages of the work. Most apparent in this regard is the course of
the first movement. In itself a perfectly constructed, organically interlaced
monothematic sonata movement of a type whose construction is rare after
Beethoven, it presents an intensification and increasing concentration of
the A minor anguish which answers the question posed in the introduction.
As such, it provides what is a dead end, the path which will not lead to
successful resolution across the course of the work.

This expressive quality is mirrored in the thematic process, which increasingly cuts down and intensifies fragments drawn from the initial material,
highlighting the characteristic figure of the fifth–minor-sixth chromatic
neighbour, a topos of anguish and pain, and obsessively concentrating on
a repeated accented $\hat{2}$–$\hat{1}$ in the closing theme. An analysis adequate to
the almost miraculous growth and interrelationship of themes across this
movement would take up more space than is possible here and probably
necessitate an annotated copy of the score, bar-by-bar. Nevertheless, it will
facilitate matters if I present the basic growth of the movement's three main
thematic ideas from one to another (Ex. 4.6).

The second theme, b. 59, grows from the second half of the first (bb. 30–2), which itself is a variant of the shape found between bb. 28 and 29 in its first half, the rising octave contracted into a sixth.[7] The intervening passage (bb. 35–58) develops this motive in a modified repetition of the first theme's bb. 41–6, recurrences of this motive in bb. 51 (Vln I) and 55 (Vla) highlighting the characteristic $\hat{5}$–$\hat{6}$–$\hat{5}$ anacrusis with grace-note, which itself is repeated for an entire bar before the second subject appears in b. 59. This anacrustic motive is taken up as the tail of the closing theme, bb. 77–85, whose head motive is derived from notes 4–6 of the second subject (the descent g–f♯–e), the development of which (bb. 71–6) emphasises the two-note descent characteristic of the closing theme, the offbeat *forte* and *sforzando* accents replaced in b. 77 by their realignment to the metric emphasis of the half bar. The new $\hat{2}$–$\hat{1}$ figure can also be seen as a transposition of the ever-present $\hat{6}$–$\hat{5}$ anacrusis motive.

What adds especially to the sense of natural, organic growth is the fact that the new themes grow from the latter sections of the previous subject, which themselves draw from their earlier part. The themes grow as if part of an ongoing cycle.[8] Connections between this movement's thematic variants and other movements do exist – the second theme, for instance, shadows the dactylic figuration preceding the finale's own second theme (this is especially notable at bb. 178–80 in the recapitulation) – but these are largely incidental and arise out of the work's common thematic substance as much as constituting intentional thematic allusion; at best they mirror their positions in their respective movements.

Cyclic recurring themes

Ongoing development and recall which forms the wider structural aspect of this work is provided by the network of connections stemming from the two thematic strands, *a* and *b*, outlined above. These strands and their ongoing transformation form the underlying thread of the work and enact its psychological journey and narrative.

As outlined earlier, the quartet can be seen to problematise and finally to resolve the conflict between the music and emotional world of the A major introduction and the conflicting A minor first movement which succeeds it, lying behind which is the question posed by the quotation from 'Frage'. The

---

[7] See also Kohlhase, 'Brahms und Mendelssohn', p. 64.
[8] Cf. Wulf Konold, 'Mendelssohn und der späte Beethoven', in Johannes Fischer (ed.), *Münchener Beethoven-Studien* (Munich: Emil Katzbichler, 1992), p. 189.

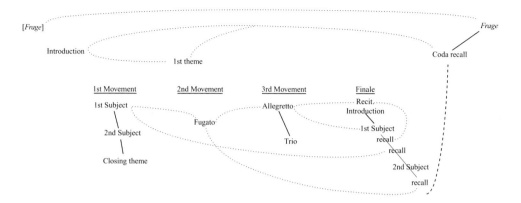

Fig. 4.5 Quartet Op. 13: detailed outline of multilevel cyclic structure showing internal links within movements and cyclic recall in finale.

two are initially poles apart, both thematically and expressively, the course of the work being to explain and reconcile them. The *a* strand corresponds to the calm of the opening adagio introduction, 'outside' the main course of the intervening work, the *b* strand to the more anguished response of the monothematic first movement, carried across to constitute the principal thematic substance of the work.

Process of theme b

Principal themes of each movement are derived from the *b* theme, the archetypal variant of which is the first movement's first subject. While there is an ongoing development of this material across the quartet, at the same time these variants appear as if different ideas. The process of the work is to draw these apparently different themes together in the finale and retrospectively reveal their underlying unity. In other words, while outwardly different with individual identities, the themes of each movement are merely different surface manifestations of an underlying common essence, which is finally revealed as such by the explicit recall and merging of music from preceding movements in the finale. The corresponding strategy is complex to explain, but more lucid in its musical realisation: a thematic idea is developed and evolves across the four movements, though this is largely sub-perceptible, until the last movement recalls and synthesises these different manifestations, making their affinities explicit, and by doing so finally liquidates this theme (Fig. 4.5).

Ex. 4.7 Quartet Op. 13, first movement: potential similarity between introduction and first-subject material.

The first subject of the opening movement is largely new, but is importantly foreshadowed in two of its aspects in the closing bars of the introduction (bb. 12–16, Ex. 4.7). The characteristic dotted rhythm derives from
the all-important quotation of 'Ist es wahr?'; the significance of this rhythmic figure is highlighted in the way its appearance in b. 13 is set up as the
first dotted rhythm in the piece (save for its immediate premonition at the
preceding half cadence).

This rhythm, combined with the descent over a fifth, is found in the
immediate response to the question of bb. 13–15, which, seemingly insignificant in itself, prepares in embryo the characteristic figure of the first subject.
We shall see later the full implications and provenance of this phrase. In this
light, theme *b* is clearly distinguished from the *a* material of the introduction
which precedes the quotation of 'Ist es wahr?'; the characteristic rhythm and
falling fifth are notable by their total absence from the introductory bars,
an absence which suggests conscious contrast between the two sections.[9]
The two, in other words, inhabit diametrically opposing worlds, separated
by the question posed in bb. 13–15.

The process of variation and transformation of this theme across the
four movements is tabulated in Ex. 4.8. The first subject can be split up
into two segments, the initial principal motive (b. 26) and the more anonymous quaver figuration concluding it (b. 32), itself a variant of the former.
Both of these will be important in later movements. Besides the growth and
evolution of this theme into the movement's second and closing subjects,
outlined above, two other variants produced in the course of the exposition
should be noted for their use in later movements. The unstable, climactic
variant at bb. 46–50 is an intensification of the initial idea, though with a
melodic diminution of its descent on its repeat in bb. 49–50 that points up

---

[9] Unless one sees the arpeggiac figure of bb. 10–11 as prefiguring, vaguely, b. 16, which itself
grows into the first subject at b. 23, but this is so removed that, to all practical purposes, *a* and *b*
are entirely separate in content.

Ex. **4.8** Quartet Op. 13: development of *b* material across the four movements.

Ex. **4.9** Quartet Op. 13, first movement: combination of *b*-material elements from first and tail segments.

the connection between this principal segment and the derived figuration of the second (Ex. 4.9). This will be explicitly recalled at the corresponding place in the finale (IV: 71). The cadential eight bars of the exposition meanwhile grow from the secondary figuration in b. 85, to outline a diminished seventh, b. 86. This is important since, besides linking up to the recall of the introductory semiquaver figuration from bb. 18–23 at the start of the development, b. 93, and thus connecting the two, drawing what could be conventional diminished sevenths into the thematic nexus of the movement, it connects forwards to the middle section of the slow movement and ultimately the recitative opening the last.

The slow movement, ternary in basic outline though substantially more complex in actuality and with a partial synthesis of contrasting sections in the reprise, takes its opening F major from the world of the quartet's introduction, returning to theme *a*. This section is contrasted with a D minor fugato, built from theme *b* (b. 24, Ex. 4.8 II). This is probably not heard as especially related thematically to the first movement, though on closer inspection it is – the purpose of the finale is to draw the separate though related strands together. The main modification here is the incorporation of an upper neighbour, ♭$\hat{6}$, to the $\hat{5}$-descent. This is new, though it is strongly prefigured in the first movement. The entry of the first subject in b. 26 of the first movement is introduced by statements of the theme in imitation in the three lower parts, entering on e (Vla, b. 23), and f twice (Vln II b. 14 and Vlc b. 24, given in reduction in Ex. 4.8), before returning to e in the first violin, initiating the first subject. This oscillation between $\hat{5}$ and ♭$\hat{6}$ is a characteristic trait of the movement, the topos of pain and anguish adumbrated in the subsidiary themes of the exposition, and can indeed be seen to extend out of the initial e–f trill of b. 18, which forges the link from the calm of the introduction to the A minor first movement.[10] The fugato subject variant, then, continues an ongoing process in its thematicisation of the ♭$\hat{6}$ neighbour figure.

The tail of the fugal subject suggests affinities with the subsidiary cadential segment of shape *b*, which are increasingly realised in the music in bb. 36 (Vln II) and 38 (Vln I) (Ex. 4.10). Further elaboration on this tail segment, bb. 44–5, grows into a new *poco più animato* variant, bb. 46ff., over a new homophonic accompanimental texture. This version shows even greater affinity with the first movement's first subject, intensified by the syncopated, breathless feel, and also, in the diminutions of the descending scale, the developments of the quaver figuration across the same movement. After extensive and masterful working-out and a steady rise in tension produced by the reintroduction of contrapuntal elements, the subject in inversion, and a long dominant pedal, the music disintegrates into a recitative-like flourish in the first violin. This cathartic release, leading to the reprise of the opening F major adagio theme, is a direct premonition of the recitative texture and gestures of the finale's introduction, and connects the animato fugato variant and first movement diminished-seventh figuration to this world.

---

[10] The actual first subject might itself allude to such a topos, as Christopher Reynolds has pointed out – the minor-key descent from $\hat{5}$ to $\hat{1}$ outlining the 'Es ist vollbracht' motive familiar from the St John Passion and used frequently by composers to express or depict spiritual suffering and anguish (including Mendelssohn himself for the aria 'Es ist genug' from *Elijah*). Reynolds, *Motives for Allusion: Context and Content in Nineteenth-Century Music* (Cambridge, MA: Harvard University Press, 2003), pp. 147–57.

Ex. 4.10 Quartet Op. 13, second movement: ongoing derivation of *b* material in central fugato.

The third movement is entitled *Intermezzo*, and thus is seen to present an escape from the tension of the surrounding movements, a momentary interlude from the sweep of the work.[11] It is correspondingly the only movement not to be explicitly recalled in the finale, though it nevertheless derives its material from the underlying substance of the work. The intermezzo itself is a clear variant of the *b* theme, in overall contour close to the first movement version, but with the ♭$\hat{6}$ neighbour and following ascending filled-out third deriving from the preceding fugato (Ex. 4.8 III).

The finale opens with a recitative-introduction, with two contrasting sections – a recitative proper and a following figurative passage treated in imitation. The first of these can be seen to be a further transformation, albeit loose and hidden by the octave transferral, of the principal *b* shape; now the emphasis on ♭$\hat{6}$ is such that the melodic line starts on this scale degree. The second is more obviously drawn from – indeed possibly

[11] As Donald Mintz has described it, this movement, like the canzonetta of Op. 12, forms a part 'during which the over-all dramatic development of an entire composition is temporarily abandoned' (Mintz, 'The Sketches and Drafts for Three of Felix Mendelssohn's Major Works', p. 257).

is – the subsidiary figuration. Again, as in the fugato subject, the two segments are presented in chronological order; here the opaqueness of the recitative's possible connection is made up for by the now almost-explicit identity of the second half.

The first group of the exposition, from b. 28, mirrors this dual layout. The main subject elaborates the $\hat{5}$–$\hat{1}$ descent – the initial $\hat{5}$–$\flat\hat{6}$–$\hat{5}$ neighbour further extended, continuing the process seen in the recitative, forming an anacrusis reminiscent of the second subject of the first movement – but in the first two bars the $\hat{5}$ cover-note is filled out underneath with a compound melody, which only returns to $\hat{5}$ to commence the $\hat{5}$–$\hat{1}$ descent in the second and third bars (Ex. 4.8 IV: 29). The following reprise of the introductory figuration that grows of this first theme's tail (bb. 47– 63, shown previously in Ex. 4.5) is important for a number of reasons: it matches the order of segments in the first movement's first subject and the two contrasting sections in the finale's introduction, it parallels the first movement, and by returning to the introductory material it makes the first explicit manifestation of the process of thematic recall which is to pervade this movement. (The lapse into the music of the presumably discarded introduction, which is overt, even blatant by b. 60, is startling and unexpected, even though it has been prepared over the preceding bars.)

This first explicit recall – albeit only of the introduction to the same movement – is nonetheless a turning point, since a few bars later (b. 71), the first movement's first subject makes a reappearance in the intensified form from I: 46–50. Since the finale had been paralleling this movement anyway, this recall does not come as so much of a shock. The affinities between various themes have been made more apparent, since two of the three ideas so far heard in the exposition are common both to the finale and to the first movement.

The second subject is then interrupted by a reprise of the recitative material from the introduction (b. 105), which is now treated in fugal imitation, a process which highlights the $\hat{5}$–$\flat\hat{6}$–$\hat{5}$ head-figure common to both finale recitative and second movement fugue. After the second subject has resumed following this interruption and brought about the exposition's concluding cadence, the actual fugal subject from the slow movement enters, taking the place of the recitative's fugal recall (b. 164). This continues the fugal-imitative process perhaps initiated in the imitative treatment at b. 105 of the (recalled) figuration from b. 9 of the introduction, and which has spread over the equally disparate recitative material. As Charles Rosen has observed, this fugal treatment 'transforms recitative into fugue. In the development that follows, the main theme of the finale is combined with both the recitative motif and the slow-movement fugue melody. Recitative and fugue are radically opposed textures, and Mendelssohn's synthesis is unprecedented.'[12]

Thus the finale has recapitulated material from the first and second movements and its own introduction. The purpose of these memories flooding back into the course of the music is to call attention to the pervading thematic unity underlying the four movements, which will eventually liquidate itself and lead to the recall of the very opening.[13] The last stage in this process is accomplished by the movement's coda. These extraordinary twenty bars present a synthesis and liquidation of the work's material, continuing and completing the process of this movement (Ex. 4.11).

First the fugue subject appears over the tremulous semiquavers of the recitative's accompaniment, thus merging the two – in Rosen's words, completing the cycle of metamorphosis and transforming the slow-movement fugue into a recitative.[14] This subsides, the rhythmic movement attenuating gradually into semibreves, and at b. 350 gives way to an echo of the first movement. This is not a direct quotation, but an allusion that merges elements of all three themes, which had after all owed their substance to each other (Ex. 4.12). The (augmented) dotted upbeat and descending fifth draws from the original *b* shape, while the initial octave leap refers to both the intermediate version of this (the rising sixth in bb. 31–2 extended to an octave in b. 51) and its consequent development into the first movement's second theme (cf. Vln I bb. 68–9); finally, the grace-note decorating the $\hat{2}$–$\hat{1}$ descent at the end calls back to this accented motive in the closing theme and the $\flat\hat{6}$–$\hat{5}$ with grace-note in the second theme from which this last theme grew.

Hence this figure synthesises elements from across the entire movement, in doing so dissolving them and revealing, as it were, their thematic substrate. This leads into the finale's main theme at b. 357, the two movements' substances connected in one continuous line, which articulates the same tonic to subdominant (Am–Dm) movement as the fugato-recitative some bars earlier (the importance of these harmonies will be explained later).

The final stage in this diffusion and dissolution is the unaccompanied passage for the first violin, bb. 365–72. The first three bars present the final

[12] Rosen, *The Romantic Generation*, p. 579. There is a precedent, of course, in Mendelssohn's Op. 6 Piano Sonata.
[13] Krummacher, *Mendelssohn – Der Komponist*, p. 377.
[14] Rosen, *The Romantic Generation*, p. 579.

Ex. 4.11 Quartet Op. 13, finale's coda: synthesis and liquidation of thematic elements.

Ex. **4.12** Quartet Op. 13, finale's coda: fusion of earlier *b*-theme first-segment variants.

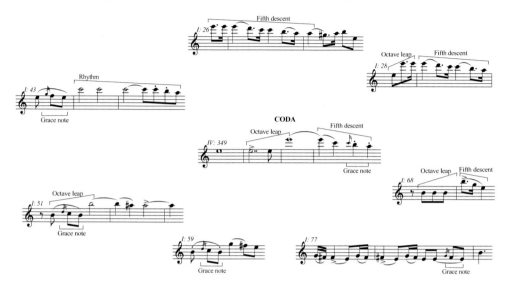

Ex. **4.13** Quartet Op. 13, finale's coda: fusion of earlier *b*-theme tail-segment variants.

statement of *b*, in the two segments of the main theme. The first half is the
fugato subject, now in its original $\frac{3}{4}$ time signature, but which has across
the course of the movement and coda been merged with the rest of the
work's material, and has been seen as identical to the principal segment
of the *b* theme. The second half is now the familiar descending figuration
of the second segment of the main theme, though here it could allude to
almost any part of the work (Ex. 4.13): the original figuration at I: 33; its
modification into bb. 178–9 which connects to the dactylic rhythm of IV: 78;
the reprise of the original figure in the recitative figuration of the finale; the
animato section of the slow movement; or, connecting back to the first half

here and commenting retrospectively on a connection only covert earlier, the development of the fugal theme's tail at II: 38.

Thus these three bars present the final substrate of the *b* theme, the variants of both segments, which are now seen as relating back to almost anywhere in the work – the distilled essence behind all the appearances. Such a synthesis has effectively dissolved the theme – through the merging and fusion the individual identities of the numerous variants have been sublated. The final five bars, marked 'recit.', are now almost athematic: even the thematic substance of the recitative opening the movement, to which this section relates in generic topos, is largely absent. The last two bars seem to refer back to the very opening of the work, the phrase that followed the question posed by 'Frage' there.

Here, after sinking from e^1 through $d\sharp^1$ and d^1, the music connects up finally to the $c\sharp^1$ of the quartet's opening, which now enters in the wake of the exhaustion and final dissolution of the material of the four intervening movements. The introduction is the final part of the work to be recalled, imparting the introduction–coda frame that is the last and most important of the quartet's cyclic procedures. It is at once a recall of the past – a return to the beginning – yet also the goal of the four movements, the end to which they had all been leading, part of an onward trajectory.

To understand how this can be both a recall of the past and yet part of the present which arises out of the teleology of the work, one must follow the course and development of the *a* strand – the music of the introduction's adagio – across the work.

Development of theme a and the converging of both strands

The introduction in its reprise at the work's coda is not identical to its first appearance, but is the result of a process of development across the work. The initial problem of the quartet revolved around the disparity between the idyllic A major introduction and the very different world which the first movement plunged us into in response to the question posed from 'Frage'. However, across the work the two emotional worlds gradually converge, and the recall here in the coda is the final resolution of the conflict – the meeting of the ideal and the actual. This is achieved in part by the working-out and eventual disintegration of the anguished A minor world of the inner movements in the finale, but is also effected by the gradual infiltration of elements of one strand in the other. As seen in the opening movement, the two are utterly dissimilar, without any thematic aspect in common. By the end of the work, however, the adagio strand has incorporated aspects of *b*,

Ex. 4.14 Quartet Op. 13, introduction, second movement and coda: motivic affinities and infiltration.

Ex. 4.15 Quartet Op. 13, introduction and second movement: harmonic affinities.

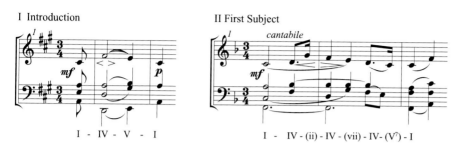

I Introduction

I - IV - V - I

II First Subject

I - IV - (ii) - IV - (vii) - IV- (V⁷) - I

and conversely *b* of *a*, and the two are seen as not so dissimilar. The two ways meet, and this can lead into the full quotation from 'Frage' that lies behind them both.

The key to the modification of *a* and the anticipation of the ultimately successful resolution of the work is the F major vision of the slow movement. This is the first glimpse of the ideal world of the quartet's introduction since the loss of that vision in the fall and precipitation into the A minor of the first movement, succeeding the enigmatic query posed by 'Frage'. The first bars of the second movement do not explicitly connect to the introduction, but are nonetheless reminiscent of the same world, returning to the major mode, the tempo 'adagio', and the $\frac{3}{4}$ time signature, for the first time in the piece. The motivic constituents are also the same (Ex. 4.14)[15] – the rising fourth followed by descending second, *a*, and a characteristic, similarly articulated dotted-crotchet and three-quaver figure, heard in inversion (*b*) – and, even more significantly, it echoes the emphasis on degree 6̂ and the subdominant tendency of the local harmonic movement, the most important features of the introduction (Ex. 4.15). By b. 9, the latent affinity is seeping out to the surface of the music, bb. 8–12 echoing almost exactly bb. 7–10 of the introduction in the uninverted, prime form of motive *b*. What was initially similar has grown into the same.

This passage also, however, reveals the growing influence of the descending *b* shape, previously noted for its complete exclusion from the introduction. From b. 12, substituting for the passage of the introduction that distantly anticipates the descending shape of b. 16 and hence *b*, a scalic descent is introduced which is reminiscent of the *b* figuration of I: 33 (see Ex. 4.13). This descent is prefigured in the preceding bars, growing out of the returning motion from the leap of the fourth in the first bar, until it makes

---

[15] Cf. Kohlhase, 'Studien zur Form in den Streichquartetten von Felix Mendelssohn Bartholdy', 78; Konold, 'Mendelssohn und der späte Beethoven', p. 190.

its thematically significant appearance in bb. 12–14. Of course, descending scalic fragments are one of the most common elements of musical language, but the introduction had been remarkable for their complete absence. Here they infiltrate and grow into a shape which echoes the *b* motive that had been all-prevalent across the course of the preceding movement. The other characteristic element of theme *b* that had been totally excluded from the introduction was the dotted rhythm which was initiated by the pivotal *Ist es wahr?* and went on to become a defining trait of the ensuing first movement. Here it is heard twice in the first three bars, merging a rhythmic feature of the *b* theme with a motivic constituent – the rising fourth – of *a*.

In other words, we see the start of a gradual process of merging *b* with *a*, and an initial approach towards reconciling the two worlds. However, this process is incomplete in the slow movement. After nineteen bars of the F major adagio, the vision is disturbed by the almost unworldly tones of the D minor fugato, which, in its minor mode and return to the substance of the *b* theme, is heard as an intrusion of the world of the first movement. This movement, however, can be read as a redemptive reworking of the first, which effects a partial but incomplete rapprochement between the two worlds. As in the first movement, a calm major-key adagio utilising theme *a*, 18 and 19 bars respectively, is succeeded by a more pained minor-key section, drawing from theme *b* and taking up the bulk of the movement. Whereas in the first movement the thematically disparate opening does not return and is consequently heard as a separate introduction unrelated to the ensuing movement, in the second the adagio – which, as we have seen, is now at least partially related to the fugue through its incorporation of the falling *b* motive – does return at the end and is combined in this reprise with the fugato theme, effecting a partial synthesis. This synthesis, however, is premature, and only hints at the final resolution which has to be earned through the struggle of the next two movements, the final realisation of the underlying unity behind all the separate appearances in the work and the converging of both paths.

Just as theme *a* saw the infiltration of aspects of its opposite, so the *b* theme now begins increasingly to show the influence of *a*. Most notable in the opening adagio is the emphasis on $\hat{6}$, the crest of a four-note motive, underpinned by a broad subdominant movement. While, as previously explained, the $\flat\hat{6}$ neighbour-note of the fugato's subject has been prepared across the preceding movement, it can also be seen as the first stage towards the infiltration of elements of the adagio. This is seen more palpably in the ensuing intermezzo. The $\flat\hat{6}$ neighbour is now harmonised with the subdominant, afforded an individual autonomy, and the thematic shape,

Ex. 4.16 Quartet Op. 13, third movement: individual harmonisation of ♭6̂ as part of gradual fusion of thematic and harmonic cyclic elements.

III Opening theme

i - iv - VII⁷ - III

which itself develops out of the fugue's modifications of *b*, outlines a similar four-note motive to the opening bars of the adagio (Ex. 4.16).

The D minor of the finale's recitative introduction refers back to that problem tonality of the second movement fugato, which disturbed the F major vision of what will eventually lead to the coda, and relates the two – fugato and recitative – together, the feature that the finale will so ingeniously explore. It can also, however, be seen as a larger manifestation of the local harmonic subdominant tendencies, which is the result of the infiltration of *a*'s material on *b* as seen in the middle two movements. As with the provenance of the upper-neighbour sixth in the slow movement, the subsequent tonal argument is determined by the convergence of more than one process.

This D minor, subdominant of the third and fourth movements' home tonality of A minor, is prepared at the end of the intermezzo, which in its uneasy vacillations between A⁷ and Dm echoes the subdominant harmony of the opening bars whilst simultaneously alluding to the future fourth-movement coda, fragmenting remnants of intermezzo and trio. The recitative, which enters urgently in the wake of the intermezzo's disintegration, seems torn between the conflicting poles of the slow movement's D minor fugato and its opening F major adagio (the consequent C⁷ chord, bb. 13–20, which, however, does not resolve to the aspired tonic but slips upward to the diminished seventh on C♯ which served at the opening as vii⁷ of D minor). The ensuing lead-in to the finale's first theme then fails to tonicise the home tonality of A minor, which is linked merely through repetition of the familiar e–f oscillation from the first movement. The resultant off-key introduction and tonally unstabilised main theme (note the veering towards the subdominant at b. 32) easily disintegrates back into the D minor void of the recitative (b. 60, and again at b. 239 triggering the recapitulation). A fleeting hope of the F major vision of *a* is seen again, preceding the caesura between the recapitulation of first and second subjects (the characteristically spaced F major $^6_4$, bb. 277–8, referring back to the reprise of the adagio in II), but this only gives way to a second, greater build-up preparing the second-subject recapitulation.

The eventual redemption of D minor is intimated in the fourth-movement coda, where the chord of A major, foreshadowing the final return of the introduction twenty bars later, is realised by treating A as the dominant of D, the transformation moreover being emphasised by the subdominant *major* (bb. 333–41). Just as at the close of Beethoven's Op. 131, the resolution to the tonic major – the raising of the third – is effected through treating it as V of iv. The consequent Am–Dm oscillation in the remaining bars of the coda is part of the liquidation of the memories of previous movements, which can lead finally to A major and the recall of the opening.

The coda

It is left to the coda of the work to complete the development of theme *a* and relate the two strands, *a* and *b*, to each other.[16] The reprise of the introduction in the work's coda completes the process of retrospective assimilation in the same way as the preceding bars of the finale fused the seemingly disparate strands of the *b* theme. The introduction's material now combines with the related slow movement: the first six bars stem from the former; the next two from both; and these form the link to the recall of the *b* scale from the end segment of the slow movement (Ex. 4.14). The first theme of the slow movement, in forming a partial mediation between the two worlds, forms a halfway stage between the introduction and the attained goal of the coda. Thus while the return to the introduction in the coda is a return to the past, it is also a past which is reinterpreted in light of the intervening journey, and made into the goal of the present. Cyclic recall and linear teleology are fused.

Finally, the dissolution of *b* and its succession by the cyclic recall of the opening, *a*, now call attention to the affinities between the two caused by the infiltration and merging of motivic constituents seen across the inner movements. Besides this now realised incorporation of the scalic figure

---

[16]   As Friedhelm Krummacher eloquently describes it, the coda 'lifts the veil from the until-now latent connections' between the different themes of the work (*Mendelssohn – Der Komponist*, p. 379).

of *b* into the true adagio substance of the previously polarised opening, the opening contour and emphasis on degree $\hat{6}$ are now retrospectively related back to that of the heads of the fugato, recitative and finale themes, synthesised and liquidated in the last bars preceding this recall. In the wake of the final collapse of the anguished *b* material, the transformed infiltration of *a* takes its place. The first has led to the second, their material has increasingly converged, and the two paths – the actual and the ideal, past and present – have met.

With this meeting, the quartet finally links up with the song that had prefaced it. The modified reprise of the opening adagio leads directly from the descending *b* figure into a return of the question, *Ist es wahr?*, posed in the thirteenth bar of the work. Previously, the music had subsided uneasily and escalated into the A minor first movement. Now, after the struggle of the intervening four movements, their final dissolution and the summoning up of the past introduction, the music leads gently and as if naturally into the end of the song 'Frage', from which the question had originated. Present on the printed page at the opening, it is now realised in the audible experience of the music, the last cyclic touch, the final level attained. It is marked *con moto*, and the effect is of joining the song mid-flow; it is as if this song had always been present, throughout the work, at a different aesthetic level or strand of time. The song is the essence behind the work, which is only now finally revealed.[17]

The whole work has, in effect, been leading, spiralling towards this, though this is only realised on its appearance. The thematic material of the quartet is finally revealed as stemming from this source, mere intimations presaging the final resolution of 'Frage'. The answer given to the question – a descending fifth with dotted anacrusis – is now seen as the source for the initially unconnected main theme of the first movement and the resulting *b* material (Ex. 4.17). Running throughout this first movement was the characteristic pervasive rhythm and contour of this theme, but what was once restless and impassioned, an anguished minor-key variant, is now resolved to a serene, peaceful recollection.

Even the process of modification to the *b* motive in the first movement mirrors that in the original song. In the latter, the *Ist es wahr?* figure is heard twice, its answer varied the second time, paralleling the modification of the first movement's main theme, b. 26, at b. 46 (which is the version recalled

---

[17] In this sense, the quartet is the inverse of Carolyn Abbate's reading of the Op. 19 *Venetianisches Gondellied*, where 'the noumenal piece that shimmers behind the phenomenal piece' is the central section that begins following the framing introductory idea (*Unsung Voices*, p. 49).

Ex. 4.17 'Frage' Op. 9 No. 1, and Quartet Op. 13: thematic provenance of quartet's
material in earlier song.

in the finale, emulating the statement of the second half of the song heard
in the coda).[18]

   This retrospective connection finally binds up the two families of thematic
strands, beyond the affinities sensed increasingly towards the work's end.
The D minor of the fugato and recitative, which had clouded the finale, is
now resolved into the relaxed subdominant leanings of the work's last bars.
This harmony had connected up to the subdominant progression opening
the adagio; now this in turn leads to the D major inclination of the first bars
and the IV–I^7 swell of the codetta (bb. 393–4, which is subtly altered from
the simpler IV$^6_4$–I of 'Frage' here, emphasising the finality of these bars and
the resolution of the whole quartet).

Cyclical form and time

Such a retrospective revelation has great significance in the context of cyclicism. Musical form is an enigmatic concept, in that it is intentional and
retrospective; it is not part of the audible experience of a work and does
not exist in a concrete ontological sense, but is created retrospectively in the
mind of the listener.[19] Form is considered to be a simultaneous, atemporal
entity, standing outside the temporally contingent process of the music yet

[18] Kohlhase, 'Studien zur Form in den Streichquartetten von Felix Mendelssohn Bartholdy', 78.

[19] I am speaking of what is commonly categorised as 'architectural' form, as opposed to
    'processual' form (a distinction made frequently by Dahlhaus). This is broadly true irrespective
    of whether one is referring to generic form or to a unique example. In the former, the model is
    still drawn from previous experience, and the relationship of the specific work with the
    archetypal model is only comprehended in its totality *ex post facto*. The expectation arising
    from previous hearings of a work is similarly still retrospective, since it presupposes a prior
    knowledge that is nevertheless *a posteriori* in relation to its first hearing. See on this matter Carl
    Dahlhaus, *Esthetics of Music*, trans. William Austin (Cambridge University Press, 1982), esp.
    'Toward the Phenomenology of Music', pp. 74–83.

intrinsically bound up with it. Carl Dahlhaus, drawing on a long history of phenomenological consideration, speaks in this context of 'the subjective impression of an instantaneous formal whole', in which 'the end of a musical work brings together its parts into a whole'. It is this 'sublimated moment in which the non-contemporaneous appears as an imaginary simultaneity, through which form, in the emphatic sense, is constituted'.[20]

Two of the most celebrated writers on time and memory, Henri Bergson and Marcel Proust, are particularly insightful on this matter. Henri Bergson's theories of temporal duration and the actions of memory provide a useful model here for understanding musical form.[21] Though in reality experienced time is a non-homogenous medium that cannot be reduced to homogenous space, our 'Platonising' intellect seeks to spatialise this lived experience through memory. 'By allowing us to grasp in a single intuition multiple moments of duration, [memory] frees us from the movement of the flow of things.'[22] Spatialising *past* time is possible, indeed habitual, but not time *passing*; hence this type of architectural understanding of a particular work's form is necessarily retrospective, achieved through memory.[23] It is the interaction of these two processes – the spatial and temporal – that gives rise to this 'contradictory idea of succession in simultaneity'.[24]

Marcel Proust, similarly, writes perceptively on the operations of the (musically trained) mind on the gradual assimilation of music through the memory of repeated hearings until it becomes conceivable as a whole: 'at the third or fourth repetition my intellect, having grasped, having consequently

---

[20] Carl Dahlhaus, 'Musik und Zeit', in Carl Dahlhaus and Hans Heinrich Eggebrecht, *Was ist Musik?* (Wilhelmshaven: Noetzel, 1985), pp. 177–80. For important earlier accounts see Roman Ingarden, *The Musical Work and the Problem of its Identity*, trans. Adam Czerniawski (London: Macmillan, 1986), pp. 70–9 and 93–7, and Victor Zuckerkandl, *Sound and Symbol* (Princeton University Press, 1956), pp. 151–264. A useful overview of musicological, theoretical, cognitive and philosophical approaches to this issue of musical form is also provided by Barbara R. Barry in *Musical Time: The Sense of Order* (Stuyvesant, NY: Pendragon Press, 1990), esp. pp. 58–69. The question of the perception of large-scale form has received relatively slight attention from empirical perspectives, in part as the issue is as much cultural-philosophical as a subject for cognitive psychology. A summary of existing experimental literature is provided in Eric Clarke, 'Rhythm and Timing in Music', §III 'Form Perception', in Diana Deutsch (ed.), *The Psychology of Music* (San Diego Academic Press, 1999), pp. 476–8.

[21] See especially Henri Bergson, *Time and Free Will: An Essay on the Immediate Data of Consciousness*, trans. F.L. Pogson (London: George Allen and Co., 1910), pp. 98–110. Indeed, the relation between the two – music and philosophy – is reciprocal in Bergson, since music and musical metaphors provide an invaluable and omnipresent means for this philosopher to convey to the reader his concept of time.

[22] Henri Bergson, *Matter and Memory*, trans. N.M. Paul and W.S. Palmer (London: George Allen and Unwin, 1911), p. 303.

[23] Bergson, *Time and Free Will*, p. 221.   [24] *Ibid.*, p. 228.

placed at the same distance, all the parts, and no longer having to exert any effort on them, had conversely projected and immobilised them on a uniform plane'.[25] Music, therefore, has the capacity 'to make visible, to intellectualise . . . realities that [are] outside Time'.[26] This theme was later elaborated upon by Claude Lévi-Strauss in his rather Proustian-entitled 'Ouverture' to *Le Cru et le cuit*. Music's relationship to time, claims Lévi-Strauss, 'is of a rather special nature'. It is as if it needs time 'only in order to deny it'.

Below the level of sounds and rhythms, music acts upon a primitive terrain, which is the physiological time of the listener; this time is irreversible and therefore irredeemably diachronic, yet music transmutes the segment devoted to listening to it into a synchronic totality, enclosed within itself. Because of the internal organisation of the musical work, the act of listening to it immobilises passing time; it catches and enfolds it.[27]

Historically, this idea of 'structural listening', in which the intellect overcomes music's temporal transitoriness by relating the memory of the past with the events of the present, is already nascent in the writings of early nineteenth-century authors such as Schelling and Jean Paul.[28] Indeed, as Reinhart Koselleck observes, such notions of the necessity for retrospective understanding of time were becoming common in early nineteenth-century Germany: 'It makes sense to say that experience based on the past is spatial since it is assembled into a totality, within which many layers of earlier times are simultaneously present, without, however, providing any indication of the before and after.'[29] From the viewpoint of its formal phenomenology, then, the beginning and end of a musical work are somehow both simultaneous in time but yet separated by time. Hence the cyclical format pursued by

---

[25] See Marcel Proust, *Within a Budding Grove*, in *Remembrance of Things Past*, trans. C.K. Scott Moncrieff and Terence Kilmartin, 3 vols. (Harmondsworth: Penguin, 1981), vol. I, pp. 570–2; *The Captive*, in *Remembrance of Things Past*, vol. III, pp. 378–9. The quotation above is taken from *The Captive*, p. 379.

[26] Proust, *Time Regained*, in *Remembrance of Things Past*, vol. III, p. 971.

[27] Claude Lévi-Strauss, *The Raw and the Cooked (Mythologiques, vol. I)*, trans. Doreen Weightman and John Weightman (New York: Harper & Row, 1969), p. 16.

[28] See the section of Schelling's *Philosophie der Kunst* concerning music (§ 77–83, in *Werke*, vol. V, pp. 491–506), or Hoeckner, *Programming the Absolute*, pp. 55–6 and 68, who refers to Jean Paul's *Flegeljahre*. Jean Paul was a particular love of the young Mendelssohn's household: Schumann later relates Mendelssohn's almost encyclopaedic knowledge of the popular German author ('His literary erudition was prodigious. He knew all the important passages of the Bible, Shakespeare, Goethe, Jean Paul (as well as Homer) by heart.' 'Erinnerungen an Mendelssohn', p. 104).

[29] Koselleck, *Futures Past*, p. 260, referring specifically to a letter from K.F. Reinhard to Mendelssohn's mentor Goethe.

Mendelssohn here, where the end is the beginning yet not a return but part of the present, can be seen to relate intimately to our internal perceptions of form and time.

It is this conception of form as relating to time which is not external, ontological, but subjective, experienced, which separates Mendelssohn's and the later Romantics' cyclicism from their earlier precedents. Thematic recall in cyclic works is not merely a part of the past, in quotation marks as it were, but constitutes a memory dredged up from the consciousness of the music. It is more complex, inasmuch as it replaces a separate, singular strand of time with a multilayered interaction of strands, where past and present, memory and actuality combine.[30] The underlying temporal conception is thus shifted away from the Newtonian external mechanism of the Enlightenment – 'Absolute, true or mathematical time, of itself, and from its own nature, flow[ing] equably without relation to anything external'[31] – to the internal experience of the Romantic era – from an external objective reality to the human subject. Time is now generated through the Self, through the Kantian contingencies of space and time or the inherent nature of human consciousness itself. 'Time is not something that subsists for itself or attaches itself as an objective determination to things, and consequently remains as residue when abstracted from all subjective conditions of the intuition of them', but rather 'the *a priori* formal condition of any appearance at all . . . Time is therefore merely a subjective condition of our (human) intuition . . . and in itself, outside the subject, is nothing.'[32]

Indeed, where Kant resubjectivised time, his successors would go even further. Herder would claim that 'in actuality every mutable thing has the measure of its own time within itself; this exists even if there were no other; no two things in the world have the same measure of time . . . There are therefore (one really can make this bold statement) at any one time in the universe innumerably many times.'[33] Bergson, later, would similarly hold

[30] Just as in St Augustine's claim that in reality to our consciousness there is not one time but rather 'three times, a present of things past, a present of things present, a present of things to come' (Augustine, *Confessions*, trans. Henry Chadwick (Oxford University Press, 1998), XI.xx (26), p. 235). The Romantic views of an internal, subjective time described below mark a decisive return to an Augustinian conception.

[31] Isaac Newton, *The Mathematical Principles of Natural Philosophy*, trans. Andrew Motte, rev. Florian Cajori, 2 vols. (Berkeley, CA: University of California Press, 1934), vol. I, p. 7.

[32] Immanuel Kant, *Kritik der reinen Vernunft*, in *Werke*, vol. III, pp. 80–2.

[33] Johann Gottlieb Herder, 'Genese des Begriffs der Zeit, nach Datis der menschlichen Natur und Sprache', from *Eine Metakritik zur Kritik der reinen Vernunft* (1799), ed. Friedrich Bassenger (Berlin: Aufbau Verlag, 1955), p. 68; compare this with Kant's assertion that time 'has only one dimension: different times are not simultaneous, but succeed each other . . . Difference times are only parts of the same time' (Kant, *Kritik der reinen Vernunft*, pp. 78–9). Novalis, following

that 'In reality there is no one rhythm of duration' but rather 'many different rhythms'. 'Wherever anything lives, there is, open somewhere, a register in which time is being inscribed.'[34] These accounts contain implicitly what Proust would make explicit: not only are there at any moment multiple instantiations of the individual times of living beings in the world, but the time of our consciousness is itself composed of multiple, intertwining strands. For Proust, life is 'careless of chronology, interpolating so many anachronisms into the sequence of our days'.[35] In the section 'The Intermittencies of the Heart' from *Cities of the Plain*, Proust describes in detail the multiple layers of time resulting from the interweaving of memory that make up our individual selves, foreshadowing the final revelations of *Time Regained*.

Time in this work is not linear – or, rather, there is not one time but several strands, which coexist, cross and converge even whilst their musical realisation takes place linearly and temporally – a highly Proustian conception, 'as though Time were to consist of a series of different and parallel lines'.[36] The flashback or linear two-level presence readings of the form given earlier are not wrong, but simplify the situation. The introduction and coda are somehow simultaneous, or succeed each other directly, yet between the two lie the four internal movements which answer the question of the introduction and thus precede the coda. ('Frage', itself, in the quartet is not cyclical in the musical sense of the term, since it does not appear in the work before the coda (excepting the three bars of *Ist es wahr?* in the introduction and the song's printed existence on the page at the start). It is rather related to the broader cyclic conception of multivalent strands of time, in the sense that it is continually present behind the work, but outside until the very end.) In the same sense as the phenomenology of form then, the sections of this work are both closely contingent upon and bound up with time and their temporal situation, but yet stand outside and above it.

Herder, would concur on this multiplicity of subjective times: 'Kronologie ist die Lehre von der Zeitlängenbestimmung eines Factums – eines zeitlichen Individuums . . . jedes zeitliche Individuum [hat] seine Sfäre, seine Skala' (Novalis, *Allgemeine Brouillon*, Fragment 474, in *Schriften*, vol. III, p. 340).

[34] Bergson, *Matter and Memory*, p. 275; *Creative Evolution*, trans. Arthur Mitchell (New York: Henry Holt, 1911), p. 16. Bergson only claims for a single, though unique, duration of each conscious being: see the 'Introduction to Metaphysics', in *The Creative Mind*, trans. Mabel L. Andison (New York: Citadel Press, 1992), p. 185.

[35] Proust, *Within a Budding Grove*, in *Remembrance of Things Past*, vol. I, p. 691.

[36] Proust, *Cities of the Plain*, in *Remembrance of Things Past*, vol. II, p. 784. See on this point also Kramer, 'Multiple and Non-Linear Time in Beethoven's opus 135', 135.

This perception of form is enabled through memory. Thematic recall within the quartet is a process of remembrance and recollection. The acceleration of memories, prompted by the until-now subconscious similarities between the events of the work, leads to the regaining of the past in the coda, which yet arises from the present – the immanent process of the finale. Mendelssohn's process of musical recall hence upholds Bergson's view that memory 'only becomes actual by borrowing the body of some perception into which it slips'; 'the past leaves the state of pure memory and coincides with a certain part of my present'.[37] This leads to the final goal of the work, which has been arrived at through the process of memory, of bringing the past back into the present, thus understanding and actualising it. Here, it reveals the essence behind the work.

'Frage' itself is both a memory and an unseen goal – the paradox of a memory of something not previously heard. It is part of the lost past of the work, something oblivious to the main course of the music, which had been present on the page but not audibly. Such a musical emulation of the ontological status of lost memory curiously parallels the ideas of Bergson and Proust. The object of memory is apparently not physically present – whether in the matter of the brain or the audible substrate of the music – but nevertheless is there somehow, 'outside' the subject's consciousness, of indeterminate ontology, its recall being prompted by association or thematic affinity. For Bergson, 'there is not, there cannot be in the brain a region in which memories congeal and accumulate'. To ask where memories are stored is (mistakenly) to confuse the inextricably temporal with concepts drawn from the spatial.[38] Or as Proust famously describes in the lead-up to the initial revelation of the *petite madeleine* near the beginning of *À la recherche*, 'The past is hidden somewhere outside the realm, beyond the reach of intellect, in some material object (in the sensation which that material object will give us) of which we have no inkling.'[39] As we have seen, in Mendelssohn's work the recovery of the 'lost' memory of 'Frage' is the last in a series of increasingly clear recollections across the finale of the quartet, and is led to by the convergence of the related thematic strands. It is this recovery of the lost past which forms the redemptive goal of this work.

---

[37] Bergson, *Matter and Memory*, pp. 72, 181.

[38] *Ibid.*, pp. 160, 191–3. For the quotidian perception of the present 'The past has not ceased to exist: it has simply ceased to be useful' (p. 193).

[39] Proust, *Swann's Way*, in *Remembrance of Things Past*, vol. I, pp. 47–8.

Ist es wahr? Interpretation and context

In the context of the composer's life, the song at the end – 'Frage' – actually is a memory of the past. The 'thema' of the quartet is a love song, written earlier that summer by the eighteen-year-old Mendelssohn. The use of the Beethovenian *Ist es wahr?* motive from the song as the pivotal question of the quartet and Mendelssohn's attaching the song facing the quartet's first page seems an attempt to provide the audience with a hermeneutical key to the meaning of the work, albeit one which, like Beethoven in his Op. 135, can make the quartet seem even more enigmatic and elusive.

One should be wary of reading too much or too specifically into such a clue, particularly in the case of Mendelssohn, whose own feelings on the indeterminacy of words faced with music are justly famous. One should not think, however, that general poetic or even programmatic responses to this composer's music are invalid – clearly not, given the celebrated examples of his concert overtures and 'Reformation', 'Italian' and 'Scottish' symphonies.[40] As Clive Brown has recently argued, Mendelssohn's aesthetic views supported the Romantic beliefs of self-expression and personal experience,[41] and the A minor Quartet furthermore comes in the middle of a period in which the young composer was heavily under the influence and mentorship of A.B. Marx.[42] Mendelssohn, however, while indisputably associating his music with particular emotional or poetic experiences, nevertheless did not believe that these were really compatible with literary exegesis, and, without wishing to become bemired in musical-programmatic aesthetics, it seems advisable to keep discussion within the context of general expressive and poetic features rather than attempting to reduce the music to specific programmes of the sort which Mendelssohn expressly rejected.[43]

The text of the song reads as follows:

Ist es wahr?	Is it true?
Dass du stets dort in dem Laubgang,	That you wait there for me
An der Weinwand meiner harrst?	In the arbour by the vineyard wall?

---

[40] Even some of these works, though, are slightly problematic in ascribing an authorial intention for a clear poetic or programmatic meaning, as will be considered at greater length in Chapter 6.

[41] Clive Brown, *A Portrait of Mendelssohn* (New Haven, CT and London: Yale University Press, 2003).

[42] See Judith [Silber] Ballan, 'Marxian Programmatic Music: A Stage in Mendelssohn's Musical Development', in R. Larry Todd (ed.), *Mendelssohn Studies* (Cambridge University Press, 1992), pp. 149–61.

[43] See Mendelssohn's vexed response to highly specific programmatic readings of Beethoven's Ninth provoked by circulation of A.B. Marx's ideas on the work, *ibid.*, p. 156.

Und den Mondschein und die Sternlein	And ask the moonlight and the stars
Auch nach mir befragst?	About me too?
Ist es wahr? Sprich!	Is it true? Speak!
Was ich fühle, das begreift nur,	What I feel, can only be understood
Die es mitfühlt, und die treu mir	By she who feels as I do, and is true to me
Ewig, treu mir ewig bleibt.	Forever, remains forever true.

(The authorship of the text is in fact unclear; Mendelssohn gave the poet as 'H. Voss', a possible pseudonym of his classics teacher and part-time poet Gustav Droysen, though Sebastian Hensel claimed the composer had actually written the verses himself.[44]) The song mirrors the quartet in its almost cyclic construction around the question *Ist es wahr?* It falls into two sections, separated by the repetition of the query in the thirteenth bar (the same, coincidentally or otherwise, as its first appearance in the quartet). The second part initially modifies the material of the first, but continues afresh and into something new, the layout approximating [Question?] A; [Question?'] A', thus similar to the recall–development of the quartet's adagio introduction in the coda. This second half provides the climax and resolution of the song, though the question posed – Is it true? – Is not really answered affirmatively. It is this latter half which is the part recalled at the end of the quartet.

Mendelssohn had fallen in love earlier that summer, though we do not know who the girl was or what, if anything, became of it, and this song came out of this experience. To judge by the lack of any further details on the matter, however, and the general mood, the restless, passionate tone of the resulting quartet, one may presume the outcome was not ultimately happy. This might explain the apparent emotional gulf between the world of the song, written back at the start of that summer, and the strong allusions to late Beethoven, particularly Op. 132, from which the quartet takes its bearings.[45]

---

44 Hensel, *Die Familie Mendelssohn*, vol. I, p. 133; Gustav Droysen, 'Johann Gustav Droysen und Felix Mendelssohn-Bartholdy', *Deutsche Rundschau*, 111 (1902), 195. The names 'W. Voss' and 'J.N. Voss' were both pseudonyms of Droysen's, though 'H. Voss' is unidentified. Droysen's *noms de plume* should also not be confused with that of the real poet Johann Heinrich Voss (1751–1826). If Mendelssohn had in fact written the verses himself, this piece of evidence would support the idea that the work held a deep personal significance for him, as later letters reveal. See further on this issue Douglass Seaton, 'With Words: Mendelssohn's Vocal Songs', in Douglass Seaton (ed.), *The Mendelssohn Companion* (Westport, CT and London: Greenwood Press, 2001), p. 664.

45 It should, however, be noted here as a cautionary word that the major part of the quartet (composed between July and October) must have already been written before Beethoven's Op. 132 was published in September 1827 (the end of the first movement is dated 28 July in the

These latter affinities have been noticed by nearly every commentator on the work.[46] Similarities include the layout of the first three thematic events of the first movement, in ambiguous relationship with each other (an adagio introduction, followed by semiquaver figuration ushering in the first subject proper of the exposition, similar in dotted rhythm and shape: however, Beethoven's is resolved over the course of the first movement, Mendelssohn's only across the whole work); a central F major adagio forming the emotional heart of the work; and a march-like penultimate movement, leading directly to an impassioned recitative and into the A minor finale, with similar accompanimental textures. The quartet can of course be taken as a homage to the Viennese master, who had died earlier that year, but both in the further contextual layer of 'Frage' and the wholly individual use of the ideas taken from Beethoven, Mendelssohn is going far beyond a simple emulation of his model and into something completely new.[47]

The anguished tone of the four inner movements of the quartet may be taken as an answer, or even an imploring for an answer, to the question set from 'Frage' in the introduction. The affiliation here with late Beethoven is particularly close. Kerman has memorably described the latter's late works as 'battering at the communications barrier';[48] in its use of recitative, Op. 132 is the direct model for Mendelssohn's own A minor Quartet. The first movement takes its thematic substance from the eventual answer to the question revealed in the coda, but in a pained, minor-key version.[49] The

autograph); commentators are left to speculate as to whether or not Mendelssohn had access to a pre-publication copy of Beethoven's work, a situation for which there is no corroborating evidence. (Indeed, despite the clear influence of various other Beethoven works elsewhere, only the recitative preceding the finale of Op. 13 is indubitably modelled on Op. 132.)

[46] For instance Philip Radcliffe (*Mendelssohn* (London: J.M. Dent, 1954), pp. 93–4), Joscelyn Godwin ('Early Mendelssohn and late Beethoven', 280–4), Friedhelm Krummacher (*Mendelssohn – Der Komponist*, esp. pp. 161–6; 'Synthesis und Disparaten: Zu Beethovens späten Quartetten und ihrer frühen Rezeption', *Archiv für Musikwissenschaft*, 37 (1980), 111–21), Wulf Konold ('Mendelssohn und der späte Beethoven', pp. 185–91; *Felix Mendelssohn Bartholdy und seine Zeit*, pp. 111–38), Ariane Jessulat (*Die Frage als musikalischer Topos: Studien zur Motivbildung in der Musik des 19. Jahrhunderts* (Berlin: Studio, 2000), pp. 145–93), and Uri Golumb ('Mendelssohn's Creative Response to late Beethoven: Polyphony and Thematic Identity in Mendelssohn's Quartet in A-major Op. 13', *Ad Parnassum*, 4 (2006), 101–19).

[47] Thus, in Harold Bloom's familiar terminology, Mendelssohn's quartet is at the very least a remarkably strong misreading of Beethoven's Op. 132 (if indeed Op. 132 is the primary influence at all).

[48] Joseph Kerman, *The Beethoven Quartets* (New York and London: W.W. Norton & Co., 1966), p. 194.

[49] Hans Kohlhase in particular has called attention to the semantic dimension of the near-quotation of the musical phrase associated with the words 'Was ich fühle, das begreift nur' within the first movement (bb. 46–8, Ex. 4.13; 'Brahms und Mendelssohn', p. 79, n. 32). For another consideration of the quartet's hermeneutic potential see Mathias Thomas, *Das*

'recitatives' of the quartet can be related back to the song's demand in b. 15, 'Sprich!', following the second statement of *Ist es wahr?* Previously the unstable V_4^6 on which the music had been left was answered by an accented e pedal in b. 2. On its second appearance, the urgency is such that the vocal part now takes over this instrumental voice, its e^2 'Sprich!' imploring an answer, but to which the accompaniment merely repeats the request. It is hard not to see this as an urgent, impassioned demand for communication in response to the original question of 'Frage'. The song's reply, the pedal e, can indeed be seen to account for the use of this characteristic feature across the work, such as the recapitulation over a $_4^6$ in the first movement and its parallel in the finale. The appearance of 'Frage' in the final page of the work is the resultant response to the plea to speak, as the finale's opening recitative leads at last into song.

'Frage' had not answered the question unconditionally, but had left it in hopeful faith. Now, in the quartet, the recall of the end of 'Frage' comes not so much as an affirmation but as a memory, charged with the quality of nostalgic recollection. The words of this last section, 'What I feel, can only be understood / by she who feels as I do, and is true to me / Forever, remains forever true', are now seen in a mood of sublimated resignation; it is as if the whole work is a monument to this ideal, probably unattained, but sublimated, fixed into a work of art. The quartet embodies a deeply Romantic theme, one of love, loss, yearning for the unobtainable – the memory of what might have been, but possibly never was. The recall of the past is the final goal, which captures this fugitive experience and thus transcends it.

The song, 'Frage', and the quartet itself indeed stand in an analogous relationship towards each other. 'Frage' is a beautiful but fleeting episode, part of the vanished past, but which is recaptured and actualised into the full substance of the quartet, forming 'a minute freed from the order of time'.[50] Art, as Proust would believe, becomes 'the sole means of rediscovering Lost Time'.[51] The song, in itself a miniature of touching simplicity, is nevertheless what would be of only fleeting significance, were it not immortalised in the quartet to which it gave growth. Life and art are interlinked.

In this sense, the quartet can be thought of as offering an alternative redemptive strategy from Beethoven's work, not through the drive towards

Instrumentalwerk Felix Mendelssohn-Bartholdys: Eine systematisch-theoretische Untersuchung unter besonderer Berücksichtigung der zeitgenössischen Musiktheorie (Göttingen: Hubert, 1972), pp. 225–6.

[50] Proust, *Time Regained*, in *Remembrance of Things Past*, vol. III, p. 906.

[51] *Ibid.*, vol. III, p. 935.

transcendence seen in the still equivocal A major of the coda of Op. 132, but a more Romantic process of loss, memory and nostalgic recall, the recapturing of a lost experience from the past as the final goal of the music. Just as in the first movement of Schumann's later *Fantasie*, the work is a search for the meaningful quotation at the end, which proves to be the essence behind everything leading up to it, Schlegel's *leiser Ton*.[52] Like the Schumann piece, the *ferne Geliebte* is a hermeneutical clue. Within a work which might ostensibly pay sincere homage to the figure of Beethoven, a highly personal message to the distant beloved is encoded, enshrining this secret love in permanence. Mendelssohn differs in the complex cyclic arrangement, which provokes this apparition of memory and binds up his work more strongly.

Form and expression are intrinsically related in this work. The complex, interlinked cyclical procedures enact a compelling emotional and psychological narrative, which spirals towards the revelation of 'Frage' as the answer to the whole quartet – the reply to the question posed at the outset, which retrospectively explains the entire journey. The complex, many-stranded musical argument, the radical formal procedures, are simultaneously the means by which the quartet realises its expressive goal. As Charles Rosen has succinctly put it, 'the subtlety of the young Mendelssohn's procedure is intellectually breathtaking, but it ends up as deeply expressive'.[53]

Opus 13 and Proust

The figure who lies behind much of this discussion is Marcel Proust. The spirit of Proust's budding grove, the *jeunes filles en fleurs*, seems to permeate the A minor Quartet. The quartet and the song that lies behind it inhabit the same world of youthful idealism, of beauty, of young love – the past which is recaptured and made permanent in *À la recherche du temps perdu*. Yet also and more significantly it mirrors the narrative structure, the formal teleology, the cyclic conception of time, the past found through the present, and its subsequent concretisation into art.

[52] Schumann prefaced his work with a quotation from Friedrich Schlegel: 'Durch alle Töne tönet / Im bunten Erdentraum / *Ein* leiser Ton gezogen / Für den, der heimlich lauschet.' A subsequent piece that may draw on Mendelssohn's design is Richard Strauss' *Metamorphosen*, whose themes gradually evolve towards the quotation from Beethoven's Third Symphony near the close. Beyond this similar design, what makes the analogy more compelling is the common use in both works of the dotted minor descent $\hat{5}$–$\hat{1}$ as the primary thematic material, and the emphasis throughout on its imitative treatment on degrees $\hat{5}$ and $\hat{6}$.

[53] Rosen, *The Romantic Generation*, p. 578.

Much of the thinking behind my discussion of the cyclic nature of time in Op. 13 has been based on Proust. Proust's work provides a theoretical model for conceptions of time, cyclicism and memory that normal music theory does not deal with. While this is not the only path to understanding Mendelssohn's music – a Hegelian interpretation, along the lines suggested earlier, could also prove rewarding – it is nevertheless an immensely fruitful one in relation to the present quartet.

Mendelssohn and Proust are an unlikely pairing, two artists with apparently little in common. Yet the connection between the two – and this work in particular with *À la recherche* – is not as slight as might at first be imagined. Proust's work grew out of the synaesthetic, *Wagnérien* world of the French *fin de siècle*. As Nattiez has argued, following Anne Henry, the influence of Schopenhauer led Proust to look to music for a 'redemptive' model for literature,[54] a tendency which may be seen as a manifestation of Walter Pater's dictum that all Romantic art aspires to the state of music:[55]

It is not monuments or paintings but music that serves as a guiding thread for the Narrator on his journey towards aesthetic revelation: music, like the quest – and like *À la recherche* itself – unfolds in time. Through the play of transformations, reminiscences and perpetual responses that it arouses in us, it is like a microcosm of our relationship to the world as inscribed in time and as conditioned by it. In particular, music imitates, in its thematic development, the workings of involuntary memory, and this analogy is encapsulated in 'the little phrase' that returns from one movement to another in the manner of Franck's cyclic sonatas.[56]

Music, for Proust, possesses the capacity to disclose 'something truer than all known books': 'literary, that is to say intellectual expression describes [life], explains it, analyses it, but does not recompose it as does music, in which the sounds seem to follow the very movement of our being, to reproduce that extreme inner point of our sensations'.[57]

[54] Anne Henry, *Marcel Proust, théories pour une esthétique* (Paris: Klincksieck, 1981), Jean-Jacques Nattiez, *Proust as Musician*, trans. Derrick Puffett (Cambridge University Press, 1989).

[55] Walter Pater, 'The School of Giorgione', in *The Renaissance: Studies in Art and Poetry*, ed. A. Phillips (Oxford University Press, 1986), p. 86. Pater's formulation is very close to some of Friedrich Schlegel's earlier hyperboles to music: calling music 'the highest of all arts', Schlegel goes on to claim 'Every art has musical principles and when it is completed it becomes itself music' (*Literarische Notizen* (1798), quoted by Andrew Bowie in *Aesthetics and Subjectivity*, p. 246).

[56] Nattiez, *Proust as Musician*, pp. 38–9.

[57] Proust, *The Captive: Remembrance of Things Past*, vol. III, p. 381. Proust's first statement in particular bears close comparison with Mendelssohn's celebrated claim that 'What the music that I love expresses to me are not thoughts too unclear for words, but rather those too definite' (letter to Marc-André Souchay, 15 October 1842, *Briefe*, vol. II, p. 337; Proust also claims in his

Proust scholarship has produced numerous studies concerning the author's relationship with music – not just the ubiquitous search for the *petite phrase* of the Vinteuil Sonata, but attempts to explain the structure of Proust's novel with reference to cyclic works. The two composers most frequently mentioned in this context are Beethoven and César Franck. It is the late quartets of the former, which aspire most closely to cyclicism, which are widely accredited with influencing Franck's later more extensive essays in the form – the same works to which Mendelssohn's early quartets are the earliest and (at the very least) equally successful artistic responses. Franck, in addition (a fact that is not always appreciated), was heavily influenced by Mendelssohn's cyclic instrumental works; the Belgian composer's first essay in the genre, for instance, the early F♯ minor Piano Trio Op. 1 No. 1 (1840), is highly indebted to Mendelssohn's example (above all the B minor Piano Quartet Op. 3). Irrespective of whether or not Proust knew Op. 13, scholarship has shown considerable evidence for his work's connection to two composers whose works are intimately related to Mendelssohn's quartet.[58] The possibility of a closer connection is, however, tantalisingly suggested by a comment made by Charlus in *Cities of the Plain*: enthusing over Beethoven's Op. 132 – a possible model for Mendelssohn's quartet – he comments on 'the sublime, imperishable phrase which the virtuoso of Berlin' (Proust adds in parentheses 'we suppose M. de Charlus to have meant Mendelssohn') 'was to imitate unceasingly'.[59] The most famous of these allusions to the first subject of Op. 132 is, of course, the first movement of Mendelssohn's Op. 13.

I do not mean to suggest a necessary, direct causal connection between Mendelssohn's work and Proust – that this work may have influenced the writing of *À la recherche* – since this situation seems highly unlikely. But

correspondence to have read Mendelssohn's letters (see n. 59 below)). Recent scholars such as Douglass Seaton and John Michael Cooper have called attention to the similarity between Mendelssohn's aesthetics of music and Schopenhauer's near-contemporaneous views, however different the two figures might have been in other respects.

[58] In this context, it is also noteworthy that Proust seems to have associated Mendelssohn and César Franck in his mind; see *The Fugitive* (*Remembrance of Things Past*, vol. III), p. 649.

[59] Proust, *Cities of the Plain*: *Remembrance of Things Past*, vol. II, p. 1043. The word 'virtuoso' is not necessarily intended to be derogatory here, but is a mannerism of Charlus' ornate language (though it is probably fair to say that Proust's taste in music, very much of his time, was not immune from the then-prevalent Wagnerian ideological view of Mendelssohn: see his letter to Marie Scheikévitch, 27 February 1917, in Marcel Proust, *Selected Letters*, Vol. 3 *1910–1917*, ed. Philip Kolb, trans. Terence Kilmartin (London: Harper Collins, 1992), p. 365; further, on the disparity between Proust's undoubted love for and insight into music and his more questionable expertise, see Cormac Newark and Ingrid Wassenaar, 'Proust and Music: The Anxiety of Competence', *Cambridge Opera Journal*, 9 (1997), 163–83).

Proust's work came out of an aesthetic backdrop with strong associations to the Mendelssohn quartet, and the relationship between two works is no less strong or relevant for being in all probability unintended. Indeed, Proust himself would advocate the very same stance concerning the irrelevance of 'authorial intentions' and the aesthetic reality of thematic recurrences and connections across unrelated cultures and times – the 'profound affinity between two ideas or two feelings . . . a subtle harmony that others are deaf to between two impressions or two ideas'.[60] As the language of our day suddenly 'strikes at us from a passage of the *Iliad*' or an ancient crisis reveals an unexpected similarity with our own mundane lives, so such extratemporal connections 'show how the basic substance of humanity, often indivisible and as though intermitted, is still a living reality to be found where least we expect it'.[61]

The justification for making this analogy between the two is due to the remarkable affinities in treatment of time, narrative and memory, and not least the strong similarities in their works' structures. The Proust scholar J.M. Cocking, for instance, argues for Franck's Quartet as the model for the structure of *À la recherche*.[62] While this composer is more obviously connected to Proust's world than Mendelssohn, if one really wishes to seek a musical model for Proust, the work which parallels his masterpiece far more closely than any other is the A minor Quartet.

In both works, an external cyclic frame encloses the intervening action, which leads to the end which is concurrent with the beginning; the resulting complex, multistranded conception of time is entirely congruent with Proust's theories. This intervening action follows the search for the vision held at the outset, following a mythopoetic fall from grace – the night the young Marcel's mother stayed in his room at Combray, or the chasm the quartet plunges into following the question of 'Frage'. This vision is glimpsed intermittently across the work, what seem to be intimations of the ideal world, and is finally found at the end, through the recapturing of the fugitive experience of lost time in art. This is foreseen in the realisation of the underlying unity behind separate appearances – a timeless Platonic or

---

[60] Marcel Proust, *Contre Saint-Beuve*, trans. Sylvia Townsend Warner as *By Way of Saint-Beuve* (London: Hogarth Press, 1984), pp. 193–4.

[61] Proust, *Jean Santeuil*, trans. Gerard Hopkins (Harmondsworth: Penguin Books, 1985), pp. 3–4. Also note the more worldly discussion between Marcel and Saint-Loup in *The Guermantes Way* of the temporal recurrence of events found in military history (*Remembrance of Things Past*, vol. II, pp. 108–17).

[62] J.M. Cocking, 'Proust and Music', in *Proust: Collected Essays on the Writer and his Art* (Cambridge University Press, 1982), pp. 109–29.

Schopenhauerian essence which connects different events across time, the different manifestations of an underlying thematic idea across the four movements.

The realisation itself is enabled through the workings of memory, the acceleration of increasingly clear recollections flooding back towards the end of the narrative – the irregular paving stones, the Guermantes' reception in *Time Regained*, the literal recalling of the first and second movements in the finale of the quartet. These memories call attention to the fundamental unity behind everything, to the essence behind the surface forms; how such events, whilst occurring in time, are by the fact of their repetition somehow above time, 'a fragment of time in the pure state', the cyclic principle which enables Mendelssohn to recall the introduction as the coda, and leads to the goal of the lost memory of 'Frage'.[63] In both, the lost experience is recaptured after much struggle through memory, and fixed for all time into a work of art; the redemption is found in the past, not a retreat back into it, but in its timelessness as found in the present.

The two works even outline two opposing paths – the innocent world of love, beauty and art of Swann's way, the idyll of the adagio opening (theme *a*); the maturer world of society, power and tradition of the Guermantes, the strife of the first movement's answer (theme *b*). The first is lost and is succeeded by the second, but gradually the characteristics of both cloud and infiltrate each other, and finally they are seen to lead to each other: their ends connect.[64]

The question we could ask is whether Mendelssohn is implicitly realising in music an archetypal trajectory which was to form the basis of Proust's great novel eighty years later. The eighteen-year-old composer's work does not go through the same length of disillusionment, half a lifetime for Marcel, but it presents a similar redemptive strategy. It is a young man's work, a youthful epiphany, crystallising the universal experience of early love into a permanently important work of art. It recaptures a similar experience to Proust, but from its own time, not from the vantage of middle-age. The reason why there is no other work comparable to the A minor Quartet for what it does, its unique mood and emotional soundscape, is due to the fact

---

[63] Proust, *Time Regained*, in *Remembrance of Things Past*, vol. III, p. 905.

[64] The analogy between the two is irresistible; however, in the interests of intellectual honesty, I should note that their respective levels probably should be seen as differing. In Proust, Swann's and the Guermantes' ways are of largely equal status, whereas in Mendelssohn the *a* theme is closer to being an idyllic vision of future resolution external to the main process of the work, which itself is formed of the *b* theme. However, the fact that both are initially entirely distinct and subsequently infiltrate and converge across the work suggests the further parallel here.

that no other composer could have realised a structure and narrative of such emotional maturity and technique at that age.

Perhaps we should just leave it by saying that music can enact through its own means a powerful emotional and psychological journey which proved highly potent for Romantic artists. To end on an appropriately Proustian note, we could suggest any (unintentional) similarity between the two works is due to the latent affinities – recurring essences – which lie behind great works of art, separated, yet related, through time.

5 | Overcoming the past

The E♭ Quartet Op. 12

> If all time is eternally present
> All time is unredeemable.
>
> T.S. Eliot, *Four Quartets*, 'Burnt Norton', I

The E♭ Quartet Op. 12, Mendelssohn's second numbered quartet, was composed two years after the A minor Quartet, in 1829.[1] Work on the composition had started in the spring of 1829, but completion was delayed over Mendelssohn's first visit to England in the summer, and it was finally completed only in September of that year in London. Ostensibly the E♭ Quartet is a more relaxed and predominantly sunny work, though the closer it is examined the more ambivalent the balance held in this piece becomes between the youthful lyricism of its immediately apparent lighter side and the darker memories that at times break through.[2] Like its earlier companion, the quartet presents a thorough working-out of cyclic procedures. Unlike the A minor work, though, its composer left little by way of a hermeneutic clue as to its underlying inspiration or to provide an extramusical key for its understanding. Yet an initialled dedication on the title page – 'B.P.' – gives some indication as to a similar inspiration and concern as the A minor Quartet.[3]

'B.P.' stands for Betty Pistor, a noted Berlin beauty with whom Mendelssohn was obviously much enamoured. A year older than

---

[1] The numbering of the two quartets – Quartet No. 1 in E♭, Op. 12 (1829), and Quartet No. 2 in A minor Op. 13 (1827) – thus contradicts their order of composition.

[2] This (superficially) untroubled nature is reflected in the quartet's reception, this being probably the most popular of the composer's quartets in the nineteenth and early twentieth centuries. The second-movement canzonetta, the most easy-going and least complex part of the work, has become by far the most popular movement from a Mendelssohn quartet, commonly taken out of context or arranged as an encore, and thus becoming emblematic of (what is taken to be) the composer's style.

[3] The autograph manuscript of the quartet is now in the Bibliothèque nationale, Paris (Conservatoire MS 191). On hearing of the engagement of Betty Pistor to Adolf Rudorff in 1830, Mendelssohn instructed his friend Ferdinand David, who was then in possession of the manuscript, subsequently to change the initials to 'B.R.' The episode is related in Ernst Rudorff, 'From the Memoirs of Ernst Rudorff', trans. Nancy B. Reich, in R. Larry Todd (ed.), *Mendelssohn and his World* (Princeton University Press, 1991), pp. 265–9.

Mendelssohn, she had started attending the Friday rehearsals of Zelter's *Singakademie* at the age of fourteen, where Felix and Fanny were already regular members. With Felix's younger sister Rebecca, the three had formed a close friendship by 1826, and an incident in January 1828 suggests that Mendelssohn's feelings may well have been amorous by this time.[4] From the memoirs of her future son, we learn that Mendelssohn, some time early in 1829, had told Betty that he was thinking of writing a quartet for her, though she seems not to have taken this statement as anything other than a tease on Mendelssohn's part. When she eventually found out several decades later that this intended work was in fact the Eb Quartet, the fact evidently came as a surprise to her. Her son maintained that though 'the memory of the dear friend of her youth . . . remained an incomparably dear and sacred possession', 'Betty's feelings for Felix Mendelssohn were never mixed with any elements of passion.'[5] While we will probably never know exactly the nature of their relationship, it is just possible that Betty Pistor was the same girl as inspired the A minor Quartet.[6]

The connection between the quartets in fact runs deeper. These two pieces are Mendelssohn's two early cyclic works in the genre: the composer was not to write another quartet (or indeed, any significant chamber work) for another eight years – the longest gap in his short creative life – and none of his subsequent chamber works would revert so openly to the cyclic design realised in these two youthful masterpieces. Both share a concern with using cyclic procedures to suggest notions of musical memory, reliving often dark and painful experiences and finding their ultimate salvation in an

---

[4] Mendelssohn had apparently reacted over-sensitively to the laughter of two of her friends he had heard when paying a visit to Betty's house, apparently thinking it aimed at himself and his relationship to Betty. See Rudorff, 'From the Memoirs of Ernst Rudorff', pp. 261–2.

[5] *Ibid.*, p. 269.

[6] No information is available as to who the girl behind Op. 13 might have been. Larry Todd conjectures that the earlier quartet was also inspired by Betty Pistor (*Mendelssohn: A Life in Music*, p. 176). This is quite possible since she was definitely known to Mendelssohn at the time, though for a number of reasons this seems unconvincing to me. The apparent sudden inspiration of the song 'Frage' (on which Op. 13 is based) in June 1827 and the difference in time between the two quartets would seem to argue against a connection. Why, after all, would Mendelssohn have written a quartet for Betty in 1829, informing her of his intention, writing her initials on the title page, and referring to the work as his 'quartet for B.P.' in his letters from the next few years, if he had already composed another quartet inspired by her two years earlier, to which he had given no hint of a dedication? Moreover, why did he refrain from giving an indication on Op. 13 as to who inspired it? Was this a youthful affair that had to remain hidden both from public and family sight? (A letter of Fanny Mendelssohn to her brother just before her marriage in 1829 has been read as confessing to a similar experience; see David Warren Sabean, 'Fanny and Felix Mendelssohn-Bartholdy and the Question of Incest', *The Musical Quarterly*, 77 (1993), 710–11.) The issue is unclear, and will probably always remain so.

Ex. 5.1 Quartets in A minor Op. 13 and in E♭, Op. 12 (1829): comparison of opening bars.

Op. 13, opening

Op. 12, opening

acceptance of and reconciliation with this time, as both works end with the nostalgic recall of their own musical past. Notable in both is the vacillation between two levels, between the present and the past, a light and a dark side of human experience, and the conflict between an ideal and a more troubled reality. And despite their tonal disparity, as I will suggest later, might the extensive use of A minor for the greater part of the E♭ Quartet's expanded first-movement development section not refer back to the tonality of the earlier work?

In thematic content and several details of general design the E♭ work also seems to present a crystallisation and echo of parts of the A minor Quartet. One could even suggest that Op. 12 presents a recomposition of Op. 13, starting from similar basic material but giving rise to a radically different cyclic design. Their introductions, both adagio and seventeen bars in length, proceed from the same two basic motivic building blocks, and are developed in similar fashion, repeating these two segments immediately and reaching a climax through an ascending sequence built out of the second (Ex. 5.1). Both also emphasise a significant move to the subdominant in their opening bars, outlining the progression $I^{(7)}$–IV–V–I.

Their respective slow movements follow similar contours, sharing the same general mood and $\frac{3}{4}$ time signature, in each case being formed from a transformation of the material of the quartet's introduction. Perhaps most strongly in this regard, the 'scherzo' movements – in Op. 12 a canzonetta placed second, in Op. 13 an intermezzo – share a similar design and contrast of mood, both forming an interlude in the course of their respective works.

Yet the differences between the two – above all, in their cyclic structure and general plot – are vital in coming to an understanding of each quartet's particularity. While the problem of the A minor Quartet arose out of the relationship between motto-introduction and first movement, that of the

E♭ is between the material and mood of the first-movement exposition and a new theme that enters mysteriously in the development and goes on to dominate this section, recurring again in the coda and twice more in the development and coda spaces of the finale, mirroring the opening movement. The recall of the past here is not the calm, if bittersweet memory of a love song, however, but a more unsettling F minor theme that brings trouble in its wake. Rather than suggesting a nostalgic embrace of the past, the effect is more akin to some dark memory, a distressing episode which continually recurs, disturbing the overriding mood of relaxed lyricism and breaking down the implied form of the work. Remarkably, here, the finale is in the 'wrong' key, C minor, characterised by a passionate turmoil which would seem more in place in the composer's Op. 13 quartet than the predominantly serene mood of the rest of the E♭ work.

The analogy with the notion of trauma might seem particularly appropriate here. Musical recall, the desire for repetition, is obviously a basic premise of musical structure, but in cases where this occurs contrary to or beyond the level of traditional requirements, such recall can unquestionably impart a strong sense of memory, as if music is modelling human consciousness and its concomitant temporal levels. The E♭ Quartet's structure, its cyclic narrative-plot, can be argued as constituting a musical model for an emotional-psychological condition analogous to the psychoanalytical idea of trauma. Both are concerned with time and the workings of memory, the intrusive and unwanted recall of dark and painful experiences which upset the course of the present and recur several times. The process of the work is to wrestle against these unwanted relapses and ultimately break free of them.[7]

The minor-key angst of the finale stems from the unresolved appearance of the new development theme in the first movement, its minor-key tonality and thematic basis stemming from this source. To understand why the cyclic re-emergence of this earlier theme should prove so disruptive, we must examine closely the remarkable structure of this earlier movement, where it first appears.

---

[7] My reading of the quartet in this chapter proceeds from this idea of trauma, and Sigmund Freud's codification of the concept in particular, as a useful way of interrogating Mendelssohn's work, though obviously such a theoretical tool will invariably distort certain aspects of the music it seeks to explain. The refined chiaroscuro of Mendelssohn's work might therefore appear slightly exaggerated in the lurid expressionist hues of Freud, though I hope through such an approach a genuine aspect of the work (and one that is moreover often overlooked) will also be brought out.

First movement

The first movement is a prominent example of a type of sonata deformation particularly characteristic of Mendelssohn. The structure of this movement is remarkably complex in its ambiguity between several different formal types. Its basic form is a sonata with slow introduction and a new theme introduced into the development section; such a description misses, however, the remarkable subtlety and tension of this movement resulting from the play of elements from the sonata, sonata rondo or sonata with a new development theme, or, indeed, a sonata where the real contrasting second theme enters in the development section and thus breaks down the whole idea of the sonata upon which the movement was originally premised.[8]

This new theme is the F minor idea which is introduced at b. 107. This design – what I will call the development breakthrough / new-theme deformation – was to prove a particular favourite of Mendelssohn's. In this, a new (if related) theme enters in the development section and is recapitulated in the coda, hence presenting us with a parallel two-strophe design where the recapitulation mirrors the exposition and the coda the development. Normally, the new material in the development is tonally resolved in its subsequent appearance, but in the present quartet this new theme, upon its return in the coda, is again unresolved, necessitating its later reappearance in the finale.

The idea of introducing a new theme in a sonata-form movement's development section was not actually new in Mendelssohn's time. Mozart in particular had a noted penchant for introducing new material into the development section of his instrumental forms, and several of Beethoven's works also feature this design, though in only a few notable examples is this fundamental to the course of the movement in question.[9] Most significant here is the first movement of the 'Eroica' Symphony. Here the famous new E minor theme enters from the debris of the movement's climax (b. 284),

---

[8]   The basic underpinning of sonata form is most apparent (see Kohlhase, 'Studien zur Form in den Streichquartetten von Felix Mendelssohn Bartholdy', p. 81); however, other commentators have also suggested elements of sonata rondo (Krummacher, *Mendelssohn – Der Komponist*, pp. 318–24), or even the idea of a sonata with second subject in the development section (Hans Keller, 'Mendelssohn's String Quartets', *The Listener*, 74/1895 (22 July 1965), 141, and 'The Classical Romantics', p. 200).

[9]   Examples in Mozart's music include the first movements of the 'Hunt' Quartet K. 458, Horn Concerto K. 495 and Piano Trio K. 502. Beethoven's use of new development-section material has been detailed by Bathia Churgin in 'Beethoven and the New Development Theme in Sonata-Form Movements', *Journal of Musicology*, 16 (1998), 323–43.

seemingly unconnected thematically yet strangely compelling in its appearance. This event, standing outside the immanent course of the music, is finally subsumed into the work in its reappearance in the coda, as the distant E minor tonality is resolved into the tonic E♭.[10]

This can be seen as another variant of the breakthrough idea discussed in relation to Op. 13. The significance of this new theme is that it disrupts the immanent logic of the music and the previous structural plan of the movement, whilst paradoxically seeming a natural outcome of the preceding music. It does not quite negate the integrity of the exposition and the contrasting opposition of first- and second-subject groups there, but does at least seem to suggest another level of musical discourse present in the work. With Mendelssohn this idea is taken up and extended further; indeed, in the present quartet and the 'Italian' Symphony, it is arguable that the generative opposition between first and second subjects is actually replaced by that between the exposition and the new development theme. In several of Mendelssohn's works the development section becomes a potential space where an external breakthrough event intrudes and thus breaks down the subsequent course of the movement. These intrusions can easily give the impression of another, separate aesthetic level, and thus strongly suggest some particular musical narrative or expressive meaning.[11]

The paralleling of this development breakthrough in the coda often further gives rise to the parallel formal design spoken of above, where the recapitulation and coda mirror the exposition and development. This is familiar from the Beethoven 'four-part model' of sonata form with its often extensive coda forming the so-called second development and resolution of any anomalous material, pertinently here such new development events.[12]

---

[10] The new theme's reappearance in the coda is initially in F minor, though subsequently moves for its second half to E♭ major. The theme had also been heard in E♭ minor in the closing stages of the development. As this example shows, though, the tonal resolution of extraneous musical events in a sonata movement is seldom as straightforward as some commentators would suggest. See particularly James Hepokoski, 'Beyond the Sonata Principle', *Journal of the American Musicological Society*, 55 (2002), 91–154, or, more generally, with regard to historical claims of harmonic versus thematic approaches, Bonds, *Wordless Rhetoric*.

[11] For instance, Thomas Grey has written perceptively of the breakthrough of the 'voice of nature' theme in the overture to *Die erste Walpurgisnacht* ('The Orchestral Music', in Douglass Seaton (ed.), *The Mendelssohn Companion* (Westport, CT and London: Greenwood Press, 2001), p. 502). Martin Witte has likewise considered the 'storm' section in the first movement of the Third Symphony an anomalous, external intrusion (Witte, 'Zur Programmgebundenheit der Sinfonien Mendelssohns', in Carl Dahlhaus (ed.), *Das Problem Mendelssohn* (Regensburg: Bosse, 1974), p. 124).

[12] See Robert G. Hopkins, 'When a Coda is More than a Coda: Reflections on Beethoven', in Eugene Narmour and Ruth Solie (eds.), *Explorations in Music, the Arts, and Ideas: Essays in Honor of Leonard B. Meyer* (Stuyvesant, NY: Pendragon Press, 1988), pp. 393–410.

In several of his works Mendelssohn extends this tendency into becoming what can be thought of as the underlying plan. As opposed to a binary (exposition / development-recapitulation) or three-part (exposition / development / recapitulation) structure, we are instead asked to hear the music working against a parallel two-strophe design, where each strophe is further divided in two (exposition–development / recapitulation–coda). Usually in this design the new development-space event is resolved or, if fleetingly suggested, fully revealed, in its coda reappearance. Examples include the overture to *Die erste Walpurgisnacht*, the finale of the First Symphony Op. 11, the first movements of the Piano Quartet Op. 3 and the Third and Fourth Symphonies Opp. 56 and 90, the Adagio of the E♭ Quartet Op. 44 No. 3, and the sonata / sonata-rondo designs of the finales of the two Piano Trios Opp. 49 and 66, where new 'redemptive' material in the development-space episode is finally brought into the home tonality and resolves the work's conflict.[13] The resolution of expositional material in the recapitulation is still present, but this is subsidiary in structural and emotional trajectory to that in the coda, which is heard as the culmination and telos of the movement.[14] In the present quartet, however, the reappearance of this F minor theme in the first-movement coda will not offer any harmonic or emotional resolution, and its impact will consequently be carried across the entire four-movement span of the quartet. It is thus to prove the defining cyclic element in this work.

The first movement takes its substance from the slow introduction, which serves as the thematic source of the work. Unlike several of Beethoven's later

[13] Krummacher notes the similarities of the E♭ Quartet's first movement with these sonata-rondo designs, which feature a short statement of the first subject as a refrain between the exposition and development and a cantabile new theme which returns in the coda (*Mendelssohn – Der Komponist*, p. 319). What, however, is crucially different about the present quartet is that the minor-key new theme is not tonally resolved in its coda reappearance, but unchanged. This is almost the inverse of the procedure in the two trios, where the major-key new theme, when brought back in the tonic, 'redeems' the surrounding minor-mode movement. A variation of this design is found in the finale to the 'Reformation' Symphony (1830), where the external introduction (Luther's chorale 'Ein' feste Burg ist unser Gott') is incorporated into the fabric of the main movement during the development, a structure similar to the first movement of the *Lobgesang* (1838–40).

[14] This structure was later taken up by Robert Schumann, who in several works from the mid-1830s onwards followed a similar parallel design with the coda mirroring the development, often with the recapitulation of new material introduced in that section, and in several cases strong parallels between the first movement and finale (e.g. the F♯ minor Piano Sonata Op. 11, *Presto passionate* Op. post (1835), *Concert sans orchestre* Op. 14, *Fantasie* in C, Op. 17, Symphony No. 4, String Quartet Op. 41 No. 3, and the Piano Quintet Op. 44 and Quartet Op. 47). See Linda Correll Roesner, 'Schumann's "Parallel" Forms', *19th-Century Music*, 14 (1991), 265–78.

works or Mendelssohn's previous quartet, it does not appear again, its function being to generate the material of the ensuing allegro. Both analytically and hermeneutically, it can be read as forming a gradual emergence of thematic substance from fragmentary beginnings, as if conjuring solid form out of the dim recesses of the unconscious.

The quartet materialises out of the *piano* E♭ chord of the *Adagio non troppo* introduction. This passage, in its fragmentary, hesitant phrases and unstable tonal direction, may potentially be read as a musical correlate of a process of recollection. The immediate turn to the subdominant through the tonic seventh has at any rate often been seen as alluding to the opening to Beethoven's 'Harp' Quartet Op. 74, another work in E♭ whose slow introduction recalls the *gestus* and topic of remembering.[15] More personal is the naked tritone in the first violin's melodic voice (g^1–d♭^{2}) which turns this opening (tonic) E♭ into a dominant seventh of its subdominant. Both this interval and the ambiguity between tonic and dominant functions will become important features in the work's design.

After a hesitant close back on the tonic and a fermata, the two motivic segments of these opening bars (*a* and *b*, Ex. 5.2) are repeated, now in a developed variation. (Both motives are actually related; indeed *b* can be thought of as a variant of *a*, common to both being a rising shape followed by stepwise movement down. The metric irregularity of these first three bars – b. 3 starting on an imperceptible second-quaver beat and seemingly compressed into one bar for *a*'s two – is also notable in contributing to the hesitant effect of this opening.) Motive *a* now traces an ascending perfect fifth then falls a semitone, c^2–g^2–f♯^{2}, still outlining the interval of a tritone, but in a shape that will become familiar from material later in the movement's development section. Even more significantly, the harmony and tonal direction is changed, moving this time in a Phrygian progression from a C minor $^6_3$ to the dominant of G minor, keys that will again reveal their significance later.

The repetition of segment *b* is now extended, imitative entries in successive instrumental voices bringing the music round through an implied cycle-of-fifths progression to the tonic E♭ (b. 9). The spare, linear,

---

[15] For instance A.B. Marx's account of Beethoven's quartet (and late quartets as a whole) reads the opening as an unfolding of memory (Marx, *Ludwig van Beethoven*, vol. II, p. 312). The initial move from I to IV by means of ♭$\hat{7}$ is in fact a characteristic of many E♭ major works: examples include the E♭ Prelude from Book I of Bach's *Das wohltemperierte Klavier* and the Fourth Cello Suite, Haydn's last Piano Sonata H. 52, Mozart's Piano Quartet K. 493, Beethoven's Trio Op. 1 No. 1, and later Schumann's Piano Quintet Op. 44. The c♯/d♭ in b. 7 of the *Eroica* can be thought of as a conscious playing with this schema.

Ex. 5.2 Quartet Op. 12, first movement: thematic derivation of introduction and exposition material.

chromatic writing of these bars and the slightly archaic contrapuntal tone could be thought of as imparting a sense of temporal and emotional distance, a searching quality to the music so far, as if summoning up something from the depths of memory. This is indeed an apt analogy for the musical process of this introduction, which through the gradual development of its opening motivic constituents grows from an initial short-breathed, fragmentary state into the beginnings of what will form the thematic material of the *Allegro non tardante*. This passage unfolds in texture and range; at bb. 7–9 a composite upper voice shared between the violins outlines the embryonic shape of the following allegro, extending the downward step of *a/b*'s appoggiatura into a scalic descent from $\hat{8}$ to $\hat{3}$ (see Ex. 5.2).

The exposition itself is a fine example of the organically evolving lyrical monothematicism characteristic of this composer. No truly new material is introduced, the music growing across this section in a manner that suggests a continual variation and motivic recombination of preceding themes.[16] The initial phrase draws its opening from motive *a*, combining this with the 8̂–3̂ descent that had materialised out of the development of this figure in bb. 8–9 (motive *a* having furthermore just been heard at the preceding cadence of the introduction, bb. 16–17). Its continuation (bb. 21–5) suggests a loose version of bb. 10–11, a connection that is confirmed in the extended consequent phrase (bb. 29–37), which echoes the introduction almost exactly. A transition section (bb. 37–58) offers a further variant of the first theme and at the same time prepares the second subject: its melodic diminution follows that introduced to the head of the consequent phrase (b. 27) and that of the quaver accompanimental figure of bb. 21 and 29 which was taken up by the upper voice in b. 33. The second subject (b. 59), while distinct from the first theme, nevertheless displays a clear family resemblance. Specifically, it derives from the diminution found in b. 39, and its continuation is a barely disguised further transformation of the corresponding bars of the first subject (compare bb. 63ff. with 22/30ff., motive *b*); thus it is the product of a continual process of variation and transformation carried across the exposition. Most fundamentally, however, the general descending contour and common rhythm ♩♩♩ | ♩♩♩♩ unmistakably resemble the first subject. Thus the contrast between the two themes is only minimal, and, after a subdominant-minor-inflected version of the second subject transfers this theme from starting on scale-degree 5̂ to degree 8̂, the reappearance at b. 86 of this first subject in the dominant to seal the exposition (taking up this b♭^{2} from b. 71) seems entirely natural.

This technique of continuous lyrical evolution is similar to that seen in Op. 6, and highly suitable for imparting the exposition's relaxed, melodious character. Here, though, there is something rather static about the overarching unity of this exposition; the second subject is not strongly differentiated from the first, and the section rather periphrastically ends up returning to the opening theme.[17] Despite the continual variation, nothing has really

---

[16] Both Donald Mintz and Friedhelm Krummacher call attention to the lack of motivic working and conventional development across this movement and their replacement by a variation procedure more suited to sustain the lied-like thematic substance. (See Mintz, 'The Sketches and Drafts for Three of Felix Mendelssohn's Major Works', pp. 129–33; Krummacher, *Mendelssohn – Der Komponist*, pp. 320–3.)

[17] Returning to a closely related version of the first subject at the close of a sonata exposition is also a common feature in many classical sonata forms, and widely enough used by

Ex. 5.3 Quartet Op. 12, first movement, new development theme.

happened; unlike the otherwise similarly lyrical A major Quintet, there is no opposing tendency which seems likely to generate any further musical argument.

The development section starts as if it were the exposition repeat, the music returning to the tonic with a statement of the first subject, a ploy that had been used before by both Haydn and Beethoven.[18] (The description of this movement as tending towards the sonata rondo would thus be technically accurate, but not relevant to the structure in the way the music is experienced. Since a repetition of the exposition is expected, the return to the first subject in the tonic following the close of the exposition will be heard as if a repeat is just starting; part of the peculiar expressive impact of this movement hinges on this misinterpretation of development section as repeated exposition.[19]) It soon becomes clear, though, that this 'repeat' is not quite proceeding as the exposition should do. The first subject's consequent phrase (b. 101) is slightly modified in harmony, the hint of C minor now more strongly suggested, as rhythmic movement slows and the music subsides through an imperfect cadence in F minor onto a sustained *pianissimo* dominant, C. From over this static harmony a new melodic idea appears in the second violin (Ex. 5.3).

There is a sense of otherness about this theme, which, although previously unheard, has the quality of memory to it. Partly this is due to the uneasy second inversion of the F minor chord, imparting a dream-like, suspended quality, the slowing of rhythm and *pianissimo* dynamic, and the theme's repetitive, undevelopmental nature, its harmony swinging between I_4^6 and

---

Mendelssohn in other instances. Here the effect is just more static than normal, due to the lack of internal tension and contrast.

[18] See the Sonata Hob. 51 and first 'Razumovsky' Quartet, Op. 59 No. 1. By Mendelssohn's standards, such a return without any transition would have been surprisingly unsubtle for a real exposition repeat.

[19] Krummacher's hypothetical division of the movement into a four-strophe sonata-rondo refrain/episode structure is thus an accurate reflection of the form as printed on the page or understood retrospectively (synchronically) but not of how the form is experienced in time (diachronically; *Mendelssohn – Der Komponist*, p. 319). Despite some of Beethoven's late quartets, and indeed Mendelssohn's Op. 13 (which, as the autograph shows, had the exposition repeat removed at a later stage), an exposition repeat would have been considered standard for the first movement of a quartet and a sonata-rondo design unusual.

V^7 without ever cadencing strongly to the implied tonic of F minor. What is further uncanny about the theme is that, while it is new and different from anything preceding it, there is yet something familiar about it. Time almost seems to stand still. The enigmatic nature of this theme's appearance, its uncertain provenance, and its anomalous position within the expected form imparts a sense of remoteness and mystery.

Though nonetheless related to those of the exposition, this F minor theme is the first really contrastive material in the quartet, differing from the earlier themes in thematic outline and, most importantly, mode. Hans Keller even calls it the second subject, which may seem rather paradoxical, were one not to remember that Mendelssohn had only a year before written another sonata-form movement with a second subject that undeniably does enter halfway through its development section, namely the scherzo of the A major Quintet Op. 18.[20]

In fact, Keller's interpretation is an extremely perceptive insight into the radically inverted structure of this movement. The exposition was notable for its absence of any strongly differentiated subject group, the second theme growing smoothly from the first, and the development started as though it were the exposition itself, returning to a statement of the first subject in the tonic as if feigning the expected exposition repeat. The appearance now of the first really contrastive material following the first subject in this erstwhile repeat of the exposition almost suggests we are listening to the real exposition, which has been covered over – 'repressed' – by the first. In terms of scale, for instance, the size of the development section surpasses that of the exposition by 84 bars to 76, an unusual feature for Mendelssohn, which suggests in itself a far greater importance placed on this section than normal. And from its opening, the development runs parallel to the exposition in several important respects, in a manner which suggests a recomposition or second rotation of this first section.

In thematic layout, the events of the development mirror those of the exposition: the new theme takes the place of the continuation of the first subject and transition, bb. 30 and 37, the two passages that are most closely related to it, and the subsequent reintroduction of the second subject (b. 123) and first-theme closing-statement (b. 131) follows the succession found in the exposition, reinforcing the suggested rotational thematic structure (Fig. 5.1).

---

[20] Keller, 'Mendelssohn's String Quartets', and 'The Classical Romantics', p. 200. For consideration of the Quintet, see Vitercik, *The Early Works of Felix Mendelssohn*, pp. 163–80.

Exposition

1	Tr	2	C
18	37	59	85 93

Development

1	New theme	2	1 / C	[further development]
94	106	123	131	176

Fig. 5.1 Quartet Op. 12, first movement: formal parallelism of exposition and development.

The harmonic sequence of this development rotation likewise parallels the exposition in several respects. The new F minor theme seems unable to close cadentially or develop, instead being restated in sequence up a tone in G minor before modulating further to A minor, where the music remains for the greater part of the section. This harmonic template parallels the transition of the exposition (the corresponding place in the thematic cycle), where a rising linear intervallic pattern moves from Eb through F minor to G minor and from there, via a diminished seventh on A, to V/V (bb. 45–58, Ex. 5.4). Here, the penultimate stage of the progression becomes massively prolonged, replacing the stable dominant secondary area Bb with the tritonally dissonant A minor.

The harmonic symbolism of the juxtaposition of Eb major with its antithesis A minor is unambiguous; such a polar opposition of harmony and mode suggests the furthest point of remove, a void.[21] No warning of this

[21] As noted, tritonal relationships are particularly prevalent in (and between) several of Mendelssohn's early works; this idea was returned to more radically in the G minor Piano Concerto Op. 25 (1832), where the exposition moves in minor thirds up from G minor, via a brief transitional statement of second-subject material in the normal secondary area of Bb, to an extended interpolated passage in Db. A potential source (again with notable hermeneutic implications) would have been Beethoven's 'Battle' Symphony (*Wellingtons Sieg*) Op. 91, in which the C major march symbolising the French army returns limping away in F♯ minor, in defeat. This work, despite its embarrassment for most modern listeners, was extremely popular in Beethoven's time and highly regarded by A.B. Marx, who published an account explicitly calling attention to this feature in 1825. Given the closeness of Marx's relationship with Mendelssohn during this period and the influence of the critic's views on music's programmatic content, it seems almost certain that Mendelssohn would have known of this feature and its hermeneutic potential.

Ex. 5.4 Quartet Op. 12, first movement: harmonic parallelism of exposition and development.

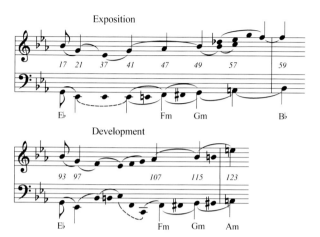

key had been given in the exposition, though the interval of the tritone had been set out right at the start of the quartet as the very first melodic event. Its careful outlining there thematicised this interval melodically, which is now paralleled at the higher level of the movement's harmony.

The entirety of the development section from the introduction of the new theme is in the minor mode, a remarkable change from the exposition, which apart from a few hints of the minor – the modulating sequence at bb. 45–54 in the transition, the touch of subdominant minor in bb. 71–4 – was relatively unclouded. The appearance of this new theme seems somehow to cast a shadow over the music: it disrupts the implied form of the movement, undermines the significance of the expositional material (specifically the generative contrast of first and second subject), and acts as the catalyst for a very extensive, anguished working-out of previous ideas as its unexpected arrival plunges the previously serene exposition material into the extremity of the tritonally distant A minor. In view of its unexpected intrusion, its quality of otherness or reminiscence, and the strife this new theme causes, it seems appropriate here to introduce the idea of trauma.

The term trauma stems from the Greek τραύμα (wound), which in psychoanalytical use can be defined as 'a psychic injury, especially one caused by emotional shock the memory of which is repressed and remains unhealed' or 'the state or condition so caused'.[22] In the lecture 'Fixation to Traumas – the Unconscious', Freud applies the term 'traumatic' to 'an experience which

---

[22] *Oxford English Dictionary*, 'trauma': 2.a, 'Psychoanalysis and Psychiatry'.

within a short period of time presents the mind with an increase of stimulus too powerful to be dealt with or worked off in the normal way', which results 'in permanent disturbances of the manner in which the energy operates'.[23] The excess psychical energy – for Freud, invariably negative – seeks to be discharged or 'abreacted'; only when the experience is too painful for the conscious mind to cope with is it involuntarily repressed into unconscious parts of the psyche, where this energy finds a way of discharging itself through neurotic symptoms. Patients suffering from traumatic symptoms appear to be fixated to a particular portion of the past, 'as though they could not manage to free themselves from it and were for that reason alienated from the present and the future'. This traumatic event is commonly repeated in dreams, a manner in which this excess energy may be 'cathected' (transferred to a different ideational object): in Freud's words, 'It is as though these patients had not finished with the traumatic situation, as though they were still faced by it as an immediate task which has not been dealt with.'[24]

The use of psychoanalysis has been established as a valid (if sometimes contentious) approach to understanding an artist's creative process, but in Mendelssohn's quartet the analogy might be taken further. Mendelssohn's work may be seen as tracing the process of the unconscious mind – Freud's 'primary process' – within itself, as an integral part of its structure. Such an approach – the correlation between the internal structure of a work of art and the psychological processes that may have contributed to its creation – is far less established. I would suggest, though, that if we wish to view a work of art, in Freudian terms, as the manifestation of the composer's 'primary process', it is not unreasonable further to assert the possibility of a connection between the work's structure and the structure or process of this psychological drive which created it.[25]

This is effectively taking up a project Hans Keller left unfinished, the illumination 'of the actual elements of musical structure and texture' by psychoanalysis.[26] In his writings on music and psychoanalysis, Keller

---

[23] Sigmund Freud, *Introductory Lectures on Psychoanalysis*, vol. I, *The Penguin Freud Library*, trans. James Strachey (Harmondsworth: Penguin, 1991), p. 315.

[24] *Ibid.*, pp. 313 and 315.

[25] For Freud, art, a creative manifestation of the primary (unconscious) process, is a sublimation of unsatisfied libido which can help the artist overcome a descent into neurosis (see, for instance, the *Introductory Lectures*, pp. 423–4). Such a view could easily fit with some aspects of the known biographical inspiration of Mendelssohn's quartet.

[26] Hans Keller, *Music and Psychology: From Vienna to London, 1939–52*, ed. Christopher Wintle (London: Plumbago Books, 2003), p. 197. The two principal works of Keller's here are 'Manifestations of the Primary Process in Musical Composition' (contained in the volume

examined the procedures typically found in the development section of sonata-form movements, using terms taken from Freud's *The Interpretation of Dreams* (specifically, displacement, condensation, and representation through the opposite) to describe the modification expositional material undergoes in the development. Keller believed that the development constituted a modification of the exposition's themes closely analogous to the process of dream-work (the operation of the mind during sleep, which transforms unconscious desires into the coded manifestation of dreams), arguing that the development's relation to the exposition equals 'in many respects the relation of manifest dream-content to latent dream thought'.[27] Implicitly, music, as artistic creativity, is allocated the function of dream-manifestation or phantasy, and the compositional process is viewed as a direct corollary of the primary process.

The E♭ Quartet's structure is being interpreted here primarily as a musical analogue of the psychological concept of trauma, but it is also possible to conjecture an autobiographical cause for such a parallel – the (probably unrequited) affair with Betty Pistor. As Hans Kohlhase has suggested, the new theme here in the quartet might conceivably be connected with the person for whom the work was written.[28] By the sublimation of the past into art, Mendelssohn might be seen in this work as engendering a critical distance between the ego and the inhibiting memory of the original experience, which enables him to move on; in Freud's words, the 'ego becomes free and uninhibited again'.[29] The extended use of A minor in the development section of this movement could even be read as referring back to the Op. 13 quartet. So far there had been no hint of the impassioned world of that work in the apparently sunny E♭ work, but the elusive memory of the F minor theme now pitches the quartet back into this seemingly suppressed time. If we are to take it that Op. 13 was inspired by the same love affair as Op. 12, then one could even go so far as to posit an autobiographical meaning to this sudden reversion.[30]

Music and Psychology) and 'Dream-Work and Development in Sonata Form' (unpublished draft MS, Cambridge University Library, n.d.). Both papers, incomplete drafts from the late 1940s and extremely similar, deal with the procedures typically found in the development section of sonata-form movements.

[27] Keller, 'Dream-Work and Development in Sonata Form', p. 4.
[28] Kohlhase, 'Studien zur Form in den Streichquartetten von Felix Mendelssohn Bartholdy', p. 80.
[29] Freud, 'Mourning and Melancholia', in *Metapsychology: The Theory of Psychoanalysis*, vol. XI, *The Penguin Freud Library*, p. 253.
[30] In this case, however, one need not argue that the underlying trauma has to relate only to one specific instance in Mendelssohn's life: the event which causes the symptoms to appear need not be the original trauma. As Freud and Breuer were to argue, hysteria and traumatic neuroses are seldom caused by one experience, but rather by several which accumulate; they are, in

Ex. 5.5 Quartet Op. 12, first movement: modulation preceding new theme, bb. 101–5, and hypothetical rewriting.

Modulation from E♭ to V / Fm

Hypothetical resolution to V / Cm

It is questionable whether the F minor theme, on its first appearance, constitutes a memory. I would contend that this theme has the quality of emotional and temporal distance to it even at its first appearance, alongside an uneasy impression of familiarity, which gives it the flavour of reminiscence.[31] But certainly when the same theme appears again in the coda of the movement, and further, twice in the finale, undeveloped and almost unchanged, it is hard not to hear it now as a memory of the past, if only a musical past.

The new theme enters, as we have seen, from a static prolonged dominant of F minor (bb. 105–6). (The subsidence of the first subject into the haze of this texture may suggest an opening to the emergence of memory, similar to the blurred diminished-seventh sonorities in the Op. 6 Sonata.) This harmony is in fact a surprise deflection from what might have been expected to be C minor: the F minor chord of b. 104 would easily (and more usually) resolve up to G at b. 105, tracing a iv–V imperfect cadence in C minor (Ex. 5.5). This tonality, as the relative minor, would indeed be a more conventional key for a subsidiary passage in an E♭ work, one which moreover has not hitherto featured in the exposition, and its substitution here raises the question as to why it seems to have been averted.

Freud's noted phrase, 'overdetermined' (*überdeterminiert*; see Josef Breuer and Sigmund Freud, *Studies on Hysteria*, vol. III, *The Penguin Freud Library*, pp. 245–6 and 289). Accordingly, an unhappy love affair in 1829 could easily have awoken memories of a similar experience two years earlier. The composer's later inability to complete an opera following the public failure of *Die Hochzeit des Camacho* in 1827 would be a perfect example of such behaviour.

[31] Perhaps coincidentally, the new F minor theme echoes the opening of Mendelssohn's own Piano Quartet in that key, Op. 2, written six years earlier (see Chapter 1, Ex. 1.2).

Though the new theme has been described as being in F minor, it is in truth poised on an unstable first inversion of that key, emphasising this 'missing' C in the bass. While F minor is always implied, only once does the $^6_4$ support resolve up to the tonic root (b. 111), and this is with a $\hat{5}$ in the melodic voice, forming the start of a modulation up a tone to G minor. The possibility suggests itself that in fact the passage is not in F minor at all, but rather the Fm $^6_4$ is just a $^{\flat 6}_4$ suspension above a C (major) tonic.[32] The ambiguity is left open here; indeed, since the following statement of the theme in sequence is now in G minor but with the root of the tonic provided (bb. 115ff.), the reading of the previous passage as F minor becomes more probable – but the question remains as to how many times this harmony will have to be heard before we start hearing it as iv$^6_4$–I instead of I$^6_4$–V, in C rather than in F minor.[33] Indeed, in this ambiguous relationship between tonic and dominant, the very opening bars of the quartet are brought back, the tonic seventh moving to the subdominant, I^7–IV heard effectively as V^7–I in A♭.

The theme itself has the appearance of unreality or distance, stemming not only from its enigmatic presence here. Besides the tonal uncertainty and suspended $^6_4$ harmony, a certain fixated quality is imparted by the repetition of the same two-bar motive which, rather than being developed, is merely sequenced up a tone at the end of the inconclusive eight-bar phrase, where it repeats itself. Repetition without development threatens to stop the ongoing experience of time in the movement; rather than a telos-driven progression through time, such reiteration results in a static (fatalistic?) circularity that Freud would find reminiscent of dream-states. A further feature of the theme's presentation is its spatial distancing at its original appearance. The first violin, normally the primary musical voice in the quartet, is here silent, while the new theme emerges mysteriously in the other three instruments. The sense of otherness engendered here connects the passage all the more strongly to the sense of an external voice, distinct and distanced from the consciousness of the present and emanating from the unconscious memory of the past.

---

[32] Since the dominant resolution of the $^6_4$ is here a seventh (C^7, b. 106), F minor is clearly implied, but this still does not mitigate against hearing this tonic as under-defined and therefore potentially chimerical.

[33] This ambiguity between C and F minor in Mendelssohn's quartet exhibits an intriguing parallel with the dualistic tonal systems of nineteenth-century theorists such as Moritz Hauptmann (later a colleague of Mendelssohn in Leipzig) and Hugo Riemann, in which minor triads are considered inversions of major triads. While the root of C major is therefore C, C is also considered the root of F minor, which, in opposition to a major triad, is built downwards.

Ex. 5.6 Quartet Op. 12, first movement: thematic affinities between successive themes in development section.

What is also uncanny about this theme is the sense in which it is new, but yet somehow already familiar. In fact, just as the development section presented a darkened mirror of the exposition, so the new theme forms the shadowy double of those of the exposition. This connection is fully revealed in the central section of the movement. After the statement on G minor, the new theme moves up to a diminished seventh functioning as V of A minor, as if about to repeat itself again in sequence (b. 122). Now, however, rather than hearing a further statement of this development theme, the melodic line turns into the second subject, which we now realise is very similar to this new theme. After eight bars, the first subject in turn replaces the second, taking up and intensifying the imitative, canonic texture characteristic of the latter. All three themes, by their juxtaposition, are shown to be related; common to each is the ♩♪♪ rhythm and descending contour (Ex. 5.6). The relationship is not organically composed-out, the music growing from one theme into the next in continuous motivic development, but the three are merely placed next to one another, disparate entities whose connection is wholly intentional.

Though, as Krummacher remarks, all three themes are shown to be closely related, in terms of tonality, mode and affective content, the passage is starkly uncompromising.[34] Rather than imparting a unity to the music, this connection darkens the perception of the previously contented major-key exposition material. The two seem to come from a common source. This is perhaps the root of the music's 'trauma': the new development theme is nothing other than the *unheimlich* side of the *heimlich* exposition.

For Freud, 'the uncanny is that class of the frightening which leads back to what is known of old and long familiar'.[35] In his famous essay *Das Unheimliche* of 1919, Freud investigates the ambiguous relation manifested

---

[34] Krummacher, *Mendelssohn – Der Komponist*, pp. 320–2. For Krummacher, this passage forms the dynamic culmination of the movement, the similarity between the themes' head-motives demonstrating how all three are variations of the same fundamental idea.

[35] Sigmund Freud, 'The Uncanny', in *Art and Literature*, vol. XIV, *The Penguin Freud Library*, p. 340.

in language between the familiar and the frightening. In German, *heimlich* can mean both 'homely, cosy, comfortable and familiar', yet also 'secret, concealed, or hidden away'. The *unheimlich* is the uncanny, eerie, uneasy, uncomfortable, used often in conjunction with words denoting fear, terror and the supernatural; that which Schelling had previously described as everything 'that ought to have remained secret and hidden but has come to light'.[36] The *unheimlich* is only antithetical to the first definition of *heimlich*: the word *heimlich* is therefore 'not unambiguous'. *Heimlich*, as it begins to signify the secret, the hidden, and therefore dangerous, thus becomes increasingly ambivalent, until it finally coincides with its opposite, *unheimlich*.[37] In Freud, the uncanny is the flip side of the homely and familiar, related back to traumatic childhood experiences that lurk half-repressed in the preconscious realm of the mind, as exemplified in E.T.A. Hoffmann's story *The Sandman*. The uncanny is therefore the frightening element of that which has been repressed and now reappears – the returning past.[38]

Here in Mendelssohn's quartet, the new F minor theme reveals itself as the dark twin of the E♭ major exposition. The 'trauma' of the development, repressed from the consciousness of the work, is merely the flipside of the *heimlich* exposition, as the apparently cheerful exposition material finds a ghostly double, its *Doppelgänger*, in this new theme.[39] In effect, Mendelssohn presents us with two expositions – a light, lyrical, predominantly relaxed one, and the darker, minor-coloured, agonised one which unfolds here. Such a structure fundamentally splits the shell of the sonata template down the middle. Rather than the generative process of the music arising out of the contrast of first and second subjects internal to the exposition, here it is between the exposition and development sections, a relationship which will have to be worked out at the larger level of the recapitulation and coda, and, even further, at the broadest level across the whole work. In this, the E♭ quartet is the inverse of the A minor, where the polarity is between the 'external' introduction and subsequent first movement. Such designs, beyond their radical deformation of accepted form, are here the motivation for the cyclic processes of their works. The minor-key angst of the finale and the return of this new development theme within that movement are merely the final consequences of this bipolar split in the music, which originated back in the first movement.

---

[36] Quoted by Freud, 'The Uncanny', p. 345.   [37] *Ibid.*, pp. 345 and 347.   [38] *Ibid.*, pp. 363–4.
[39] Similar to the story of Heine's spurned lover in his poem of that name; Schubert had composed his famous setting of Heine's poem only a year before Mendelssohn's quartet.

The relationship of E♭ to its relative C minor (and the F minor theme associated with the later) takes further this idea of bipolarity. The complementarity of the tonic and relative minor will, as we shall see, become notable throughout the quartet, C minor commonly used as a substitute or replacement for its relative E♭. Similarly, in a manner typical of much Romantic music, the major and minor modes of the same tonic can be thought of as near-equivalents. As suggested above, the F minor $^6_4$ of the new development theme can in fact be viewed alternatively as a suspension above a C major tonic, which substitutes for the more normal C minor tonality suggested by the previous bars. Not only then are the themes of the exposition and the new development theme related to one another like the two sides of a coin, but so are the key areas associated with the two, mirroring the emotional–psychological bipolarity running throughout the work.[40] This feature will become increasingly fundamental in the piece later, reaching a climax in the finale, which, instead of the expected E♭, enters in C minor and grows from the material of the first-movement development theme.

Much of this tonal ambivalence stems from the unstable grounding of the exposition in the join between introduction and exposition. The return to the tonic at b. 10 of the introduction had been deflected to ii, prolonging the drive to a full cadence over the next few bars. A pre-cadential I$^6_3$ in b. 15 seems finally to be leading the harmony round to an imperfect cadence in preparation for the start of the allegro (IV–ii$^{8-7}$–V$^{(7)}$). However, on the last chord of this sequence the bass line stays fixed to the F of the preceding ii, thus ending the introduction with an unstable-sounding V$^4_3$. This harmonic anomaly, while not outlandish, is nevertheless disconcerting. Harmonically it is slightly 'wrong', being neither a cadential tonic $^6_4$ nor passing by step to the ensuing opening of the allegro, and the effect is of a delayed cello voice which does not resolve as expected to the dominant B♭.[41] The resolution

[40] Psychological bipolarity, the notion of the psyche being split by two opposing tendencies – the un- or preconscious and the conscious, the id and the ego or id and superego – is an important part of Freud's thinking. See, for instance, *Introductory Lectures on Psychoanalysis*, p. 342, or 'Beyond the Pleasure Principle'. In this context, it might be useful to think of this work's background structure not as mono-tonal, governed by a single tonic (as Schenker would have it), but dual-tonal (after the manner of Robert Bailey), formed out of a complex of tonic and relative where the latter forms a secondary centre.

[41] This particular passage has affinities to an idea heard near the end of *An die ferne Geliebte* for the words 'ein liebend Herz geweiht' (song no. 6, bb. 71–2), heard again in E♭ though resolving more conventionally in Beethoven's work from V$^4_2$ to I$^6_3$. It seems at any rate to have been echoed by Schumann in the first movement of his *Fantasie*, bb. 79–81, the allusion particularly apparent when the same section is repeated in E♭ near the end of the movement at the same pitch (c^2–f^2–e♭^{2}–d^2, bb. 261–3). Here Schumann 'resolves' the bass F, but only to a further dissonance, a diminished seventh. For both composers the typically 'Romantic' unresolved

of this dominant second-inversion at the opening of the allegro is then undercut by the use of another unexpected inversion – V^4_3 moving to I^6_3 – and subsequently by an interrupted move to the submediant supporting the downbeat tonic E♭ in the melody.[42] Something seems to be rather strange about the harmonic underpinning of this movement. Vitercik has suggested that

> The bass-line motion over the join between the introduction and the Allegro non tardante suggests a iv–V–I progression in C minor that reinforces this submediant turn by gently playing it against the sense of the progression as V–I–vi in E♭ major.... There is a friction between the bass line as implied root-motion and the chord grammar of the passage that blurs the harmonic sense in these first moments of the theme, giving a delicate emphasis to the submediant tinge that colours its opening measures.[43]

While the prominent B♭ upbeat in the melody would deny the possibility of actually hearing this opening as in C minor, Mendelssohn is nonetheless offsetting any clear definition of the home tonality. Historically this harks back to the join between maestoso and allegro at the start of Beethoven's other E♭ quartet, Op. 127, where the two passages are connected by a subdominant chord which bridges the two, giving rise to a notable absence of structural dominants across the work. In this quartet Mendelssohn is similarly expanding the functional language of tonality, moving fluidly to relative minor and subdominant areas as tonic substitutes in a manner that was to become a feature of early Romantic music.[44]

The opposition between E♭ tonic and C minor areas, as heard in the first five bars of the quartet and again here, will become one of the primary generative motives of the work. Essentially, the harmonic irregularity here undercuts the foundation for the allegro exposition. While its opening theme clearly derives from the preceding adagio, its harmonic support is slightly insecure. The exposition's lack of strong harmonic foundation, E♭ undercut by its relative C minor, displays the unsure grounding of its erstwhile happiness.

The return to the recapitulation is also a remarkable conception. Startlingly, the first subject is now underpinned by a root position tonic

---

appoggiatura-figure must surely have held connotations of romantic yearning or unresolved desire, as it did later with Wagner, Bruckner or Mahler.

[42] The discontinuity here is further apparent in the disjunct cello line across the join (F–g–c¹, bb. 17–18).

[43] Vitercik, *The Early Works of Felix Mendelssohn*, p. 272.

[44] This feature of early Romantic music has been discussed by Rosen in *The Romantic Generation* (see especially pp. 342–4) and in William Kinderman and Harald Krebs (eds.), *The Second Practice of Nineteenth-Century Tonality* (Lincoln, NE: University of Nebraska Press, 1996).

triad – the most normal harmony imaginable, for the first (and only) time in the work. How Mendelssohn manages to make this root position tonic sound so extraordinary is particularly noteworthy. Charles Rosen has suggested that

> Mendelssohn here manipulates the most traditional elements of Classical form to achieve a deeply unclassical effect. The cadence on V of vi is traditional, and so is the device of surrounding a tonic (E flat) by the mediants (C and G) balancing each other .... Ending with a half cadence drained of all force on the leading tone, D, and then raising the pitch gently and unobtrusively a modest half step to E flat is Mendelssohn's own contribution and resembles nothing he could have heard .... there is no suggestion of a dominant in the six bars marked pianissimo preceding the theme.[45]

The retransition is not a modulation but the harmony just slips back from a D major chord, via a sustained b♭ and g, to settle on an E♭ chord, which with apparent surprise is the right harmony for the return of the main theme, which tentatively starts under tempo as if it can hardly believe the illusion of its reappearance. Though, as Rosen notes, 'since the theme is harmonised for the first time here with the tonic in the bass, it gains a quiet stability that it never had until this moment',[46] the lack of any dominant preparation and therefore true modulation cannot but make this re-entry of the exposition material appear slightly unreal. The start of the exposition was destabilised by the underpinning non-tonic harmony; astonishingly the stable root-position tonic in the recapitulation now is heard as illusory, plucked out of the air, simply due to its lack of preparation. Reversing the sequence of the exposition, the previously stable cadence to the root-position tonic in the fourth bar of the theme is now interrupted by being deflected to the submediant.[47]

The familiar is defamiliarised. The homecoming to the tonic – and the tonic major triad itself – is made to sound unhomely.[48] The recapitulation

---

[45] Rosen, *The Romantic Generation*, pp. 583–4.   [46] *Ibid.*, p. 584.

[47] See Mathias Thomas, *Das Instrumentalwerk Felix Mendelssohn-Bartholdys*, pp. 158–9. As Vitercik has noted, the harmonisation of the opening bars of this first subject is never quite the same any two times in the movement, the recall of this theme being continually reinterpreted (*The Early Works of Felix Mendelssohn*, p. 273). This is similar to the use made of a primary theme in a rondo-type structure (leading credence to the view of this movement as displaying affinities to such forms). The idea of the rondo – the continual returning to earlier ideas, which several commentators read into the structure of this movement – can be viewed as a further manifestation of this 'compulsion to repeat' in the movement.

[48] The recapitulation of Schubert's Sonata D. 960 has been read in similar fashion by Nicholas Marston in 'Schubert's Homecoming', *Journal of the Royal Music Association*, 125 (2000), 248–70.

proceeds as if the events of the development had never happened, but the lack of foundation points to this fragile self-illusion. The development, the trauma emanating from the unanticipated appearance of the F minor theme, is forcibly repressed by the ego in an attempt to maintain at least some semblance of order, but this order, conforming to generic expectation, is imposed from without.

In accordance with most standard theories of sonata form, the recapitulation fulfils its obligatory purpose, the second subject being resolved to the tonic. This recapitulation is heavily abridged, on the continuation of the first subject's consequent phrase the first violin continuing straight into the start of the second subject (b. 194), thus eliding the music over the transition material. Since in the exposition the transition had grown into the second subject, this replacement underscores the commonality of the material of the exposition, the second subject substituting for the transition material from which it had grown. In the development rotation this material had already been replaced in the thematic cycle by the new theme. Thus this passage had merely been functional in its initial mediating between first and second subjects, and having no further use in the movement is consequently discarded.

As we have seen from this movement, though, the events of the exposition are less important than the conflict between exposition and development, the exposition's second subject and dominant tonality subordinated to that of the F minor development theme. Conventional twentieth-century accounts of sonata form determine that any non-tonic material introduced before the movement's recapitulation needs to be resolved tonally by its restatement and harmonic grounding in the recapitulation or, more usually if introduced in the development section, the coda – the so-called sonata principle.[49] Correspondingly we may be expecting a return to the development theme, but heard now in the tonic, either E♭ minor or fully transformed to the tonic major, thus grounding the anomalous theme tonally and resolving the conflict of the movement. Instead, we are presented with the recall of the new theme in F minor again, with no sense of resolution projected.

After an extension of the second subject material, the recapitulation prolongs the climactic anticipation of the closing first theme for five bars, picking out the three-note descent familiar from the development theme (bb. 222–4). The closing statement of the first theme subsides, continuing its melodic descent, touching on the subdominant (b. 230) and then

---

[49] See Hepokoski, 'Beyond the Sonata Principle', 100ff.

F minor (b. 231), returning more insistently (b. 233). This transition from recapitulation to coda now echoes more clearly than ever the introduction to the movement (bb. 10–13), moving chromatically, via a German sixth, to a V_4^6 of F minor, and the reappearance of the development theme, as before. This relapse into the introduction reveals how this passage had effectively given birth to the F minor theme, just as it had to the exposition; the *heimlich* and the uncanny arise from the same source.

No resolution is offered to the F minor theme (though the marking *tranquillo* might suggest a more reflective aspect or sense of distance); the eight-bar phrase makes as if to modulate up to G minor, but its last two bars are repeated, then again in augmentation, stretching out the rising fifth / semitone descent of motive *a*. Just as in the coda of the E major Sonata, this motivic link connects up to the reappearance of the first subject, which, in its halcyon lyricism, peacefully brings the movement to its close. The two opposing themes are placed side by side; the latter grows out of the end of the former, but there is no resolution.[50] The enigmatic question of the new development theme, its meaning and tonality, are left unresolved.

There is correspondingly a strong sense of uncertainty to this coda, amidst the serenity. At its reappearance, the development theme still refuses to offer any satisfactory reconciliation. The import of the F minor theme will have to be carried, across the larger level of the work, to the later movements. Thus this opening movement's highly expressive structural deformation will operate as the cyclic principle across the quartet.

Later movements

For this quartet, the usual position of scherzo and slow movement is inverted, an intermezzo-like canzonetta preceding the Andante espressivo third movement, which, by its *attacca* close, serves as a large-scale upbeat to the fourth. The last two movements together thus create what is effectively a composite, run-on finale.

[50] Greg Vitercik reads the harmonic reinterpretation of the opening of the first subject, the underpinning of the downbeat e♭ (b. 259) with a $C_{♭3}^4$, as resolving the F minor tonality of the anomalous development theme that precedes it (*The Early Works of Felix Mendelssohn*, p. 276). (Since it is a second-inversion F chord, if now a seventh with a raised third, it is possible that Mendelssohn is referring back to this characteristic sonority.) It is hard, though, to see how a minim second inversion of an F_5^7 chord here (which is only a neighbour harmony between the B♭$_4^6$ upbeat and B♭$_3^5$ of b. 259$^{3-4}$) supporting the first subject could in any sense resolve the entirely separate F minor theme, let alone contribute to a perceptible impression of such resolution.

Ex. 5.7 Quartet Op. 12, second movement, canzonetta and trio.

The canzonetta fulfils the function of an interlude within the design of the quartet, similar in function to the intermezzo of Op. 13. While this movement is an example of the composer at his most easy-going and charming (or *heimlich*), this does not disguise a certain nostalgic, backward-looking quality, as its title perhaps implies.[51] Its wistfully tinged G minor has sometimes been read as conjuring up the Italy of Goethe's Mignon, 'wo die Zitronen blühn', the memory of lost childhood and happiness;[52] certainly, there is something regretful about its dreaming. Although the thematic connection between the outer section and the rest of the work is only slight, the trio, is closer to the rising-fourth / descending-sixth $\hat{5}$–$\hat{8}$ / $\hat{8}$–$\hat{3}$ outline of the first-movement introduction (motive *a′*) and first subject, and even closer to the brief B♭ major second-group theme of the finale (b. 64, Ex. 5.7).

The Andante espressivo third movement, meanwhile, is an example of the inward, *ausdrucksvoll* slow movement Mendelssohn took up from late Beethoven. Its cantabile melodic line in the opening section and more discontinuous, recitative-like outbursts hail back to the elder composer's cavatina from Op. 130, as does the lyrical transformation of the second group at b. 39 to the *Grosse Fuge*.[53] This *espressivo* style is exemplified in the rather free, non-schematic approach to form. An outline of A B A′ B′ [A″] can be distinguished underneath the fluid surface, corresponding harmonically to an abridged (slow-movement) sonata, with the more fragmentary B section moving at its end to the dominant. At its return, though, this second section

---

[51] As Donald Mintz describes the second movement of Op. 44 No. 1, 'This is not a minuet, it is a recollection of a minuet, a recollection of times past and times lost' ('The Sketches and Drafts for Three of Felix Mendelssohn's Major Works', p. 13).

[52] Goethe, *Wilhelm Meisters Lehrjahre*, opening of bk III (*Poetische Werke*, vol. VII, p. 91).

[53] Apropos of Op. 130, only a year before Mendelssohn had written to Adolf Lindblad 'Do you know [Beethoven's] recent Quartet in B♭ major? ... there is a *Cavatina* in E♭ in which the first violin sings throughout, and the world sings with it.' Dahlgren, *Bref till Adolf Fredrik Lindblad från Mendelssohn*, pp. 19–20.

Ex. 5.8 Quartet Op. 12, third movement, opening.

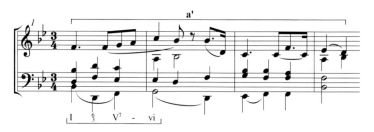

Ex. 5.9 Quartet Op. 12, third movement, B section and subsequent transformation.

is developed almost beyond recognition, subject to a process of continuous growth across the movement.

The first A section is the only closed section in the movement, its twelve bars forming a self-contained lyrical phrase. Starting with a transformation of the introduction / exposition material of the first movement (corresponding in thematic outline $\hat{5}$–$\hat{8}$–$\hat{3}$, and exhibiting the same interrupted harmonisation of $\hat{8}$ with vi, Ex. 5.8), the melodic line seems to imply an expansive period with a passing cadence to ii (C minor, b. 8), but closes slightly perfunctorily with the return of the head motive, reinterpreted to supply the end cadence and rounding off the phrase as it had started (bb. 11–12).

The B section is more discontinuous in both material and texture. Its opening reverts to the G minor of the second movement, though it almost immediately departs from this key, typifying this section's harmonic instability – and stresses thematically the $\hat{3}$–$\hat{2}$–$\hat{1}$ descent familiar from the first movement's development theme. This characteristic motive is successively extended into a scalic falling fifth, which is later taken up in this section's recapitulation (B′, b. 45, preceded by a further rhythmic diminution, bb. 34–41, Ex. 5.9).

Both appearances lead to the disintegration of the music into recitative-like passages which recall almost explicitly the climax of the first-movement development section (b. 156). The contrast between the A section's major tonality, continuous lyrical line and ascending scalic movement on the one hand, and this passage on the other, recalls that between the exposition and new development theme, a parallel which is strengthened by the links of each to the first movement. This reversion into recitative suggests an urgency to communicate, an imploring for an answer, such that the rational discourse of the music is broken by this overwhelming need to speak. Both times the request seems to go without eliciting a response, the concluding three-note ascent being separated off, from which the music grows back into the reprise of the A section (bb. 23–9; 54–7).

The second appearance of A is not separated from the following B section but subtly merged, the music evolving into a passage that seems new but which in fact forms a further development of the B material. The opening section had moved via V^6_3/ii to a cadence on ii (C minor, bb. 7–8). At its reappearance, the same G^6_3 chord breaks in a beat earlier (b. 34), offering a mild disturbance (proleptic, as it will prove, of the start of the finale), but this chord is now sustained and leads seamlessly into an eloquent new variant of the second-group material. The subtle blurring of formal outline here, the new section's intricate rhythmic interplay, and the continuous thematic evolution, results in an extended section that seems, rather than being a recapitulation of the second group, as forming the culmination of the movement.

This final balm of the opening theme in the coda is strangely unsatisfying. Both times the music of the recitative passages has managed to find its way back to the more placid lyricism of the opening theme, but in neither does the question posed by the recitative really seem to have been answered. Mirroring the modulation from dominant back to tonic at the retransition (bb. 25–9), the music now vacillates between the movement's tonic B♭ and subdominant E♭, ending on an imperfect-sounding cadence on B♭ with 5̂ in the treble, as if anticipating an imminent return to the quartet's home tonality of E♭ in the finale. Effectively, the Andante is heard functioning as a slow introduction to the finale, a large-scale dominant, which will lead on without break.

Contrary to all expectations, however, the finale bursts in, *attacca*, with strident G chords, functioning as V / C minor. The surprise is almost complete, though by now we should be starting to realise that such interruptions are becoming a structural principle of the quartet. In fact, the interruption of a B♭ dominant by V / C minor recalls just that between the first movement's slow introduction and allegro exposition, the third movement and finale mirroring these two sections at a larger structural level. What was just an understated hint of submediant colour there, though, has now materialised into the true tonality of the ensuing movement. This same G dominant chord is familiar from the preceding movement, where it twice interrupted the course of the first theme. Its intrusion here, following the return of the first theme in the third movement's coda, consequently directly parallels its previous appearances. The opening of the finale in C minor may be a shock, but nevertheless it is one that has, if obliquely, been forewarned.

The main body of the finale – a sonata-form structure over two-thirds of the total length of the movement – is in this 'wrong' key of C minor. The appearance of a minor-key movement characterised by such agitated passion within a work as ostensibly serene in its lyricism as this quartet is a surprise, though the unresolved presence of the new theme in the first movement, the darkness of that movement's development section, and the still-unresolved issue of the andante's recitatives point to the fragile foundation of that beguiling lyricism. Earlier, the conflict between the light and dark sides of the music's experience had managed largely to repress the latter, though at times their memory – the F minor theme – broke through. Like psychological trauma, the memory of the experience remains deep down at some subconscious level, however, and recurs without warning, shattering the harmony of the present.

The very existence of an extended sonata-form movement in C minor as the finale of a quartet whose home tonality is E♭ drastically upsets the expected structure of the work. The movement 'should' be in E♭, and the finale will correspondingly have to find its way round to that key if the work is to find any resolution.[54] This change in the fate of the work is in

---

[54] This structure proved quite popular later in the nineteenth century; the idea of an off-tonic minor key opening to a finale to an ostensibly major-key work is followed in later pieces such as Brahms' Third Symphony (also deriving its cyclic close from this quartet of Mendelssohn's), several of Bruckner's symphonies, and Mahler's and Elgar's First Symphonies.

An interesting parallel with this structure can be found in settings of the Roman Catholic mass, where the final movement, the Agnus Dei, sometimes started in the relative minor of the work's overall tonic, moving to the security of the home tonic only for the final Dona nobis pacem (the most imposing example would be Beethoven's *Missa Solemnis*, which charts a progression from B minor to D major). What makes this analogy especially noteworthy is the tradition in Austrian mass settings for the return to the home tonic and the end of the Agnus Dei to be fused simultaneously with a recall of the opening material of the entire mass, imparting a cyclic frame to the work mirrored almost precisely in Mendelssohn's quartet (the final E♭ section here consists largely of a recall of the first movement). Beethoven's Mass in C is a clear example of this cyclic tendency; other instances include Haydn's *Nikolaimesse*, Mozart's 'Coronation' Mass K. 317, and Diabelli's 'Pastoral' Mass. Though Mendelssohn was a Lutheran, he knew and respected the Catholic church music of the past; the possibility of some allusion here is intriguing. A religious reading of this work might speculate here as to how far the C minor Molto allegro could constitute Mendelssohn's *miserere nobis* and the final return to the security of the first movement a plea for peace with the past, not triumphant but pious.

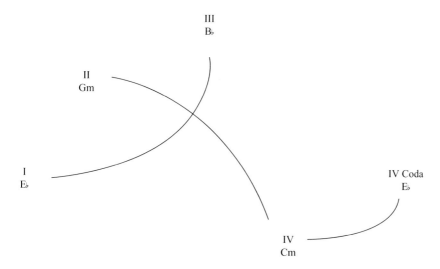

Fig. 5.2 Quartet Op. 12: chiastic tonal design of work.

fact nothing other than the largest-scale manifestation of the polar Eb/Cm opposition that has run through this quartet from the introduction onwards. The dual key structure of the quartet is now seen reflected in the tonalities of the separate movements, the two complementary poles of Eb and C minor setting up their own dominants in the inner movements (G minor, II, and Bb major, III), an interlocking or chiastic design where movement I relates to III and movement II to IV (Fig. 5.2).

This conflict is even reflected in the harmonic structure of the finale's exposition, which, although charting a large-scale move from C minor to the dominant minor G as the secondary tonal area, incorporates brief passages of Eb and Bb major interpolated within each tonal group, as if residues of the 'proper' course of events.[55] Associated with this tonal duality was the opposition between the enigmatic new development theme and the exposition. The C minor tonality of the finale alludes to the ambiguity surrounding the establishment of the first-movement exposition, as Vitercik indeed suggests,[56] but further and more importantly, it relates to the still unresolved development theme.

This C minor movement forms the full realisation and working-out of the F minor theme which disrupted the course of the opening movement. On its

---

[55] As Greg Vitercik has suggested, it almost seems as if Mendelssohn has written 'a double exposition, establishing both C minor and Eb major in the first group, and both G minor (the dominant key of C minor) and Bb major (the dominant of Eb major) in the second.' *The Early Works of Felix Mendelssohn*, p. 279.

[56] *Ibid.*, pp. 279 and 290.

Ex. 5.10 Quartet Op. 12, finale, exposition: thematic metamorphoses of development-theme material.

appearance in that movement, the theme markedly was never developed or modified, seemingly existing in an autonomous, intangible space, its presence, like the memory of a past event, remaining fixed and unchangeable. Almost the entire material for this movement – again largely monothematic, with a proliferation of variants of the opening material – derives clearly from the new F minor theme, as opposed to that of the rest of the quartet, which stems mainly from the contrasting exposition material (Ex. 5.10).

The opening theme picks up the $\hat{5}$–$\hat{3}$–$\hat{2}$–$\hat{1}$ motive of the development's new theme. Though rhythmically related to the other material of the first-movement exposition, that theme had nevertheless remained distinct in its diastematic contour, outlining the sixth from $\hat{5}$ to $\hat{3}$. What was heard there over an uncertain F minor dominant is, however, now unmistakably in C minor. (Aspects of this material – the descending scalic tarantella-like figures found here and in the introduction – also mark a further derivation of material from the third movement (see especially b. 34), which had seemed to allude to this first-movement 'trauma' theme at its outset (bb. 13–14).) This opening theme is successively transformed across the exposition, the tarantella style of the movement being particularly suited to

such a proliferation of related ideas. One theme, the momentary B♭ interpolation (Ex. 5.10e), may appear slightly extraneous alongside the other
variants, though aspects of it are prepared by the second group's first theme
(Ex. 5.10c).

The relationship of this movement to the 'trauma' theme is made explicit
by the reappearance of this F minor theme in an episode that occupies the
development space of the movement (bb. 106–19). After the exposition has
concluded in G minor, hollow octave Cs again pre-empt the materialisation
of this theme, once more perched unstably above the F minor $^6_4$ chord.
(The move to the subdominant for the development is again unusual,
though one could note that the reversion to the pitch C at the end of the
exposition might seem to imply a return to the tonic for an exposition repeat,
distantly recalling the first movement's ambiguity here.) The presence of
this theme from an earlier movement is here even more uncanny: unlike
the first movement, now it actually is a memory, the regression into a past
thought lost, a ghostly presence that has all along haunted the work. The
repetition of the same thing is, for Freud, one of the primary sources of the
unheimlich – the factor of involuntary repetition that transforms what would
otherwise seem quite innocent into something uncanny and 'forces upon us
the idea of something fateful and inescapable'. Related to the unconscious
mind's compulsion to repeat the traumatic experience, it 'recalls the sense
of helplessness experienced in some dream-states'.[57]

For once, the theme is slightly altered, the tail segment modified to sustain
F minor (bb. 112–15), a moment of personal pathos allowed to register
(significantly the marking is *espressivo*), as if the implacable memory is
beginning to yield. And indeed the theme is becoming more integrated into
the material of the quartet. To make the connection between the agitation
of the finale and this theme explicit, the three-note descent is broken off and
heard to grow into the tarantella material of the movement (bb. 120–8), as
the movement embarks upon a recapitulation. The F minor theme is shown
to give birth to the music of this movement; the otherwise inexplicable
neurosis of the finale is merely the outermost manifestation of this repressed
memory, which is here revealed as its cause. At the same time, though, the
theme is at last being faced up to, the finale working-out what was unable
to be developed in the first movement.[58]

---

[57] Freud, 'The Uncanny', p. 359.
[58] Cf. Freud, 'if the original experience, along with its affect, can be brought into consciousness,
the affect is by that very fact discharged or "abreacted", the force that has maintained the
symptom ceases to operate, and the symptom itself disappears.' Breuer and Freud, *Studies on
Hysteria*, p. 37.

This disruption retrospectively unifies the movement with the rest of the work. The interruption of the cyclic development theme, though initially destroying the integrity of the finale, binds it all the more closely to the previous movements, and, since this theme subsequently grows back into the material of the finale, the initial breakthrough event is subsumed *ex post facto* into the immanent course of the movement. The unexpected structural paralleling of the finale with the opening movement is further suggested, both movements incorporating the intrusion of the 'trauma' theme as a new episode in their development space, a feature which will eventually prove decisive in the redemption of the finale. The resulting design is comparable to Rosen's formulation of cyclic form as analogous to the Romantic fragment. Speaking of the Octet, in a phrase perhaps more apposite to the present quartet, Rosen suggests:

> The sense of the cyclical return as both inside and outside the finale relates it directly to the fragment. Perceived both as a quotation from an earlier movement and as a theme derived from its new context, the cyclical return simultaneously attacks and reaffirms the integrity of the individual musical structure: it displays the double nature of the fragment.[59]

The relatively straightforward repetition of the exposition in the sonata recapitulation is now necessary to show how this material grows from and relates back to the first-movement development theme. In a typical Mendelssohnian touch, generic demands are reinterpreted as the necessary outcome of the work's own individual processes. Such repetition could of course also be interpreted as a neurotic fixation, an inability to break out of an obsessive circle of repetition, characteristic of the symptoms of trauma.

The hints of F minor are increasingly prevalent across the recapitulation, this tonality and the ab–g–f descent of the first-movement development theme being continually emphasised. The new bridge section between first and second groups moves, in passing, to F minor (bb. 151–3) touching on the distinctive ab–g–f–c motive of the 'trauma' theme in the second violin (the same voice that has always stated this theme), while the second group's first theme mirrors the exposition's move to the subdominant by translating Gm–Cm to Cm–Fm (b. 162). Now the climactic continuation (bb. 165ff.) modifies the diminished harmony and ascending thematic contour of the exposition's bb. 50–3 to an F minor chord and descending ab–g–f (Ex. 5.11).

---

[59] Rosen, *The Romantic Generation*, p. 92.

Ex. 5.11 Quartet Op. 12, finale: modification of exposition material in recapitulation.

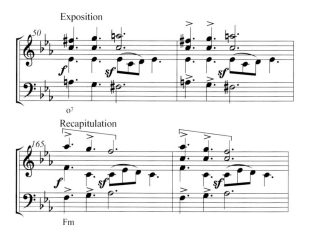

Most tellingly, when the B♭ major interpolation within the second group is reprised (bb. 181ff.), the melody seems to outline not the expected E♭ but rather C major,[60] though the accompanying harmony (a third-inversion C[7]) instead suggests that this C is actually the dominant of F minor, playing off the same ambiguity between tonic and dominant that has been a feature of the quartet. To make this connection unmistakable, the ensuing three-note descent in the melodic line is altered from its previous [8̂]–7̂–6̂–5̂ to [8̂]–6̂–5̂–4̂, consequently outlining the all-pervasive a♭–g–f motive (b. 183, Ex. 5.12).

It is difficult to determine whether this passage is actually in F minor or C, and it therefore proves easy for the music to return to the C minor tonic at b. 189, the tints of F minor heard now as local oscillations to the minor subdominant.[61] At b. 196, the music swings again from C[7] to F minor. Crucially, the descending tetrachord c–b♭–a♭–g above this harmony foreshadows the climax of the work in the coda; it has grown out of the third descent of the 'trauma' theme in the previous bars (bb. 183ff.), and,

---

[60] E♭ would correspond to the tonal transposition of the B♭ exposition passage in the recapitulation, though since this initial B♭ is an unprepared tonal shift up a third from the more likely G (major/minor) the reappearance of the theme in C major would correspondingly be more normal. Mendelssohn here reinterprets this original ploy in the formal process of the movement. A similar technique is found in the opening movement of Op. 44 No. 2.

[61] The initial harmony of B♭⁴ in b. 182 suggests C as V/Fm, though when this phrase is repeated at b. 184 the b♭ is missing, being underpinned by a straight C major chord which has been weakly tonicised on the preceding beat (the b♮ of b. 183⁴). E♭ (the real tonic of the piece and the expected key for this passage) is then touched upon in a sequence which moves via F minor harmony to C minor (b. 189), which is now heard as the true tonic, F minor reconstituted as a local oscillation to the subdominant (bb. 189–90).

Ex. 5.12 Quartet Op. 12, finale: modification of exposition material in recapitulation.

metrically realigned, now prefigures the coda (bb. 229ff.) at the same pitch. F minor harmony is further touched upon in the closing stages of the recapitulation, bb. 200 and 215 (the latter incorporating the aʹ–g–f descent in viola and cello voices), and in passing, bb. 219–20. The final cadence (b. 223), a C♮⁷ first inversion replacing the expected C minor tonic, seems projected to swing the tonality round to F, but the music instead deflects immediately to V⁶₅ of C minor (b. 225), which leads directly into the work's coda.[62]

From a formalist perspective, emphasising the subdominant is common towards the end of sonata-form recapitulations; as Charles Rosen has influentially formulated it, a move to the subdominant in the recapitulation balances the sharpward direction of the dominant in the exposition, contributing to a relaxation of harmonic tension accumulated across the movement.[63] Here, though, this harmonic tendency is further drawn into a formal process which enables the work finally to achieve some degree of resolution. What is crucially different about this sonata movement is that it is in the wrong key – C minor as opposed to E♭ major. The prominence of F minor and the associated thematic third-motive in the development and recapitulation refers directly to the unresolved F minor theme of the first movement, but this itself is to prove the means for escaping from the

[62] It is possible to see this C⁷ finally resolved 11 bars later by the crucial pivot Fm harmony of b. 234, which picks up the still unresolved seventh of b. 223.
[63] Rosen, *The Classical Style*, p. 79.

Ex. 5.13 Quartet Op. 12, finale: transformation of new theme in coda's E♭ breakthrough.

pervading C minor angst of the finale and finally reaching the true tonality of E♭.

Coda

The pivotal point of the quartet – the *peripeteia* of the drama – is the transformation of the F minor theme at b. 235, which forms the decisive breakthrough to E♭ major. An impassioned dotted figure, underpinned by the descending crotchets from b. 191 in the cello, follows on directly from the dominant of b. 228, suggesting a last, crucial struggle with the problems of the work. The rising third in the melody is now expanded into a sixth, c^2–a♭^{2} (bb. 233–4), from which materialises the principal motive of the development theme. Now, however, the harmony is a clear root-position F minor. In a supreme effort of will, the melody, rather than descending back down to c^2, rises up to b♭^{2}, under which is pinned a $^6_4$ of E♭ major (Ex. 5.13). This is the crux and turning point of the movement; from this dominant, E♭ is finally regained.

The resolution to the quartet's real tonic key is enabled through treating this F minor harmony as v/V, the motive used as the crucial pivot from the finale's C minor, down the harmonic cycle of fifths to B♭ (B♭$^6_4$–^{7}, bb. 235–6), and from there to E♭. The ambiguity running throughout the quartet between C and F minor, between 'dominant' and 'tonic', is settled in favour of the latter. Thus the trauma stemming from the F minor theme – the C minor Molto allegro – is finally transcended through the theme itself. To extend the psychoanalytical analogy, by being faced up to, through the conscious return to the root cause, the work manages to overcome itself.[64]

---

[64] As famously stated by Breuer and Freud in their *Studies on Hysteria*, 'we found, to our great surprise at first, that *each individual hysterical symptom immediately and permanently disappeared when we had succeeded in bringing clearly to light the memory of the event by which*

By managing to rise to b♭ and thus realising the dominant of the home key E♭, the quartet is stopped from spiralling into an endless cycle of neurosis.

The key of E♭ is triumphantly heralded in b. 237 with a return of the coda's martial figures in the true tonic, though the quartet will not conclude quite as simply. At bb. 241ff., the music retraces the crucial Fm–B♭$^6_4$ progression, now fully integrated into its true E♭ context (I$^6_3$–ii$^6_5$–I$^6_4$); above the $^6_4$ appears a close variant of an idea which was found in the coda of the first movement (b. 271), preparing, perhaps, for the imminent recall of that section. When returned to a second time, this Fm$^6_3$ is lingered over in the first violin, dropping out into an unaccompanied passage virtually constituting a recitative (bb. 253ff.; note the *espressivo* and *ad lib.* markings). In almost identical fashion to Op. 13, the violin recalls the past once more, glancing back one final time to the F minor theme from the first movement which had dominated the quartet. Now on its second statement, the motive moves from f^2 up to c^3, completing the process seen in the breakthrough passage. The motive had originally always fallen to its low c; across the course of the finale's exposition the music had striven to rise to the upper c (b. 57), but only now, following on from the b♭^{2} of b. 235, is c^3 finally attained. From under this pitch, the other instruments quietly enter with the full theme (b. 259); the quotation of the theme's opening bars in the first violin leads, by the associative power of memory, to the actual reappearance of this memory.[65]

Throughout the work, the F minor theme has always been stated in the second violin, its companion silent.[66] The effect is of different spatial or temporal levels, a memory external to the narrative/protagonist voice of the first violin.[67] For the first time now, this memory in the other instrumental voices is voluntarily recalled by the first violin. The effect is of looking

---

    it was provoked and in arousing its accompanying effect' (*Studies on Hysteria*, p. 57; emphasis in original).

[65] In accordance with the theories of Freud, memories can occur spontaneously, or 'aroused in accordance with the laws of association' (*ibid.*, p. 67).

[66] The one exception is the sequential repetition in G minor at its first appearance in the first movement, but this is taken up by the first violin after the initial F minor statement in the second violin. Since in this G minor statement the harmony is changed for the only time to a more stable root position and this sequence leads to the transformed reprise of the second and first subjects of the exposition in the minor key, it seems fair to suggests that the 'trauma' is initially distinct from the narrative voice of the first violin, but, on materialising in the external second violin, spreads to (infects?) the first.

[67] In several other works Mendelssohn's use of the violin(s) suggests at times its literal voicing of the first-person 'aesthetic protagonist'. In the 'Reformation' Symphony the violins are silent throughout the introduction, only materialising in b. 33 with the shimmering external voice of the Dresden Amen. Likewise in the Third Symphony, the violins are held back until the long, expressive cantilena at b. 17, suggesting for the first time the presence of a first-person narrative voice (see Chapter 6).

back in recollection, consciously summoning up the past which has been overcome. The work does not end with the initial triumph of the E♭ major breakthrough, but, having reached its home, recollects the painful journey in tranquillity.

This recall leads into the first theme from the opening movement, entering on the back of the F minor theme, mirroring almost identically the coda to the first movement, which now concludes the quartet. This confirms the latent parallelism of the finale with that movement, already suggested by the reappearance of the first-movement development theme in the finale's development episode. The redemption of the movement – the tranquil refinding of this initial theme – is achieved in part by this association with the first movement.[68] As Rosen states, 'the coda to the finale seems almost inevitable when it arrives, as it simply returns to the coda of the first movement, coming out of the same motives and ending in the same way, as the opening theme dies into silence'; what Hans Keller describes as 'one of music history's most organic "cyclic" forms'.[69] The first theme is slightly varied from its appearance in the first-movement coda, the climactic high g^3 (bb. 287–91) extended by two bars to three-and-a-half (prolonging a final revisiting of the C minor harmony that has been so prominent across the work),[70] the following bar augmented, and two small passages repeated or subjected to octave transposition.

The first violin finally descends down three octaves from its climactic g^3 as the work ends, *pianissimo*, in nostalgic recall. The memory of the F minor theme still remains; on its recall, the theme, though transformed in the breakthrough of b. 235, is still above an inconclusive $^6_4$ of F minor, neither resolved tonally nor melodically closed. The memory has been overcome, but the past is unable to be changed, which is why, when recalled for this last time, the theme is still unresolved. This bittersweet, half-resolved / unresolved quality takes up a typical Romantic theme of love, loss, and distance, both emotional and temporal. In Keller's view, 'this Quartet is one of his profoundest and most original inspirations .... The passion behind [it] is, naturally, youthful, but its serenity and resignation aren't.'[71] Or, to

---

[68] One could also note the psychological tendency for association between disparate events which, though unconnected, occurred temporally in close proximity (noted in Breuer and Freud, *Studies on Hysteria*). The close succession of the first subject and trauma theme in the opening movement thus 'connects' the two.

[69] Rosen, *The Romantic Generation*, p. 586; Keller, 'The Classical Romantics', p. 201.

[70] Cf. Vitercik, *The Early Works of Felix Mendelssohn*, p. 276. This pitch, taken up from bb. 34, 90, 126, 149 and 178, is the highest in the movement, a good example of sensitivity to long-range registral relationships in Mendelssohn's writing.

[71] Keller, 'The Classical Romantics', p. 211.

give the final word to Eliot: 'only in time can the moment in the rose-garden / Be remembered ... / Only through time time is conquered.'[72]

The past that in 1827 had been nostalgically embraced is now seen in Op. 12 as being double-sided. In the E♭ Quartet the past is not only a halcyon vision of distant happiness but reveals a darker, more sinister aspect. Rather than a place to tarry 'in sessions of sweet, silent thought', the past has a more destructive claim on the individual, the memory of whose experiences are now revealed to have a negative impact on the self, an inhibition of the psyche which must be shaken off in order to live the present. Never again was Mendelssohn to return to the musical past at the conclusion of an instrumental work. The cyclic works which followed in the next few years would allude only in passing to their own history, and by 1842, with the completion of the Third Symphony, literal recall would be sublated into a larger musical process where every movement would form a transformation of the same basic material, but where there was no going back to that heard in previous movements. It is to these works that we turn now.

---

[72] Eliot, 'Burnt Norton', II, *Collected Poems*, p. 192.

6 | Cyclicism in Mendelssohn's mature music

The years after 1829, with the composition of the E♭ Quartet, show a development away from the idea and principles of cyclical form espoused so brilliantly in these early chamber works. In fact, it is not just cyclic works which are discarded but instrumental music in general: Mendelssohn was not to complete another chamber work until eight years later, in 1837, when the Op. 44 set of quartets demonstrate a 'new way' – a new formal clarity and masterly handling of generic demands which has often been seen as issuing in a more classical or classicist period in Mendelssohn's music.[1]

The reasons for this change are complex and multifaceted, and have been a stumbling block for many attempts at understanding the composer's life. Certainly, biographical factors offer some explanation for a break in Mendelssohn's life at this time which could conceivably have influenced a stylistic change in his music by the later 1830s. The years from 1829 onwards were those of Mendelssohn's travels, the famous journeys to England, Scotland and Italy, which formed the inspiration for so many of the compositions from the next years. These *Wanderjahre*, besides their immediate service as a formative artistic *Bildung*, were an opportunity for the young composer to establish contact with the leading figures of European musical life and decide on the most profitable place for his future vocation.[2] Within a year of returning to Germany Mendelssohn had embarked upon his professional career in Düsseldorf as musical director of the town.

The series of personal setbacks in the composer's private and professional life during the early 1830s have also been held accountable for a crisis Mendelssohn seems to have experienced at that time.[3] Despite the undoubted success of the St Matthew Passion revival of March 1829, this achievement should not overshadow the growing disillusionment and frustration Mendelssohn felt with the musical life of Berlin, and the relatively

---

[1] See Krummacher, *Mendelssohn – Der Komponist*, for the most detailed and cogently argued account of Mendelssohn's compositional development.

[2] See Mendelssohn's letter to his father from Paris, 21 February 1832 (*Briefe*, vol. I, pp. 320–3).

[3] Krummacher, *Mendelssohn – Der Komponist*, pp. 56–7.

scarce opportunities he found there for presenting his music.[4] The events surrounding the attempts to get his new 'Reformation' Symphony performed after 1830 upon his return from Britain only added to his disappointments.

Most significant in this regard was the debacle in 1831–2 of the succession to the Berlin *Singakademie*, where Mendelssohn, against his own instincts, let himself be entered into the leadership battle with the more experienced but largely mediocre C.F. Rungenhagen, only to fall victim to what seems likely to have been an anti-Semitic campaign against him. This was not the first time that Mendelssohn's success and prodigious ability aroused jealousy and resentment in colleagues; unfortunately neither would it be the last.[5] This episode left Mendelssohn with a lasting bitterness towards Berlin, which resurfaced a decade later in the unsatisfactory time working for the Prussian government in the early 1840s. To make matters worse, the deaths early in 1832 of his two closest mentors, his teacher Carl Friedrich Zelter and Goethe, left Mendelssohn with a profound feeling of loss. Mendelssohn's close friend and violin teacher Eduard Rietz, the dedicatee of the Octet, had died that January, and Hegel himself the year before. The letters of the time speak eloquently of Mendelssohn's state of depression and lethargy.[6]

It was in response to this period of despondency and uncertainty that Mendelssohn resolved in 1833 to leave Berlin and establish his professional career in Düsseldorf and, later, Leipzig. Two years later the death of his father, Abraham, severed a further close spiritual link, and forced

---

[4] This point is well brought out by Paul Jourdan, 'Mendelssohn in England, 1829–37', unpublished PhD thesis, University of Cambridge (1998), who rightly emphasises just how important Mendelssohn's success in England in 1829 was for the composer. It is indeed ironic that Mendelssohn's biggest native success was not with his own music but with Bach's. His most ambitious project – the opera *Die Hochzeit des Camacho* – had proved an embarrassment when finally brought to the stage in 1827 when, due largely to the machinations of Spontini and the indisposition of its leading singer, it was pulled off the stage after only one performance. The overture to *Calm Sea and Prosperous Voyage* had likewise been rejected by the *Singakademie* Orchestra and Mendelssohn had only been able to secure a performance of *A Midsummer Night's Dream* in Stettin.

[5] On this episode see W.A. Little, 'Mendelssohn and the Berliner Singakademie: The Composer at the Crossroads', in R. Larry Todd (ed.), *Mendelssohn and his World* (Princeton University Press, 1991), pp. 65–85.

[6] For instance, as the composer wrote to Klingemann on 5 September 1832, 'for some weeks now I have been feeling so unspeakably low and deeply depressed that I can't even express my mood to you' (Karl Klingemann [d.J.] (ed.), *Felix Mendelssohn-Bartholdys Briefwechsel mit Legationsrat Karl Klingemann in London* (Essen: Baedeker, 1909), p. 100). Mendelssohn later thought of this time as one of illness – 'for it really is an illness, and an illness of the worst kind, this uncertainty, these doubts and this insecurity' (*Briefe*, vol. II, p. 1).

upon Mendelssohn new responsibilities as head of his family. (As he would later acknowledge to Klingemann, with the death of his father his 'youth had ended' and his life taken on a new seriousness.[7]) In 1836, finally, Mendelssohn met and became engaged to Cécile Jeanrenaud, whom he married the following spring. The years of youthful freedom and experimentation were now effectively over, and the responsibilities of a family and career upon him.

These years provide a convenient and plausible biographical cut-off point within Mendelssohn's life which could partly explain some stylistic differences in his later music. However, none of this really answers quite why cyclic form, in the sense used by Mendelssohn in the late 1820s, was abandoned, or what the artistic reasons for the possible shift of direction in his music, perceived by many observers, might have been.

Obviously such an issue is unlikely to be reducible to one simple explanation but is more likely the result of a constellation of motives. In part, Mendelssohn's avoidance of the cyclic procedures of the Op. 6 sonata and A minor and E♭ quartets might stem from a desire not to repeat himself, to avoid turning the highly expressive formal innovations of those works into a mannerism. As was suggested before, such structures are unique, one-off conceptions which cannot really be taken up as generic formal templates: they work *against* or above accepted formal moulds, deforming generic structure and expectations. (It would, after all, become quite tiresome if every multimovement instrumental work by a composer were to end serenely in returning to the music of its beginning.) It must also be observed that not all of Mendelssohn's compositions from the years 1825–9 are themselves in cyclic form: one of his most beautiful and accomplished pieces from these years, the A major Quintet Op. 18, has (at least in its final, published version) nothing so overtly radical about its design, while still achieving a highly sophisticated integration of lyricism into its essentially monothematic evolving structure that foreshadows the works of the later 1830s.[8]

It could also be argued that the way started here in these early cyclic works had no further potential, Mendelssohn having exhausted the possibilities of such structures. Friedhelm Krummacher in particular has claimed that

---

[7] Letter to Klingemann, 14 December 1835, in Klingemann, *Felix Mendelssohn-Bartholdys Briefwechsel*, pp. 194–6.

[8] As noted, the first version of the Quintet does in fact feature a possible allusion to one of the themes from the trio of the original third-movement 'Minuetto' in its finale, though Mendelssohn's decision to replace this movement with the present slow movement in 1832 effectively destroyed this cyclic feature.

the integration and total unity of material evidenced in the Op. 12 Quartet admitted of no continuation; the integration is such that contrast between themes within the movements is so minimal as to preclude any further internal development, and thus threatens the very basis of the sonata conception. Mendelssohn's subsequent works – Op. 44 in particular, which is seen by Krummacher as a paradigm of his mature style – offer a classical synthesis of the form/content duality to which the earlier cyclic compositions had presented only individual solutions.[9]

Moreover, Mendelssohn's growing sense of personal identity may have been leading him to assert his independence from the mantle of Beethoven, to whose all-pervasive presence the younger composer had sometimes come rather close. (At a performance of the Op. 13 Quartet in Paris in 1832 a member of the audience, according to the composer's account, leaned over to Mendelssohn and whispered in his ear '"Il a cela dans une de ses sinfonies." "Qui?" said I, rather alarmed. "Beethoven, l'auteur de ce quatuor," said he, with an important air. It was bittersweet!' commented Mendelssohn.[10]) While Mendelssohn had gone considerably further in cyclic unity and sophistication in his early works than had Beethoven, the influence of the latter still sometimes hung too closely around the younger composer's music; it is arguable that one of the reasons why Mendelssohn rejected the B♭ major Piano Sonata of 1827 is that, unlike Op. 13 in comparison with Beethoven's Op. 132 or indeed Op. 12 with the latter's Opp. 74 and 127, its debts do not begin to repay its obvious model, let alone transcend it. The importance of this influence is revealed in a letter Fanny Hensel wrote to her brother in 1835, following the composition of her own E♭ Quartet – which is, like Felix's early works, highly indebted to late Beethoven – in which she confesses how she still had not got over her Beethoven phase, a period and influence which Felix had happily worked through and overcome by this time:

I believe it results from the fact that we were young precisely during Beethoven's last years, and it was thus reasonable for us to absorb his way of doing things . . . You've lived through it and progressed beyond it in your composing, and I've remained stuck in it.[11]

---

[9] Krummacher, *Mendelssohn – Der Komponist*, pp. 324 and 382–4.

[10] 'He has that in one of his symphonies.' 'Who?' 'Beethoven, the author of this quartet.' Letter to Fanny Hensel, Paris, 21 January 1832 (*Briefe*, vol. I, p. 315).

[11] Letter, Fanny Hensel to Felix Mendelssohn, 17 February 1835, in Fanny Hensel, *The Letters of Fanny Hensel to Felix Mendelssohn*, ed. and trans. Marcia J. Citron (Stuyvesant, NY: Pendragon, 1987), p. 490.

One could even suggest that Mendelssohn's widening experience and growing awareness of his historical views and his position vis-à-vis the past made the composer more conscious of the musical past, and less willing to retreat into this world (if that is what it was) within his music. As Susanna Großmann-Vendrey has suggested, the years following the St Matthew revival of 1829 and the direct exposure to Europe's classical past during Mendelssohn's *Italienische Reise* of 1830–1 – on the way to which the composer had his last and most intellectually fruitful stay with Goethe in Weimar – saw a maturing of Mendelssohn's view of his historical and cultural past, and his position therein.[12] James Garratt has claimed that the possibly naïve identification with the musical heritage Mendelssohn had grown up with was here replaced by a more sophisticated awareness of the gap between the irretrievability of the past and the reality of the present.[13] Whether or not one agrees with this conjecture, it is noticeable that from this time on Mendelssohn never moves back to the memory of the past within his musical works. Indeed, the implication of the procedure of the Op. 12 Quartet, as argued in the previous chapter, is of a new fear of the past and the need to escape or overcome its overpowering force.

What is even more important than all these factors, however, is surely Mendelssohn's growing concern with the question of the intelligibility of instrumental music, and how this relates to both the idea of cyclical form and to programme music. After the E♭ Quartet, only one major instrumental work in the following years would return to music heard in past movements, and this following the more simple Beethovenian model – the programmatic 'Reformation' Symphony in D minor, posthumously published as Op. 107.[14]

---

[12] Großmann-Vendrey, 'Mendelssohn und die Vergangenheit', p. 78; *Felix Mendelssohn Bartholdy und die Musik der Vergangenheit*, p. 28.

[13] Garratt, 'Mendelssohn and the Rise of Musical Historicism', pp. 60–5.

[14] Krummacher has shown that Mendelssohn made plans for further chamber works in the early 1830s (including a possible pair of piano trios and another quartet), though never took these ideas any further (*Mendelssohn – Der Komponist*, pp. 90–1). Douglass Seaton has also called attention to an unpublished song-cycle dating from May 1830, in which the music of the final song returns to the close of that of the first, a cyclic structure not unlike that of Op. 12 which precedes it (Douglass Seaton, 'Mendelssohn's Cycles of Songs', in John Michael Cooper and Julie D. Prandi (eds.), *The Mendelssohns: Their Music in History* (Oxford University Press, 2002), pp. 214–15; further, see John Michael Cooper, 'Of Red Roofs and Hunting Horns: Mendelssohn's Song Aesthetic, with an Unpublished Cycle (1830)', *Journal of Musicological Research*, 21 (2002), 300–14). The 'Italian' Symphony is also sometimes named as an example of a cyclic work, though despite several possible allusions to earlier moments in its finale (and strong parallelisms and motivic links between movements) there is no literal citation of earlier themes in the manner seen in Mendelssohn's works of the 1820s (and still present in the 'Reformation' Symphony).

This work, in so many ways a pivotal composition within Mendelssohn's oeuvre, is highly instructive as to Mendelssohn's growing dissatisfaction with the possibilities of cyclic form and, most crucially, the related idea of programme music, and rewards a more detailed examination here.

The 'Reformation' Symphony (1830)

The 'Reformation' Symphony, written in 1829–30 and first performed in 1832, was conceived by Mendelssohn as a major work and one of which he had high hopes and aspirations. A symphony, after all, was at this time a major statement of artistic intent, and in the years following Beethoven Mendelssohn had, as Schumann later remarked, taken the 'crown and scep-tre' with his concert overtures,[15] quickly becoming the leading instrumental composer of the era. As his first attempt in the genre since the youthful C minor Symphony of 1824 (published in 1830 as Symphony No. 1, Op. 11) and following the success of the *Sommernachtstraum* and *Meeresstille* over-tures, not to mention the chamber masterpieces of the intervening years, Mendelssohn had every right to be hopeful of a new symphony from his pen. Yet by 1838 he had turned vehemently against the work, even going so far as to declare in a letter to his friend Julius Rietz that there was no work of his that he would rather see consigned to the flames than his D minor Symphony.

This remarkable volte-face, as Judith Silber Ballan has pointed out, demands critical scrutiny. What was it in the symphony that Mendelssohn took such exception to in 1838, even though only eight years previously he had described it as something he 'was very pleased with'?[16] While the com-poser's perfectionism was responsible for much fault-finding with what he had written, the level of self-criticism here is extreme even for his standards. The problem Mendelssohn had with the work cannot be due merely to the protracted and ultimately disheartening labour he undertook to obtain its performance, or merely accountable to the lukewarm critical reception the work elicited at this first appearance.[17] It lies, rather, with the entire

---

[15] Schumann, 'Sinfonie von H. Berlioz' (*NZfM*, 3 (1835)), *Gesammelte Schriften*, vol. I, p. 70.

[16] Judith Silber [Ballan], 'Mendelssohn and the Reformation Symphony: A Critical and Historical Study', unpublished PhD thesis, Yale University (1987), p. 42.

[17] The second performance, immediately prior to Mendelssohn's harsh comments, had anyway been a public success. The ordeals behind the premiere are summarised by Judith Silber [Ballan] in 'Mendelssohn and his *Reformation* Symphony', *Journal of the American Musicological Society*, 40 (1987), 310–36.

aesthetic upon which the symphony was conceived, the very notion of a programmatic symphony, and the uneasy relationship its programmatic elements (which are intimately linked with its cyclic procedures) hold with more abstract musical demands.

To investigate the roots of the composer's dissatisfaction, one must look more closely at the aesthetic which lay behind the symphony, namely the theory of musical representation of A.B. Marx. In the late 1820s Mendelssohn had been, as remarked, deeply under the influence of A.B. Marx, some fourteen years his elder but one of his closest friends. The *Sommernachtstraum* and *Meeresstille* overtures had been written under this influence, and as Judith Silber Ballan has argued, the 'Reformation' Symphony was designed as a symphonic expression of Marx's theoretical views.[18] Marx had argued that all great works of music were based on a fundamental idea, the *Grundidee*, which, while not being entirely explicable through verbal formulations, could nevertheless be substantially expressed in words.[19] Through this ability of music to express such ideas or concepts, Marx held, a great composer could even encapsulate historical events within a musical work; all the work needed was a programmatic title to signal to the audience what the music relates to. This is what Marx's idol Beethoven had done in his then most celebrated (and now most reviled) composition, *Wellingtons Sieg*, where the victory of the British general over Napoleon at Vitoria in 1813 is enacted through the use of opposing themes to signify the French and British armies respectively (namely the popular melodies 'Malbrouck s'en va-t-en guerre' and 'Rule Britannia'). The expression of the great cultural event in German history that was the Reformation through musical means was therefore entirely realisable within Marx's system.

This is evidently how Mendelssohn's symphony was received, though the critics were divided regarding the success of such a project. At its premiere in Berlin in 1832, the critic Ludwig Rellstab had commented unfavourably on the aesthetic under which the work had been written:

To music is open only the world of feelings, and in this world music does without, and should do without, any more explicit or precise designations . . . . Never has an endeavour seemed more wrong-headed than that which the *Musikalische Zeitung* of Herr Marx espoused: that is, to trace a specific course of intelligible thoughts in

[18] [Silber] Ballan, 'Marxian Programmatic Music: A Stage in Mendelssohn's Musical Development', and 'Mendelssohn and the Reformation Symphony', pp. 85–98. See also R. Larry Todd, *Mendelssohn: The Hebrides and other Overtures* (Cambridge University Press, 1993), pp. 69ff.
[19] Adolph Bernhard Marx, *Über Malerei in der Tonkunst: Ein Maigruß an die Kunstphilosophen* (Berlin: Finke, 1828).

every piece of music, thereby reading things into a piece and out of a piece that are entirely foreign to it. We simply think that Herr Mendelssohn has let himself be too strongly influenced by this notion.[20]

Across the 1830s, however, Mendelssohn began increasingly to shun this more explicit type of programme (or poetic) music he had espoused in his earlier days. *Die schöne Melusine* in 1834 was to be his fourth and last poetic overture; the 'Reformation' Symphony was rejected outright, the 'Italian' Symphony discarded indefinitely, and upon its completion in 1842 the 'Scottish' Symphony had now no indication as to its provenance.[21] This was simultaneously accompanied by a gradual cooling of the formerly extremely close musical friendship between the two figures, which precipitated into an outright break in 1839. The reasons for this were more personal than aesthetic, but there is no doubt that Mendelssohn began to view Marx's theories with more scepticism.[22]

As Mendelssohn famously wrote in a letter to Marc-André Souchay a few years later, expressing what must be considered his mature aesthetic views on the matter,

People often complain that music is so ambiguous, and that what they are supposed to think when they hear it is so unclear, whereas words would be understood by everybody. But for me it is exactly the opposite, and not just with whole books, but also with individual words, which seem to me so ambiguous, so unclear, so liable to misunderstanding in comparison with good music, which fills the soul with a thousand things better than words. What the music that I love expresses to me are not thoughts too unclear for words, but rather those too definite.[23]

Mendelssohn did not necessarily retract completely from the Marxian standpoint of the intelligibility of instrumental music, or, likewise, from the notion of the musical idea, but, more importantly, he did begin to question the necessity for a programmatic verbal outline to support a piece of music and the spate of literary interpretations this easily spawned. Even as far back in 1827 he had written to his sister, half in jest, half in exasperation, at the

[20] Ludwig Rellstab, *Iris im Gebiete der Tonkunst*, 3/47 (23 November 1832), 187–8, cited in [Silber] Ballan, 'Marxian Programmatic Music', p. 160.

[21] See Thomas Schmidt-Beste, 'Just how "Scottish" is the "Scottish" Symphony? Thoughts on Form and Poetic Content in Mendelssohn's Opus 56', in John Michael Cooper and Julie D. Prandi (eds.), *The Mendelssohns: Their Music in History* (Oxford University Press, 2002), pp. 147–65.

[22] See, for instance, Werner, *Mendelssohn: A New Image*, pp. 280–1, [Silber] Ballan, 'Marxian Programmatic Music', p. 161.

[23] Mendelssohn, letter to Marc-André Souchay, 15 October 1842, *Briefe*, vol. II, p. 337.

consternation Marx had let loose on the town of Stettin with his journalistic explanation of Beethoven's Ninth Symphony, whose German premiere was being given on that occasion:

O Marx! Marx! What a disaster he has created. Here they find his view of the symphony entirely wrong. So, for example, city councillor Schafer says 'It is every graduation of joy. The first movement is the joy of men and youths –' 'and the spirits of hell' interrupts Treasurer Mayer. 'No,' Koelpin says, 'the scherzo is the spirits of hell.' 'Wrong', says Registrar Gebhard, 'the scherzo is childish joy. When the drum plays, that's the boy turning a somersault, and not until the trio does he learn to walk.' 'In the last vocal movement is an immense lamentation!' says the blond government councillor Werth. 'No, jubilation.' 'No, bravado....'[24]

If a work is sufficiently well written it should, according to Mendelssohn's belief, convey such meaning without the need to resort to titles, let alone a programme. (This was the matter to which he had been referring in the famous letter to Souchay, who had been requesting indicative titles for some of the composer's *Lieder ohne Worte*.) Conversely, if the music does require a programme then the musical ideas must be insufficiently well formed and therefore ambiguous.

The 'Reformation' Symphony is cyclic in the sense that elements from earlier movements reappear in the closing stages of its andante third movement, acting as a transition to the finale. In the familiar revised version of the symphony this consists of one clear instance of cyclic recall, namely a reference back to the first movement's second subject – a characteristic motive, drawn from the symphony's opening material, turning from minor to major within its first two bars. The first version of the symphony was indeed more cyclic still, incorporating reminiscences of several of the themes of the previous three movements and foreshadowing the finale in a recitative-like transition between the slow movement and finale. These twenty-eight bars were cut by the composer in November 1832 before the premiere on the fifteenth of that month.[25] It is possible, in addition, to trace

---

[24] Unpublished letter, Mendelssohn to his family, Stettin, 19 February 1827, cited by [Silber] Ballan, 'Marxian Programmatic Music', pp. 156–7.

[25] The revised manuscript is dated 11 November 1832. This passage was first transcribed by Silber in her dissertation ('Mendelssohn and the Reformation Symphony'), and subsequently included by Wulf Konold in *Die Symphonien Felix Mendelssohn Bartholdys*, pp. 365–8. Consideration of some possible cyclic thematic links between this passage and other movements in Mendelssohn's symphony is given by Wolfgang Dinglinger in 'The Programme of Mendelssohn's "Reformation" Symphony, Op. 107', in John Michael Cooper and Julie D. Prandi (eds.), *The Mendelssohns: Their Music in History* (Oxford University Press, 2002), pp. 119–20.

numerous connections between the themes of different movements which are perhaps less transparent than those in some of Mendelssohn's other cyclic works but still relatively straightforward.

Beyond these straightforward cyclic procedures, Mendelssohn similarly introduces music from sources external to the movement in which they are heard, specifically pre-existent musical themes, which thus have an impact mildly akin to cyclically recalled material. These are the liturgical melodies of the 'Dresden Amen' twice within the first movement and, most obviously, the Lutheran chorale 'Ein' feste Burg ist unser Gott' in the introduction to the finale and subsequently throughout the course of that movement. The former appears both at the end of the andante introduction as the result of a subtle process of thematic growth, and as an interpolation between the climactic end of the expanded development section and the limp re-entry of the first subject as recapitulation. In both instances the theme appears to issue from some external source, notwithstanding the implied thematic relationship with both the introductory material and the derived first subject.[26] Luther's famous hymn, meanwhile, appears in the off-tonic introduction to the finale as a breakthrough from the G minor slow movement that had preceded it. Absent from the finale's exposition, it is reintroduced only in stages within the development section of that movement, and finally fully integrated in the later stages of the recapitulation.

While it has been claimed that the Dresden Amen was not widely known outside its home town at the time and would therefore not have seemed remarkable to Mendelssohn's contemporaries, Luther's chorale was known to everyone in Protestant Germany as perhaps *the* musical embodiment of their religion, and would have undoubtedly have signified something.[27] Moreover, the sustained passage of close imitative polyphony of the first movement's introduction could have been easily recognised as the *stile antico* of the Palestrina school, the ideal church music over which E.T.A. Hoffmann had lyricised and which the Heidelberg jurist and antiquarian A.F.J. Thibaut (whom Mendelssohn had met in 1827) made the subject of his famous *Über Reinheit der Tonkunst* (1825).

---

[26] See Hermann Deiters' review of the publication in 1868 (*Allgemeine musikalische Zeitung*, 3 (1868), col. 349–50, 356–7), Thomas, *Das Instrumentalwerk Felix Mendelssohn-Bartholdys*, p. 243, or Konold, *Die Symphonien Felix Mendelssohn Bartholdys*, p. 109.

[27] Silber [Ballan], 'Mendelssohn and the Reformation Symphony', pp. 99–106. Indeed, no one seems to have noticed that the Dresden Amen was an already existing theme until Wilhelm Tappert in 1903 ('Das Gralthema in Richard Wagners "Parsifal"', *Musikalisches Wochenblatt*, 34/31–2 (30 July 1903), 421).

These extrinsic, cyclic or extramusical elements undoubtedly relate to the programme of the work, the narrative or story Mendelssohn is attempting to convey musically. The question is, what are we (and what was the listener in Mendelssohn's day) to make of them? The potential problem stemming from the incorporation of these elements is that such external quotations invite, even demand, hermeneutic explanation. It might sound paradoxical to suggest that such overt programmatic gestures actually resulted not in more comprehensibility but rather in less, but it seems that one of the problems Mendelssohn's audience had with this work is with this very notion of intelligibility. The problem with the 'Reformation' Symphony is that the work, with its quotations of earlier themes and pre-existent liturgical melodies, is not sufficiently comprehensible without some kind of (verbal) hermeneutic key to explain these unconventional procedures.

This seems at any rate to have been the root of the composer's dissatisfaction with the work. In 1837, unbeknown to many subsequent commentators, a further (and final) performance within Mendelssohn's lifetime was put on, in Düsseldorf on 12 December with his friend Julius Rietz (brother of the late Eduard) conducting. Wolfgang Dinglinger has rightly called attention to this occasion as fundamental to understanding Mendelssohn's subsequent disavowal of the work two months later.[28] Mendelssohn did not attend the performance but knew of it and asked after it in a letter to Rietz. What is revealing is that the composer had appeared to request that no information concerning the programmatic title ('Reformation') or as to any of the intended programmatic content should be made known to the public; the symphony should and must stand on its own, as music, and its (programmatic) meaning must be comprehensible from the music alone, without help from a verbal exegesis. Rietz's reply revealed to Mendelssohn that this was not the case:

The 'Reformation' Symphony was performed, albeit not with that title, and was enthusiastically received. People were racking their brains trying to figure out what it was supposed to mean, and I quietly enjoyed their various conjectures but was careful not to reveal the correct interpretation.[29]

It was in response to this that Mendelssohn let forth his strongest criticism of the work: 'I can no longer tolerate the 'Reformation' Symphony, and of all my compositions it is the one I would most like to see burnt. It

---

[28] Dinglinger, 'The Programme of Mendelssohn's "Reformation" Symphony', pp. 131–3.

[29] Unpublished letter, cited in *ibid.*, p. 131.

will never be published.'[30] The public had been unable to understand the author's intention from the music by itself: the meaning of the work is not sufficiently conveyed in the music, but requires further clarification; this, Mendelssohn sees, is a problem with his work.

Later, in 1841, Mendelssohn confessed to Rietz where the problem lay:

> The fundamental ideas [*Grundgedanken*] in … my Reformation Symphony … are interesting more through what they mean than for what they are in and of themselves; … both must connect and meld into each other …. The most important thing … is to make a theme (and everything similar) interesting in its own right.[31]

There had been a dislocation between the meaning intended by the composer and the ability of the music to convey this meaning. The rather explicit programmatic elements had not helped salvage the work, since the musical substance was insufficiently developed in its own right, and therefore they stood out as extrinsic factors, requiring extra-musical explanation.[32]

Musical meaning and the challenge of instrumental music

This aspect – the determinacy of instrumental music – which led to the rejection by the composer of what had until then been his most ambitious work, the 'Reformation' Symphony, would become one of the most pressing aesthetic questions for Mendelssohn in the following years, and to a large extent the subsequent course of his compositional career can be explained by his response to this issue. This is, after all, one of the most concerning challenges for any creative artist – whether or not their work can be understood – and one which Mendelssohn, with his deeply felt sense of ethical responsibility, felt duty-bound to resolve.

Mendelssohn had reached artistic maturity at a pivotal moment within music history and the history of musical aesthetics. If, as James Garratt has

---

[30] Letter, Mendelssohn to Rietz, 11 February 1838, originally published in Max Friedländer, 'Ein Brief Felix Mendelssohns', *Vierteljahrsschrift für Musikwissenschaft*, 5 (1889), 484, cited in Silber [Ballan], 'Mendelssohn and the Reformation Symphony', p. 6.

[31] Letter to Rietz, Leipzig, 23 April 1841, *Briefe*, vol. II, p. 282.

[32] Hermann Deiters felt much the same way about the symphony in his 1868 review of the first publication. Commenting on the first movement, Deiters held that 'the composer sought to make the form serve a distinct idea here', and, despite his admiration for much in the piece, still felt that 'we cannot look upon the all-too-prominent role of an idea, to the detriment of the form, without some reservations.' Review of the first publication of Symphony No. 5 in D minor ('Reformation'), *Allgemeine musikalische Zeitung*, 3 (1868), col. 349–50, 356–7; trans. Thomas Grey in Douglass Seaton (ed.), *The Mendelssohn Companion* (Westport, CT and London: Greenwood Press, 2001, pp. 534–43, p. 538.

suggested, Mendelssohn's historical situation as the first major composer to be dispossessed of a lingua franca makes him also, in some ways, the first musical modern,[33] then the composer's situation vis-à-vis the question of the intelligibility of instrumental music makes him no less so. The pupil of Hegel, friend and sometime follower of Marx and fellow expositor of Beethoven was acutely aware of the sometimes fragile status of instrumental music with regard to musical meaning.

The emancipation of instrumental music – the 'Idea of Absolute Music', as Carl Dahlhaus has famously described it – was an achievement of the late eighteenth and early nineteenth centuries, which, so one might believe, was a fait accompli by Mendelssohn's time.[34] Almost as soon as instrumental music was declared autonomous, however, it had come under attack, from both adherents of the old aesthetic (such as Hegel) and those of a new one demanding greater semantic content which necessitated as often as not an explicit conjunction with a verbal text – a confused battle which raged across the remainder of the nineteenth century. Beethoven, of course, occupied a pivotal position here; to many seen as the emancipator of absolute music, he was also to others (such as A.B. Marx) a figure who had invested instrumental music with a previously unheard semantic content and communicative power, even one who had exhausted the potential of instrumental music per se (as Wagner would later contest, not of course without considerable self-serving interest). Even if it had not been his music but rather Haydn's or Mozart's that had inspired the first wave of Romantic authors of the 1790s to declare instrumental music as the realm of the Absolute, it was Beethoven who was best placed to raise the status of the composer to musical priest of the Beyond.[35] As the first major composer to reach maturity in the years immediately following Beethoven's death, Mendelssohn felt this challenge acutely. Indeed, one could profitably view Mendelssohn's entire aesthetic project as a challenge to the view expressed by Hegel, in the lectures on

---

[33] Garratt, 'Mendelssohn and the rise of Musical Historicism', p. 55.

[34] Carl Dahlhaus, *The Idea of Absolute Music*, trans. Roger Lustig (Chicago, IL and London: Chicago University Press, 1991); further, Bellamy Hosler, *Changing Aesthetic Views of Instrumental Music in Eighteenth-Century Germany* (Ann Arbor, MI: UMI Research Press, 1981), John Neubauer, *The Emancipation of Music from Language: Departure from Mimesis in Eighteenth-Century Aesthetics* (New Haven, CT: Yale University Press, 1986), and Mark Evan Bonds, *Music as Thought: Listening to the Symphony in the Age of Beethoven* (Princeton University Press, 2006).

[35] See Lydia Goehr, *The Imaginary Museum of Musical Works: An Essay in the Philosophy of Music* (Oxford University Press, 1992), pp. 205–42, and Tia DeNora, *Beethoven and the Construction of Genius: Musical Politics in Vienna, 1792–1803* (Berkeley and Los Angeles, CA: University of California Press, 1996).

aesthetics that the composer had attended, that music in itself 'is addressed to feeling generally and in the abstract, and this can be expressed in the medium in only a general way' – as an attempt almost to disprove Hegel's aesthetic distrust of untexted music.[36]

Instrumental music was, as we have seen for Mendelssohn, not *less* meaningful or clear than words, but *more* determinate.[37] The succession of poetic overtures written partly under the influence of Marx and in some ways as an aesthetic realisation of his system – *A Midsummer Night's Dream, Calm Sea and Prosperous Voyage, The Hebrides, The Fair Melusine* – can be viewed as a successful refutation of the idea that music could not communicate meaning without recourse to words (as indeed the 'Reformation' Symphony could be viewed as a warning of its dangers). For Marx, the young composer's *Meeresstille* had surpassed Beethoven's own setting of the same pair of poems, published only a few years previously, which had unfortunately still relied on a choral expression of Goethe's text. Indeed, with this work, held Marx, Mendelssohn had gone one stage further than Beethoven's Ninth Symphony, by expressing solely through musical means what previously had been the preserve of words.[38] (Interestingly, this comparison, also much to Mendelssohn's advantage at the expense of Beethoven, was also Schumann's view of the overture.[39])

After 1829, however, Mendelssohn was becoming increasingly aware and self-conscious of this question of intelligibility. The reaction to his cyclic works was without doubt fundamental in this. As we have seen, the reception, not just among the public but by Mendelssohn concerning the programmatic meaning of the 'Reformation' Symphony, was a major blow. Even more important here was surely the response to his A minor Quartet, Mendelssohn's most complex and thoroughgoing composition in cyclic form, the pinnacle of his early experiments in this style, and a work which, as he confessed, held great personal significance for him.

The problem with cyclic music, at least in the complex form exhibited in the A minor Quartet, is that the radical, experimental structure adopted is

---

[36] Hegel, *Aesthetics*, vol. II, p. 953 / *Werke*, vol. XV, p. 216. For Dahlhaus, Mendelssohn's 'distrust of words' was a central element in his efforts as a composer (Carl Dahlhaus, *Klassische und Romantische Musikästhetik* (Laaber Verlag, 1988), p. 141).

[37] Useful discussion of this aspect of Mendelssohn's thought in relation to his song aesthetic has been given by Douglass Seaton, 'The Problem of the Lyric Persona in Mendelssohn's Songs', in Christian Martin Schmidt (ed.), *Felix Mendelssohn Bartholdy Kongress-Bericht Berlin 1994* (Wiesbaden: Breitkopf & Härtel, 1997), pp. 167–86, and following this by John Michael Cooper, 'Of Red Roofs and Hunting Horns', 280–97.

[38] Marx, *Über Malerei in der Tonkunst*, pp. 59–60. See [Silber] Ballan, 'Marxian Programmatic Music', p. 159.

[39] Schumann, *Schwärmbriefe* (*NZfM*, 3 (1835)), in *Gesammelte Schriften*, vol. I, pp. 116–17.

liable to confuse listeners. Such structures work against traditional models and expectations; they break down generic form. Breaking norms obviously poses questions to the listener: a return to music heard in the past is prone to be heard as a quotation, and thus more readily suggests some programmatic or literary basis. Obviously this need not be the case for all works in the form; the more general type of transformatory cyclicism is unlikely to raise such problems and might in fact aid understanding by demonstrating an underlying unity or logic behind the separate movements of a work. Likewise, when thematic recall is treated in passing – particularly as in the Octet, where the return of the scherzo in the finale is a brief and potentially witty gesture with a precedent in one of Beethoven's most famous works – the momentary flashback can be integrated fairly unproblematically by the listener; as Krummacher remarks, the Octet is quite exceptional for an early nineteenth-century work for its almost uniformly *un*problematic reception.[40] But when the finale of a string quartet consistently disintegrates into snatches of previous movements, followed by an utter dissolution of material and ends in the quotation of a song never before heard in the work, even the intelligent listener of the 1830s was likely to be disorientated. These departures from established musical expectations are exceptional, and thus suggest some (programmatic) extra-musical cause or literary-hermeneutic basis.

Thomas Schmidt, in his important thesis investigating the aesthetic underpinnings of Mendelssohn's instrumental music, has usefully illuminated Mendelssohn's position in relation to the question of (musical) language and meaning by comparing the composer's aesthetic views with the *Sprachphilosophie* developed by Johann Gottfried Herder in the late eighteenth century and continued by Wilhelm von Humboldt, a colleague well known to Mendelssohn's family in Berlin.[41] Put briefly, this theory views language as an organic growth and expression of the particular society in which it developed. Language is the unique expression of a shared culture, an 'expressivist' aesthetic related to the Romantic notion of art and culture as a self-expression or overflowing of a person's or people's individuality.[42] It follows from this that the deepest and most semantically precise form

[40] Krummacher, *Mendelssohn – Der Komponist*, p. 32.
[41] Schmidt, *Die ästhetischen Grundlagen der Instrumentalmusik Felix Mendelssohn Bartholdys*, pp. 171ff. See, for example, Herder's *Abhandlung über den Ursprung der Sprache* (1772) or Humboldt's *Über die Verschiedenheit des menschlichen Sprachbaus* (1827–9).
[42] The term 'expressivist' is Isaiah Berlin's (see 'Herder and the Enlightenment', in Earl Wasserman (ed.), *Aspects of the Eighteenth Century* (Baltimore, MD: Johns Hopkins Press, 1965), pp. 47–104). This romantic notion of expressive overflowing is treated at length by Abrams in *The Mirror and the Lamp*.

of communication is that between members of the same specific culture in the language which they have developed through their shared experience.[43] Within any such form of communication, the user must navigate a course between the twin dangers of a language which is too widely comprehensible and descends into convention and banality, and one which is conversely too specialised and therefore comprehensible only to an initiated few.

Within music – or indeed any other form of communication – the case is arguably hardly that different.[44] If a composer writes in too common and comprehensible a style he runs the risk of descending into triviality and commonplace; too esoteric and personal and no one will understand it and his significance as an artist – his entire *raison d'être*, is surrendered. Mendelssohn was aware of the former clearly enough. In particular, his letters abound in (sometimes rather chauvinistic) criticisms of common, low and unsophisticated music – folk music of other countries, the popular music of the time, the piano virtuosi of his day – and, like many other artists of the time (Schumann, through his criticism, is probably the most widely read), the necessity for music to be poetic and avoid at all costs the conventional, prosaic or trivial.[45] Now he was beginning to realise that perhaps he had gone too far in the opposite direction: his music was descending into the vortex of incomprehensibility.

The problem with these radical early cyclic works is that they were not understood even by immediate members of Mendelssohn's family, those with whom the composer shared the most intimate cultural and aesthetic ties. (It also cannot be overemphasised how important Mendelssohn's family environment was for the composer throughout his life.) In 1832 Mendelssohn's father wrote a bemused letter admitting his bewilderment at what Mendelssohn was meaning in his Op. 13 Quartet and upbraiding his son for letting loose such incomprehensible madness on an unsuspecting

---

[43] The incipient nationalism in this theory was soon taken up by other figures. Richard Taruskin has commented in the context of Mendelssohn's later reception on the perversion of this theory of uniqueness and implicit cultural pluralism from a (inclusive) cultural nationalism into an (exclusive) ethnic or overtly racial version by nationalists later in the nineteenth century, most crudely by Wagner in *Das Judentum in der Musik* (Taruskin, *The Oxford History of Western Music*, 6 vols. (Oxford and New York: Oxford University Press, 2005), vol. III, pp. 166–79).

[44] Mendelssohn's views on instrumental music in fact suggest that musical language was, for the composer, closely comparable – indeed an even more precise – form of communication than conventional language.

[45] See Schmidt, *Die ästhetischen Grundlagen der Instrumentalmusik Felix Mendelssohn Bartholdys*, pp. 111ff. Indeed, it seems that Mendelssohn was not particularly receptive to most music outside the serious culture of German art music from Bach to Beethoven he had grown up in – his own particular tribal 'language'. A letter to Zelter of 13 September 1822 criticises the yodelling of the Swiss mountain villagers for its parallel fifths, and his reaction to Berlioz's music is perhaps the most prominent example of the restricted range of his appreciation.

world. Mendelssohn's reply adopts an uncharacteristically defensive tone, which seeks to defend his work but seems to deflect the question.

You appear to mock me about my A minor Quartet, when you say that you have to rack your brains to find out what the composer was thinking about in such instrumental works, when often the composer had not thought about anything. I must defend my quartet, for it is very dear to me; all the same, its success depends too much upon its performance.[46]

(It would have to be admitted, though, that Abraham Mendelssohn was never the most receptive to modern music, disliking even most Beethoven, so that his confusion over the quartet is hardly difficult to understand.) What was perhaps of more concern was that Mendelssohn's sister Fanny, undoubtedly his closest musical confidante, could offer no support of her brother here. Similarly, the sheer ingenuity of his quartet's cyclic construction seemed to be too difficult for most listeners to comprehend:

Many people have already heard it, but has it ever occurred to any of them (my sister excepted, along with Rietz and also Marx) to see a whole in it? One praises the intermezzo, another this, another that. Phui to all of them![47]

Despite its extreme cyclic integration, the complexity of his quartet was such that most listeners were unable to perceive the higher unity of the whole composition, and instead focused only on individual moments.

Perhaps the final confirmation came two years later, following the composition of Mendelssohn's fourth and last programmatic-poetic overture. Having sent a copy of the manuscript of *Das Märchen von der schönen Melusine* to Fanny for her criticism, Mendelssohn was less than pleased to receive her reply, which, while enthusing over the work, asked him a seemingly innocuous question regarding which story he had in mind.

Now I really must be cross. You! You ask me which tale you are to read? How many are there, then? And how many do I know? And don't you know the story of the 'fair Melusina'? And would it not be better to wrap oneself up in all conceivable sorts of instrumental music without a title, when one's own sister (you raven-sister! [*Rabenschwester*]) doesn't appreciate such a title?[48]

---

[46] Letter to his father, Paris, 31 March 1832, *Briefe*, vol. I, pp. 329–30. This profession that his work may well have meant nothing recalls one of Goethe's stranger comments concerning his own poetry – that there were in fact no ideas behind it (6 May 1827, in Eckermann, *Gespräche mit Goethe*, pp. 648–9).

[47] Letter to Adolf Lindblad, 22 April 1828, in Dahlgren, *Bref till Adolf Fredrik Lindblad från Mendelssohn*, p. 20.

[48] Letter to Fanny Hensel, 7 April 1834, *Briefe*, vol. II, pp. 36–7.

While we might view Mendelssohn's insistence on the determinacy of instrumental music slightly more leniently, we must bear in mind that, for him, to have created semantic ambiguity in the listener, and his sister at that, was to have failed as a composer. The problem here, which Mendelssohn found impossible to ignore, is that his own sister – the one person in the world to whom he felt the closest artistic and spiritual empathy – could not understand the meaning of his music without asking him for verbal clarification. (Later, upon its first performance, someone asked Mendelssohn what the overture was actually about, a question which, on Schumann's account, prompted Mendelssohn's somewhat flippant retort, 'hmm, a *mésalliance*'.[49]) It is notable here that this, in 1834, is the last programmatic overture Mendelssohn ever wrote, coinciding as it does with the decline in cyclic works within the composer's oeuvre.

The cyclic and programmatic works Mendelssohn had written in the late 1820s and early 1830s had too often proven incomprehensible even to Mendelssohn's closest colleagues. He was, in short, in danger of retreating into the solipsistic madness of his own private language in his music.

Cyclic form in Mendelssohn's 'middle-period' works and the question of intelligibility

The solution to this impasse lay in the approach adopted by Mendelssohn in his music from the later 1830s onwards. In these works, the overtly radical forms and gestures of some of his earlier pieces are replaced by a surface conformity to generic structures and expectations, which nevertheless conceals a far more complex and subtle process underneath the superficial impression of normality. The classical poise of these works is the result of a balance between generic conformity and an immensely skilled command of compositional technique, where all the elements of Mendelssohn's musical style are held in a subtle balance. As Krummacher has demonstrated in great detail, the extremity and even slight ostentatiousness of his earlier music is replaced by a more understated but yet more complex use of counterpoint, thematic derivation, motivic saturation of accompanying voices and relationship to generic form. In particular, the process of thematic accompaniment, counterpoint and developmental variation that Mendelssohn

---

[49] Schumann, 'Erinnerungen an Mendelssohn', p. 102; also see the footnote to his review 'Ouvertüre zum "Märchen von der schönen Melusine"' (*NZfM*, 4 (1836)), *Gesammelte Schriften*, vol. I, p. 143.

developed here proved crucial for later composers (such as Brahms and Dvořák), transforming the structures and language associated with the so-called classical style into a new Romantic means of construction.[50] Poetic elements are still present, but they are always intimately bound up with the more 'purely musical' aspects of the music's construction, and not dissociated as was the case with the 'Reformation' Symphony. Thus Mendelssohn's mature music achieves a remarkable synthesis between form and content.[51] In this, Mendelssohn was bearing out Schumann's famous claim for him as 'the highest [brightest, most brilliant] musician of our age, the one who sees most clearly through the contradictions of the era and is the first to reconcile them'.[52] Or, as Wagner was later to admit privately, 'the greatest purely musical genius since Mozart'.[53]

As Krummacher has argued, the problem facing Mendelssohn was one of creating a comprehensible musical *form*. The problems in understanding his cyclic and programmatic works of the 1820s and early 1830s had arisen from a surplus of signifying content without recognisable form, as if bearing out Hegel's criticism of instrumental music. To this end Mendelssohn strove to give to instrumental music an intelligible design, which necessitated his music's structure embodying a clear relationship to recognisable models.[54] Yet the structures Mendelssohn creates underneath the superficial appearance of normality are remarkably varied and complex, as has been long recognised by those familiar with his music. This balance between generic conformity and individuality does of course vary according to genre and

---

[50] Krummacher, *Mendelssohn – Der Komponist*; also see Thomas Christian Schmidt-Beste, 'Mendelssohn's Chamber Music', in Peter Mercer-Taylor (ed.), *The Cambridge Companion to Mendelssohn* (Cambridge University Press, 2004), pp. 141–4.

[51] See Krummacher, *Mendelssohn – Der Komponist*; Schmidt, *Die ästhetischen Grundlagen der Instrumentalmusik Felix Mendelssohn Bartholdys*, pp. 318–27.

[52] Schumann, review of Mendelssohn's Piano Trio No. 1, Op. 49, 'Trios für Pianoforte und Begleitung' (*NZfM*, 13 (1840)), *Gesammelte Schriften*, vol. I, pp. 500–1.

[53] Reported by Hans von Bülow in *Ausgewählte Schriften: 1850–92* (Leipzig: Breitkopf & Härtel, 1896), p. 371.

[54] Mendelssohn's advice to his sister, concerning her E♭ Quartet, is revealing here as to the composer's aesthetic views concerning this question of form: 'I must take to task the compositional style of the work in general, or if you wish, the form [*Form*]. I would advise you to pay greater heed to maintaining a certain form, particularly in the modulations – it is perfectly all right to shatter such a form, but it is the contents themselves which must shatter it, through inner necessity; without this, such new or unusual formal turns and modulations only make the piece more vague and diffuse. I have noticed the same error in some of my more recent pieces . . . I feel I am right in having more respect than before for form and proper craftsmanship, or whatever the technical expressions are.' (Unpublished letter, 30 January 1835, quoted by Günter Marx in the preface to Fanny Hensel, String Quartet in E♭ (Wiesbaden: Breitkopf & Härtel, 1988).)

audience target-group within Mendelssohn's music, as Thomas Schmidt has suggested. The expectations and musical expertise of the audience for private, domestic music-making – middle-class, largely female, as epitomised in some of the *Songs without Words* – would, for instance, obviously be different from that of the *bürgerliche* society attending a symphony concert, the needs of the large-scale choral societies and festivals from that of the musical connoisseur at a chamber concert.[55] Hence we observe the difference between the Mendelssohn of the large-scale public works such as the *Lobgesang*, *Paulus* and *Elijah*, and that of the great chamber works, a division which historically has given rise to some extraordinary critical misconceptions.

Within this new formal aesthetic, cyclic elements still have a role, but are more discreetly integrated into the music than were the procedures of Mendelssohn's youth. Mendelssohn's earlier cyclic style had been denoted by its synthesis of ongoing thematic development across the four movements and the cyclic recall of past material within them. The explicit recall and literal reminiscence of earlier works is by and large discarded; continuity between these two periods is maintained, however, by the continuation of this process of inter-movement thematic development.[56]

In this, Mendelssohn avoids the danger of confusion and incomprehensibility, by maintaining an external conformity to established forms. There is not the flamboyance of Mendelssohn's earlier cyclic works (even though this can be so impressive), but this is counterbalanced by the more understated technique of thematic growth and metamorphosis across the movements of his work. (There is a sense, after all, in which the radical cyclic structures of his youth are a bit ostentatious, a display of technical dexterity that Mendelssohn in later life, given his upbringing and distrust of virtuoso display, may have come to frown on.) At the same time, one is faced with the paradox that the new style, due to the very fact of its subtlety, is seemingly more conventional. What is distinctively Mendelssohnian about this, however, is the extreme sophistication and technical strength of the music, which is hidden under this veneer of the utmost normality.

Given this subtlety of Mendelssohn's new style, what constitutes a cyclic connection is obviously going to be open to interpretation. In some cases, where a work demonstrates only loose affinities in construction between different movements one might be excused for doubting the relevance of

---

[55] Schmidt, *Die ästhetischen Grundlagen der Instrumentalmusik Felix Mendelssohn Bartholdys*, pp. 191–6.

[56] Except for a few texted works (such as the *Lobgesang* or *Elijah*), where thematic recall is prompted by clear dramatic reasons, overt cyclic recall or reminiscence is eschewed in all Mendelssohn's later music.

Ex. 6.1 Piano Trio No. 2 in C minor Op. 66 (1845): thematic relationships.

calling too much attention to such cyclic procedures. In other cases the connections are so ubiquitous as to make the contention not only reasonable but highly meaningful to understanding the piece. Thomas Schmidt, for instance, has drawn attention to the thoroughgoing use of a rising motive $\hat{5}$–$\hat{8}$–$\hat{3}$ throughout the composer's C minor Piano Trio Op. 66 (Ex. 6.1).[57]

While this particular idea is so prevalent within Mendelssohn's music as almost to constitute a personal *idée fixe* (the first Trio Op. 49 is similarly based on this figure, Ex. 6.2), the extremely consistent use here does indeed seem to point to a meaningful and indeed intended connection between the parts of the work. (As Schmidt has gone on to show, the melody of the

---

[57] This example is based on that given by Schmidt, *Die ästhetischen Grundlagen der Instrumentalmusik Felix Mendelssohn Bartholdys*, p. 323.

Ex. 6.2 Piano Trio No. 1 in D minor Op. 49 (1839): thematic relationships.

Ex. 6.3 Quartet in E♭, Op. 44 No. 3 (1838): relationship between third movement and finale.

Ex. 6.4 Quartet in D, Op. 44 No. 1 (1838): circular allusion to opening at close of finale.

chorale that forms the decisive breakthrough in the second trio's finale was modified by the composer to become far more closely allied with that of this constitutive motive in that work.)

In the Op. 44 quartets, however, the links between movements are more general and in some cases could easily be due to characteristics of Mendelssohn's style rather than to any intended connections. (This set is in many ways the most 'classical' opus of Mendelssohn's musical output, as shown by the decision uniquely to publish all three quartets together, and radical surface gestures are on the whole suppressed in favour of a more restrained employment of musical elements.) The ubiquitousness of first themes starting with rising arpeggios in the E minor Quartet Op. 44 No. 2 is undoubtedly a unifying feature, but on the other hand is a general characteristic of Mendelssohn's mature style, as Friedhelm Krummacher has shown. A variant of this procedure is found in the E♭ Quartet, the third of the group, whose finale tacitly takes up a figure from the preceding adagio (Ex. 6.3).[58]

Other connections are more unassuming than in Mendelssohn's previous works, such as the clear though nevertheless rather general allusion to the opening of the D major Quartet Op. 44 No. 1 – the arpeggiac climb to a F♯² $\hat{3}$ in the first violin over tremolo string accompaniment – in the last bars of the finale (Ex. 6.4). (This is after all no more radical than Haydn's procedure in his 'Hornsignal' Symphony.) The finale nonetheless does seem

---

[58] Noted earlier by Werner, *Mendelssohn: A New Image*, p. 360.

Ex. 6.5 Cello Sonata No. 1 in B♭, Op. 45 (1838): thematic relationships.

set on revisiting the gestures of the opening movement in its continued exploration of the registral space around this top F♯ in its primary theme.

However, in the first Cello Sonata Op. 45, the close relationship between finale and first movement is so transparent as to still any doubts as to the relevance of such a connection.[59] The angular intervals of the first theme of the opening movement are smoothed out into the gentle conjunct motion of the finale's main theme, a process of thematic resolution that Réti would probably have held up as exemplary (Ex. 6.5). This work, one of the hidden secrets of Mendelssohn's chamber music, imparts a graceful roundness to its three-movement form from these connections – the relaxed sonata-rondo finale balancing the aspiring lyricism of the first movement, and the central andante fulfilling a dual role as slow movement and intermezzo-like scherzo substitute. This latter movement balances the unfolding of its lyrical central section within the encasing G minor material, whose characteristic rhythm persists throughout this inner section. Even this movement hides a variant of the primary idea of the outer movements within its second phrase.

In order to explore this aspect of Mendelssohn's later music in sufficient depth, I will take one of his most important mature works as a final case study. This is the Symphony No. 3 in A minor, popularly known as the 'Scottish'. As the only mature instrumental symphony that the composer published this work occupies a highly important position within Mendelssohn's oeuvre, and critical reception since its day has stressed its position as arguably the finest symphonic work in the fifty years between

<hr/>

[59] See also Todd, *Mendelssohn: A Life in Music*, p. 367; Newman, *The Sonata since Beethoven*, pp. 302–4.

Beethoven's Ninth and Brahms' First.[60] Beyond this, the symphony is one of the most important cyclic works of the first half of the nineteenth century, a fact that was recognised as early as its first performance.[61] This is the successful work in Mendelssohn's eyes that the 'Reformation' and 'Italian' Symphonies were not and, as such, potentially highly instructive as to the composer's aesthetic aims. In a sense, it must improve where the previous works had failed for the composer – its cyclic processes should be more subtly integrated into the overall fabric of the work, the programmatic and poetic elements should never intrude to the detriment of the musical substance, and it should sustain sufficient musical interest in its own terms.[62] It thus stands as both a paradigm of Mendelssohn's mature cyclic style and as perhaps its highest example.

MENDELSSOHN'S MATURE CYCLICISM

Symphony No. 3 in A minor ('Scottish') Op. 56

The Symphony in A minor Op. 56 drew its initial inspiration from Mendelssohn's 1829 visit to Britain, though the symphony's gestation was protracted, being completed only in 1841–2 and receiving its first performance under the composer's baton in March 1842. Critics at the time were almost unanimous in their praise for the work: the *Allgemeine musikalische Zeitung* (*AmZ*) stated that 'Mendelssohn's symphony is in our opinion the greatest accomplished in the genre since Beethoven, uniting rich fantasy and the highest formal skill with the most beautiful interplay of themes',[63] Schumann considered that with respect to 'beauty and delicacy of structure' the new symphony was comparable to Mendelssohn's overtures, and was

---

[60] For example Hans von Bülow, in the famous 'open letter' following the appearance of Brahms' Symphony No. 1 (Bülow, *Ausgewählte Schriften*, pp. 369–72).

[61] For example Robert Schumann's much-cited review in *NZfM*, and the anonymous reviewer for *AmZ*.

[62] John Michael Cooper has argued that one reason for suppressing the 'Italian' Symphony was its lack of overriding thematic unity, unusual within Mendelssohn's symphonic oeuvre and thus potentially a source of dissatisfaction for the composer (*Mendelssohn's Italian Symphony*, pp. 153–4).

[63] *Allgemeine musikalische Zeitung*, 47 (1845), col. 362, referring to the Prague performance under Kittl, cited in Konold, *Die Symphonien Felix Mendelssohn Bartholdys*, p. 231, who provides a good digest of contemporary sources regarding the symphony's early reception (pp. 229–35).

'no less rich in delightful instrumental effects',[64] while Macfarren called it 'a work to raise the author to the highest pinnacle of musical repute'.[65] What is most interesting from the view of the present study is the particular attention that was drawn in several early reviews to the symphony's inter-movement thematic unity and the organic nature of the work's form. The *AmZ* again stated that though the symphony 'is similar in layout and form to those previously introduced in the genre, the important difference is that the single movements ... are not in themselves self-standing independent pieces, but are intimately connected to each another and therefore form just one large movement',[66] while August Kahlert, following the publication of the symphony, similarly drew particular attention to the work's thematic unity, devoting several pages to explication of the thematic working and commenting that 'the entire work is characterised by internal proportion, fine spiritual cohesion of all ideas, and firmly delineated forms'.[67] Robert Schumann's comments are perhaps the most famous, and due to their importance are worth repeating again here:

> The ground-plan of the symphony is distinguished by the intimate relation of all four movements to one another; even the melodic contours of the main themes of the four movements are related, as the most cursory inspection of the thematic material will verify. More than any other symphony, it forms a tightly woven, complete whole: across the four movements, character, key and rhythm are only slightly contrasted. As the composer himself has indicated in a prefatory note, the four movements are to be performed directly after each other, without the customary long pauses in between.[68]

Cyclic themes and thematic connections between movements

Two main groups or families of themes run throughout the symphony – the first based on the ascending fourth / minor-third $\hat{5}$–$\hat{8}$–$\hat{3}$ that is so familiar throughout Mendelssohn's oeuvre (*a*), and the second a more general shape based on a descending scale (*b*), often subsidiary to the former (Ex. 6.6).[69]

[64] Robert Schumann, 'Sinfonien für Orchester' (*NZfM*, 18 (1843)), *Gesammelte Schriften*, vol. II, p. 133. This was high praise given Schumann's regard for Mendelssohn's overtures.
[65] George Macfarren, Review of Mendelssohn Symphony No. 3, *Musical World*, 17 (1842), 185–7, reprinted in part in Brown, *A Portrait of Mendelssohn*, p. 402.
[66] *AmZ*, 44 (1842), col. 258, quoted by Konold, *Die Symphonien*, p. 230.
[67] *AmZ*, 45 (1843), col. 344, quoted by Konold, *Die Symphonien*, p. 233.
[68] Robert Schumann, 'Sinfonien für Orchester', *Gesammelte Schriften*, vol. II, pp. 132–3.
[69] The use of cyclic themes in this work was first systematically investigated in 1979 by Rey M. Longyear in 'Cyclic Form and Tonal Relationships in Mendelssohn's "Scottish" Symphony',

Ex. 6.6 Symphony No. 3 in A minor Op. 56 (1829–42): cyclic themes *a* and *b*.

Both of these shapes grow out of the slow introduction to the symphony, the opening of which was the idea Mendelssohn jotted down on that memorable evening in Edinburgh, where the idea of the symphony first came to him (see Fig. 6.4).

The introduction's opening motive, outlining the rising fourth / minor-third of theme *a*, is transformed into the allegro theme of the following sonata-form first movement (Ex. 6.7). From this, it is developed into a variety of shapes. The first theme's concluding phrase (b. 75) is formed from a developed variation of its opening (b. 63), and gives rise to a further derivation that serves as the transition theme (b. 126). This theme's motivic constituents, a rising fourth and filled-in third, are then reordered as the lyrical closing theme (b. 181), whose conclusion (b. 189) features another variant of the concluding pendant that aligns it more clearly with the initial motive. From here it turns up in a pentatonic-inflected guise as the bubbling clarinet melody of the scherzo. The adagio third movement is initially less clearly derived from either theme group, though the continuation of the first subject demonstrates a potential connection.[70]

The finale features two further metamorphoses of this theme: the second theme of the first group with an inverted variant (bb. 14 and 37), and the second subject's first theme that follows (b. 66). Finally, in the maestoso coda, this thematic shape is reformulated and then liquidated in two related variants that are simultaneously a simplification and resolution of the finale's derivations (compare IV: bb. 397–8 with bb. 14–17) and a return to aspects from the first movement (the prominent scale-degree $\hat{6}$ from the opening movement's first subject (b. 64), now resolved to the major mode).

Subsidiary to this is the other, looser thematic idea – a descending minor scale, often dotted (*b*, Ex. 6.8). This can be heard in the introduction's continuation – a long, expressive cantilena for the unaccompanied violins (b. 17) – a secondary theme of the first movement's first subject (b. 99), the

In Theory Only, 4 (1979), 38–48. Later in the 1980s Greg Vitercik modified Longyear's model into two families which are more commensurate with my own analysis (Vitercik, *The Early Works of Felix Mendelssohn*, pp. 292–3).

[70] See Longyear, 'Cyclic Form and Tonal Relationships in Mendelssohn's "Scottish" Symphony', p. 41.

Ex. 6.7 Symphony No. 3: thematic metamorphoses of *a* theme.

Ex. 6.8 Symphony No. 3: thematic metamorphoses of *b* theme.

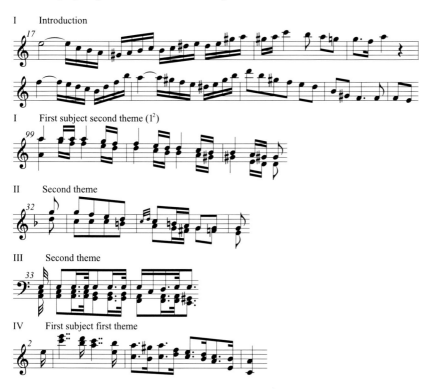

second subjects of the scherzo and the slow movement (b. 32 and b. 33, the latter as a solemn, almost funereal *lamento*), and the fierce opening of the finale (marked *guerriero* – warlike – on the title page). This last appearance is subsequently transformed into the true C major second subject of the finale (b. 82), which will eventually give way to a more unadorned major variant by the end of the exposition (b. 109).

This second group of themes in fact grows out of the first at the symphony's opening, where the concluding phrase of the introduction's first theme (bb. 14–16), a descent from $\hat{5}$ to $\hat{1}$, is immediately taken up by the violins in their ensuing unaccompanied cantilena, which forms the basis of the *b* theme (see Ex. 6.9).

The extreme unity of musical material across the symphony is, as Schumann claimed, groundbreaking, in that it goes far beyond traditional links between movements found in earlier symphonies and even surpasses most later attempts in its sophistication. Indeed, the only work of the time to approach Mendelssohn's design is by Schumann himself, his D minor Symphony (later published as No. 4), which had been premiered barely two

Ex. 6.9 Symphony No. 3, introduction: motivic derivation of second theme from end of first.

months earlier. The parallels between the two works are fascinating given the virtual simultaneity of their creation and common origin in Leipzig. Comparison of the two is instructive as to Mendelssohn's mature style and the notable differences between his and his friend's aesthetic approaches: while aiming for a similar goal, the two achieve it through completely different means.

What is particularly distinctive about Mendelssohn's procedure is the simultaneous coexistence of a formal procedure of great strength and complexity with the appearance of the utmost normality; his work feels like a lyrical Romantic symphony, incorporating this extremely intricate cyclic process within an attractive melodic exterior. Schumann's Fourth Symphony is, on the surface, a more overtly radical work, departing more clearly from standard formal models, whose material is formed through the successive transformations of a more basic thematic idea. (To be rather schematic, the difference between the two could be characterised by saying that in Mendelssohn's best works the composer shows the reconciling of almost intractable problems, largely through his mastery of the means of the genre – not avoiding but transcending; Schumann's, when he departs from the limiting features, hence being seen as more innovatory.[71] There is no particular reason to privilege either position.) The subtlety of Mendelssohn's design is probably one reason why his symphony has not been so widely celebrated for its cyclic qualities, despite their undoubted presence.

The nub of Mendelssohn's achievement here is his reconciling of developmental logic within lyrical, song-like melodies, both at the inter-movement level and across the work. Carl Dahlhaus has claimed in this context that Mendelssohn was the only nineteenth-century composer to reconcile the Romantic desire for lyrical, lied-like melody with the ongoing teleological process seen as requisite for the symphonic style; more generally, the only

---

[71] This quality of Mendelssohn's music was recognised by the more perceptive critics of the time, including Macfarren in relation to the present symphony and of course Schumann himself in his celebrated 'Mozart of the nineteenth century' label – the composer 'who sees most clearly through the problems of the age and is the first to reconcile them.' (Schumann, *Gesammelte Schriften*, vol. II, pp. 500–1.)

composer of his generation really to resolve the conflicting demands of form and content in his instrumental music.[72] At a time when musical form was disintegrating either into the simple, schematic designs of the miniature characteristic piece or into 'formless' rhapsodic structures, the mere residue of its material-content,[73] Mendelssohn uniquely was able to overcome the miniaturist tendency in contemporary music and solve the issue of the creation of large-scale Romantic symphonic designs. This is exemplified for Dahlhaus particularly in the thematic process of the first movement of the 'Scottish' Symphony, which he sees as an ideal-type of Mendelssohn's technique.[74] This example is worth exploring in greater detail here in order to understand the relationship and intersection of cyclic thematic techniques with wider formal issues in the composer's mature music.

Cyclic thematic manipulation and formal process: first movement

The strength of Mendelssohn's achievement stems from his capacity to derive lyrical songlike themes from the continuous development of motivic constituents – effortlessly to draw what appear as self-contained themes into an ongoing thematic process. The subtlety of his procedure is demonstrated as early as the introduction, where the embryonic shape of the *b* theme is derived from the tail of the ballad-like opening paragraph (Ex. 6.9).

   This apparently simple opening melody belies its ostensible artlessness in its internal process of motivic developmental-variation (Ex. 6.10). The first four-bar unit outlines two important shapes – the ascending arpeggiation e^1–a^1–c^2 and the implied embryonic descent c^2–b^1–a^1–$g\sharp^1$. Its continuation (bb. 5–8) varies the material of the first bars, restating the opening in sequence up through the tonic triad (a^1–c^2–e^2), now elaborating more clearly the second-half descent from e^2 ($\hat{5}$) down to $g\sharp^1$, broken only by

---

[72] Carl Dahlhaus (ed.), *Das Problem Mendelssohn* (Regensburg: Bosse, 1974), pp. 7–8; *Nineteenth-Century Music*, trans. J.B. Robinson (Berkeley and Los Angeles, CA: University of California Press, 1989), p. 158 (the essentialised symphonic qualities that Dahlhaus demands and the implicitly Beethovenian orientation of their aesthetic values may, however, be open to debate). Krummacher's entire project in *Mendelssohn – Der Komponist* can be seen as a detailed substantiation of Dahlhaus' claim.

[73] Dahlhaus, *Nineteenth-Century Music*, pp. 87–8.

[74] *Ibid.*, pp. 156–8. A detailed consideration of this movement from a similar perspective has also been given by Siegfried Oechsle in *Symphonik nach Beethoven: Studien zu Schubert, Schumann, Mendelssohn und Gade* (Kassel: Bärenreiter, 1992), pp. 247–371.

Ex. 6.10 Symphony No. 3, introduction: internal developmental-variation.

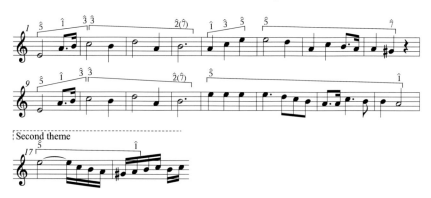

Ex. 6.11 Symphony No. 3, first movement: motivic derivation of second theme from end of first.

a consonant skip to a¹ midway through. Upon its repetition in the consequent phrase, this final portion is revealed as a full scalic descent from $\hat{5}$ to $\hat{1}$ (bb. 13–16). This concluding gesture is immediately taken up by the violins, entering for the first time at b. 17 with a recitative-like passage that successively transforms this five-note fall into a larger scalic descent, which clearly foreshadows the *b* theme that will appear explicitly at b. 99.

This process of derivation is paralleled in the ensuing allegro, where the second statement of the opening theme is modified in its second phrase into a descending scale $\hat{5}$–$\hat{1}$ (bb. 90–1, repeated at bb. 93–4), emphasising the b♭ familiar from the Neapolitan harmony of the introduction's climax, which similarly prepares the forthcoming *b* material (Ex. 6.11). Even the parallel thirds of the *b* theme – characteristic also of its later appearance in the scherzo – may be seen to be foreshadowed in the tenths between the bass line of the opening andante and the implied melodic voice (Ex. 6.12).

Thus, despite their surface contrast, both *a* and *b* themes reveal a latent thematic connection stemming from a subtle process of contrasting derivation originating in the opening bars.

Ex. 6.12 Symphony No. 3, introduction: linear reduction of opening theme.

The process of thematic metamorphosis of *a* material across the exposition is no less sophisticated. The allegro first theme (1¹, b. 63) – a more
ornamented version of the andante's austere melodic outline – is presented
three times in sequence on a, c and e, outlining the scale degrees of the
tonic minor triad that will each be significant as tonal areas in their own
right in both the opening movement and finale.[75] The second appearance
is unchanged except for the new harmonic context, but the third segment
modifies the material to circumscribing its initial fourth b–e, reflecting the
harmonic movement from the dominant back to the tonic, which is subsequently developed in the concluding fourth phrase into outlining an initial
ascending fourth followed by a scalic descent from 8̂ (Ex. 6.13).

The subsequent development of this material in the transition theme at
b. 126 takes up this fourth from the tail of the first subject, running it in
contrapuntal combination with the head of the first theme in a justly celebrated passage to which Dahlhaus rightly calls attention (Ex. 6.14).[76] This
new variant is not identical with the closing version of bb. 75ff. but is rather
a further development of it, whose second half enlarges the initial leap of
a fourth to span a sixth b¹–g²–e² (5̂–3̂–8̂ in E minor), distantly recalling
the opening 5̂–8̂–3̂ of 1¹. As Dahlhaus notes, this contrapuntal combination of closely related themes lends itself to a developmental function; this
passage's quality of invertible thematic counterpoint will be realised later
by Mendelssohn in the development section, but it is here the start of a
passage of fifty-six bars that presents an intensive further development of
the material heard thus far in the exposition. This passage takes the place
of an expanded second subject group, starting on V/v but being tonally
unstable and essentially developmental, threatening to slip all the while to C
major, the more usual relative-major secondary area, and thus postponing
any stable secondary theme or sense of harmonic arrival until b. 181.

---

[75] These diatonic shifts are echoed in the earlier *Hebrides* Overture, and have prompted R. Larry
Todd to speak of a particular 'Scottish' or more precisely 'Ossianic' manner in Mendelssohn's
oeuvre ('Mendelssohn's Ossianic Manner', pp. 152–3).

[76] Dahlhaus, *Nineteenth-Century Music*, p. 157.

Ex. 6.13 Symphony No. 3, first movement: internal developmental-variation of first subject.

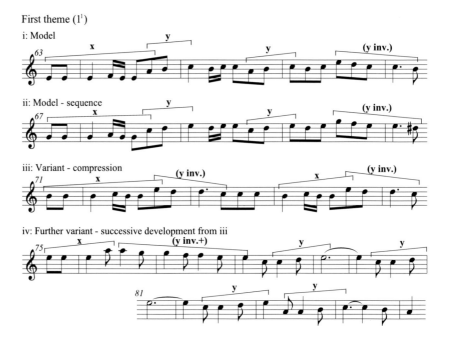

Ex. 6.14 Symphony No. 3, first movement, transition theme.

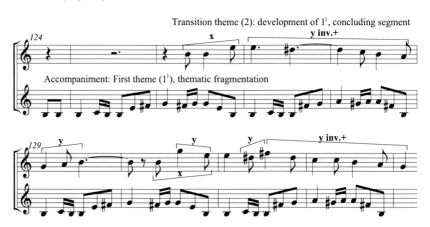

This closing theme (3) now takes up and develops the second part of the transition theme, modifying its subsequent rising sixth $\hat{5}$–$\hat{3}$ (b^2–g^3) and scalic descent from this g^3 (Ex. 6.15).

Effectively the motivic constituents of the first thematic shape – a rising fourth and filled-in third – have now been reordered across the exposition

Ex. 6.15 Symphony No. 3, first movement, closing theme.

into the final filled-in third followed by rising fourth. In addition, the harmonic sonority underlying the third bar of this theme recalls the pungent c♯–d and embedded tritone of the transition (bb. 137 and 145) that formed the pivotal movement back from C major to the dominant of E minor, which had subsequently been reiterated in sequence in the bars immediately preceding the theme (bb. 153–8, 177–80; also cf. 121–3 and the future 'storm' section of the development and coda).

What is distinctly Mendelssohnian about the thematic process seen across the exposition of this symphony is the sense in which each theme grows from the latter stages of the preceding one, yet despite the transparent motivic logic there is no sense in which the themes that result are ever merely an accumulation of motivic constituents instead of memorable themes or melodic entities in their own right.[77] This is partly what distinguishes Mendelssohn's from Brahms' later procedure – the developmental variation of small-scale melodic constituents which, while similar in many respects to Mendelssohn's process, is rarely used to create lyrical melodic phrases but combined to form sentences analogous to Dahlhaus' description of musical prose[78] – or indeed the different technique of thematic transformation exhibited in Schumann's Fourth Symphony and, following this, by Liszt in his B minor Sonata, where the thematic material involved is less strongly melodically characterised, consisting of a simple diastematic shape which is subjected to surface variation or reconfigured. This process of successive

---

[77] Donald Mintz has spoken of Mendelssohn's technique in this respect as giving the appearance not so much of the building of 'ever new themes' out of a motive, but rather of the absorption of a motive 'into ever new themes' ('The Sketches and Drafts for Three of Felix Mendelssohn's Major Works', p. 404). However, despite the appearance of natural melodic simplicity, this lyrical veneer is in fact attained by Mendelssohn foremost through his intricate motivic work.

[78] Carl Dahlhaus, 'Musical Prose', in *Schoenberg and the New Music*, trans. Derrick Puffett and Alfred Clayton (Cambridge University Press, 1987), pp. 105–19; also see his 'Issues in Composition', in *Between Romanticism and Modernism*, trans. Mary Whittall (Berkeley and Los Angeles, CA: University of California Press, 1980), pp. 40–78.

growth – the tendency to derive later themes from concluding stages of earlier ones – as well as the constructive principle of drawing on two contrasting families of themes which nevertheless possess a latent relationship, is similar in many ways to that of Mendelssohn's earlier works (Op. 13 is a clear example). Mendelssohn's mature music is as 'organic' as his earlier compositions, but the incorporation of lyrical themes into this developmental process is even more refined, as is the use of counterpoint and thematically derived accompanimental texture (as exemplified in the combination of themes in the first-movement exposition of this symphony).

This evolutive connection between successive themes enables Mendelssohn to avoid the danger of a symphonic movement disintegrating into a mere succession of static melodic phrases. Syntactically the phrases are rarely closed off and discrete, in spite of their pronounced lyrical-quadratic quality. This is achieved through the frequent overlapping of phrase beginnings and endings (e.g. bb. 84–5), the tendency for musical repetitions to become modified developments that evolve harmonically towards a new goal (compare bb. 84–99 with 63–84), and the keeping of strong cadential articulations to a minimum (the entire passage bb. 99–181). The only two themes after the opening andante theme (which, as the initial inspiration and thematic source for the rest of the symphony, might be seen as to some extent separate from the rest) to be pronouncedly quadratic in phrase-syntax are the initial allegro theme 1^1 and the closing theme. The former elides its last bar with the first of its modified repetition (bb. 84–5), and this following passage modifies its later part in order to build a powerful harmonic preparation for the ensuing second theme (1^2, b. 99). The closing theme, on its arrival, is the only stable and harmonically and syntactically closed theme in the exposition. By delaying its arrival until the last part of the structure Mendelssohn avoids any strong cadential articulation until the very end of the exposition, which is consequently heard as one long continuous section that finally attenuates into the stasis of its close.

Following the intensive process of development exhibited across the exposition, the development section itself is less concerned with thematic and motivic development than with the juxtaposition and contrapuntal recombination of themes, its main part taking up the invertible thematic-complex of the transition.[79] Before this, however, its opening presents a magical new direction, which hints towards the as yet unrealised 'storm' section of the coda. Some commentators have seen this storm material as unrelated to the

---

[79] See Konold, *Die Symphonien Felix Mendelssohn Bartholdys*, p. 269.

remainder of the movement – an external intrusion, 'a foreign interpolation . . . a movement within a movement', as Martin Witte has it.[80] However, the growth of this passage's largely athematic chromatic scales out of the material of the first subject is made clearly enough at the start of each appearance in the development and coda. Following the utter stasis at the close of the exposition, the bare e sustained in the strings is miraculously met in the woodwind with the unexpected fifth c♯–g♯, transforming what had been $\hat{1}$ of E minor into $\hat{3}$ of C♯ minor. The ascending third $[\hat{1}–\hat{2}–\hat{3}]$ of the first subject's second motive is repeated, trancelike, before the entire texture is shifted down a tone to B minor, where the phrase is restated. The undisguised parallel fifths of this passage recall the rising-third shifts of the first subject's opening statement, now sounding even more primitive and primeval. The following sequential repetition that would have led back to the tonic A minor is converted into a diminished seventh, which leads instead into the minor mode of the relative C that had been tantalisingly suggested in the exposition. This harmony alternates with that of the diminished seventh, drawing out the scalic motion of the original motive into a conjunct turning figure (subsequently rhythmically diminuted), which forms the basis of the storm music that erupts fully in the return of this section in the coda.

Such is the thoroughness of the developmental logic with which Mendelssohn derives themes within the exposition that this ongoing developmental tendency threatens to downplay the traditional function of the development section. As would become increasingly prominent later in the nineteenth century, the constant developmental tendency of material in the earlier stages of the movement undermines the very existence of a separate development section. Furthermore, the large-scale repetition of material demanded by the formal imperative for recapitulation (material which had itself grown so organically in the exposition) ran contrary to Romantic desires for constant development and organic growth: the aesthetic idea that a repetition must always be somehow new, changed in light of its intervening experiences. Yet without some sense of large-scale formal recurrence the very notion of musical form, in the strong sense, is endangered, and such was the artistic status and generic importance of the sonata model that few composers concerned with large-scale instrumental music in the nineteenth century could abandon the structure altogether.

---

[80] Witte, 'Zur Programmgebundenheit der Sinfonien Mendelssohns', p. 124. Also see Mathias Thomas, who speaks of 'a more or less athematic passage', *Das Instrumentalwerk Felix Mendelssohn-Bartholdys*, p. 152.

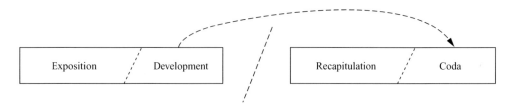

Fig. 6.1 Symphony No. 3, first movement: parallel structure.

Mendelssohn's response to this problem was to rethink fundamentally the functions of the traditional sections of sonata form. Thus the development section, after having briefly hinted at new material, is designed more as a circular transition back to the restatement of the exposition in the recapitulation. This latter section is newly varied now with the addition of a new lyrical countermelody in the cellos and, as normal with Mendelssohn, drastically curtailed, since it leads directly to the coda, which is hence heard as the goal of the movement. This coda takes up the as yet unrealised potential of the new material of the development section (the storm passage), thus mirroring the earlier section. The design manifested in this symphony therefore follows Krummacher's model for Mendelssohn's mature style – a structural reworking of the basic sonata template with the development section designed as a lead-back to the recapitulation, which itself is often drastically shortened, and extra weight added to the coda, which often mirrors the development.[81] The resulting parallel two-strophe design thus maintains the teleological drive across the movement through to its end, while still preserving the formal articulation of the sonata (Fig. 6.1).

It is hard to resist speaking of a Hegelian process of *Aufhebung* in the approach to form seen here: Mendelssohn preserves the outline of the sonata model, whilst simultaneously altering its sections' internal functions in light of the demands of the material, transcending the model, which nevertheless still retains its importance.

The reason why Mendelssohn is normally concerned to under-articulate the double return of the recapitulation is related to this desire for onward teleological drive. The first-subject reprise is kept to a minimum, being used just to articulate the return at this stage of the movement's form, but in the interests of maintaining a sense of ongoing momentum this point of return is typically blurred or elided. Characteristic Mendelssohnian devices

---

[81] See, for a brief summary, Krummacher, 'On Mendelssohn's Compositional Style', pp. 556–8; also cf. *Mendelssohn – Der Komponist*, p. 324, and Kohlhase, 'Studien zur Form in den Streichquartetten von Felix Mendelssohn Bartholdy', p. 100.

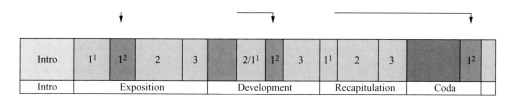

Fig. 6.2 Symphony No. 3, first movement: rotational shifting of contrasting 1^2 theme.

for this include the introduction of a new countermelody, often beginning some bars prior to the onset of the recapitulation and hence heard as a continuation from the preceding music (as is realised most beautifully here in the symphony), or the recapitulation over a tonic $^6_3$ or $^6_4$ chord, undercutting the tonal grounding and hence creating a harmonic need for closure which stretches from the end of the exposition to the coda. This structure was important for many later Romantic approaches to sonata form, being taken up by Schumann and later by Brahms.[82]

The actual goal of the sonata-form movement is the restatement at the climax of the coda of the *b* theme (1^2), which had been excised from the recapitulation and thus saved for this final reappearance. This theme had always seemed catalytic in its effect, its first appearance tightening up the tempo from *Allegro un poco agitato* ($\downharpoonright. = 100$) to *Assai animato* ($\downharpoonright. = 120$), and its final entry here is a fitting point for the internal sonata movement to peak and dissolve into the return of the introduction as the frame to the movement. This holding back of the second theme is in fact the final stage in a process of rotational shifting of this material across the internal sections of the movement. In the development, the 1^2 theme had been delayed until after the transition material (which, however, can also be heard as functioning simultaneously as a surrogate first subject due to its incorporation of the latter's material in its contrapuntal complex), and subsequently its appearance is shifted to after the recapitulation's closing theme in the coda (Fig. 6.2). Its final transformation here is further reminiscent of elements of the *a* theme in its outline $\hat{8}$–$\hat{5}$ $\hat{3}$–$\hat{1}$ $\hat{5}$, suggesting a partial (though incomplete)

[82] Peter Smith has described this feature in Brahms's music as 'continuous linear evolution' (Smith, 'Liquidation, Augmentation, and Brahms's Recapitulatory Overlaps', *19th-Century Music*, 17 (1994), 237–62, and 'Brahms and Schenker: A Mutual Response to Sonata Form', *Music Theory Spectrum*, 16 (1994), 77–103). A few precedents for this harmonically ungrounded recapitulation are found in Beethoven's music (e.g. the Eighth Symphony, the 'Appassionata' and Op. 90 Sonatas), though Mendelssohn appears to have been the first to exploit it extensively in his works from the 1820s onwards.

Ex. 6.16 Symphony No. 3, first movement, coda: possible synthesis of *a* and *b*.

merger of the two opposing themes, an idea which will be paralleled more strongly in the second movement (Ex. 6.16).

This interplay between continuous thematic development and architectonic formal design demonstrates the remarkable synthesis of structure and process in Mendelssohn's music, bearing out Dahlhaus's claim for him as the only composer of the age to resolve the competing claims of form and content in his instrumental music:

Though seemingly contradictory, Mendelssohn's combination of lied melodies, counterpoint, and motivic association is thoroughly tenable on its own terms and served as a starting point for his attempt to establish and vindicate symphonic form in a different manner from Beethoven .... [W]e should marvel that Mendelssohn was successful at all in handling continuous lied melodies as though they were complex, intrinsically antithetical themes – that is, in dissecting these melodies and modifying and recombining the parts without making his technique look heavy-handed and extraneous. In any event, it is wrong to say that Mendelssohn simply filled in traditional symphonic form without tackling its problems. That Mendelssohn was able to solve the problem that brings this form to life, and to solve it so completely that we are hardly aware of its existence, should not blind us to the fact that its difficulties were virtually insurmountable and remained so for a full century.[83]

It might seem therefore that, given this unique and exemplary position, the status of Mendelssohn's symphony as one of the greatest symphonic works ever penned is impregnable. But, as so often with this composer's music, there must be a catch somewhere. Mendelssohn's achievement here is, according to Dahlhaus, at the expense of his music's claim to monumentality. This contention is worth interrogating a little further here, since it will lead to important hermeneutic and biographical issues which need to be investigated before offering a reading of Mendelssohn's symphony and consideration of the later movements.

---

[83] Dahlhaus, *Nineteenth-Century Music*, pp. 157–8.

Interpretative issues: the 'Scottish' Symphony
as overdetermined

The reasons for believing that Mendelssohn's Third and Fourth Symphonies abandon their claim to monumentality – as with the seemingly related assertion that his music departs from Beethovenian models in ways qualitatively different from other comparable nineteenth-century composers – is never spelled out by Dahlhaus; in some ways this might seem an unlikely assertion to make, given that in terms of sheer scale the present symphony is as long as any of Beethoven's (with the exception obviously of the Ninth), comparable to Brahms' and longer than any of Schumann's.[84] In fact, of instrumental symphonies written before the later nineteenth century, only Schubert's Ninth outspans it. What Dahlhaus' unstated motivation may well be is the belief, iterated frequently in his consideration of the symphony, that Mendelssohn's symphony is a folkloric work – a travelogue of his journey through Scotland, a purveyor of the musical picturesque. As what is essentially a glorified musical landscape painting, Mendelssohn's symphony therefore cannot help failing to achieve true monumentality and the grandeur appropriate to the pure Germanic symphony. This seems confirmed in Dahlhaus' frequent designation of the work as the *Schottische Symphonie*, never as the more neutral 'Symphony No. 3 in A minor' as Mendelssohn published the work, and as he describes Schumann's First Symphony (*die Erste Symphonie*), rather than the equally applicable 'Spring' Symphony, which, for Dahlhaus, makes a claim, if ultimately unsuccessful, to monumentality.[85] But this cannot avoid leading to a fundamental question concerning Mendelssohn's work, which finally needs to be asked here. What evidence is there that Mendelssohn's symphony really is a musical landscape painting, an incarnation of the musical picturesque? How justified are we in taking Mendelssohn's work as a musical embodiment

---

[84] It is unclear, for instance, what attributes are possessed by the 'Reformation' and *Lobgesang* Symphonies (both of which Dahlhaus considers monumental) that are absent from the A minor and A major works. John Michael Cooper has similarly taken issue with Dahlhaus' assertion in relation to the 'Italian' Symphony, pointing out several aspects of Mendelssohn's design (especially in the 1834 revisions) that suggest not just a desire for greater scale and monumentality but also a clear desire to face up to Beethoven's legacy (Cooper, *Mendelssohn's Italian Symphony*, pp. 149–51 and 194). For consideration of some of the unexamined ideological issues underlying Dahlhaus' viewpoint see Sanna Pederson, 'On the Task of the Music Historian: The Myth of the Symphony After Beethoven', *repercussions*, 2 (1993), 5–30.

[85] Carl Dahlhaus, *Nineteenth-Century Music*, pp. 156–8, German original in *Die Musik des 19. Jahrhunderts (Neues Handbuch der Musikwissenschaft, 6)* (Wiesbaden: Athenaion, 1980), pp. 128–30.

of his experiences in Scotland? In short – is the 'Scottish' Symphony even Scottish?

As Thomas Schmidt-Beste has recently shown, there is no evidence that Mendelssohn ever considered the completed work 'Scottish' or approved of this designation for publication. Only the very beginning of the symphony, the sixteen-bar theme, jotted down in Holyrood Palace on 30 July 1829, which later became the introduction, was explicitly described as part of his 'Scottish' Symphony.[86] During the composer's Italian sojourn of 1830–1 brief mention is made to his inability to work further on the symphony since the Italian climate was not conducive to his 'Scottish mists', but after 1832 no mention is made of the symphony until Mendelssohn resumed work in 1841, when the Scottish appellation has been completely dropped. The compositional genesis of the composition across the thirteen years from conception to birth has long been unclear, but it appears that it had progressed little further from the introduction until the composer resumed the composition in 1841.[87] Effectively, the composition seems to be a work of the early 1840s.

It was only in the 1850s that the Scottish label first became attached to the work – following Julius Benedict's biography, which mentioned the Scottish genesis publicly for the first time – and it was not until two decades later that this name became widespread, following the publication of Mendelssohn's letter of 1829 in Sebastian Hensel's *Die Familie Mendelssohn*.[88] This is significant since, as we have seen, across the 1830s Mendelssohn grew increasingly doubtful concerning the possibilities of titled programmatic instrumental

---

[86] Schmidt-Beste has called attention to the fact that Mendelssohn's wording in his letter – 'I think I have found the beginning of my "Scottish" Symphony' – suggests as much that the composer had gone to Scotland with an idea for writing a Scottish Symphony already existent in his mind. 'Just how "Scottish" is the "Scottish" Symphony?', p. 158.

[87] A draft page for the first movement exposition which provides a valuable clue to the composer's work on the piece was found by Douglass Seaton in Berlin, who dated it as 'after 1834'; more recent research has suggested that the sheet dates from no earlier than 1837 and possibly some time after. For research on the genesis of the symphony see Douglass Seaton, 'A Study of a Collection of Mendelssohn's Sketches and Other Autograph Material, Deutsche Staatsbibliothek, Berlin, Mus. Ms. Autogr. Mendelssohn 19', unpublished PhD thesis, Columbia University (1977), pp. 211–39, and 'A Draft for the Exposition of the First Movement of Mendelssohn's "Scotch" Symphony', *Journal of the American Musicological Society*, 30 (1977), 129–35; Hiromi Hoshino, *Menderusuzon no 'Sukottorando kokyokyoku' [Mendelssohn's Scottish Symphony]* (Tokyo: Ongaku no Tomosha, 2003); Thomas Schmidt-Beste, editor's introduction to critical edition of score, *Sinfonie Nr. 3 a-Moll op. 56: Leipziger Mendelssohn-Ausgabe, I.5* (Wiesbaden: Breitkopf & Härtel, 2005), pp. xxii–xxvii.

[88] Julius Benedict, *Sketch of the Life and Works of the Late Felix Mendelssohn Bartholdy* (London: John Murray, 1850), pp. 14–15.

music, abandoning the genre of the poetic concert overture he had effectively created, and both retracted the 'Reformation' title to his D minor Symphony and then withdrew the work. Nothing here implies that the composer might not have still privately considered the work Scottish, which is perfectly possible, though there is no indication of this in any of his correspondence.[89] But it raises the problematic question of whether a piece whose initial inspiration came over a decade before its actual composition and saw a fundamental change in the artist's aesthetic views in the interim can really be said to be still the same as the initial conception which forms barely 1 per cent of the completed work. And irrespective of whether the symphony may still have been 'Scottish' for Mendelssohn in 1842, it is at least significant that the composer wished the work to stand as a piece of instrumental music with no picturesque title or connotations derived from such a verbal guide.

The implications of all this for a critical consideration of the symphony are obviously important. While early critics were quick to point to a 'folkish' tone in the new work, the precise geographical provenance of this feature was rarely specified. (Only one early critic in England seems perceptively to have noted similarities of construction and orchestral colour with the earlier *Hebrides* and suggested a partial Scottish or northern mood to the piece.[90]) Indeed, a musician as sensitive as Schumann made the famous mistake of confusing the A minor symphony with the 'Italian', having learnt from 'third hand' that the early part of the symphony had been written in Italy, which prompted a rhapsodic hyperbole to 'that blessed land'. In the absence of any specific colouring or locale, such a tendency can easily be viewed as nothing more than a reaction to the pronounced tendency in the symphony for the use of lyrical, songlike themes; there is nothing to suggest that this is in any way picturesque, let alone an attempt to paint another land in musical terms. Indeed, given Mendelssohn's expressed contempt for the folk music he had encountered on his travels in Britain – 'so-called national airs, that is to say, the most infamous, vulgar, false rubbish'[91] – it seems most unlikely that he would have persevered creating a symphony which contains and celebrates this heritage. Likewise, the notable use of

---

[89] The only instance is a letter to his mother of 1842 describing how the dedication to Queen Victoria fitted 'the Scottish piece very prettily', though this statement is clarified in the dedication letter to the Queen as indicating only that the 'the first idea for it came about during my earlier journey through Scotland'. See Schmidt-Beste, 'Just how "Scottish" is the "Scottish" Symphony?', pp. 156–7.

[90] The anonymous reviewer in the *Athenaeum*, 764 (18 June 1842), 549 (*ibid.*, p. 149).

[91] Letter from Llangollen, 25 August 1829 (Hensel, *Die Familie Mendelssohn*, vol. I, p. 264).

medium-scale phrase repetition in the work (e.g. the first themes of the first and second movements or the finale's coda) could be intended to suggest a more primitive or folklorish construction, but this could alternatively be viewed as a new attempt at monumentality. (This tendency, in marked contrast to Mendelssohn's more usual procedure in his chamber music of a continuous Beethovenian development, could be aptly viewed as a response to the recent discovery of Schubert's C major Symphony, whose simpler, more static, monumental style might reasonably have provided Mendelssohn and Schumann with an alternate model for symphonic construction following its performance in 1840.[92])

The work sustains the possibility of multiple readings. It can be seen simultaneously as a piece of 'absolute' instrumental music, a poetic or 'characteristic' work, or even – possibly – a piece of programme music.[93] (Indeed, the verbal over-determination – the ability to be simultaneously a pure, abstract symphony, a piece of musical landscape painting, a mythic history, an Ossianic work – is the perfect exemplification of Mendelssohn's protest that words are too imprecise and vague for music, and not the other way around.) All such views have a potential claim on the critic.[94] It is only problematic when one of these views – and one which runs contrary to the composer's designation and claims for the work, whilst nevertheless basing its sole justification on a misinformed and mistaken knowledge of these claims – is taken as an exclusive reading. The 'Scottish'

---

[92] Larry Todd has pointed to Schubert's work in the sketches for an unfinished symphony in C major dating from 1844–5, which would have been, if completed, Mendelssohn's last symphony. In the exposition of this work the opening theme, a simple diatonic melody outlining the tonic triad, is restated twice within the opening section of the exposition, each time with increased orchestral backing. The relative simplicity of construction here differs from Mendelssohn's normal (chamber music) style, with its more sophisticated process of developmental variation, and suggests a desire for greater breadth and monumentality that Todd surmises may draw on Schubert's Ninth and Beethoven's Third as models. (R. Larry Todd, 'An Unfinished Symphony by Mendelssohn', *Music & Letters*, 61 (1980), 293–309.)

[93] The symphony thus inhabits the space 'between absolute and programme music' outlined long ago by Walter Wiora and continued in much German-language discussion of the symphonic output of Mendelssohn and Schumann (see Walter Wiora, 'Zwischen absoluter und Programmusik', in Anna Amalie Abert and Wilhelm Pfannkuch (eds.), *Festschrift Friedrich Blume zum 70. Geburtstag* (Kassel: Bärenreiter, 1963), pp. 381–8; Witte, 'Zur Programmgebundenheit der Sinfonien Mendelssohns'; Ludwig Finscher, '"Zwischen absoluter und Programmusik": Zur Interpretation der deutschen romantischen Symphonie', in Christoph-Hellmut Mahling (ed.), *Über Symphonien: Beiträge zu einer musikalischen Gattung (Festschrift für Walter Wiora)* (Tutzing: H. Schneider, 1979), pp. 103–15).

[94] The poetic aspects, while not explicitly authorised by the composer, are nevertheless genuine qualities of many listeners' experience of the music, and have become part of the work's cultural meaning irrespective of whether or not the symphony was actually intended by Mendelssohn to be 'Scottish'.

view risks peripherising the symphony as picturesque. Dahlhaus' view of the symphony recalls Wagner's faint praise of the composer of the *Hebrides* as a 'musical landscape painter of the first order', albeit one who does not deny the compositional mastery demonstrated by his composition. As Thomas Grey has pointed out, by reserving for Mendelssohn a position of a painter of picturesque backdrops, Wagner was seeking to marginalise the composer as a mere imitator of the external world (and a foreign one at that), unable to delve deeply into the (German) soul.[95] Wagner's criticism, as so often, reveals if anything a latent fear of his own inclinations; the unjustified depiction of Mendelssohn as a visual impressionist is more a cover for Wagner's own tendency to musical mimesis – the 'great actor', as Nietzsche would claim, who sought to reduce musical logic and compositional craft to the accompaniment of a stage pantomime.[96]

The A minor Symphony, by being divested of its authorial designation as a pure instrumental symphony and turned into the decorous scene-painting of a foreign land, consequently is easily heard as cosmopolitan, impersonal, un-German – in other words, the product of a 'Jewish' mentality. This more-or-less anti-Semitic influenced reception of the work has arguably overshadowed the full significance of the symphony and the scale of Mendelssohn's symphonic achievement. The stature of Mendelssohn's work was clearly recognised by Hans von Bülow in 1877, in the famous open letter declaring Brahms' First 'The Tenth', following the emergence of Brahms as a symphonic composer and the decisive re-establishment of the symphonic lineage of Beethoven, Mendelssohn and Schumann.

I furthermore confess that for me, in spite of my partial admiration for Schubert's [C major Symphony], for certain movements in Schumann's (II, 3 and III, 1, 4, etc.), as a complete work of art Mendelssohn's 'Scottish' Symphony (No. 3, A minor) occupies first place among the post-Beethovenian symphonies[97]

George Macfarren similarly, in England, was of no doubt concerning the significance of the new symphony:

[W]hen the time shall come, which cannot be remote, when all the world shall own this generation has added one to the great Trinity of Genius that has stood over instrumental music, I shall exult to have been one who could appreciate the merit, and has, however worthless, paid his tribute of acknowledgement to the original

---

[95] Thomas Grey, '*Tableaux vivants*: Landscape, History Painting, and the Visual Imagination in Mendelssohn's Orchestral Music', *19th-Century Music*, 21 (1997), 69.

[96] See Steinberg, 'Schumann's Homelessness', pp. 47–65; *Listening to Reason*, pp. 98–9; Nietzsche, *Der Fall Wagner*, § 7–8, in *Sämtliche Werke*, vol. VI, pp. 26–32.

[97] Bülow, *Ausgewählte Schriften*, pp. 369–72.

identity of style, the grandeur of conception, and the powers of development which this symphony displays, and which, in aftermen's esteem, shall place as equals, Haydn, Mozart, Beethoven, and Mendelssohn.[98]

Ruins and historical memory: the first movement

Despite the seemingly intractable issues surrounding the Third Symphony's 'Scottishness', it is still possible, I believe, to reconcile the historical conception of the work with a hermeneutic understanding of the symphony, by offering a reading of the work stemming from knowledge of this biographical backdrop. The entire symphony grows from the initial introduction theme, the sombre, mournful melody for violas and woodwind opening the symphony, which was the first element to come to the composer in 1829. Of Holyrood Palace, Edinburgh, Mendelssohn had written back to his family:

In the deep twilight we went today to the palace where Queen Mary lived and loved. There is a little room there with a winding staircase leading to it; there, in this tiny room, they found Rizzio and dragged him out; three rooms further on is a dark corner where they murdered him. The chapel below is now roofless. Grass and ivy thrive there, and at the broken altar where Mary was crowned Queen of Scotland. Everything is ruined, decayed, and the clear heavens shine in. I think today I have found there the beginning of my 'Scottish' Symphony.[99]

While we know very little concerning the actual poetic intent of Mendelssohn's symphony, we do know that this one particular passage was prompted by a definite place and time. This first element can thus be taken to stand for the ruins of Holyrood Chapel, the initial setting for the symphony and site of Mendelssohn's first inspiration (see Fig. 6.3).

In the symphony this introductory paragraph gives way to a beautiful and highly expressive passage for unison violins, thus far silent in the piece, whose metrically free outpouring and recitative-like gestures introduce a more personal, emotive quality hitherto absent from the piece. Like the emergence of the warmly lyrical second subject in the *Hebrides*, this passage might suggest the emergence of a human presence on this desolate scene, the first person singular or narrative voice.[100] In cinematic or pictorial terms, the scene pans back to reveal the narrator or composer deep in contemplation of the vista, like a figure from a Friedrich painting in rapt communion with the

---

[98] Macfarren, *Musical World*, pp. 185–7 (Brown, *A Portrait of Mendelssohn*, pp. 404–5).
[99] Letter to his family, Edinburgh, 30 July 1829, in Hensel, *Die Familie Mendelssohn*, vol. I, p. 244.
[100] See Steinberg, 'Schumann's Homelessness', pp. 63–5, and Grey, '*Tableaux vivants*', 70.

Fig. 6.3 Louis Jacques Mandé Daguerre, *The Ruins of Holyrood Chapel* (*c.* 1824).

landscape. The development of this passage combines the violins' cantilena with the head-motive of the first theme, moving from the relative major C to F major, and then in sequence up to the Neapolitan B♭, which gives way to a depleted reprise of the opening theme, now decorously intertwined with the violin arabesques, open-ended as the music slows to a dominant chord preparing the main allegro.[101] This climax on the Neapolitan chord is the only time in the introduction that the violins 'voice' the opening theme, suggesting perhaps at the height of the section a full identification with the scene and opening to memory; in Thomas Grey's words, 'as gesture, the introduction re-enacts a characteristic progression from melancholy

---

[101] Thomas Grey has made the pretty analogy between the violins' intertwining figure and the ivy tendrils creeping round the ruined stones of the chapel, as spoken of by the composer in his letter ('*Tableaux vivants*', 57).

reminiscence to passionate surge of identification (as the past becomes present in the singer's mind), before relapsing into contemplative silence'.[102]

This introduction returns once again at the very end of the movement, the final blows that seemingly culminate the movement's stormy coda disintegrating into the melancholy reminiscence of the final part of the introductory theme. This particular framing device – the introduction–coda deformation – as James Hepokoski has noted, may be often read as alluding to a narrative frame, suggesting that the enclosed sonata-space activity is to be heard as subordinate to the surrounding frame.[103] Thomas Grey has similarly suggested that the movement could be read in terms of 'a familiar narrative framing technique, so that the central Allegro assumes the character of a narrated past in relation to the "present" scene of narration projected by the introduction'.[104] Suddenly the scene before us has become populated with the historical figures and legendary deeds of the past, just as Mendelssohn in his letter merges the present scene with the imaginative reconstruction of the events it had witnessed nearly three centuries before.

This imaginative recreation of the past, the ability to move between different time levels – how it was, how it is, even (implicitly) how it might become – is a perfect instance of historical self-consciousness. Mendelssohn's work reveals a thickening and deepening of temporal experience, the consciousness of the transience of human actions and workings within the dimension of time. The spatial scene becomes temporal; the present is shown, for a moment, in the glory it once possessed in the past, before the vision dissolves back into the decay of the present. This contrast between past and present is further embodied in the thematic construction of the movement, where the principal theme of the allegro takes up the introduction's melody in a more adorned version. Thus in 'physical' terms the introduction preserves just the bare thematic outline, stripped of all its ornamentation, of the previously complete theme, which is heard issuing from a semi-mythical history; the andante, the present tense, is heard as the 'ruined' version of the interposed allegro, the narrated past (Ex. 6.17). At the very end of the

---

[102] Grey, '*Tableaux vivants*', 57. Also see Konold, *Die Symphonien Felix Mendelssohn Bartholdys*, p. 259, who speaks of the restatement of the introduction's opening passage as 'an intensification of memory – or distant history – that increasingly takes shape'.

[103] Hepokoski, *Sibelius Symphony No. 5*, p. 6; James Hepokoski and Warren Darcy, *Elements of Sonata Theory: Norms, Types, and Deformations in the Late-Eighteenth-Century Sonata* (New York: Oxford University Press, 2006), pp. 304–5.

[104] Grey, '*Tableaux vivants*', 56. Also see the same author's 'The Orchestral Music', p. 450: 'The musical character of the Andante con moto is also that of an introduction in a literary or poetic sense: it conveys the feeling of a narrative frame, a lens through which the "events" of the following Allegro – or perhaps the symphony as a whole – are to be viewed.'

Ex. 6.17 Symphony No. 3: (a) Introduction (b) First movement, first theme.

a Introduction (historical present: ruins)

b First movement, first theme (historical past: ornamented, temporally 'earlier' version)

introduction this connection is hinted at as, following the process of dissolution and liquidation of material, the introduction theme is pared down
to its barest outline (upper woodwind, bb. 59–63). The trope of ruins,
as beloved by the Romantic imagination, here finds its perfect musical
embodiment.[105]

The entire movement is suffused with this unmistakable sense of loss,
transience and decay, an almost overwhelming burden of past history weigh-
ing painfully upon the opening of the symphony. The course of the movement is ultimately nothing more than a return to this state, the internal
sonata form subordinated to the status of narrated myth, in quotation
marks as it were, whose insubstantiality is underlined by its withering away
back to the dark minor $^6_4$ of the introduction. This theme of loss, dejection, Romantic melancholy and a semi-mythical Scottish past, spoken of
in Mendelssohn's letter and encapsulated perfectly in his opening movement, is (notwithstanding the possible allusion to Schiller's *Maria Stuart* in
Mendelssohn's letter) utterly Ossianic.

Larry Todd has spoken perceptively of an 'Ossianic manner' in several of
Mendelssohn's works inspired by Scotland or the literary construction of
this country by authors such as Macpherson and Scott.[106] These include the
Hebrides Overture, whose successive titles – 'Overture to the Lonely Isle',
'The Isles of Fingal' and 'Ossian in Fingal's Cave' – unmistakably allude
to James Macpherson's notorious reconstructions of Scottish (or Celtic)
mythology, the F♯ Minor Fantasie Op. 28 (first entitled *Sonate Ecossaise*)

---

[105] See on this point Rosen, 'Ruins', *The Romantic Generation*, pp. 92–4. Mendelssohn's
description of the ruined chapel in Edinburgh might recall the iconic paintings of ruined
gothic abbeys by Casper David Friedrich a few years earlier. For both Friedrich and
Mendelssohn, the ruin is a bleak reminder of the transitoriness of human achievements and
an affirmation of their protestant faith in the sole intransience of the divine.

[106] Todd, 'Mendelssohn's Ossianic manner', pp. 137–60. A recent account of this 'Nordic' aspect
of Mendelssohn's music has been made by Balázs Mikusi in 'Mendelssohn's "Scottish"
Tonality?', *19th-Century Music*, 29 (2006), 240–60.

and, most directly of all, an unpublished dramatic scena from 1846, 'On Lena's Gloomy Heath', whose words are taken from Books III and IV of Macpherson's epic *Fingal*. The 'Scottish' Symphony is of course the largest and most imposing member of the group, though its Scottish or Ossianic connection is, as we have seen, the most uncertain. Its opening is obviously directly related to Scotland, though, and the character of the first movement ties in perfectly with this reading. The return of the introduction at the close of the movement is like the semi-mythic bard moving out of his narration and returning to the world of the present, giving voice to his dejection and all-consuming melancholy:

Often have I fought, and often won in battles of the spear. But blind, and tearful, and forlorn I now walk with little men. O Fingal, with thy race of battle I now behold thee not. The wild roses feed upon the green tomb of the mighty king of Morven. – Blest be thy soul, thou king of swords, thou most renowned on the hills of Cona!

Battles . . . where I often fought; but now I fight no more. The fame of my former actions is ceased; and I sit forlorn at the tombs of my friends.[107]

Whether or not the immediate inspiration for the piece came from Holyrood Palace and Mary Queen of Scots, Mendelssohn's symphony is nevertheless the perfect encapsulation of this gloomy 'Scottish' melancholy and sense of an irrecoverable lost heroic past, crystallised in Macpherson's *Fragments of Ancient Poetry* and fragmentary reworkings of 'lost' epics such as *Fingal* and *Temora*.

One might therefore think that, as such, the symphony as a whole could be analogised as a potentially Ossianic work, particularly given the prevalence of Scottish readings of Mendelssohn's piece, but I would like to suggest an alternative viewpoint, one which takes into consideration the composer's own creative development in relation to the work. The most significant feature of the symphony in this regard is that it traces what is ultimately a positive, redemptive course, from this almost overwhelming sense of the past to a triumphant, affirmative coda; it does not remain in this frozen state of isolation and loss but succeeds in overcoming it. Like the composer's own experiences from the work's conception in 1829 to its final completion a decade later, the symphony moves forward, starting from this initial memento of the vanished past but building this into a larger work, which is not exclusively defined by the composer's experiences in Scotland

---

[107] James Macpherson, *The Poems of Ossian*, ed. Howard Gaskill (Edinburgh University Press, 1996), pp. 79 and 104. The passages cited form part of the conclusions to book III and the final book VI of Macpherson's *Fingal*.

Fig. 6.4 Mendelssohn's sketch for the start of his 'Scottish Symphony', dated Edinburgh, 30 July 1829.

or this past moment in time but reflects on the distance travelled since then.[108]

This process, embodied in the symphony, hence mirrors the progression of Mendelssohn's cyclic music from the literal cyclic return of the works of the later 1820s to the ongoing cyclical transformation of the later 1830s and 1840s. While the symphony's introduction, dating from 1829, returns at the end of the first movement in the manner of the composer's cyclic works of this time, Mendelssohn rejects this as an ultimate solution and instead seeks salvation in its organic growth and transformation into the final goal of the

---

[108] Mendelssohn's original sketch is given in Fig. 6.4. As Schumann wrote, poeticising upon his own hypothetical version of events, the (somewhat erroneous) biographical information he had picked up seemed 'of interest for the evaluation of the particular character of this piece. Just as when an old, yellowed page suddenly slips from an old and neglected volume, recalling to us times long past, and those times rise again to their full brilliance, so that we forget the present, so might well the master's imagination have been flooded by happy memories when he happened upon these old melodies he had once sung'. Schumann, 'Sinfonien für Orchester', *Gesammelte Schriften*, vol. II, p. 132, translation slightly modified from that of Thomas Grey in Seaton, *The Mendelssohn Companion*, p. 543.

fourth-movement coda.[109] In this sense the symphony, taken as a whole, could be thought of as an 'anti'-Ossianic work.

This process is seen immediately by the character of the scherzo, following the opening movement without break, which, while structured as a parallel to the previous movement, forms its antithesis. What is most remarkable about the first movement is its unremitting absorption – obsession, even – with the minor mode: the only section in the entire movement which is in the major is the brief statement of the closing theme in E major at the end of the development, and this passage itself can be heard as no more than a prolongation of the dominant of A minor, the theme's alternation between tonic and subdominant harmony neatly recontextualised as V–I–V over a dominant pedal. Despite the fleeting hint of C major in the exposition, the secondary tonal area is firmly in E minor, the movement moving between the poles of its A minor tonic and its minor dominant. This is entirely inverted in the lithe scherzo, whose sonata form articulates the movement between the tonic F major and more usual C major dominant. The sequence of thematic events also directly parallels the first movement: the first subject is formed from a cheerful major-key transformation of the first movement's first subject (note how the initial $\hat{5}$–$\flat\hat{6}$–$\hat{5}$–$\hat{8}$ of the earlier movement is turned into the pentatonic $\hat{5}$–$\hat{6}$–$\hat{8}$ of the movement's second motivic segment), and the second subject, which grows yet again from an elaborated tail-piece of the first, is a direct transformation of the preceding movement's secondary theme (Ex. 6.18).

The first movement had hinted at a synthetic process in the combination of *a* and *b* themes in the last section of the introduction and following this in the transformation of the *b* theme at its last appearance in the coda. The process of the second movement is more obviously affirmative and synthetic. As has been often noted, the first subject is briefly 'recapitulated' wittily in the entirely wrong key, E♭, and on regaining the correct dominant pedal and after an expectant build-up of this theme, proceeds in the 'real' recapitulation from entirely the wrong theme, the second subject, now stated *fortissimo*. The first subject is never actually afforded its own independent

---

[109] This progression is further paralleled in Mendelssohn's two *Infelice* arias, dating from 1834 and 1843 respectively. While the 1834 setting returns to a brief, bittersweet reminder of the vocal melody that accompanied the words 'Ah, ritorna, età dell'oro' in the solo violin towards its end, the later 1843 version eschews this literal citation in favour of the transformation of a melody that had initially appeared in G minor into B♭ major in the coda, thus overcoming and transcending its past. See John Michael Cooper, 'Mendelssohn's Two *Infelice* Arias: Problems of Sources and Musical Identity', in John Michael Cooper and Julie D. Prandi (eds.), *The Mendelssohns: Their Music in History* (Oxford University Press, 2002), pp. 43–97.

Ex. 6.18 Symphony No. 3, second movement: motivic derivation of second subject from end of first.

recapitulation, but underneath the tutti statement of the second theme the cellos and lower woodwind scurry away in semiquaver figures drawn from this material (the superimposition of first and second subjects at the recapitulation can also be heard above the din of the latter in the third and fourth bars of the theme in the woodwind). This undercutting of the recapitulatory point by desynchronising the thematic and harmonic recapitulations is highly characteristic of Mendelssohn, as is the tendency to synthesise opposing thematic subjects at the culmination of the movement, either in the recapitulation or as the coda (the present movement is of such brevity that the recapitulation effectively functions as a coda, the remainder of the movement being left to the liquidation of the music in a Romantic trope of farewell and fading into the distance).

In place of the long, weighty minor-key opening movement, Mendelssohn has given us a bucolic major-key scherzo, as brief as it is cheerful, negating the overbearing mood of melancholy hanging over the first movement. This movement has frequently been read as Scottish through its pentatonic melodic character, the characteristic anapaestic ('Scotch-snap') rhythm of the melody's fourth bar ($\frac{2}{4}$ ♪♩♪), and even the possibly 'rustic' sounding orchestration (whose brilliance belies its erstwhile naïveté), though it is decidedly not the ancient mythical Scotland of Macpherson.[110] Persisting with a Scottish reading, this could be seen as turning out from the solitary world of melancholy and burden of past history embodied in the first movement into the fullness of everyday life characterising the ordinary country folk, similar to the progression that characterises the similarly self-absorbed protagonists in *Faust* or *Manfred*.

---

[110] The first influential Scottish reading of this movement was provided by Julius Benedict in his *Sketch of the Life and Works of the Late Felix Mendelssohn Bartholdy*, pp. 38–9.

Ex. 6.19 Symphony No. 3: harmonic templates of third movement second theme and first movement first subject.

III Second theme

I First subject

The slow movement that follows, a lyrical adagio, derives its processional character from the constant alternation of two themes drawn somewhat more loosely in this case from the *a* and *b* ideas, similarly vacillating between the major and minor poles associated with each theme group. While the head-motive of theme *a* is outlined only in the second half of the first subject, thematic semiquaver fragments from the preceding scherzo are taken up from the start as part of its accompaniment.[111] The second theme that follows (b. 33) seems to allude to the descending scalic figure of the *b* theme, though is closer in several respects to earlier versions of the *a* theme from which the second family grew. The descending *lamento* bass recalls the initial source of the *b* theme – the closely comparable descent of the bass line in the symphony's introduction – and, what is more remarkable, the harmonic template of this theme is an exact replica of the first movement's first subject – the harmonic shifts a–C–V/e across the four-bar melodic phrase-units (Ex. 6.19).

This second theme is unusual in the sense that in tonal function it serves merely as a bridge section, starting from the tonic A (major/minor) and ending on a dissonant diminished seventh that, functioning as an altered V/V of E, leads into the secondary tonality of E major, formed through a return of the second section of the first theme. Effectively there is a dislocation of thematic and harmonic structures in the movement, since the thematically distinct 'second subject' functions only as a modulatory bridge between the two appearances of the first subject, which serves tonally as both first and second subject. The resulting form is hence an interaction between a double-variation or sonata-rondo thematic structure and a simpler sonata or abridged-sonata harmonic design, with further elements of rotational structure suggested by the return of the ostensible introduction at the start

[111] Konold, *Die Symphonien Felix Mendelssohn Bartholdys*, p. 283.

of the short development section and its further return at the close of the movement. (The characteristic iv^6–V^7 Phrygian progression at the start of the adagio – a linking modulation between the scherzo's F major and the third movement's A major/minor – is also later subtly recontextualised as an expressive $\sharp IV^6_5$–V^7 dissonance at the melodic climax of the first subject, as is made explicit by its reappearance in the movement's final bars.)

The apparent interruption of the serene progression of the opening melody by the more ominous second theme cannot but help suggest some conflict between two contradictory forces, besides a strong spatial or temporal sense of separation. This is seen even at the beginning and end of the movement, one bar of first-subject material being counterpoised with the insistent rhythmic figure of the second theme – in the introduction as a solemn warning in the horns, at the close now just a muffled drum-beat, as if emanating from the distance, the threat (which is perhaps fulfilled in the explosive A minor start of the fourth movement's Allegro guerriero) subdued but not gone. Some commentators have heard this Adagio as a musical depiction of a scene from Scotland's past, whether concerning Queen Mary (the sweet, 'feminine' lyricism of the first theme counterpoised with the heavy tread of the more threatening march-theme, which with its lamento bass could suggest mourning for the unhappy queen),[112] an allusion to Sir Walter Scott's *The Lady of the Lake* (the harp-like accompaniment to the instrumental melody in pizzicato strings, and the (possibly fortuitous) scansion of its opening bars with Scott's 'Ave Maria'),[113] or a quasi-operatic scena (a wife pleading with an ancient warrior about to go to battle and death),[114] though for many others the movement has seemed less Scottish than German, or simply Mendelssohnian.

Rotations and cycles: the A major coda

The culmination of the symphony is formed by a thematically distinct (though nevertheless closely related) A major second coda to the fourth movement's A minor sonata form. Mendelssohn's guide in the published

---

[112] Todd, 'Mendelssohn', in D. Kern Holoman (ed.), *The Nineteenth-Century Symphony* (New York: Schirmer, 1997), p. 95.

[113] Roger Fiske, *Scotland in Music: A European Enthusiasm* (Cambridge University Press, 1983), p. 147. Mendelssohn had indeed set Scott's famous poem back in 1820. Ludwig Finscher has gone so far as to describe the entire work as a 'Walter Scott Symphony' ('"Zwischen absoluter und Programmusik"', pp. 114–15).

[114] Grey, '*Tableaux vivants*', 63–9.

programme describes these last two sections as 'Allegro guerriero and Finale maestoso', linking the two sections while separating their differences (though true to form the composer later removed the descriptive 'guerriero' and replaced it by the more abstract *vivacissimo*). This new 'breakthrough' coda as the end of a work is, as James Hepokoski has described, a symphonic innovation of Mendelssohn's in this symphony.[115] A precedent might be seen in Beethoven's overture to *Egmont*, whose coda forms an independent major-key triumphant breakthrough, though Mendelssohn's design is more notable given its symphonic context and is also more closely integrated with the rest of his work. (More generally, the coda's hymn-like topos, $\frac{6}{8}$ time signature and status as an additional fifth section to the symphony might recall the final 'Shepherd's Hymn of Thanksgiving' from the 'Pastoral' Symphony.) Robert Schumann had noted this in 1843, when he exclaimed:

> The conclusion of the symphony as a whole is sure to provoke conflicting opinions. Many will expect the symphony to conclude in the character of the last movement, while instead, rounding out the whole in cyclic fashion, it recalls the opening introduction of the first movement. We simply find this conclusion poetic; it is like an evening mood corresponding to a beautiful morning.[116]

Its significance can be seen in the tendency in later Romantic symphonies for independent apotheoses or epilogues to finales which form both the culmination of the finale and a summing-up of the work as a whole; two examples from the later 1840s and 1850s show Schumann taking up this design (Symphonies Nos. 2 and 3), the latter paralleling Mendelssohn directly in the use of a rotational finale structure followed by an independent culminatory coda featuring the cyclic recall or transformation of earlier themes, while later uses include Bruckner in his Third, Fifth, Seventh and Eighth Symphonies, Tchaikovsky's Fourth and Fifth, Mahler's Fifth, Elgar's First, or in modified form Brahms' Third and Elgar's Second.

Though Schumann obviously approved of Mendelssohn's innovation and was quick to take it up, it seems to have proved a problem for some critics in the twentieth century that was not always apparent to those in the nineteenth, despite the palpable fact that for many other listeners following Schumann the coda is one of the highlights of the work and forms a fitting

---

[115] James Hepokoski, 'Beethoven Reception: The Symphonic Tradition', in Jim Samson (ed.), *The Cambridge History of Nineteenth-Century Music* (Cambridge University Press, 2002), p. 428.
[116] Robert Schumann, 'Sinfonien für Orchester', *Gesammelte Schriften*, vol. II, p. 133.

and memorable end to the symphony.[117] The musical reasons why this should be the case are rarely specified and not at all obvious, since the coda is clearly thematically integrated with the preceding movement and the outcome of the process of the movement and of the overall cyclic structure of the work. Indeed, to be fully understood the coda must be viewed both from the four-movement cyclic design of the symphony and from the individual process of the finale.

The coda to Mendelssohn's symphony is (as outlined before) the last stage of the process of thematic metamorphosis across the work. While it relates directly to the music of the preceding movement, the coda also is heard, as Schumann suggests, as a direct corollary and transformation of the symphony's introduction, thus imparting an external frame to the four movements of the symphony as a whole, just as the introduction had enclosed the first movement by its return at its close. Indeed, the composer's wording in his note links the two sections together in the same way as the symphony's introduction led to the first movement: 'Introduction und Allegro agitato. – Scherzo assai vivace. – Adagio cantabile. – Allegro guerriero und Finale maestoso.'[118] This opening theme had returned not just at the end of the introduction but also at the close of the first movement, effectively subordinating the process of the opening movement to the events of the frame, as if (as in Op. 13) the question posed by the introduction has still not been answered or adequately resolved. Now this unresolved formal question is re-engaged, but rather than returning to the unsatisfactory melancholy of the opening, this theme is transfigured in a major-key apotheosis, which similarly stands 'outside' the main course of the work but relates to and is the outcome of it. The design of the symphony can hence be thought of as a series of ever increasing returns to this framing idea, like a series of Russian dolls nestling inside each other (Fig. 6.5).

Thus the A major coda is both the final stage of the process of thematic transformation that spans the entire work and a transformed return to the opening of the symphony – the paradox of a one-way, progressive cycle, or, as Schumann's analogy suggests, the same as the opening but the reverse – a sunset to a dawn (or, given the major-key transfiguration, a glorious dawn to the opening dusk, a darkness to light scenario). The coda is also the

[117] A good summary of these negative views is provided by Peter Mercer-Taylor in 'Mendelssohn's "Scottish" Symphony and the Music of German Memory', *19th-Century Music*, 19 (1995), 68–9.

[118] Ludwig Finscher comments on the resulting formal symmetry that the A major coda makes the finale 'an exact mirror-image of the first movement' ('"Zwischen absoluter und Programmusik"', p. 114).

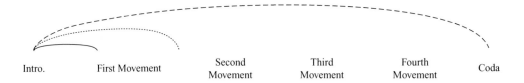

Intro.   First Movement   Second   Third   Fourth   Coda
                                            Movement   Movement   Movement

Fig. 6.5 Symphony No. 3: successive cyclical returns of the introduction across the symphony.

Ex. 6.20 Symphony No. 3, finale, second half of exposition: harmonic layout.

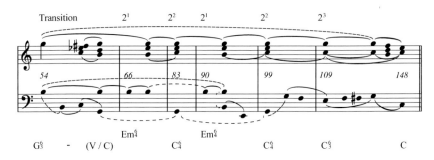

outcome and logical resolution of the particular thematic and harmonic processes of the finale. Most clearly, its A major is the tonal counterweight to the large section of tonic major expected in the finale's recapitulation but unexpectedly missing there. The entire tonal argument of this finale stems from the idiosyncratic harmonic structure of Mendelssohn's exposition.

The finale's exposition charts a large-scale course from A minor to the relative major, C. Within this general design, however, the musical realisation of this standard harmonic plan is far more complex (Ex. 6.20). The bridge theme at b. 37, growing out of and taking the place of the first group's second theme at its repetition, moves from the tonic A minor, via d to G, which is set up as the expected V / C major, the relative (b. 66). The empty leading note b, sustained low in the violins, fails, however, to materialise into C major, but is instead reinterpreted as the dominant of E minor, over which enters the second subject's first theme (2^1). After sixteen bars of this surprise tonality, C major reasserts itself in a blustery new transformation of the *b* theme material that had opened the movement, but this dies away again onto the b pedal and the process repeats itself. This block-like juxtaposition of two opposing tonalities is not unlike passages of the scherzo's development, the implied dominant of one key giving way to an unconnected third-related key and then switching back belatedly and without any warning to the key initially prepared, even subsequently repeating both parts of this process.[119] The process here surely alludes to the exposition of the first movement, where the progression had been from the tonic A minor to the more unusual (though typically Mendelssohnian) dominant minor, E, with C major as merely a brief interpolation within that secondary tonality. Here, E minor is heard as an interruption within the C major secondary tonal area, the movement paralleling the first while forming a redemptive reworking of it.

C major, the expected relative of the tonic minor and the tonality originally anticipated, wins out in the end, a substantial closing section of thirty-eight bars confirming the key re-established in the previous eleven bars by returning to an even closer variant of the opening material (2^3, $= 1^1$), transformed into C major (bb. 109–47). Thus the exposition closes firmly in the secondary key expected at the medial caesura, the momentary interpolations of E minor material that had threatened to destabilise its course heard merely as remnants of the first movement's exposition.

In the recapitulation, however, this entire section is missing. The bridge theme, which had been substantially worked out in the development, is cut out entirely and the music leads straight from the first group into a single statement of 2^1, heard now in the tonic minor over a dominant $^6_4$ pedal (b. 225), before moving into the movement's coda. The C major second-subject material that followed 2^1 – all fifty-eight bars of the second group's original eighty, expected now in A major – seems to have disappeared. All that is left of it is at best the two bars of F major at the start of the (sonata-movement) coda (b. 290), conforming to a downward translation of the e–C progression of the exposition's second group, sounding the theme in its original 1^1 / 2^3 version as part of a Phrygian progression ♭VI–V to the dominant of A minor, which is heard as the start of a new section or further rotation of the movement's basic materials.[120]

To understand what has happened to the missing second-subject material we must examine more closely the particular thematic structure of Mendelssohn's finale, which, as James Hepokoski has claimed, is one of the most important early sonata movements in rotational form.[121] What is

---

[119] A process named 'double alienation' by Warren Darcy – the preparation of a 'wrong' secondary tonality by the 'right' tonality's dominant ('Bruckner's Sonata Deformations', in Timothy L. Jackson and Paul Hawkshaw (eds.), *Bruckner Studies* (Cambridge University Press, 1997), p. 272). A similar effect (here of 'secondary alienation') is achieved in the first movement of the E minor Quartet Op. 44 No. 2 (1837) and in the first *Caprice* Op. 33 No. 1.

[120] This progression could also allude to the start of the slow movement – a Phrygian iv⁶–V⁷ in A minor, moving from the Scherzo's F major to the Adagio's A major/minor.

[121] Hepokoski, *Sibelius Symphony No. 5*, p. 7.

Exposition							Development				Recapitulation		[Coda?]	Coda	A major Coda
1	Bridge	2^1	2^2	2^1	2^2	$2^3(=C)$	1	Bridge	2^1	$1^1 / (2^2)$	$1^1 / (2^3)$	2^1	$1^1 / (2^3)$	2^1	
Am	– V/C	Em^6_4	C^6_4	Em^6_4	C^6_4	C^6_3	C	Dm	Am^6_4	– V	Am	$^6_4$	–	Am – V	A
1	37	66	82	90	98	109	147	182	225	237	245	270	290	361	396

Exposition	Development	Recapitulation	[Coda?]	Coda	A major Coda
Rotation 1	2	3	4		Coda
Rotation 1	2	3		?	Coda
Rotation 1	2		?		Coda

Fig. 6.6 Symphony No. 3, fourth movement: table showing thematic layout and alternate structural rotations.

notable about the thematic layout of the exposition is that the second group's
second theme (2^2), whose C major forms the structural opposition with the
tonic A minor, is little more than a rhythmically transformed version of the
opening theme, and the ensuing closing section (2^3) is transparently just a
major-key modification of the opening. Effectively, 2^2 and 2^3 are identical
to 1^1, save for their mode and tonality. The process of the movement is the
gradual merging of 2^2 and 2^3 with 1^1 across each structural division of the
form, thus eliding the beginning and end of each rotational cycle across
the movement.

The course of thematic events in the development section follows closely
that of the exposition / first rotation (see Fig. 6.6). The bridge theme, which
itself had formed a development of aspects of the first group, is subjected to
a lengthy working out on its arrival (b. 182), giving rise to a fugato section
utilising its as yet unrealised contrapuntal potential. In this the finale yet
again echoes the opening movement of the symphony, paralleling the use
to which the comparable transition theme in the first movement had been
put. This culminates in a *fortissimo* climax on the first second-subject theme
(2^1) over a second inversion of A minor, seemingly heralding the imminent
arrival of the recapitulation. The last eight bars of the section, preceding
the recapitulation at b. 245, present a minor-key version of the thematic
material of $2^{2/3}$,[122] now heard in a transitional role leading harmonically to
the return of the tonic root position at b. 245 and linking thematically with
the almost-identical 1^1 that returns now at the recapitulation. This linkage
of the end of one rotation and the beginning of the next is demonstrated
by the new accompanimental material for 1^1, a rising arpeggio figure in
flutes and clarinets, which is taken from the accompaniment to 2^3. The
presentation of the main part of the second subject group has been cut out
in the movement's second rotation and elided with the return of the first
subject at the start of the third. Effectively, the end of one strophe and the
beginning of the next have begun to overlap and merge.

This process is carried further in the recapitulation or third rotation. As is
usual with Mendelssohn, the reprise is highly concise, removing internally
repeated material and the bridge theme that had been so thoroughly worked
out in the development, leading straight through into 2^1. The logic of
excising the bridge material is compelling, since it had already been used
to such a great extent in the development rotation (sustaining thirty-four

---

[122] Just as, it will be noted, the minor-key closing theme of the first movement was presented in a
brief major-key transformation at the closing stages of that development section, the exact
inversion of the finale's process.

bars there), and the second-subject material that takes its place in the third rotational cycle is closely linked to it, not just through the characteristic intervals of its three head notes but also in its distinctive dotted rhythm (which in the former's contrapuntal working is probably more significant than its actual melodic contour). Following the process of the development rotation, where the remaining second-group material had been afforded only eight bars before combining with the onset of the third rotation of the first subject material, the second and third themes are now not heard at all, or, if they are, it is as part of the fourth rotation or coda, which simultaneously forms the first subject (bb. 290ff.). (This is again suggested by the rising arpeggios noted in the first theme's accompaniment at b. 290, new to this 1^1 theme in the recapitulation but characteristic of both the accompanying ascending scale-figure of 2^2 (see bb. 82ff., horns and lower strings) and especially the identical striding arpeggios of 2^3 (bb. 109ff., oboe and clarinet).) The second-group material and the first theme have now totally combined.

A further implication of this process, however, is that by combining rotations it becomes increasingly difficult to state where one rotation ends and another begins; put differently, the coda section which appears to begin at b. 290 could mark the beginning of the fourth rotation, but it might alternatively be the continuation of the third, since the beginning and end of each are nearly identical.[123] This is supported not only by the accompaniment to the passage, which suggests, as outlined, the thematic version of 2^3, but by the continuation of this 'coda' section, which increasingly focuses on and develops a characteristic dotted rhythmic figure, familiar from the bridge theme and its working in the development, but which is most strongly parallel to that used the end of the exposition (bb. 135ff.) – the continuation of 2^3. Thus we are simultaneously in the fourth rotation and also in the third; the movement's structural outline is beginning to break up irrevocably.

---

[123] This ambiguity manifested between end of recapitulation and start of coda is well made by Wulf Konold in *Die Symphonien Felix Mendelssohn Bartholdys*, pp. 331–3. Though the material of bb. 290ff. might seem as relating most obviously to a minor-key version of the latter stages of the exposition (bb. 109ff.), this interpretation downplays both the peculiar formal structure and process of Mendelssohn's movement and the resultant phenomenal effect of the music. While the minor-key restatement of secondary material that had appeared in the major in the exposition is not unusual (being a characteristic particularly of Mozart's minor-key sonata forms), in Mendelssohn's work, where such material is differentiated from the first subject only by its mode, any minor-key statement will be heard automatically as a statement of the first subject. This formal division at b. 290 is further emphasised by Mendelssohn's marked *ritardando* in the previous bars, a notation used sparingly by the composer.

This final section is set for a bitter stand-off that to many listeners unmistakably suggests a battle – the contrary motion of the upper and lower strings grinding out a three-note chromatic motive and a slow but unwavering chromatic ascent; the polarising of the orchestral texture into two opposing groups with a third echoing out bare octaves, like the clang of metal on metal, sword on shield.[124] This passage is a large-scale and highly dramatic conflagration of the movement's remaining thematic material. The first-subject and later second-subject themes have already combined and merged, and the bridge section largely spent itself out in its fugal working in the development. Now the latter is alluded to for the last time, in conjunction with the codetta material from the latter stages of the exposition's structure. Following the catastrophic pile-up in this coda (the climax reached on a *fortissimo* B♭ Neapolitan chord and upper f^3 in the violins (b. 346), echoing the climax long before of the first movement introduction) there is nothing left save for a bleak *pianissimo* statement of the remaining 2^1 theme in the clarinet, accompanied by an empty sustained fifth a–e in the strings, *ppp*.[125] (It is difficult not to think that the Sibelius of *En Saga* and the First Symphony must have remembered this theme in its desolate appearance here in the solo clarinet winding its way above the freezing wastes of the open-spaced strings.) Essentially what Mendelssohn's process across the movement has achieved is the gradual merging and breakdown of its formal strophes accompanied by the liquidation of material within the movement.

It is from this state of utter exhaustion that the coda ushers in its major-key transformation of the *a* material. Its opening picks up the head-motive of the second-subject theme immediately preceding it and something of its rhythm, and its second segment is likewise closely comparable with that of the 1^2 theme (Ex. 6.21). Thus, following the breakdown and liquidation of the finale's material, the second coda enters with a subject drawing from and leading out of this movement, which is also a return to and transformation of

[124] As Thomas Grey puts it, 'the effect is one of relentless, violent hammer strokes (bringing to mind, perhaps, the clubs, axes and spears of primitive warfare)' ('The Orchestral Music', p. 458). Or to be Ossianic, 'As waves white-bubbling over the deep come swelling, roaring on, as rocks of ooze met roaring waves: so foes attacked and fought. Man met with man, and steel with steel. Shields sound; men fall. As a hundred hammers on the son of the furnace, so rose, so rung their swords.' *Fingal*, IV, in Macpherson, *The Poems of Ossian*, p. 86.

[125] This empty fifth might again cast the listener's mind back to the close of the exposition and recapitulation in the first movement.

Ex. 6.21 Symphony No. 3, A major coda: relationship to earlier themes.

Coda

396

Finale

66

14

the symphony's introduction that returns in the wake of this dissolution.[126] Its A major tonality is likewise the long-delayed reconfirmation of that key so conspicuously missing from the recapitulation. Due to the idiosyncratic structure of the movement, the merging of second-group second theme and first subject within the development and recapitulation rotations, the large section of A major expected from the grounding of the C major goal of the exposition has been bypassed, and the second coda now finally provides this missing tonality. In theoretical terms, since the events of the recapitulation have not resolved the tonal argument set up from the exposition, such resolution must be found later, outside sonata space in the final coda.[127]

Indeed, the prevalence of the minor mode in the later stages of the finale's sonata structure is surprising given the amount of major mode throughout the symphony and especially that found in the first part of the finale. While the first movement had been an unremitting exploration of the minor mode, the second had been conversely entirely major. The Andante had meanwhile contrasted major and minor thematic groups, and the finale had charted a course from its initial dramatic reversal to the minor back to major by the end of the exposition. However, after the essential expositional closure in

---

[126] This is more or less the inverse of a process Hepokoski has identified in later rotational movements, 'teleological genesis', where the progression across the successive rotations develops and brings to the fore a new theme only previously latent in the original rotation. See James Hepokoski, 'The Essence of Sibelius: Creation Myths and Rotational Cycles in *Luonnotar*', in Glenda Dawn Goss (ed.), *The Sibelius Companion* (Westport, CT and London: Greenwood Press, 1996), pp. 121–46.

[127] On this point, see especially James Hepokoski, 'Back and Forth from *Egmont*: Beethoven, Mozart, and the Non-Resolving Recapitulation', *19th-Century Music*, 25 (2002), 127–54. A good account of another design of Mendelssohn's from this perspective has been made by Joel Haney in 'Navigating Sonata Space in Mendelssohn's *Meeresstille und glückliche Fahrt*', *19th-Century Music*, 28 (2004), 108–32.

Ex. **6.22** Symphony No. 3, A major coda: transformation of earlier themes.

C major at the end of the exposition (b. 147) there is no suggestion of major mode throughout the remaining 249 bars of the main sonata movement. Hence the external A major coda at the end of the movement is not only a logical but a necessary outcome; the symphony simply *could not* have ended with the A minor close to the sonata movement, at least if basic tenets of sonata construction are taken to be valid.

The A major coda resolves this need for A major outside sonata space, simultaneously returning to earlier material and transforming that of the finale. In topos the new finale material takes up something of the chivalric tone of the missing 2^2 material, as well as its inferred tonality. The first two incomplete statements, functioning as a gradual orchestral crescendo, lead to the full presentation of the theme in a *fortissimo* tutti (bb. 420ff.), which leads into a new continuation that even more clearly relates to the finale material of the bridge/fugato theme (bb. 430–3) and missing 2^3 material (bb. 435–43, Ex. 6.22).

The contrasting theme which appears now at b. 444 is in fact the last stage in the process of thematic metamorphosis and resolution of the *a* theme across the symphony, presenting the basic fifth $\hat{5}$–$\hat{8}$, ornamented with the $\hat{6}$ auxiliary note, in a simple and effective liquidation of the symphony's essential thematic substrate. At b. 464 the first theme returns again for the last time, to round off the coda and conclude the symphony with a burst of celebration.

The coda therefore provides the resolution of the finale, specifically its modal imbalance; the ultimate outgrowth of the process of thematic metamorphosis that spans the entire work; and a summing-up and frame to the work as a whole, returning to the idea of the first movement introduction, now transformed. To put it in the language of music-theoretical orthodoxy, it provides 'unity' and closure to the symphony as a whole.

The reason for some of the twentieth-century dissatisfaction with the symphony's conclusion is hence rather mystifying, given the extremely strong thematic, tonal and topical connections with the preceding move-ment; in analytical terms there seems to be little problematic about it.[128] Indeed, Mendelssohn's entire design seems not only admirable but highly innovatory and influential. This criticism seems to betray, rather, the twentieth-century distrust of victory; the belief that happy conclusions are somehow 'not real', the wish perhaps to return to the Ossianic melancholy of the opening. Some, like Jenkins and Visocchi, find the threefold statement of the same theme disagreeable as a culmination of the work, but it should be pointed out that this structural repetition has all along been a feature of the symphony's thematic presentation (the first subjects of both first and second movements) and that only the third of these statements is complete; that they do not actually form the culmination of the work but rather the theme grows until it covers the whole orchestra before moving onto a final variant which liquidates this theme; and that Mendelssohn's procedure is anyway hardly any more simplistic than Beethoven's in the first movement of the 'Eroica' or the presentation of the 'Joy' theme in the Ninth, let alone Bruckner's later examples.[129] How this victory could be seen as unprompted is likewise hard to see: if we persist with an extramusical battle analogy for the finale,[130] it does not take too great a stretch of the imagination to see that if one side has lost (the implication of the A minor clarinet coda), in all probability the other side will have won.

Moreover, unlike earlier examples of triumphant breakthrough in Beethoven (*Egmont*, even to an extent the Fifth Symphony), Mendelssohn's new material is extremely strongly integrated into the preceding music and work as a whole, and is the culmination of a far more complex and thorough process. One is left to speculate, as so often, whether the name 'Mendelssohn' instead of 'Beethoven' has been more responsible for the idea that this fea-ture is fair game for uncritical attack, almost on principle.[131] Or, similarly,

---

[128] One problem with this work's reception may well just be (as so often the case with Mendelssohn's music) that overeager critics simply have not looked at the work in question; one example is Roger Fiske, whose generally sympathetic account concludes with the analytically imprecise observation 'Mendelssohn had the original idea of introducing a brand new theme of immense grandeur to round the symphony off...If it had evolved from something earlier in the symphony all might have...been well, but the tune is not related to anything we have heard before' (Fiske, *Scotland in Music*, p. 148).

[129] David Jenkins and Mark Visocchi, *Mendelssohn in Scotland* (London: Chappell, 1978), p. 105.

[130] See Witte's influential formulation in 'Zur Programmgebundenheit der Sinfonien Mendelssohns', p. 125.

[131] As Leon Botstein has suggested, after the middle years of the twentieth century there is a rather unfair tendency to blame (particularly Jewish) figures who articulate such positive aspirations as delusionary, as if the course of twentieth-century German history should have been known to Mendelssohn a century earlier (Botstein, 'Mendelssohn and the Jews', *The Musical Quarterly*, 82 (1998), 210–19).

the symphony's association with the Victorian age – an association which is as tenuous as it is nebulous as an apparent criticism – is enough to damn the work solely through that dubious fact alone.[132] Vitercik's comments say it all when he remarks that the end sounds the 'fatal touch of Victorian profundity', as if the content of such criticism is self-explanatory.[133] There is quite simply no musical problem with the end; any problem there stems from the relation of the expressive quality it imparts with the (normally unexamined) cultural prejudices of the critic.[134]

Breakthrough and daybreak

Several interpretative readings have been given to this final A major coda.[135] From the perspective of an Ossianic or generally Scottish viewpoint, the final breakthrough might be seen as a dramatic Deus ex machina device, an exercising of poetic licence. Indeed, this reading would tie in with several aspects of the symphony thus far noted: the narrative ('Once upon a time') frame to the first movement, the ritualistic alternations of subject groups in the slow movement, the epic rotational structure of the finale. But, as we have hinted, if the symphony really were an Ossianic work, it should have ended (somehow) with the unsolved and unresolved A minor close of the main finale movement – 'on Lena's gloomy heath the voice of music died away'[136] – retreating into the desolate distance, into the Scottish mists and 'time immemorial', like his earlier overture to *Fingal's Cave* or indeed Niels Gade's *Efterklange af Ossian*. Instead of which, it transforms the material of the symphony into an affirmative peroration, which could indeed be Scottish, but which many other commentators have seen as speaking of Germany as much as of the north.

---

[132] The work was dedicated, after completion, to Queen Victoria (which makes it about as Victorian as *Tristan und Isolde* is Brazilian, I suppose).

[133] Vitercik, *The Early Works of Felix Mendelssohn*, p. 302. What exactly such 'Victorian profundity' means, how Mendelssohn's symphony, started in the Scotland of 1829 and completed in Friedrich Wilhelm IV's Berlin, is Victorian, and why this anyway would be *ipso facto* so much worse than association with any other political state is, of course, never interrogated.

[134] A point which Jenkins and Visocchi at least seem to realise (*Mendelssohn in Scotland*, pp. 104–5: 'Mendelssohn has also been criticised for the "moralising" of the tail-piece to his finale, but such an interpretation says more about the prejudices of commentators reacting against Victorian attitudes').

[135] See, for instance, Witte, 'Zur Programmgebundenheit der Sinfonien Mendelssohns', p. 125; Finscher, '"Zwischen absoluter und Programmusik"', p. 114; Grey, '*Tableaux vivants*', 62–3

[136] Macpherson, *Fingal*, IV, *The Poems of Ossian*, p. 84, a line which was set by Mendelssohn in his eponymous 1846 concert aria.

Indeed, a more generally Germanic or European style for the close of the symphony would fit in well with the biographical genesis and completion of the work. An important reading of the coda from this perspective has been given by Peter Mercer-Taylor. Drawing on similarities in melodic construction between the coda theme of the symphony and the festival song ('Vaterland in Deinen Gauen') from the 1840 Leipzig celebrations for Johannes Gutenberg (which later would achieve world-fame as 'Hark the Herald Angels Sing'), Mercer-Taylor suggests that Mendelssohn's conclusion may be read as a musical enactment of the act of celebrating nothing other than the glorious heritage of the symphony as a genre itself. In this reading, Mendelssohn's symphony actually ends with the A minor coda – 'with the pianissimo closing measures of the finale's main movement, the symphony fades into a fitting close. What remains is to dwell on its memory through the conventional strains of public celebration.' The allusion to the first movement in the coda is thus 'a stylised act of reflection . . . an object of ceremonial remembrance'.[137] This theory, while intriguing, seems irreconcilable with the experience of the work and with Mendelssohn's probable views. As we have seen, to end with the first coda would be to leave fundamental issues of the symphony still unresolved – the lack of tonic major in the recapitulation, the formal 'problem' of the first movement introduction. The death of the symphony spoken of by Mercer-Taylor is also, to my mind, greatly exaggerated. Despite the copious quantities of ink spilt over the problem of the symphony after Beethoven (a debate which, notwithstanding its undoubted foundation in historical reality, seems too often to have become a self-sustaining and self-validating discourse), there is little hard evidence to suggest that this particularly afflicted Mendelssohn directly, despite occasional assertions to that effect.

I would like instead to suggest an alternative reading, which still fits with the biographical details of composition. This derives from the strong affinities demonstrated between the present symphony and Mendelssohn's dramatic cantata *Die erste Walpurgisnacht*, started in 1831 but which similarly had to wait until the early 1840s for its final appearance. What is striking about these two compositions is that they proceed from almost identical themes, and transform their principal melodic idea into closely comparable shapes by the end.[138] Like the first movement of the symphony,

---

[137] Mercer-Taylor, 'Mendelssohn's "Scottish" Symphony and the Music of German Memory', 81.
[138] Carl Dahlhaus had noticed the similarity of the *Walpurgisnacht* opening theme with the start of the A minor Symphony and the cantata's final transformation with the motto of the *Lobgesang*, though did not follow the process of the symphony's subsequent transformations

Ex. 6.23 Symphony No. 3 and *Die erste Walpurgisnacht* Op. 60 (1830–43), initial and final thematic variants.

Symphony No. 3, opening theme, I introduction

Die erste Walpurgisnacht, opening theme, overture

Symphony No. 3, closing variant, IV coda

Die erste Walpurgisnacht, closing variant, concluding choral number

the overture to *Die erste Walpurgisnacht*, a monothematic A minor sonata movement moving to the dominant minor, is built on the rising $\hat{5}$–$\hat{8}$–$\hat{2}$–$\hat{3}$ shape familiar throughout much of Mendelssohn's music, and across the movements of the cantata this idea is developed and transformed into innumerable subsidiary variants which permeate nearly all aspects of the musical texture.[139] By the close, it has been reformed as a dotted major-key variant emphasising scale-degree $\hat{6}$ – $\hat{5}$–$\hat{6}$–$\hat{8}$, $\hat{5}$–$\hat{8}$–$\hat{3}$ – so close to the A major coda-theme of the symphony as to make it remarkable that this seems not to have been previously spotted (Ex. 6.23). The historical genesis of the two works was also, as stated, extremely similar, both being products of Mendelssohn's early years of travel that were subsequently revised or completed in the early 1840s; thus the two in a sense grew together in the composer's mind. The cantata can, I believe, be used as a useful hermeneutic key into the meaning of the symphony, if not in terms of narrative content at least in terms of its process and overall trajectory.

Goethe's text to the cantata (which the aged poet had induced Mendelssohn to tackle upon what was to be their last meeting in 1830)

any further (Dahlhaus, "'Hoch symbolisch intentioniert": Zu Mendelssohns "Erster Walpurgisnacht", *Österreichische Musikzeitschrift*, 36 (1981), 290–1).

[139] See the graphs reproduced in Dahlhaus, "'Hoch symbolisch intentioniert'", 296, and Douglass Seaton, 'The Romantic Mendelssohn: The Composition of *Die erste Walpurgisnacht*', *The Musical Quarterly*, 68 (1982), 408–9.

describes the progression away from the winter storms – both physical and metaphorical – of the opening, via the spring breezes of the awakening of the first choral number, to the final affirmation of the old and true way of the pagans' religion, which had since been threatened by the new-fangled Christians.

Und raubt man uns den alten Brauch,	And though they rob us of our old customs,
Dein Licht, wer kann es rauben?	Who can take away Thy light?

I would like to suggest that this emotional and spiritual process can be seen as mirrored in the course of Mendelssohn's symphony.

The C major final transformation of the opening motive in *Die erste Walpurgisnacht* is the last stage of a course charted from the A minor storms of winter to the C major key of light and revelation (indelible in music since its use in Haydn's *Die Schöpfung* for the words 'und es ward Licht'), explicitly articulating this word 'light' in Goethe's text. The significance of Goethe's/Mendelssohn's work has been taken up by several scholars, often being read from an Enlightenment perspective as a plea for the acceptance of religious diversity and the underlying truth in all forms of worship common to man.[140] This may be seen as part of what Leon Botstein has described as Mendelssohn's 'cultural project' on behalf of music: the desire to turn music into an ethical force for the good of humanity, promoting societal participation and the integration of community.[141] The symphony, and the thematic process seen across its four movements, hence might encapsulate a process of ethical *Bildung* or formation of character – a process in which the initial musical subject has evolved towards 'full self-disclosure', continuing the procedure seen in Mendelssohn's earlier cyclic works.

An expressly religious significance can likewise be read into this process. It has been suggested that for Mendelssohn the (Protestant) chorale was

[140] For different readings see Werner, *Mendelssohn: A New Image*, p. 203, Seaton, 'The Romantic Mendelssohn', pp. 404–5, Kramer, '*Felix culpa*', Prandi, 'Kindred Spirits', and Cooper, *Mendelssohn, Goethe, and the Walpurgis Night*. Heinz-Klaus Metzger has specifically related the work to Mendelssohn's Jewish heritage ('Noch einmal: "Die erste Walpurgisnacht", Versuch einer anderen Allegorese', in Heinz-Klaus Metzger and Rainer Riehn (eds.), *Felix Mendelssohn Bartholdy, Musik-Konzepte* 14/15 (Munich: Edition Text+Kritik, 1980), pp. 93–7).

[141] Leon Botstein, 'The Aesthetics of Assimilation and Affirmation: Reconstructing the Career of Felix Mendelssohn', in R. Larry Todd (ed.), *Mendelssohn and his World* (Princeton University Press, 1991), pp. 32–7. See further, Botstein, 'Neoclassicism, Romanticism, and Emancipation', Steinberg, 'Schumann's Homelessness', pp. 47–9, and *Listening to Reason*, pp. 97–122, esp. p. 99.

Ex. 6.24 *Antigone*, opening chorus: 'Daybreak'.

Strahl des   He - li - os, schön - stes   Licht

equivalent to or indeed a higher form of folk music (which, as we know, the composer was not particularly fond of); hence partly the use of chorales and chorale-like melodies in several of his instrumental pieces.[142] Mendelssohn's coda can of course be seen as similar in style and syntax to the part-songs and male choruses of (secular) civic celebration in *Vormärz* Germany,[143] but has also commonly been read as more specifically religious or hymn-like in topos. The opening motive especially demonstrates a connection to the 'magnificat' or hymn-tone on the numbers 7 and 9 familiar from the opening of the 'Reformation' Symphony and, as Dahlhaus has pointed out, the *Lobgesang* motto-theme and *Walpurgisnacht* final chorus.[144] Thus, like the affirmation of the old and nevertheless true way of the Blocksberg pagans in Goethe's *Erste Walpurgisnacht*, the end of the symphony presents a spiritual awakening and celebration – a revelation of the universal religious essence common to mankind across all societies, from the Highlands to Leipzig, from the primitive clans of a (fictional) Scotland of Macpherson or Scott to the home of Bach and spiritual centre of Lutheranism.[145]

More generally, reversing Schumann's expressive dawn to dusk analogy, the end of the symphony is not a sunset but rather a daybreak, a break-through of light and a final affirmative close. Like the comparable opening chorus of *Antigone* (1841; Ex. 6.24), the sun rising over the 'glorious city of

---

[142] Markus Rathey, '"Anything but National Music!": Mendelssohn's Composing of "Folk Music" on a Higher Level', paper presented at *Mendelssohn in the Long Nineteenth Century*, 15 July 2005, Trinity College, Dublin. Examples of works incorporating chorales include the first fugue from the Six Preludes and Fugues Op. 35, the 'Reformation' Symphony, *St Paul*, *Lobgesang*, the Cello Sonata No. 2, Op. 58, Organ Sonatas Op. 65 Nos. 1, 3, 5 and 6, and Piano Trio No. 2, Op. 66.

[143] Mercer-Taylor, 'Mendelssohn's "Scottish" Symphony and the Music of German Memory', 69–77.

[144] Dahlhaus, '"Hoch symbolisch intentioniert"', 291. This theme is also used by Mendelssohn in his 'Ave Maria' Op. 23 No. 2 (1830).

[145] Botstein has spoken similarly of the use of folk material in this work and the 'Italian' Symphony to 'transform the local into the universal' ('The Aesthetics of Assimilation and Affirmation', p. 24); also see Steinberg, *Listening to Reason*, p. 99. The use of a modified chorale melody in the Second Piano Trio has not dissimilarly been interpreted by Thomas Schmidt as a desire more openly to praise God through the means of instrumental music (*Die ästhetischen Grundlagen der Instrumentalmusik Felix Mendelssohn Bartholdys*, pp. 326–7).

seven gates' following the end of a terrible battle, we hear this same joyous celebration emanating now from a more northerly clime.[146]

Mendelssohn's symphony enacts a darkness-to-light narrative, a journey from the dusk of Holyrood Palace where Mendelssohn had first felt the idea of the symphony to the final triumphant dawn at the close; from the solitary Ossianic melancholy of 1829 to the public, ethical affirmation of 1842, from Edinburgh to Leipzig, the particular to the general, from the individual to the universal. In returning to the cyclic principles of his earlier music, Mendelssohn transcends the pessimistic cyclic return of the opening movement by an ongoing process of organic growth and development, and with this transforms the past into a renewed present. Thus with this symphony Mendelssohn affirmed the beliefs he had inherited from the high-minded ideals of his father and grandfather, his Protestant faith, and the humanist–classical tradition of Goethe; and with it created both his most imposing orchestral work and the renewal and continuation of the great symphonic tradition he had done so much to build.

---

[146] Steinberg has even described the opening of Mendelssohn's first choral ode – 'an ascending, arpeggiated figure' (Ex. 25), comparable with that of the coda of Mendelssohn's symphony – as 'a musical referent' for the rays of the dawn sun spoken of in Sophocles' text (Michael P. Steinberg, 'The Incidental Politics to Mendelssohn's *Antigone*', in R. Larry Todd (ed.), *Mendelssohn and his World* (Princeton University Press, 1991), p. 152). A further parallel which might seem to confirm this reading of the coda as some type of 'daybreak' is the affinity it likewise exhibits with a theme in the *Lobgesang* that answers the tenor's 'ist die Nacht bald hin?' with 'Die Nacht ist vergangen', again $\hat{5}$–$\hat{8}$–$\hat{2}$–$\hat{3}$.

Bibliography

Abbate, Carolyn, *Unsung Voices: Opera and Musical Narrative in the Nineteenth Century* (Princeton University Press, 1991).

Abraham, Gerald, *A Hundred Years of Music* (London: Duckworth, 1938).

Abrams, M.H., *The Mirror and the Lamp: Romantic Theory and the Critical Tradition* (Oxford University Press, 1953).

   Natural Supernaturalism: Tradition and Revolution in Romantic Literature (New York: Norton, 1971).

Adorno, Theodor W., *Beethoven: The Philosophy of Music*, ed. Rolf Tiedermann, trans. E. Jephcott (Cambridge: Polity Press, 1998).

Augustine, *Confessions*, trans. Henry Chadwick (Oxford University Press, 1998).

Ballantine, Christopher, 'Beethoven, Hegel and Marx', *The Musical Review*, 33 (1972), 34–46.

Bann, Stephen, *Romanticism and the Rise of History* (New York: Twayne, 1995).

Barry, Barbara R., *Musical Time: The Sense of Order* (Stuyvesant, NY: Pendragon Press, 1990).

Beddow, Michael, 'Goethe on Genius', in Penelope Murray (ed.), *Genius: The History of an Idea* (Oxford: Blackwell, 1989), pp. 98–112.

Behler, Constantin, *Nostalgic Teleology: Friedrich Schiller and the Schemata of Aesthetic Humanism* (Berne: Peter Lang, 1995).

Bekker, Paul, *Gustav Mahlers Sinfonien* (Berlin: Schuster, 1921).

Benedict, Julius, *Sketch of the Life and Works of the Late Felix Mendelssohn Bartholdy* (London: John Murray, 1850).

Bent, Ian, *Music Analysis in the Nineteenth Century*, 2 vols. (Cambridge University Press, 1994).

Berger, Karol, *Bach's Cycle, Mozart's Arrow: An Essay on the Origins of Musical Modernity* (Berkeley, CA and Los Angeles, CA: University of California Press, 2007).

Bergson, Henri, *Creative Evolution*, trans. Arthur Mitchell (New York: Henry Holt, 1911).

   The Creative Mind, trans. Mabel L. Andison (New York: Citadel Press, 1992).

   Matter and Memory, trans. N.M. Paul and W.S. Palmer (London: George Allen and Unwin, 1911).

   Time and Free Will: An Essay on the Immediate Data of Consciousness, trans. F.L. Pogson (London: George Allen and Co., 1910).

Berlin, Isaiah, 'Herder and the Enlightenment', in Earl Wasserman (ed.), *Aspects of the Eighteenth Century* (Baltimore, MD: Johns Hopkins Press, 1965), pp. 47–104.

The Roots of Romanticism, ed. Henry Hardy (London: Chatto & Windus, 1999).

Bingham, Ruth, 'The Song Cycle in German-Speaking Countries, 1790–1840: Approaches to a Changing Genre', unpublished PhD thesis, Cornell University (1993).

Birrell, Gordon, *The Boundless Present: Space and Time in the Literary Fairy Tales of Novalis and Tieck* (Chapel Hill, NC: University of North Carolina Press, 1979).

Bloom, Harold, *The Anxiety of Influence: A Theory of Poetry* (Oxford University Press, 1973).

Bonds, Mark Evan, *After Beethoven: Imperatives of Originality in the Symphony* (Cambridge, MA: Harvard University Press, 1996).

'Haydn, Laurence Sterne, and the Origins of Musical Irony', *Journal of the American Musicological Society*, 44 (1991), 57–91.

Music as Thought: Listening to the Symphony in the Age of Beethoven (Princeton University Press, 2006).

Wordless Rhetoric: Musical Form and the Metaphor of the Oration (Cambridge, MA: Harvard University Press, 1991).

Botstein, Leon, 'The Aesthetics of Assimilation and Affirmation: Reconstructing the Career of Felix Mendelssohn', in R. Larry Todd (ed.), *Mendelssohn and his World* (Princeton University Press, 1991), pp. 5–42.

'Mendelssohn and the Jews', *The Musical Quarterly*, 82 (1998), 210–19.

'Neoclassicism, Romanticism, and Emancipation: The Origins of Felix Mendelssohn's Aesthetic Outlook', in Douglass Seaton (ed.), *The Mendelssohn Companion* (Westport, CT and London: Greenwood Press, 2001), pp. 1–23.

Bowie, Andrew, *Aesthetics and Subjectivity: From Kant to Nietzsche* (Manchester University Press, 2003).

Music, Philosophy, and Modernity (Cambridge University Press, 2007).

Brinckmann, Reinhold, 'In the Time(s) of the "Eroica"', in Scott Burnham and Michael Steinberg (eds.), *Beethoven and his World* (Princeton University Press, 2000), pp. 1–26.

Brown, Clive, *A Portrait of Mendelssohn* (New Haven, CT and London: Yale University Press, 2003).

Brown, Jane K., *Goethe's Faust: The German Tragedy* (Ithaca, NY: Cornell University Press, 1986).

Brown, Marshall, *The Shape of German Romanticism* (Ithaca, NY: Cornell University Press, 1979).

Bruyne, Edgar de, *The Esthetics of the Middle Ages*, trans. Eileen B. Hennesey (New York: Frederick Ungar, 1969).

Buhler, James, 'Breakthrough as a Critique of Form: The Finale of Mahler's First Symphony', *19th-Century Music*, 20 (1996), 125–43.

Bülow, Hans von, *Ausgewählte Schriften: 1850–92* (Leipzig: Breitkopf & Härtel, 1896).

Burnham, Scott, *Beethoven Hero* (Princeton University Press, 1995).

'Criticism, Faith, and the *Idee*: A.B. Marx's Early Reception of Beethoven', *19th-Century Music*, 13 (1990), 183–92.

'Landscape as Music, Landscape as Truth: Schubert and the Burden of Repetition', *19th-Century Music*, 29 (2005), 31–41.

Review-Article 'E.T.A. Hoffmann's Musical Writings', *19th-Century Music*, 14 (1991), 286–96.

Bury, B.J., *The Idea of Progress: An Inquiry into its Origins and Growth* (London: Macmillan, 1920).

Chua, Daniel K.L., 'Haydn as Romantic: A Chemical Experiment with Instrumental Music', in W. Dean Sutcliffe (ed.), *Haydn Studies* (Cambridge University Press, 1998), pp. 120–51.

Churgin, Bathia, 'Beethoven and the New Development Theme in Sonata-Form Movements', *Journal of Musicology*, 16 (1998), 323–43.

Chusid, Martin, 'Schubert's Cyclic Compositions of 1824', *Acta Musicologica*, 36 (1964), 37–45.

Clarke, Eric, 'Rhythm and Timing in Music', §III 'Form Perception', in Diana Deutsch (ed.), *The Psychology of Music* (San Diego Academic Press, 1999), pp. 476–8.

Cocking, J.M., *Proust: Collected Essays on the Writer and his Art* (Cambridge University Press, 1982).

Condorcet, Nicolas de, *Esquisse d'un tableau historique des progrès de l'esprit humain* (Paris: Agasse, 1795).

Cone, Edward T., *The Composer's Voice* (Berkeley, CA: University of California Press, 1974).

Cooke, Deryck, 'The Unity of Beethoven's Late Quartets', *The Music Review*, 24 (1963), 30–49.

Cooper, John Michael, *Mendelssohn, Goethe, and the Walpurgis Night: The Heathen Muse in European Culture, 1700–1850* (University of Rochester Press, 2007).

Mendelssohn's Italian Symphony (Oxford University Press, 2003).

'Mendelssohn's Two *Infelice* Arias: Problems of Sources and Musical Identity', in John Michael Cooper and Julie D. Prandi (eds.), *The Mendelssohns: Their Music in History* (Oxford University Press, 2002), pp. 43–97.

'Of Red Roofs and Hunting Horns: Mendelssohn's Song Aesthetic, with an Unpublished Cycle (1830)', *Journal of Musicological Research*, 21 (2002), 300–14.

Crane, Susan, *Collecting and Historical Consciousness in Early Nineteenth-Century Germany* (Ithaca, NY: Cornell University Press, 2000).

Dahlgren, Lotte (ed.), *Bref till Adolf Fredrik Lindblad från Mendelssohn, Dohrn, Almqvist, Atterbom, Geijer, Fredrika Bremer, C.W. Böttiger och andra* (Stockholm: Albert Bonnier, 1913).

Dahlhaus, Carl, *Esthetics of Music*, trans. William Austin (Cambridge University Press, 1982).

'"Hoch symbolisch intentioniert": Zu Mendelssohns "Erster Walpurgisnacht"', *Österreichische Musikzeitschrift*, 36 (1981), 290–7.

The Idea of Absolute Music, trans. Roger Lustig (Chicago, IL and London: Chicago University Press, 1991).

'Issues in Composition', in *Between Romanticism and Modernism*, trans. Mary Whittall (Berkeley and Los Angeles, CA: University of California Press, 1980), pp. 40–78.

Klassische und Romantische Musikästhetik (Laaber Verlag, 1988).

Ludwig van Beethoven: Approaches to his Music, trans. Mary Whittall (Oxford University Press, 1991).

'Mendelssohn und die musikalische Gattungstradition', in Carl Dahlhaus (ed.), *Das Problem Mendelssohn* (Regensburg: Bosse, 1974), pp. 55–60.

'Musical Prose', in *Schoenberg and the New Music*, trans. Derrick Puffett and Alfred Clayton (Cambridge University Press, 1987), pp. 105–19.

Die Musik des 19. Jahrhunderts (Neues Handbuch der Musikwissenschaft, 6) (Wiesbaden: Athenaion, 1980), trans. J.B. Robinson as *Nineteenth-Century Music* (Berkeley and Los Angeles, CA: University of California Press, 1989).

'Musik und Zeit', in Carl Dahlhaus and Hans Heinrich Eggebrecht, *Was ist Musik?* (Wilhelmshaven: Noetzel, 1985), pp. 174–80.

'Sonata Form in Schubert', in Walter Frisch (ed.), *Schubert: Critical and Analytical Studies* (Lincoln, NE: University of Nebraska Press, 1986), pp. 1–12.

(ed.), *Das Problem Mendelssohn* (Regensburg: Bosse, 1974).

(ed.), *Studien zur Musikgeschichte Berlins im frühen 19. Jahrhundert* (Regensburg: Bosse, 1980).

Darcy, Warren, 'Bruckner's Sonata Deformations', in Timothy L. Jackson and Paul Hawkshaw (eds.), *Bruckner Studies* (Cambridge University Press, 1997), pp. 256–77.

Deiters, Hermann, Review of the first publication of Mendelssohn's Symphony No. 5 ('Reformation'), *Allgemeine musikalische Zeitung*, 3 (1868), col. 349–50, 356–7; trans. Thomas Grey in Douglass Seaton (ed.), *The Mendelssohn Companion* (Westport, CT and London: Greenwood Press, 2001), pp. 534–43.

DeNora, Tia, *Beethoven and the Construction of Genius: Musical Politics in Vienna, 1792–1803* (Berkeley and Los Angeles, CA: University of California Press, 1996).

Devrient, Eduard *Meine Erinnerungen an Felix Mendelssohn-Bartholdy und seine Briefe an mich* (Leipzig: J.J. Weber, 1869).

Dinglinger, Wolfgang, 'The Programme of Mendelssohn's "Reformation" Symphony, Op. 107', in John Michael Cooper and Julie D. Prandi (eds.), *The Mendelssohns: Their Music in History* (Oxford University Press, 2002), pp. 115–33.

Dommer, Arrey von, *Musikalisches Lexikon: auf Grundlage des Lexicon's von H. Ch. Koch* (Heidelberg: J.C.B. Mohr, 1865).

Donelan, James H., *Poetry and the Romantic Aesthetic* (Cambridge University Press, 2008).

Dostoyevsky, Fyodor, *The Brothers Karamazov*, trans. David Magarshack, 2 vols. (Harmondsworth: Penguin, 1958).

Droysen, Gustav, 'Johann Gustav Droysen und Felix Mendelssohn-Bartholdy', *Deutsche Rundschau*, 111 (1902), 107–26, 193–215, 386–408.

Eckermann, Johann Peter, *Gespräche mit Goethe in den letzten Jahren seines Lebens*, ed. Otto Schönberger (Stuttgart: Reclam, 1998).

Eco, Umberto, *Art and Beauty in the Middle Ages*, trans. Hugh Bredin (New Haven, CT: Yale University Press, 1988).

Eliade, Mircea, *The Myth of the Eternal Return* (New York: Pantheon Books, 1954).

Eliot, T.S., *Collected Poems 1909–1962* (London: Faber, 1974).

Epstein, David, *Beyond Orpheus: Studies in Musical Structure* (Cambridge, MA: MIT Press, 1979).

Ferris, David, *Schumann's 'Eichendorff Liederkreis' and the Genre of the Romantic Cycle* (Oxford University Press, 2001).

Fichte, Johann Gottlieb, *Sämmtliche Werke*, 8 vols. (Berlin: Veit, 1845–6).

Finscher, Ludwig, '"Zwischen absoluter und Programmusik": Zur Interpretation der deutschen romantischen Symphonie', in Christoph-Hellmut Mahling (ed.), *Über Symphonien: Beiträge zu einer musikalischen Gattung (Festschrift für Walter Wiora)* (Tutzing: H. Schneider, 1979), pp. 103–15.

'Zyklus', in Ludwig Finscher (ed.), *Die Musik in Geschichte und Gegenwart*, 20 vols. (Kassel and Stuttgart: Bärenreiter and Metzler, 1998), vol. IX, cols. 2528–37.

Fisk, Charles, *Returning Cycles: Contexts for the Interpretation of Schubert's Impromptus and Last Sonatas* (Berkeley and Los Angeles, CA: University of California Press, 2001).

Fiske, Roger, *Scotland in Music: A European Enthusiasm* (Cambridge: Cambridge University Press, 1983).

Forchert, Arno, 'Adolf Bernhard Marx und seine "Berliner Allgemeine musikalische Zeitung"', in Carl Dahlhaus (ed.), *Studien zur Musikgeschichte Berlins im frühen 19. Jahrhundert* (Regensburg: Bosse, 1980), pp. 381–404.

Friedländer, Max, 'Ein Brief Felix Mendelssohns', *Vierteljahrschrift für Musikwissenschaft*, 5 (1889), 483–9.

Freud, Sigmund [and Breuer, Josef], *The Penguin Freud Library*, trans. James Strachey, 15 vols. (Harmondsworth: Penguin, 1991).

Garratt, James, 'Mendelssohn's Babel: Romanticism and the Poetics of Translation', *Music & Letters*, 80 (1999), 23–49.

'Mendelssohn and the Rise of Musical Historicism', in Peter Mercer-Taylor (ed.), *The Cambridge Companion to Mendelssohn* (Cambridge University Press, 2004), pp. 55–70.

Palestrina and the German Romantic Imagination: Interpreting Historicism in Nineteenth-Century Music (Cambridge University Press, 2002).

Gell, Alfred, *The Anthropology of Time: Cultural Constructions of Temporal Maps and Images* (Oxford: Berg, 1992).

Gjerdingen, Robert O., *A Classic Turn of Phrase: Music and the Psychology of Convention* (Philadelphia, PA: University of Pennsylvania Press, 1988).

Godwin, Joscelyn, 'Early Mendelssohn and late Beethoven', *Music & Letters*, 55 (1974), 272–85.

Goehr, Lydia, *The Imaginary Museum of Musical Works: An Essay in the Philosophy of Music* (Oxford University Press, 1992).

Goethe, Johann Wolfgang von, *Kunsttheoretische Schriften und Übersetzungen*, in *Berliner Ausgabe* (22 vols.), vols. 17–22 (Berlin: Aufbau Verlag, 1965–78).

Poetische Werke: Vollständige Ausgabe, 10 vols. (Essen: Phaidon Verlag, 1999).

and Zelter, Carl Friedrich, *Briefwechsel zwischen Goethe und Zelter*, ed. Max Hecker, 3 vols. (Frankfurt: Insel Verlag, 1987).

Golumb, Uri, 'Mendelssohn's Creative Response to late Beethoven: Polyphony and Thematic Identity in Mendelssohn's Quartet in A-major Op. 13', *Ad Parnassum*, 4 (2006), 101–19.

Graham, Ilse, *Goethe: Portrait of the Artist* (Berlin: de Gruyter, 1977).

Greene, David B., *Temporal Processes in Beethoven's Music* (New York: Gordon and Breach, 1982).

Grey, Thomas, 'The Orchestral Music', in Douglass Seaton (ed.), *The Mendelssohn Companion* (Westport, CT and London: Greenwood Press, 2001), pp. 395–533.

'*Tableaux vivants*: Landscape, History Painting, and the Visual Imagination in Mendelssohn's Orchestral Music', *19th-Century Music*, 21 (1997), 38–76.

'. . . *wie ein rother Faden*: On the Origins of "Leitmotif" as Critical Construct and Musical Practice', in Ian Bent (ed.), *Music Theory in the Age of Romanticism* (Cambridge University Press, 1996), pp. 187–210.

Großmann-Vendrey, Susanna, *Felix Mendelssohn Bartholdy und die Musik der Vergangenheit* (Regensburg: Bosse, 1969).

'Mendelssohn und die Vergangenheit', in Walter Wiora (ed.), *Die Ausbreitung des Historismus über die Musik: Aufsätze und Diskussionen* (Regensburg: Bosse, 1969), pp. 73–82.

Haimo, Ethan, *Haydn's Symphonic Forms: Essays in Compositional Logic* (Oxford: Clarendon Press, 1995).

'Remote Keys and Multi-Movement Unity: Haydn in the 1790s', *The Musical Quarterly*, 74 (1990), 242–68.

Haney, Joel, 'Navigating Sonata Space in Mendelssohn's *Meeresstille und glückliche Fahrt*', *19th-Century Music*, 28 (2004), 108–32.

Hatten, Robert S., *Musical Meaning in Beethoven: Markedness, Correlation, and Interpretation* (Bloomington, IN: Indiana University Press, 1994).

Hegel, Georg Wilhelm Friedrich, *Aesthetics: Lectures on Fine Art*, trans. T.M. Knox, 2 vols. (Oxford: Clarendon Press, 1975).

Lectures on the History of Philosophy, trans. E.S. Haldane and F.H. Simson, 3 vols. (London: Kegan Paul, 1896).

Lectures on the Philosophy of History, trans. J. Sibree (New York: Dover, 1956).

The Logic of Hegel, trans. William Wallace (Oxford University Press, 1892).

Phenomenology of Spirit, trans. A.V. Miller (Oxford University Press, 1979).

Science of Logic, trans. A.V. Miller (London: Allen & Unwin, 1969).

Werke, 20 vols. (Frankfurt am Main: Suhrkamp, 1979).

Henry, Anne, *Marcel Proust, théories pour une esthétique* (Paris: Klincksieck, 1981).

Hensel, Fanny, *The Letters of Fanny Hensel to Felix Mendelssohn*, ed. and trans. Marcia J. Citron (Stuyvesant, NY: Pendragon, 1987).

Hensel, Sebastian, *Die Familie Mendelssohn 1729–1847: Nach Briefen und Tagebüchern*, 3 vols. (Berlin: B. Behr, 1879).

Hepokoski, James, 'Back and Forth from *Egmont*: Beethoven, Mozart, and the Non-Resolving Recapitulation', *19th-Century Music*, 25 (2002), 127–54.

'Beethoven Reception: The Symphonic Tradition', in Jim Samson (ed.), *The Cambridge History of Nineteenth-Century Music* (Cambridge University Press, 2002), pp. 424–59.

'Beyond the Sonata Principle', *Journal of the American Musicological Society*, 55 (2002), 91–154.

'The Essence of Sibelius: Creation Myths and Rotational Cycles in *Luonnotar*', in Glenda Dawn Goss (ed.), *The Sibelius Companion* (Westport, CT and London: Greenwood Press, 1996), pp. 121–46.

Sibelius Symphony No. 5 (Cambridge University Press, 1993).

and Darcy, Warren, *Elements of Sonata Theory: Norms, Types, and Deformations in the Late-Eighteenth-Century Sonata* (New York: Oxford University Press, 2006).

Herder, Johann Gottlieb, *Eine Metakritik zur Kritik der reinen Vernunft*, ed. Friedrich Bassenger (Berlin: Aufbau Verlag, 1955).

Hobsbawm, Eric and Ranger, Terence (eds.), *The Invention of Tradition* (Cambridge University Press, 1992).

Hoeckner, Berthold, *Programming the Absolute: Nineteenth-Century German Music and the Hermeneutics of the Moment* (Princeton University Press, 2002).

Hoffmann, E.T.A., *Poetische Werke*, 6 vols. (Berlin: Aufbau Verlag, 1963).

Hopkins, Robert G., 'When a Coda is More than a Coda: Reflections on Beethoven', in Eugene Narmour and Ruth Solie (eds.), *Explorations in Music, the Arts, and Ideas: Essays in Honor of Leonard B. Meyer* (Stuyvesant, NY: Pendragon Press, 1988), pp. 393–410.

Horton, John, *The Chamber Music of Mendelssohn* (London: Geoffrey Cumberlege / Oxford University Press, 1946).

Hoshino, Hiromi, *Menderusuzon no 'Sukottorando kokyokyoku' [Mendelssohn's Scottish Symphony]* (Tokyo: Ongaku no Tomosha, 2003).

Hosler, Bellamy, *Changing Aesthetic Views of Instrumental Music in Eighteenth-Century Germany* (Ann Arbor, MI: UMI Research Press, 1981).

d'Indy, Vincent, *Cours de Composition*, ed. Auguste Sérieyx, 3 vols. in 4 books (Paris: A. Durand, 1903–50).

Ingarden, Roman, *The Musical Work and the Problem of its Identity*, trans. Adam Czerniawski (London: Macmillan, 1986).

Jenkins, David and Visocchi, Mark, *Mendelssohn in Scotland* (London: Chappell, 1978).

Jessulat, Ariane, *Die Frage als musikalischer Topos: Studien zur Motivbildung in der Musik des 19. Jahrhunderts* (Berlin: Studio, 2000).

Jourdan, Paul, 'Mendelssohn in England, 1829–37', unpublished PhD thesis, University of Cambridge (1998).

Kant, Immanuel, *Werke*, 12 vols. (Frankfurt am Main: Suhrkamp, 1977).

Kaufmann, Walter, *Hegel: A Reinterpretation* (New York: Doubleday, 1966).

Keller, Hans, 'The Classical Romantics: Schumann and Mendelssohn', in H.H. Schönzeler (ed.), *Of German Music: A Symposium* (London: Oswald Wolff, 1976), pp. 179–218.

'Dream-Work and Development in Sonata Form', unpublished draft MS [8 pp.], Cambridge University Library, n.d.

'Mendelssohn's String Quartets', *The Listener*, 74/1895 (22 July 1965), 141.

Music and Psychology: From Vienna to London, 1939–52, ed. Christopher Wintle (London: Plumbago Books, 2003).

Kerman, Joseph, '*An die ferne Geliebte*', in Alan Tyson (ed.), *Beethoven Studies 1* (New York: Norton, 1973), pp. 123–57.

The Beethoven Quartets (New York and London: W.W. Norton & Co., 1966).

Kiesewetter, Raphael Georg, *Geschichte der europäisch-abendländischen oder unsrer heutigen Musik* (Leipzig: Breitkopf & Härtel, 1834).

Kinderman, William and Krebs, Harald (eds.), *The Second Practice of Nineteenth-Century Tonality* (Lincoln, NE: University of Nebraska Press, 1996).

Klein, Richard, 'Thesen zum Verhältnis von Musik und Zeit', in Richard Klein, Eckehard Kiem and Wolfram Ette (eds.), *Musik in der Zeit: Zeit in der Musik* (Göttingen: Velbrück Wissenschaft, 2000), pp. 57–107.

Kleist, Heinrich von, *Werke und Briefe*, 4 vols. (Berlin and Weimar: Aufbau Verlag, 1978).

Klingemann, Karl [d.J.] (ed.), *Felix Mendelssohn-Bartholdys Briefwechsel mit Legationsrat Karl Klingemann in London* (Essen: Baedeker, 1909).

Kohlhase, Hans, 'Brahms und Mendelssohn: Strukturelle Parallelen in der Kammermusik für Streicher', in Constantin Floros, Hans Joachim Marx and Peter Petersen (eds.), *Brahms und seine Zeit: Symposion Hamburg 1983* (*Hamburger Jahrbuch für Musikwissenschaft*, 7) (Laaber: Verlag, 1984), pp. 59–85.

'Studien zur Form in den Streichquartetten von Felix Mendelssohn Bartholdy', in Constantin Floros, Hans Joachim Marx and Peter Petersen (eds.), *Zur Musikgeschichte des 19. Jahrhunderts* (*Hamburger Jahrbuch für Musikwissenschaft*, 2) (Hamburg: Karl Dieter Wagner: 1977), pp. 75–104.

Konold, Wulf, *Felix Mendelssohn Bartholdy und seine Zeit* (Laaber: Verlag, 1984).

'Funktion der Stilisierung: Vorläufige Bemerkungen zum Stilbegriff bei Mendelssohn', in Heinz-Klaus Metzger and Rainer Riehn (eds.), *Felix Mendelssohn Bartholdy, Musik-Konzepte* 14/15 (Munich: Edition Text + Kritik, 1980), pp. 3–7.

'Mendelssohn und der späte Beethoven', in Johannes Fischer (ed.), *Münchener Beethoven-Studien* (Munich: Emil Katzbichler, 1992), pp. 183–91.

Die Symphonien Felix Mendelssohn Bartholdys: Untersuchungen zu Werkgestalt und Formstruktur (Laaber Verlag, 1992).

Koselleck, Reinhart, *Futures Past: On the Semantics of Historical Time*, trans. Keith Tribe (Cambridge, MA: MIT Press, 1985).

Kramer, Jonathan, 'Multiple and Non-Linear Time in Beethoven's opus 135', *Perspectives on New Music*, 11 (1973), 122–45.

The Time of Music: New Meanings, New Temporalities, New Listening Strategies (New York: Schirmer, 1988).

Kramer, Lawrence, '*Felix culpa*: Goethe and the Image of Mendelssohn', in R. Larry Todd (ed.), *Mendelssohn Studies* (Cambridge University Press, 1992), pp. 64–79.

'The Harem Threshold: Turkish Music and Greek Love in Beethoven's "Ode to Joy"', *19th-Century Music*, 22 (1998), 78–90.

'The Lied as Cultural Practice: Tutelage, Gender, and Desire in Mendelssohn's Goethe Songs', in *Classical Music and Postmodern Knowledge* (Berkeley and Los Angeles, CA: University of California Press, 1995), pp. 143–73.

Music as Cultural Practice, 1800–1900 (Berkeley and Los Angeles, CA: University of California Press, 1992).

Kramer, Richard, *Distant Cycles: Schubert and the Conceiving of Song* (University of Chicago Press, 1994).

Krummacher, Friedhelm, *Mendelssohn – Der Komponist: Studien zur Kammermusik für Streicher* (Munich: Wilhelm Fink, 1978).

'Synthesis und Disparaten: Zu Beethovens späten Quartetten und ihrer frühen Rezeption', *Archiv für Musikwissenschaft*, 37 (1980), 99–134.

'Zur Kompositionsart Mendelssohn: Thesen am Beispiel der Streichquartette', in Carl Dahlhaus (ed.), *Das Problem Mendelssohn* (Regensburg: Bosse, 1974), pp. 169–84; trans. Douglass Seaton as 'On Mendelssohn's Compositional Style: Propositions Based on the Example of the String Quartets', in Douglass Seaton (ed.), *The Mendelssohn Companion* (Westport, CT and London: Greenwood Press, 2001), pp. 551–68.

Küpper, Peter, *Die Zeit als Erlebnis des Novalis* (Cologne: Böhlau, 1959).

Lévi-Strauss, Claude, *The Raw and the Cooked (Mythologiques, vol. I)*, trans. Doreen Weightman and John Weightman (New York: Harper & Row, 1969).

Little, William A., 'Mendelssohn and the Berliner Singakademie: The Composer at the Crossroads', in R. Larry Todd (ed.), *Mendelssohn and his World* (Princeton University Press, 1991), pp. 65–85.

Litzmann, Berthold, *Clara Schumann, ein Künstlerleben: Nach Tagebüchern und Briefen*, 2 vols. (Leipzig: Breitkopf & Härtel, 1902).

Lobe, Johann Christian, 'Conversations with Felix Mendelssohn', trans. Susan Gillespie, in R. Larry Todd (ed.), *Mendelssohn and his World* (Princeton University Press, 1991), pp. 187–205.

Longyear, Rey M., 'Beethoven and Romantic Irony', *The Musical Quarterly*, 56 (1970), 647–64.

  'Cyclic Form and Tonal Relationships in Mendelssohn's "Scottish" Symphony', *In Theory Only*, 4 (1979), 38–48.

Lütteken, Laurenz, *Das Monologische als Denkform in der Musik zwischen 1760 und 1785* (Tübingen: Niemeyer, 1998).

Macdonald, Hugh, 'Cyclic Form', in Stanley Sadie (ed.), *The New Grove Dictionary of Music and Musicians*, 29 vols. (London: Macmillan, 2001), vol. VI, pp. 797–8.

  '[G♭]', *19th-Century Music*, 11 (1988), 221–37.

Macfarren, George, Review of Mendelssohn Symphony No. 3, *Musical World*, 17 (1842), 185–7.

Macpherson, James, *The Poems of Ossian*, ed. Howard Gaskill (Edinburgh University Press, 1996).

Mähl, Hans Joachim, *Die Idee des goldenen Zeitalters im Werk des Novalis* (Heidelberg: Carl Winter, 1965).

Marston, Nicholas, 'Schubert's Homecoming', *Journal of the Royal Music Association*, 125 (2000), 248–70.

  'Voicing Beethoven's Distant Beloved', in Scott Burnham and Michael Steinberg (eds.), *Beethoven and his World* (Princeton University Press, 2000), pp. 124–47.

Marx, Adolph Bernhard, *Erinnerungen aus meinem Leben*, 2 vols. (Berlin: Janke, 1865).

  Ludwig Van Beethoven: Leben und Schaffen, 2 vols. (Berlin: Janke, 1828).

  Musical Form in the Age of Beethoven: Selected Writings on Theory and Method, ed. and trans. Scott Burnham (Cambridge University Press, 1997).

  Über Malerei in der Tonkunst: Ein Maigruß an die Kunstphilosophen (Berlin: Finke, 1828).

Marx, Günter, Preface to Fanny Hensel, String Quartet in E♭ (Wiesbaden: Breitkopf & Härtel, 1988).

Mendelssohn Bartholdy, Felix, *Briefe aus den Jahren 1833 bis 1847 von Felix Mendelssohn Bartholdy* [*Briefe*, vol. II], ed. Paul and Karl Mendelssohn Bartholdy (Leipzig: Hermann Mendelssohn, 1863).

  Reisebriefe von Felix Mendelssohn Bartholdy aus den Jahren 1830 bis 1832 [*Briefe*, vol. I], ed. Paul Mendelssohn Bartholdy (Leipzig: Herrmann Mendelssohn, 1861).

Mendelssohn-Bartholdy, Karl, *Goethe und Felix Mendelssohn Bartholdy* (Leipzig: Hirtel, 1871).

Mercer-Taylor, Peter, 'Mendelssohn's "Scottish" Symphony and the Music of German Memory', *19th-Century Music*, 19 (1995), 68–82.

Metzger, Heinz-Klaus, 'Noch einmal: "Die erste Walpurgisnacht", Versuch einer
anderen Allegorese', in Heinz-Klaus Metzger and Rainer Riehn (eds.), *Felix
Mendelssohn Bartholdy, Musik-Konzepte* 14/15 (Munich: Edition Text+Kritik,
1980), pp. 93–7.

Mikusi, Balázs, 'Mendelssohn's "Scottish" Tonality?', *19th-Century Music*, 29 (2006),
240–60.

Mintz, Donald M., 'The Sketches and Drafts for Three of Felix Mendelssohn's Major
Works', unpublished PhD thesis, Cornell University (1960).

Monelle, Raymond, *The Sense of Music: Semiotic Essays* (Princeton University Press,
2000).

Montgomery, David L., 'The Myth of Organicism: From Bad Science to Great Art',
The Musical Quarterly, 76 (1992), 17–66.

Motte-Haber, Helga de la, 'Historische Wandlungen musikalischer Zeitvorstellungen', in Diether de la Motte (ed.), *Neue Musik: Quo vadis? 17 Perspektiven*
(Mainz: Schott, 1988), pp. 53–66.

Munn, Nancy D., 'The Cultural Anthropology of Time: A Critical Essay', *Annual
Review of Anthropology*, 21 (1992), 93–123.

Nattiez, Jean-Jacques, *Proust as Musician*, trans. Derrick Puffett (Cambridge University Press, 1989).

Neff, Severine, 'Schoenberg and Goethe: Organicism and Analysis', in Christopher
Hatch and David Bernstein (eds.), *Music Theory and the Exploration of the Past*
(University of Chicago Press, 1993), pp. 409–33.

Neubauer, John, *The Emancipation of Music from Language: Departure from Mimesis
in Eighteenth-Century Aesthetics* (New Haven, CT: Yale University Press, 1986).

Newark, Cormac and Wassenaar, Ingrid, 'Proust and Music: The Anxiety of Competence', *Cambridge Opera Journal*, 9 (1997), 163–83.

Newcomb, Anthony, 'Once More "Between Absolute and Programme Music": Schumann's Second Symphony', *19th-Century Music*, 7 (1984), 233–50.

Newman, William S., *The Sonata since Beethoven* (Chapel Hill, NC: University of
North Carolina Press, 1969).

Newton, Isaac, *The Mathematical Principles of Natural Philosophy*, trans. Andrew
Motte, rev. Florian Cajori, 2 vols. (Berkeley, CA: University of California Press,
1934).

Nietzsche, Friedrich, *Sämtliche Werke (Kritische Studienausgabe)*, ed. Giorgio Colli
and Mazzino Montinari, 15 vols. (Berlin and New York / Munich: de Gruyter
/ Deutscher Taschenbuch Verlag, 1980).

Novalis, *Schriften. Die Werke Friedrich von Hardenbergs (Historische-kritische Ausgabe)*, ed. Paul Kluckhohn, Richard Samuel, Gerhard Schulz and Hans-Joachim
Mähl, 6 vols. (Stuttgart: Kohlhammer, 1960–2006).

Oechsle, Siegfried, *Symphonik nach Beethoven: Studien zu Schubert, Schumann,
Mendelssohn und Gade* (Kassel: Bärenreiter, 1992).

Panofsky, Erwin, 'Et in Arcadia Ego: Poussin and the Elegiac Tradition', in *Meaning in the Visual Arts* (New York: Doubleday, 1955), pp. 295–320.

Pater, Walter, *The Renaissance: Studies in Art and Poetry*, ed. A. Phillips (Oxford University Press, 1986).

Pederson, Sanna, 'On the Task of the Music Historian: The Myth of the Symphony After Beethoven', *repercussions*, 2 (1993), 5–30.

Plotinus, *The Enneads*, trans. Stephen MacKenna, ed. John Dillon (Harmondsworth: Penguin, 1991).

Pope, Alexander, *Poetical Works*, ed. Herbert Davis (Oxford University Press, 1966).

Poulet, Georges, *Studies in Human Time*, trans. Elliott Coleman (Baltimore, MD: Johns Hopkins Press, 1956).

Prandi, Julie D., 'Kindred Spirits: Mendelssohn and Goethe, *Die erste Walpurgisnacht*', in John Michael Cooper and Julie D. Prandi (eds.), *The Mendelssohns: Their Music in History* (Oxford University Press, 2002), pp. 135–46.

Proclus, *Elements of Theology*, trans. E.R. Dodds (Oxford: Clarendon Press, 1933).

Proust, Marcel, *By Way of Saint-Beuve*, trans. Sylvia Townsend Warner (London: Hogarth Press, 1984).

   Jean Santeuil, trans. Gerard Hopkins (Harmondsworth: Penguin Books, 1985).

   Remembrance of Things Past, trans. C.K. Scott Moncrieff and Terence Kilmartin, 3 vols. (Harmondsworth: Penguin, 1981).

   Selected Letters, ed. Philip Kolb, trans. Ralph Manheim, Terence Kilmartin and Joanna Kilmartin, 4 vols. (London: Harper Collins, 1983–2000).

Quinones, R.J., *The Renaissance Discovery of Time* (Cambridge, MA: Harvard University Press, 1972).

Radcliffe, Philip, *Mendelssohn* (London: J.M. Dent, 1954).

Rathey, Markus, '"Anything but National Music!": Mendelssohn's Composing of "Folk Music" on a Higher Level', paper presented at *Mendelssohn in the Long Nineteenth Century*, 15 July 2005, Trinity College, Dublin.

Réti, Rudolf, *The Thematic Process in Music* (New York: Macmillan, 1951).

Reynolds, Christopher, *Motives for Allusion: Context and Content in Nineteenth-Century Music* (Cambridge, MA: Harvard University Press, 2003).

   'The Representational Impulse in Late Beethoven, I: *An die ferne Geliebte*', *Acta Musicologia*, 60 (1988), 43–61.

Roesner, Linda Correll, 'Schumann's "Parallel" Forms', *19th-Century Music*, 14 (1991), 265–78.

Rosen, Charles, *The Romantic Generation* (London: Harper Collins, 1996).

Rudorff, Ernst Friedrich Karl, 'From the Memoirs of Ernst Rudorff', trans. Nancy B. Reich, in R. Larry Todd (ed.), *Mendelssohn and his World* (Princeton University Press, 1991), 259–71.

Rumph, Stephen, *Beethoven After Napoleon: Political Romanticism in the Late Works* (Berkeley and Los Angeles, CA: University of California Press, 2004).

Sabean, David Warren, 'Fanny and Felix Mendelssohn-Bartholdy and the Question of Incest', *The Musical Quarterly*, 77 (1993), 709–17.

Salm, Peter, *The Poem as Plant: A Biological View of Goethe's Faust* (Cleveland, OH and London: Case Western Reserve University Press, 1971).

Schelling, Friedrich Wilhelm Joseph, *Sämtliche Werke*, ed. K.F.A. Schelling, 14 vols. (Stuttgart: Cotta, 1856–61).

Schiller, Friedrich, *Sämtliche Werke*, 5 vols. (Munich: Carl Hanser, 1962).

Schlegel, Friedrich, *Philosophie der Geschichte*, 2 vols. (Vienna: Klang, 1829).

Schleiermacher, Friedrich, *Ästhetik*, ed. Rudolf Odebrecht (Berlin: de Gruyter, 1931).

Schleuning, Peter, 'Felix Mendelssohn Bartholdys Klaviersonate E-Dur, op. 6', *Mendelssohn-Studien*, 16 (2009), 231–50.

   Die freie Fantasie: Ein Beitrag zur Erforschung der klassischen Klaviermusik (Göppingen: Kümmerle, 1973).

Schmalfeldt, Janet, 'Form as the Process of Becoming: The Beethoven-Hegelian Tradition and the "Tempest" Sonata', in Christopher Reynolds, Lewis Lockwood and James Webster (eds.), *Beethoven Forum 4* (Lincoln, NE: University of Nebraska Press, 1992), pp. 37–71.

Schmidt [-Beste], Thomas Christian, *Die ästhetischen Grundlagen der Instrumentalmusik Felix Mendelssohn Bartholdys* (Stuttgart: M & P, 1996).

   Introduction to critical edition of score, *Sinfonie Nr. 3 a-Moll op. 56: Leipziger Mendelssohn-Ausgabe*, I.5 (Wiesbaden: Breitkopf & Härtel, 2005).

   'Just how "Scottish" is the "Scottish" Symphony? Thoughts on Form and Poetic Content in Mendelssohn's Opus 56', in John Michael Cooper and Julie D. Prandi (eds.), *The Mendelssohns: Their Music in History* (Oxford University Press, 2002), pp. 147–65.

   'Mendelssohn's Chamber Music', in Peter Mercer-Taylor (ed.), *The Cambridge Companion to Mendelssohn* (Cambridge University Press, 2004), pp. 130–48.

Schopenhauer, Arthur, *Werke (Zürcher Ausgabe)*, 10 vols. (Zurich: Diogenes Verlag, 1977).

Schubring, Julius, 'Erinnerungen an Felix Mendelssohn Bartholdy', *Daheim*, 2 (1866), 373ff., trans. (anon.) in *Musical World*, 31 (12 and 19 May 1866) and repr. in R. Larry Todd (ed.), *Mendelssohn and his World* (Princeton University Press, 1991), pp. 221–36.

Schulenberg, David, *The Instrumental Music of Carl Philipp Emanuel Bach* (Ann Arbor, MI: UMI Research Press, 1984).

Schumann, Robert, 'Erinnerungen an F[elix] Mendelssohn vom Jahre 1835 bis zu s[einem] Tode', in Heinz-Klaus Metzger and Rainer Riehn (eds.), *Felix Mendelssohn Bartholdy, Musik-Konzepte* 14/15 (Munich: Edition Text + Kritik, 1980), pp. 97–122.

   Gesammelte Schriften über Musik und Musiker, ed. Martin Kreisig, 2 vols. (Leipzig: Breitkopf & Härtel, 1949).

Seaton, Douglass, 'A Draft for the Exposition of the First Movement of Mendelssohn's "Scotch" Symphony', *Journal of the American Musicological Society*, 30 (1977), 129–35.

'Mendelssohn's Cycles of Songs', in John Michael Cooper and Julie D. Prandi (eds.), *The Mendelssohns: Their Music in History* (Oxford University Press, 2002), pp. 203–29.

'The Problem of the Lyric Persona in Mendelssohn's Songs', in Christian Martin Schmidt (ed.), *Felix Mendelssohn Bartholdy Kongress-Bericht Berlin 1994* (Wiesbaden: Breitkopf & Härtel, 1997), pp. 167–86.

'The Romantic Mendelssohn: The Composition of *Die erste Walpurgisnacht*', *The Musical Quarterly*, 68 (1982), 398–410.

'A Study of a Collection of Mendelssohn's Sketches and Other Autograph Material, Deutsche Staatsbibliothek, Berlin, Mus. Ms. Autogr. Mendelssohn 19', unpublished PhD thesis, Columbia University (1977).

'With Words: Mendelssohn's Vocal Songs', in Douglass Seaton (ed.), *The Mendelssohn Companion* (Westport, CT and London: Greenwood Press, 2001), pp. 661–700.

Seidel, Wilhelm, 'Schnell–Langsam–Schnell: Zur "klassischen" Theorie des instrumentalen Zyklus', *Musiktheorie*, 1 (1986), 205–16.

Sembdner, Helmut (ed.), *Kleists Aufsatz über das Marionettentheater: Studien und Interpretationen* (Berlin: Erich Schmidt, 1967).

Silber [Ballan], Judith, 'Marxian Programmatic Music: A Stage in Mendelssohn's Musical Development', in R. Larry Todd (ed.), *Mendelssohn Studies* (Cambridge University Press, 1992), pp. 149–61.

'Mendelssohn and his *Reformation* Symphony', *Journal of the American Musicological Society*, 40 (1987), 310–36.

'Mendelssohn and the Reformation Symphony: A Critical and Historical Study', unpublished PhD thesis, Yale University (1987).

Sisman, Elaine, 'Memory and Invention at the Threshold of Beethoven's Late Style', in Scott Burnham and Michael Steinberg (eds.), *Beethoven and his World* (Princeton University Press, 2000), pp. 51–87.

Mozart: The 'Jupiter' Symphony (Cambridge: Cambridge University Press, 1993).

Smith, Peter, 'Brahms and Schenker: A Mutual Response to Sonata Form', *Music Theory Spectrum*, 16 (1994), 77–103.

'Liquidation, Augmentation, and Brahms's Recapitulatory Overlaps', *19th-Century Music*, 17 (1994), 237–62.

Solie, Ruth, 'The Living Work: Organicism and Musical Analysis', *19th-Century Music*, 4 (1980), 147–56.

Solomon, Robert C., *Continental Philosophy since 1750: The Rise and Fall of the Self* (Oxford University Press, 1988).

Sposato, Jeffrey S., 'Creative Writing: The [Self-] Identification of Mendelssohn as Jew', *The Musical Quarterly*, 82 (1998), 190–209.

Steinberg, Michael P., 'The Incidental Politics to Mendelssohn's *Antigone*', in R. Larry Todd (ed.), *Mendelssohn and his World* (Princeton University Press, 1991), pp. 137–57.

Listening to Reason: Culture, Subjectivity, and Nineteenth-Century Music (Princeton University Press, 2004).

'Schumann's Homelessness', in R. Larry Todd (ed.), *Schumann and his World* (Princeton University Press, 1994), pp. 47–79.

Stewart-MacDonald, Rohan H., 'Elements of "Through-Composition" in the Violin Concertos Nos. 23 and 27 by Giovanni Battiata Viotti', *Ad Parnassum*, 3 (2005), 99–131.

Szeskus, Reinhard, '*Die erste Walpurgisnacht*, Op. 60, von Felix Mendelssohn Bartholdy', *Beiträge zur Musikwissenschaft*, 17 (1975), 171–80.

Tappert, Wilhelm, 'Das Gralthema in Richard Wagners "Parsifal"', *Musikalisches Wochenblatt*, 34/31–2 (30 July 1903), 421.

Taruskin, Richard, *The Oxford History of Western Music*, 6 vols. (Oxford and New York: Oxford University Press, 2005).

Taylor, Charles, *Hegel* (Cambridge University Press, 1977).

Sources of the Self: The Making of Modern Identity (Cambridge, MA: Harvard University Press, 1989).

Thaler, Lotte, *Organische Form in der Musiktheorie des 19. und beginnenden 20. Jahrhunderts* (Munich: Emil Katzbichler, 1984).

Thomas, Mathias, *Das Instrumentalwerk Felix Mendelssohn-Bartholdys: Eine systematisch-theoretische Untersuchung unter besonderer Berücksichtigung der zeitgenössischen Musiktheorie* (Göttingen: Hubert, 1972).

Todd, R. Larry, 'The Instrumental Music of Felix Mendelssohn Bartholdy: Selected Studies Based on Primary Sources', unpublished PhD thesis, Yale University (1979).

'Mendelssohn', in D. Kern Holoman (ed.), *The Nineteenth-Century Symphony* (New York: Schirmer, 1997), pp. 78–107.

Mendelssohn: A Life in Music (New York: Oxford University Press, 2003).

'A Mendelssohn Miscellany', *Music & Letters*, 71 (1990), 52–64.

'Mendelssohn's Ossianic Manner, with a New Source: *On Lena's Gloomy Heath*', in Jon Finson and R. Larry Todd (eds.), *Mendelssohn and Schumann* (Durham, NC: Duke University Press, 1984), pp. 137–60.

Mendelssohn: The Hebrides and other Overtures (Cambridge University Press, 1993).

'An Unfinished Symphony by Mendelssohn', *Music & Letters*, 61 (1980), 293–309.

Toews, John Edward, *Becoming Historical: Cultural Reformation and Public Memory in Early Nineteenth-Century Berlin* (Cambridge University Press, 2004).

'Musical Historicism and the Transcendental Foundation of Community: Mendelssohn's *Lobgesang* and the "Christian German" Cultural Politics of Frederick William IV', in Michael S. Roth (ed.), *Rediscovering History: Culture, Politics and the Psyche* (Stanford University Press, 1994), pp. 183–201.

Turchin, Barbara, 'Robert Schumann's Song-Cycles in the Context of the Early Nineteenth-Century *Liederkreis*', unpublished PhD thesis, Columbia University (1981).

Turgot, Anne-Robert-Jacques, *Oeuvres de Turgot et documents le concernant*, ed. Gustave Schelle, 5 vols. (Paris: Alcan, 1913–23).

Vincent, Deirdre, *The Eternity of Being: On the Experience of Time in Goethe's Faust* (Bonn: Bouvier Verlag Herbert Grundmann, 1987).

Vischer, Friedrich Theodor, *Ästhetik oder Wissenschaft des Schönen: Zum Gebrauche für Vorlesungen von Dr. Friedrich Theodor Vischer*, 3 vols. (Reutlingen, Leipzig and Stuttgart: Carl Mäcken, 1846–57).

Vitercik, Greg, *The Early Works of Felix Mendelssohn: A Study in the Romantic Sonata Style* (Philadelphia, PA: Gordon and Breach, 1992).

   'Mendelssohn as Progressive', in Peter Mercer-Taylor (ed.), *The Cambridge Companion to Mendelssohn* (Cambridge University Press, 2004), pp. 71–88.

Webster, James, *Haydn's 'Farewell' Symphony and the Idea of Classical Style: Through-Composition and Cyclic Integration in his Instrumental Music* (Cambridge University Press, 1991).

Wendorff, Rudolf, *Zeit und Kultur: Geschichte des Zeitbewusstseins in Europa* (Opladen: Westdeutscher Verlag, 1983).

Werner, Eric, *Mendelssohn: A New Image of the Composer and his Age*, trans. Dika Newlin (London: Free Press of Glencoe, 1963).

Whitrow, G.J., *Time in History: Views of Time from Prehistory to the Present Day* (Oxford University Press, 1988).

Wilkins, Nigel, 'Rondeau (i)', in Stanley Sadie (ed.), *The New Grove Dictionary of Music and Musicians*, 29 vols. (London: Macmillan, 2001), vol. XXI, pp. 644–7.

Wilkinson, E.M., 'Goethe's *Faust*: Tragedy in the Diachronic Mode', *Publications of the English Goethe Society*, 42 (1971–2), 116–74.

Wiora, Walter, *Die Ausbreitung des Historismus über die Musik: Aufsätze und Diskussionen* (Regensburg: Bosse, 1969).

   'Zwischen absoluter und Programmusik', in Anna Amalie Abert and Wilhelm Pfannkuch (eds.), *Festschrift Friedrich Blume zum 70. Geburtstag* (Kassel: Bärenreiter, 1963), pp. 381–8.

   'Musik als Zeitkunst', *Die Musikforschung*, 10 (1957), 15–28.

Witte, Martin, 'Zur Programmgebundenheit der Sinfonien Mendelssohns', in Carl Dahlhaus (ed.), *Das Problem Mendelssohn* (Regensburg: Bosse, 1974), pp. 119–27.

Young, Edward, *Conjectures on Original Composition* (1759; repr. Leeds: Scolar Press, 1966).

Zaslaw, Neil, *Mozart's Symphonies: Context, Performance Practice, Reception* (Oxford University Press, 1989).

Zuckerkandl, Victor, *Sound and Symbol* (Princeton University Press, 1956).

Index

Made in United States
North Haven, CT
02 September 2022

23599317R00172